Forecasting and
Time Series Analysis

Forecasting and Time Series Analysis

DOUGLAS C. MONTGOMERY

Associate Professor of Industrial and Systems Engineering
Georgia Institute of Technology

LYNWOOD A. JOHNSON

Professor of Industrial and Systems Engineering
Georgia Institute of Technology

McGRAW-HILL BOOK COMPANY
New York St. Louis San Francisco Auckland
Düsseldorf Johannesburg Kuala Lumpur
London Mexico Montreal New Delhi
Panama Paris São Paulo Singapore
Sydney Tokyo Toronto

Library of Congress Cataloging in Publication Data

Montgomery, Douglas C
  Forecasting and time series analysis.

  Bibliography: p.
  1. Sales forecasting. 2. Time-series analysis.
3. Forecasting. I. Johnson, Lynwood A., joint author. II. Title.
HF5415.2.M64   658.8'18   75-31584
ISBN 0-07-042857-3

1234567890 KPKP 785432109876

*The editors for this book were Jeremy Robinson and
Lester Strong, the designer was Naomi Auerbach, and
the production supervisor was Teresa F. Leaden. It
was set in Times Roman by Computype, Inc.
It was printed and bound by The Kingsport Press.*

Contents

Preface

Statistical forecasting techniques are widely used in the management of production and inventory systems and have also found frequent application in a variety of other problem areas, including quality and process control, financial planning, marketing, investment analysis, and distribution planning. Despite the wide application of statistical forecasting techniques, there is not a text available that covers the range of short-term forecasting methods in an introductory fashion. We believe that this book serves that purpose and is suitable for both undergraduate students and professional practitioners who design forecasting systems.

This text has evolved from forecasting lectures in an undergraduate course in production and from a graduate course in forecasting at the Georgia Institute of Technology. We also benefited from experience in extension and continuing education activity and professional consulting in forecasting and production control.

The book can be used by readers with modest mathematical and statistical training, provided they skip some developments and take the associated results on faith. A reader familiar with calculus and introductory statistics can read the entire book. Certain sections and some chapters which have considerable mathematical content and which may be skipped without loss of continuity have been marked with an asterisk.

This book can be used in several ways. It contains exercises and examples and can serve as a text for a one-semester or one-quarter course or seminar on forecasting, such as is typically taught by departments of industrial engineering, management science, operations research, or business administration. Most of the widely used forecasting techniques are organized and presented in a manner that should make the book useful to professional practitioners who are developing and maintaining forecasting systems. The book also contains computer programs for several of the forecasting methods discussed.

The scope of the book is confined to short-term forecasting methods. Chapter 1 is an introductory discussion of the forecasting problem and of the methods and systems in general use today. This chapter also introduces terminology and notation used in the rest of the text. Chapter 2 discusses regression methods and introduces the moving average as a forecasting technique for certain simple time series structures. In Chap. 3 exponential smoothing methods are introduced. Single and double smoothing are presented, as well as the generalization to smoothing of order k for a polynomial of degree k-1. Direct smoothing of the coefficients in polynomial and transcendental models is described in Chap. 4. This chapter requires some knowledge of matrix algebra, and may be skipped by the reader. Chapter 5 presents both exponential smoothing methods for forecasting seasonal time series. Here results from Chap. 4 are used to develop efficient parameter updating procedures for trigonometric seasonal models. Chapter 6 discusses forecasting with time series models, with emphasis on the construction of prediction intervals. Methods for directly forecasting the percentiles of the probability distribution of the process are also described. The analysis of forecast errors and the use of tracking signals to monitor forecasting system performance are discussed in Chap. 7. Chapter 8 contains several procedures for automatic control of the smoothing constant. Chapter 9 presents the Box-Jenkins approach of time series modeling and forecasting. This chapter requires a more advanced statistical background than does the rest of the book. Finally, in Chap. 10 we discuss Bayesian methods for forecasting when little or no historical data are available.

Many individuals contributed to the completion of this book. We particularly thank L. E. Contreras and D. H. Vatz for their assistance in developing the computer programs in Appendix C, B. W. Schmeiser for providing Table A-4, and Professor J. A. White for supplying the data in Example 9-5. We are also indebted to Professor E. S. Pearson and the Biometrika Trustees, the editor of *AIIE Transactions*, the editor of *Operationl Research Quarterly*, and The Ronald Press Company for permission to use copyrighted material. We thank Dr. R. N. Lehrer for providing resources in support of this project. Finally, we thank the several secretaries involved in typing this manuscript.

Douglas C. Montgomery
Lynwood A. Johnson

Atlanta, Georgia

Forecasting and
Time Series Analysis

CHAPTER ONE

Introduction to Forecasting Systems

Our purpose is to present quantitative procedures for use in forecasting systems that routinely predict values of variables important in decision processes. These statistical methods analyze historical data in order to provide estimates of the future. Subsequent chapters will describe the nature and use of the more important statistical forecasting techniques. In this chapter we discuss certain qualitative aspects of developing a forecasting system: the nature and uses of forecasts, definition of the forecasting problem, alternative methods of forecasting, time series models, performance criteria, and other considerations in the system design process.

1-1 NATURE AND USES OF FORECASTS

We often hear of the importance of forecasts in decision-making processes. This is not unusual, since the ultimate effectiveness of any decision depends upon the nature of a sequence of events following the decision. The ability to predict the uncontrollable aspects of these events prior to making the decision should permit an improved choice over that which would otherwise be made. For this reason, management systems for planning and controlling the operations of an organization typically contain a forecasting function, which may be more or less formally defined. The following are examples of situations where forecasts are useful:

Inventory management.   In controlling inventories of purchased spare parts at an aircraft maintenance facility, it is necessary to have an estimate of the usage rate for each part in order to determine procurement lot sizes.   In addition, an estimate of the variability of forecast error over the procurement lead time is required to establish reorder points.

Production planning.   To plan the manufacturing of a product line, it may be necessary to have a forecast of unit sales for each item by delivery period for a number of months in the future.   These forecasts for finished products can then be converted into requirements for semifinished products, components, materials, labor, and so on, so that the entire manufacturing system can be scheduled.

Financial planning.   A financial manager has concern about the pattern of cash flow his or her company will experience over time.   The manager may wish a prediction of cash flow broken down by type and time period for a number of future time periods as an aid in making current decisions.

Staff scheduling.   The manager of a mail processing facility of the United States Postal Service needs a forecast of the hourly volume and mix of mail to be processed in order to schedule staff and equipment efficiently.

Facilities planning.   Decisions about new facilities generally require a long-range forecast of the activities utilizing the facilities.   This is important in the design of the facility, as well as for justification of the investment required.

Process control.   Forecasting also can be an important part of a process control system.   By monitoring key process variables and using them to predict the future behavior of the process, it may be possible to determine the optimal time and extent of control action.   For example, a chemical processing unit may become less efficient as hours of continuous operation increase.   Forecasting the performance of the unit will be useful in planning the shutdown time and overhaul schedule.

From these examples and others that easily come to mind, we see that a forecast is a prediction of future events.   The purpose of forecasting is to reduce the risk in decision making.   Forecasts are usually wrong, but the magnitude of the forecasting errors experienced will depend upon the forecasting system used. By devoting more resources to forecasting, we should be able to improve our forecasting accuracy and thereby eliminate some of the losses resulting from uncertainty in the decision-making process.   This concept is illustrated in Fig. 1-1, where as the cost of forecasting is increased, the losses associated with risk decrease. At some level of forecasting effort the sum of these costs is a minimum.

Note that the conceptual model of Fig. 1-1 is based upon the assumption of decreasing marginal value from forecasting.   That is, each additional dollar spent on forecasting results in a smaller reduction in risk losses than the previous dollar.   Beyond some point, additional resources devoted to forecasting may bring no improvement at all.   This is because it will be impossible to reduce the average forecast error below a given level, no matter how complex the forecasting process employed.

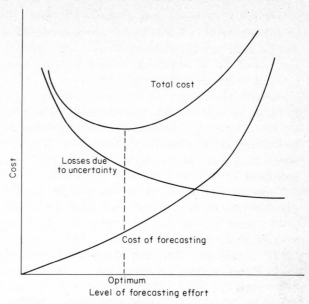

Fig. 1-1 Trade-offs in forecasting.

Because forecasting can never completely eliminate risk, it is necessary that the decision process explicitly consider the uncertainty remaining subsequent to the forecast. Often the decision is related conceptually to the forecast by

ACTUAL DECISION = DECISION ASSUMING FORECAST IS CORRECT

+ ALLOWANCE FOR FORECAST ERROR

This implies that the forecasting system should provide a description of forecast error as well as a forecast. Ideally the forecasting process should result in an estimate of the probability distribution of the variable being predicted. This permits risk to be objectively incorporated into the decision-making process.

The forecast is not an end in itself; rather it is a means to an end. The forecasting system is a part of a larger management system and, as a subsystem, interacts with other components of the total system to determine overall performance.

1-2 DEFINING THE FORECASTING PROBLEM

We shall generally assume that we are concerned with forecasting for the purpose of planning and scheduling production or inventory control, so that our interest lies with future sales of product or usage of material. Typically we shall refer to the variable of interest as "demand." Naturally this need not be the case, and the forecast may be for some other purpose and involve other types of variables. However, by assuming this common setting, we can make specific comments that illustrate principles having general applicability to other problems.

To define the forecasting problem, we must start with the decision problem. Information from the forecasting process is to be used to improve the decision process. Therefore the nature of the decisions to be made will dictate many of the desired characteristics of the forecasting system. A study of the decision problem should help answer questions about what is to be forecast, what form the forecast should take, what time elements are involved, and what accuracy is desired.

In determining what is to be forecast, we are defining the variables that are to be analyzed and predicted. The level of detail required is an important consideration. A production planning system may require a forecast of demand in units for each finished product produced in order to schedule the plant and plan inventories. On the other hand, a sales manager may require only a forecast of total sales in dollars as his or her input to the budgeting process. In the former case, the forecast is on an item basis; in the latter, it is on an aggregate basis. While these are the final forms required, they are not necessarily the variables we would use in the analysis. In production planning we might forecast at some aggregate level, say families of similar products, and then break the aggregate forecasts down to the item level in a secondary calculation. In forecasting sales dollars, we may choose to forecast the components of sales, again possibly product families, in units, convert to dollars by using predicted prices, and then add to obtain an estimate of total dollar sales.

Many factors influence the level of detail used: availability of data, accuracy attainable, cost of analysis, and management preferences. In situations where the appropriate choice of variables is not clear, one may try several alternatives and select the one giving the best performance. Typically this is done during the development of the forecasting system through simulation using historical data.

A second important class of decisions involves the following three time elements: the forecasting period, the forecasting horizon, and the forecasting interval. The *forecasting period* is the basic unit of time for which forecasts are made. For example, we might wish a forecast of demand by week, in which case the period is a week. The *forecasting horizon* is the number of periods in the future covered by the forecast. Thus, we could require a forecast for the next 10 weeks, broken down by week. The period is a week, the horizon is 10 weeks. Finally, the *forecasting interval* is the frequency with which new forecasts are prepared. Often the forecasting interval is the same as the forecasting period, so that forecasts are revised each period using the most recent period's demand and other current information as the basis for revision. If the horizon is always the same length, say T periods, and the forecast is revised each period, we say we are operating on a *moving horizon* basis. In this case, each period we reforecast the demand for the next T-1 periods and make the original forecast for period T.

The forecasting period and horizon are usually dictated by the decision process requiring the forecast. For a forecast to be of value, the forecast horizon must be no less than the lead time for implementing the decision. How much farther into the future one must forecast will depend heavily on the nature of the decision problem. Sometimes the term *forecast lead time* is used in place of forecast horizon. In some problems, the required lead time may be uncertain, as in the case of delivery time to replenish the inventory of a purchased part. There are methods to deal with this complication, but its impact is to increase the variability of forecast error. Since forecasts typically become less accurate with increasing forecast horizon, we can often improve our decision process by shortening the decision lead time, thereby reducing the required forecast lead time and permitting a quicker reaction to forecast error.

The forecasting interval often is determined by the operating mode of the data processing system that provides information on the variable being forecasted. If sales are reported monthly, there might be little basis for weekly forecast revision and a monthly forecast interval would be reasonable.

Although not an important distinction, we might point out the difference between *period data* and *point data*. Period data are indicative of a variable over a period of time. For example, the total sales for a month and the average temperature during a day each characterize a period of time. Point data represent the value of a variable at specific time points. For example, the inventory at the end of the month and the temperature at noon are point data. The difference between the two types of data has implications primarily for the type of data collection system to be used and the effect of measurement and data processing errors on results.

A third aspect of the forecasting problem relates to the required form of the forecast. As we shall see in Sec. 1-4, it is convenient to conceive of the variable of interest as being a random variable having an unknown probability distribution. The decision problem may require an estimate of some characteristic of that distribution, such as the mean, median, or most probable value (mode) for use as a forecast of the variable. Or as a measure of uncertainty, it may call for estimates of the standard deviation, a percentile, or perhaps an interval having a high probability of containing the actual value to be realized. Less frequently there may be need to predict the form of the distribution (for example, Poisson, normal, gamma). Usually the forecast will take one of the following forms: (1) an estimate of the expected value of the variable, plus an estimate of the standard deviation of forecast error, or (2) an interval that has a stated probability of containing the actual future value. The latter is called a *prediction interval*.

In certain cases, we may be less interested in predicting the value of a variable than in predicting significant changes in the process giving rise to the variable. The latter might be the case in process control, when we want to predict the time at which a process shifts to an out-of-control state.

The forecast accuracy required by the decision problem will have an effect on the forecasting system adopted. We already have illustrated the trade-offs in

Fig. 1-1. An important characteristic of a good management system is its ability to achieve optimal performance in the face of uncertainty. Improving forecast accuracy will reduce uncertainty, but the added refinement may not be economically justified.

To this point, we have discussed the impact of the decision problem on the forecasting system. There are some other factors that also should be considered in defining the forecasting problem. One has to do with the process generating the variable. If the process is known to be stable, either having constant conditions or changing slowly with time, the forecasting system may be quite different from that required when the process is highly erratic, with fundamental changes occurring often. The former would make extensive use of historical data to predict the future, while the latter would place a premium on subjective estimation and forecast control procedures to detect changes in the process.

Another factor is the availability of data. Historical data are valuable in establishing forecasting procedures, and future observations should be provided for forecast revision. The quantity, accuracy, and timeliness of this information are important. In addition, the representativeness of the data should be examined. The classical example in this regard is the problem of forecasting customer demand for a manufactured product when the company keeps records only of orders booked and shipments by period. Neither represents demand, since orders are booked before the desired delivery period, orders lost because of unsatisfactory projected delivery performance are not recorded, and shipments may take place in a delivery period different from that desired by the customer. The company will have to set up a special data collection procedure if it desires information indicative of what its customers actually want shipped by delivery period. This type of problem is most acute in oversold conditions when sales lost because of capacity constraints are not recorded.

A source of confusion about sales forecasts is the distinction between a forecast of "what can be sold" and "what will be sold." The former is an estimate of the opportunities available to the company assuming it is not capacity-bound. This is the kind of forecast required for product-mix planning. The later reflects capacity constraints and management decisions, and represents a plan or goal. It could better be called a budget than a forecast. We would expect that sales data would be correlated with budgeted sales in many types of business. This is because the managers strive to meet the "forecast."

The computational limitations imposed on the forecasting system should be defined. If only a few variables are to be forecasted infrequently, it will be possible to utilize more elaborate analysis procedures than if a large number must be analyzed often. In the latter situation, however, more effort must be devoted to development of efficient data handling and management procedures.

Two final important factors in defining the forecasting problem are the capabilities and interests of the people who will make and use the forecast. Ideally, historical information is analyzed automatically with statistical methods and a forecast is presented to appropriate management for possible modification. This introduction of judgment into the forecasting process is important, but it requires managers who are willing to participate. Often the final forecast is then provided to other managers who are to use it in their decision processes. Unless they can be convinced that the forecasting process is sound, they may make little use of the information given them.

1-3 METHODS OF FORECASTING

Methods for generating forecasts can be broadly classified as qualitative or quantitative, depending upon the extent to which mathematical and statistical methods are used.

Qualitative procedures involve subjective estimation through the opinions of experts. There usually are formal procedures for obtaining predictions in this manner, ranging from consolidation of the estimates of sales personnel to the use of Delphi-type methods to obtain a consensus of opinion from a panel of forecasters. These procedures may rely in part on marketing tests, customer surveys, sales force estimates, and historical data, but the process by which the information is used to obtain a forecast is subjective.

On the other hand, statistical forecasting procedures explicitly define how the forecast is determined. The logic is clearly stated and the operations are mathematical. The methods involve examination of historical data to determine the underlying process generating the variable and, assuming that the process is stable, use of this knowledge to extrapolate the process into the future. Two basic types of models are used: time series models and causal models.

A *time series* is a time-ordered sequence of observations (realizations) of a variable. Time series analysis uses only the time series history of the variable being forecasted in order to develop a model for predicting future values. Thus, if examination of past monthly sales of replacement tires for automobiles revealed a linear growth, a linear trend model might be chosen to represent the process and the appropriate slope and intercept estimated from historical data. Forecasts would be made by extrapolating the fitted model, as illustrated in Fig. 1-2.

Causal models exploit the relationship between the time series of interest and one or more other time series. If these other variables are correlated with the variable of interest and if there appears to be some cause for this correlation, a statistical model describing this relationship can be constructed. Then, knowing values of the correlated variables, one can use the model to obtain a forecast of the dependent variable. For example, analysis might reveal a strong correlation between monthly sales of replacement tires and monthly sales of new automobiles 15 months before. Then information about new car sales 14 months ago would be useful in predicting replacement tire sales next month. The concept is illustrated in Fig. 1-3.

An obvious limitation to the use of causal models is the requirement that the independent variables be known at the time the forecast is made. The fact that tire sales are correlated with new car sales 15 months previous is not useful in

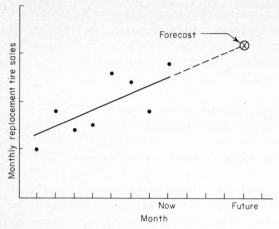

Fig. 1-2 Linear-trend time series forecast.

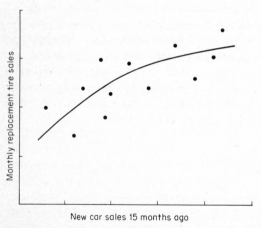

Fig. 1-3 Causal model illustrated.

forecasting tire sales 18 months in the future.   Similarly, the knowledge that tire sales are correlated with current gasoline prices is of little value, since we would not know exactly the gasoline price in any future month for which we wished to forecast tire sales.   Another limitation to the use of causal models is the large amount of computation and data handling compared with certain forms of time series models.   This will become apparent in studying Chaps. 2 and 4.

Actually, forecasting systems often use a combination of quantitative and qualitative methods.   The statistical methods are used to routinely analyze historical data and prepare a forecast.   This lends objectivity to the system and results in effective organization of the information content of historical data. The statistical forecast then becomes an input to a subjective evaluation by informed managers, who may modify the forecast in view of other relevant information and their perception of the future.

The selection of appropriate forecasting methods is influenced by the following factors, most of which were discussed in the previous section:

1. Form of forecast required
2. Forecast horizon, period, and interval
3. Data availability
4. Accuracy required
5. Behavior of process being forecast (demand pattern)
6. Cost of development, installation, and operation
7. Ease of operation
8. Management comprehension and cooperation

Ease of operation here refers primarily to the simplicity of maintaining the system. Since items are continually being added and deleted, it is desirable to have a forecasting method that is independent of the time when an item is initially introduced into the system. As we shall see in Chaps. 3 to 5, such methods exist and have considerable advantage in ease of maintenance and operation over those which require knowledge of the initialization time.

In this text we are primarily concerned with short-term forecasting, say up to a year in the future. Also we are oriented toward systems requiring periodic forecasting of many items each period. Under these requirements, the economics (as shown in Fig. 1-1) usually indicate a relatively simple forecasting procedure. Quantitative forecasting methods usually employ time series models having only a few terms. Management judgment is typically applied each period to only those items where poor forecasting performance is being experienced.

1-4 TIME SERIES MODELS

1-4.1 Characteristics of Time Series

For our purposes a time series is a sequence of observations on a variable of interest. The variable is observed at discrete time points, usually equally spaced. Time series analysis involves describing the process or phenomena that generate the sequence. To forecast time series, it is necessary to represent the behavior of the process by a mathematical model that can be extended into the future. It is required that the model be a good representation of the observations in any local segment of time close to the present. We usually do not require the model to represent very old observations, as they probably are not characteristic of the present, or observations far into the future, beyond the lead time over which the forecast is made. Once a valid model for the time series process has been established, an appropriate forecasting technique can be developed.

Several characteristic patterns of time series are shown in Fig. 1-4, where x_t is the observation for period t. In Fig. 1-4a, the process remains at a constant level over time, with variation from period to period due to random causes. Pattern (b) illustrates a trend in the level of the process, so that the variation from one period to the next is attributable to trend in addition to random variation. In (c), the process level is assumed to vary cyclically over time, as in

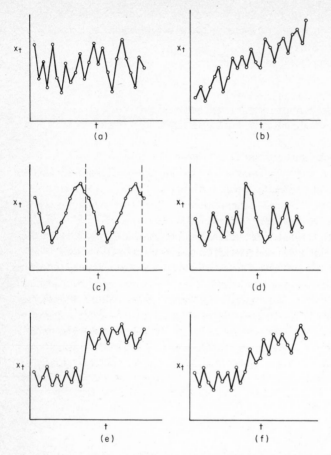

Fig. 1-4 Time series characteristics. (*a*) Constant process; (*b*) linear trend; (*c*) cyclic variation; (*d*) impulse; (*e*) step function; (*f*) ramp.

the case of a seasonal product. Seasonal variation can be attributed to some cause, such as weather (e.g., the demand for soft drinks), institutions (e.g., Christmas cards), or policy (e.g., end-of-quarter accounting). Most time series models for forecasting are developed to represent these patterns: constant, trend, periodic (cyclical), or a combination of the three.

In addition, there are patterns resulting from a change in the underlying process. A transient, or *impulse*, pattern is illustrated by (*d*). For two periods the process operated at a higher level before reverting to the original level. An example would be a temporary increase in sales caused by a strike at a competitor's plant. In (*e*), the change to a new level is permanent, and we refer to it as a *step* change. This could be caused by the acquisition of a new customer, for example. Finally, pattern (*f*) shows a process which has been operating at a constant level suddenly experiencing a trend. Since these three patterns of change are common in practice, we desire that our forecasting

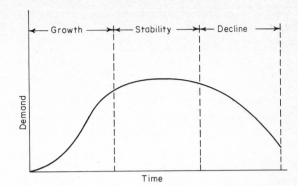

Fig. 1-5 Product life cycle.

system identify permanent changes and adjust the forecasting model to track the new process. At the same time, we wish our forecasting system to recognize random variations and transient changes and not react to these phenomena. This conflict between responsiveness and stability of the forecasting system will be discussed in more detail in later chapters.

In forecasting demand for a product, we may need to use different forecasting models during various stages in the product's life cycle. For example, Fig. 1-5 illustrates a life cycle having three distinct phases. During the growth phase, following introduction of the product, we might represent the process by a trend model, possibly with both linear and quadratic components. Once demand has leveled off, it would be desirable to switch to a constant-process model. During the final phase, when sales are declining, a trend model would again be appropriate.

1-4.2 Representation of Time Series

Many of the models used to represent time series are algebraic or transcendental functions of time, or some composite model that combines both algebraic and transcendental components. For example, if the observations are random samples from some probability distribution, and if the mean of that distribution does not change with time, then we may use the constant model

$$x_t = b + \epsilon_t \qquad (1\text{-}1)$$

where x_t is the demand in period t, b is the unknown process mean, and ϵ_t is the random component, sometimes called the "noise" in the process. The random component has an expected value of zero, and we usually assume that its variance is constant; that is, $E(\epsilon_t) = 0$ and $V(\epsilon_t) = \sigma_\epsilon^2$. Note that this is equivalent to saying that x_t is a random variable with mean b and variance σ_ϵ^2. Equation (1-1) is the appropriate model for the process illustrated in Fig. 1-4a.

To represent the process of Fig. 1-4b, we might assume that the mean of the process changes linearly with time and use the linear trend model

$$x_t = b_1 + b_2 t + \epsilon_t \qquad (1\text{-}2)$$

where b_1 and b_2 are constants. Note that the slope, b_2, represents the change in the average level of demand from one period to the next. Equation (1-3) gives a quadratic trend model:

$$x_t = b_1 + b_2 t + b_3 t^2 + \epsilon_t \qquad (1\text{-}3)$$

Cyclical variation may be accounted for by introducing transcendental terms into the model; for example,

$$x_t = b_1 + b_2 \sin \frac{2\pi t}{12} + b_3 \cos \frac{2\pi t}{12} + \epsilon_t \qquad (1\text{-}4)$$

which would account for a cycle repeating every 12 periods. In Chap. 5 we shall discuss this and other approaches to modeling periodic processes.

The models described above are of the following general form:

$$x_t = b_1 z_1(t) + b_2 z_2(t) + \cdots + b_k z_k(t) + \epsilon_t \qquad (1\text{-}5)$$

where the $\{b_i\}$ are parameters, the $\{z_i(t)\}$ are mathematical functions of t, and ϵ_t is the random component. Thus, for example, in Eq. (1-2), $z_1(t) = 1$ and $z_2(t) = t$. Note that this modeling approach represents the expected value of the process as a mathematical function of t.

Often it will be desirable to define the origin of time as the end of the most recent period T. Then we shall write the model for the observation in period $T + \tau$ as

$$x_{T+\tau} = a_1(T)z_1(\tau) + a_2(T)z_2(\tau) + \cdots + a_k(T)z_k(\tau) + \epsilon_t \qquad (1\text{-}6)$$

where the coefficients are now denoted by $\{a_i(T)\}$ to indicate that they are based on the current time origin T, and thereby distinguish them from the original-origin coefficients $\{b_i\}$.

Always keeping the origin of time on a current basis greatly facilitates the operation of a forecasting system. In Chaps. 3, 4, and 5, we shall study several models where parameter estimation and forecasting are done on a current-origin basis.

Most of this book treats models of the form (1-5); however, in Chap. 9 we shall describe a quite different approach to representing a time series. There the current observation x_t will be modeled as a function of the prior random components $\epsilon_t, \epsilon_{t-1}, \epsilon_{t-2}, \ldots$, in the following general form:

$$x_t = \mu + \psi_0 \epsilon_t + \psi_1 \epsilon_{t-1} + \psi_2 \epsilon_{t-2} + \cdots \qquad (1\text{-}7)$$

where μ and the $\{\psi_i\}$ are constants. Models of this type are commonly called *Box-Jenkins models*. It may not be obvious how a model of this form can represent a time series; yet in Chap. 9 we shall see that for certain time series this approach yields excellent results. This is particularly true for time series in which observations are highly autocorrelated, that is, where the observations are not mutually independent. *after deterministic parts are removed.*

One simple technique in model selection is to plot historical data and look for patterns. Since the model should represent the near future for forecasting purposes, we usually judge its effectiveness by how well it describes the recent past.

1-4.3 Forecasting with Time Series Models

Time series forecasting consists of estimating the unknown parameters in the appropriate model and using these estimates, projecting the model into the future to obtain a forecast. For example, let $\hat{b}_1$ and $\hat{b}_2$ be estimates of the unknown parameters b_1 and b_2 in Eq. (1-2). If we currently are at the end of period T, the forecast of the expected value of the observation in some future period $T + \tau$ would be

$$\hat{x}_{T+\tau}(T) = \hat{b}_1 + \hat{b}_2(T + \tau) \qquad (1\text{-}8)$$

Thus, the forecast simply projects the estimate of the trend component, $\hat{b}_2$, τ periods into the future. This is illustrated in Fig. 1-6.

The forecast given by Eq. (1-8) is for a single period $T + \tau$. We may wish to forecast the sum of the observations in periods $T + 1, T + 2, \ldots, T + L$. To obtain this *cumulative forecast*, we add the period forecasts as follows:

$$\hat{X}_L(T) = \sum_{\tau=1}^{L} \hat{x}_{T+\tau}(T) \qquad (1\text{-}9)$$

Cumulative forecasts are often required to predict total requirements over a lead time. They will be treated in Chap. 6.

In subsequent chapters, we shall consider a variety of techniques for estimating the unknown parameters of time series models. At this point, we observe

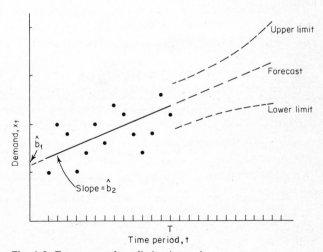

Fig. 1-6 Forecasts and prediction intervals.

only that the model of Eq. (1-5) is linear in the unknown coefficients $b_1, b_2, \ldots, b_k$, and therefore conventional least-squares methods can be used to obtain parameter estimates from historical data.

In previous sections, the concept of a prediction interval was described. It is illustrated in Fig. 1-6, where the upper and lower prediction limits are determined so that there is a specified probability of their containing the actual observation. Methods for computing prediction intervals for time series models will be discussed in Sec. 6-3.

1-5 PERFORMANCE CRITERIA

There are a number of measures that can be used to evaluate the effectiveness of a forecasting system. Among the more important are forecasting accuracy, system cost, utility of output, and stability and responsiveness properties.

The accuracy of a forecasting method is determined by analyzing forecast errors experienced. If x_t is the actual observation in period t and $\hat{x}_t$ is the forecast for that period made at some prior time, the forecast error for period t is

$$e_t = x_t - \hat{x}_t \tag{1-10}$$

For a given process and forecasting method, the forecast error is considered a random variable having mean $E(e)$ and variance σ_e^2. If the forecast is *unbiased*, $E(e) = 0$. While an unbiased forecast is desirable, it usually is more important that large forecast errors are rarely obtained. Hence a quantity such as the expected absolute error

$$E[|e_t|] = E[|x_t - \hat{x}_t|] \tag{1-11}$$

or the expected squared error

$$E[e_t^2] = E\left[(x_t - \hat{x}_t)^2\right] \tag{1-12}$$

is commonly used as a measure of forecast accuracy. Note that the expected squared error, usually called the *mean squared error*, is equal to σ_e^2 if the forecast is unbiased. As we shall see in Chap. 7, there are efficient methods for estimating these measures, either from actual system operation or from a simulation.

In analyzing the accuracy of an installed forecasting method, it is common to employ a *tracking signal test* each period. The purpose is to determine if the forecast is unbiased. The tracking signal is a statistic computed by dividing an estimate of expected forecast error by a measure of the variability of forecast error, such as an estimate of the mean absolute deviation of forecast error. If the forecasting system yields unbiased estimates, the tracking signal should be near zero. Should the tracking signal deviate from zero by more than a prescribed amount, an investigation is made to determine if the forecasting

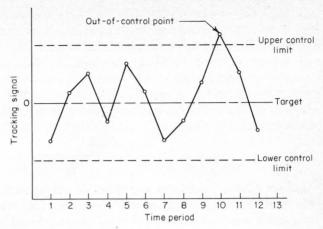

Fig. 1-7 Forecast control.

model should be modified in order to better represent the time series process, which may have experienced a change such as those shown in Fig. 1-7. Note that this form of analysis can be applied to a statistical forecast, a judgmental forecast, or a combination of the two. Tracking signal tests are described in more detail in Chap. 7.

Naturally, cost is an important consideration in evaluating and comparing forecasting methods. There are one-time costs for developing and installing the system and periodic costs for operating it. With regard to operating costs, alternative forecasting procedures may differ widely in the cost of data acquisition, the efficiency of computation, and the level of activity required to maintain the system.

The utility of the forecast in improving management decisions will depend upon the timeliness and form of the forecast, as well as its accuracy. Benefits should be measured with regard to the management system as a whole. Forecasting is only one component of this total system. The objective is to reach good decisions, and usually this can be achieved with less than perfect forecasts.

We may also wish to compare forecasting methods on the basis of their response to permanent changes in the time series process and their stability in the presence of random variation and transient changes. This can be done through simulation and, for certain statistical methods, by mathematical analysis.

1-6 CONSIDERATIONS IN SYSTEM DESIGN

We do not intend to give a comprehensive description of how one goes about developing and installing a forecasting system. The process is similar to that used for design of many other types of management information systems. Instead, we describe some considerations, not previously discussed, that are important for forecasting systems.

In choosing the forecasting interval, there is a trade-off between the risk of not identifying a change in the time series process and the costs of forecast revision. If we forecast infrequently, we may operate for a long period under plans based on an obsolete forecast. On the other hand, if we use a shorter interval, we more frequently incur not only the cost of making the forecast but also the cost of changing plans to conform to the new forecast. The appropriate forecast frequency depends upon the stability of the process, the consequences of using an obsolete forecast, and the costs of forecasting and replanning.

The data required by the forecasting system are subject to recording and transmission errors and therefore should be edited to detect obvious or likely mistakes. Small errors in magnitude will not be identifiable, but they usually will have little effect on the forecast. Larger errors can be more easily detected and corrected. Also, the forecasting system should not respond to extraordinary or unusual observations. If we are forecasting product demand, any sales transaction that is identified as nontypical or extreme should, of course, affect inventory records, but should not be included in data used for forecasting. For example, suppose a manufacturer who supplies a number of distributors acquires a new customer. The initial orders from this customer probably will not be typical of his later orders, since he is at first establishing his inventory. Methods for screening data to identify possible outliers are described in Sec. 7-5.

Simulation is a useful technique for evaluating alternative forecasting methods. This can be done retrospectively using historical data. For each method, one starts at some prior time point and simulates forecasting period by period up to the present. Measures of forecast error can then be compared among methods. If the future is expected to differ from the past, a pseudo-history can be created based upon subjective expectations of the future nature of the time series and used in the simulation. Simulation is also useful in determining parameters of forecasting techniques, such as the best smoothing constants for the exponential and direct smoothing methods to be described in Chaps. 3 to 5.

It is convenient to think of the two primary functions of a forecasting system as *forecast generation* and *forecast control*. Forecast generation involves acquiring data, using the data to revise the forecasting model, producing a statistical forecast, introducing management judgment, and presenting the results to the user of the forecast. Forecast control involves monitoring the forecasting process to detect out-of-control conditions and identify opportunities for improving forecasting performance. An essential component of the control function is the tracking signal test described in the previous section. Items that exhibit out-of-control tracking signals can be singled out for special attention by managers and efforts can be directed toward modifying their forecasting models if necessary.

Also, the forecast control function should involve periodically summarizing forecasting performance and presenting the results to appropriate management.

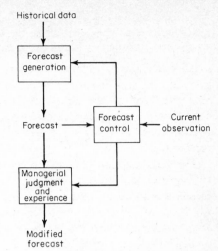

Fig. 1-8 The forecasting system.

This feedback should encourage improvement in both the quantitative and qualitative aspects of the system. A conceptual relationship between forecast generation and forecast control is shown in Fig. 1-8.

1-7 EXERCISES

1-1 Discuss the nature of forecasting systems for each of the decision areas described below. Define the forcasting problem. What time series patterns would you expect?
  a. Inventory control by a wholesale food distributor.
  b. Inventory control by a retail grocery store.
  c. Production planning by a carpet manufacturer who produces to inventory.
  d. Production planning by an automobile parts manufacturer who produces to order.
  e. Production planning by a soft drink bottler.
  f. Clerical staff planning by a large insurance company.
  g. Mail carrier staff planning by the U.S. Postal Service.
  h. Cash management by the operator of a fast-food restaurant.
  i. Food preparation at a cafeteria.
  j. Fleet management by a rental car agency.

1-2 Use a table of random normal numbers (Appendix Table A-4) to generate observations for $t = 1, 2, \ldots, 20$, from the constant process

$$x_t = 100 + \epsilon_t$$

where ϵ_t is normally distributed with mean 0 and standard deviation $\sigma_\epsilon = 10$. Plot the results. Repeat for $\sigma_\epsilon = 20$. In each case, what is the best forecast of the next observation? (Note: If u is a value from the random normal number table, the associated observation on ϵ is $u\sigma_\epsilon$, and $x = 100 + u\sigma_\epsilon$.)

1-3 Use a table of random normal numbers (Appendix Table A-4) to generate observation for $t = 1, 2, \ldots, 50$, from the following processes. Plot the results on graph paper. Assume $\sigma_\epsilon = 20$ in each case.

a. $x_t = 100 + 10t + \epsilon_t$

b. $x_t = 100 - 10t + 2t^2 + \epsilon_t$

c. $x_t = 100 + 10 \sin \dfrac{2\pi t}{12} - 20 \cos \dfrac{2\pi t}{12} + \epsilon_t$

d. $x_t = 100 + 10t + 10t \sin \dfrac{2\pi t}{12} - 20t \cos \dfrac{2\pi t}{12} + \epsilon_t$

e. $x_t = 100 + 10 \sin \dfrac{2\pi t}{12} - 20 \cos \dfrac{2\pi t}{12} - 5 \sin \dfrac{2\pi t}{6} + 30 \cos \dfrac{2\pi t}{6} + \epsilon_t$

f. $x_t = 100 + 0.8 x_{t-1} + \epsilon_t$

g. $x_t = 100 + \epsilon_t + 0.8 \epsilon_t$

h. $x_t = 100 + \epsilon_t - 0.8 \epsilon_t$

1-4 Explain the meaning of "noise" in a time series process and discuss the interpretation of σ_ϵ^2 as a measure of noise. How does the amount of noise in the process affect the ability to forecast? How do you forecast noise?

1-5 Describe circumstances under which good forecasting performance would be expected. What factors would lead to poor performance?

CHAPTER TWO

Regression Methods and Moving Averages

The development of many types of forecasting systems involves the assumption of a particular mathematical model as the underlying process for the observed data, and then the estimation of the unknown parameters in that model from historical data. Many of the forecasting techniques that we shall present utilize the method of least squares for parameter estimation. Furthermore, least-squares regression is occasionally used as a forecasting technique in its own right. This chapter provides an introduction to the method of least squares, and discusses its application to two elementary time series models in which only the most recent N observations are considered. When these N observations are all equally important, a forecasting method based on the moving average results.

2-1 REGRESSION METHODS IN TIME SERIES ANALYSIS

In this section, the notation and methodology of regression methods applied to estimating the parameters of time series models are discussed. Initially, least-squares analysis of a model with linear trend is presented, and then the general procedure for the case of several independent variables is described.

2-1.1 Simple Linear Regression

Many time series can be adequately described by a simple linear function of time. We may write this function as

$$x_t = b_1 + b_2 t + \epsilon_t \tag{2-1}$$

where b_1 and b_2 are the intercept and slope, respectively, and ϵ_t is the random deviation from the mean in time period t. We shall assume that this random error component has mean 0 and variance σ_ϵ^2, and is not correlated with random deviations in other periods. Expressed mathematically, our assumptions are $E(\epsilon_t) = 0$, $\text{Var}(\epsilon_t) = \sigma_\epsilon^2$, and $E(\epsilon_t \cdot \epsilon_{t+j}) = 0$ for $j \neq 0$.

The mean of the time series process changes linearly with time, and at time t the mean is $b_1 + b_2 t$. The parameters b_1 and b_2 are unknown constants, which we shall estimate by the method of least squares.

Assume that there are T periods of data available, say $x_1, x_2, \ldots, x_T$. Denote the estimators of b_1 and b_2 by $\hat{b}_1$ and $\hat{b}_2$. The fitted model is

$$\hat{x}_t = \hat{b}_1 + \hat{b}_2 t$$

and the difference between the fitted model and the data is called a *residual*, say

$$e_t = x_t - \hat{x}_t$$

To estimate b_1 and b_2 by the method of least squares, we must choose $\hat{b}_1$ and $\hat{b}_2$ so that the error sum of squares

$$SS_E = \sum_{t=1}^{T} (x_t - b_1 - b_2 t)^2 \tag{2-2}$$

is minimized. Therefore, it is necessary that $\hat{b}_1$ and $\hat{b}_2$ satisfy

$$\left. \frac{\partial SS_E}{\partial b_1} \right|_{\hat{b}_1, \hat{b}_2} = 0$$

and

$$\left. \frac{\partial SS_E}{\partial b_2} \right|_{\hat{b}_1, \hat{b}_2} = 0$$

This results in the following equations:

$$-2 \sum_{t=1}^{T} \left(x_t - \hat{b}_1 - \hat{b}_2 t \right) = 0 \tag{2-3}$$

$$-2 \sum_{t=1}^{T} \left(x_t - \hat{b}_1 - \hat{b}_2 t \right) t = 0 \tag{2-4}$$

Equations (2-3) and (2-4) may be rewritten as

$$\hat{b}_1 \sum_{t=1}^{T} (1) + \hat{b}_2 \sum_{t=1}^{T} t = \sum_{t=1}^{T} x_t \tag{2-5}$$

$$\hat{b}_1 \sum_{t=1}^{T} t + \hat{b}_2 \sum_{t=1}^{T} t^2 = \sum_{t=1}^{T} t x_t \tag{2-6}$$

Equations (2-5) and (2-6) are called the *least-squares normal equations*. Since $\sum_{t=1}^{T} t = T(T+1)/2$ and $\sum_{t=1}^{T} t^2 = T(T+1)(2T+1)/6$, we may easily solve the normal equations for the estimators $\hat{b}_1$ and $\hat{b}_2$. The solution is

$$\hat{b}_1 = \frac{2(2T+1)}{T(T-1)} \sum_{t=1}^{T} x_t - \frac{6}{T(T-1)} \sum_{t=1}^{T} t x_t \qquad (2\text{-}7)$$

$$\hat{b}_2 = \frac{12}{T(T^2-1)} \sum_{t=1}^{T} t x_t - \frac{6}{T(T-1)} \sum_{t=1}^{T} x_t \qquad (2\text{-}8)$$

The estimators $\hat{b}_1$ and $\hat{b}_2$ depend upon the point in time at which they are computed (that is, T). Therefore, it is occasionally convenient to denote them as a function of time, say $\hat{b}_1(T) \equiv \hat{b}_1$ and $\hat{b}_2(T) \equiv \hat{b}_2$, where T is the time at which the estimates are computed.

The forecast, made at the end of period T of an observation in some future time period, say $T + \tau$, would be denoted by $\hat{x}_{T+\tau}(T)$, and is computed from

$$\hat{x}_{T+\tau}(T) = \hat{b}_1(T) + \hat{b}_2(T)[T + \tau] \qquad (2\text{-}9)$$

As a new observation becomes available, new estimates of the model parameters may be computed.

It is frequently useful to estimate the variance of the random error component, σ_ϵ^2. If the linear trend model adequately describes the data, then we may estimate σ_ϵ^2 by

$$\hat{\sigma}_\epsilon^2 = \frac{\sum_{t=1}^{T} (x_t - \hat{x}_t)^2}{T - 2} \qquad (2\text{-}10)$$

EXAMPLE 2-1 The maintenance department of a small manufacturing company wishes to forecast the total monthly maintenance expense for the plant. Data for the past 10 months are shown in Table 2-1.

TABLE 2-1   Data for Example 2-1

Month	1	2	3	4	5	6	7	8	9	10
Maintenance expense, $	880	850	830	950	1,000	1,125	1,310	1,260	1,300	1,250

The staff industrial engineer has studied the data and decided to use a simple linear regression model with time as the independent variable. Since $\sum_{t=1}^{10} x_t = 10{,}755$ and $\sum_{t=1}^{10} t x_t = 64{,}050$, the least-squares estimators $\hat{b}_1$ and $\hat{b}_2$ from Eq.

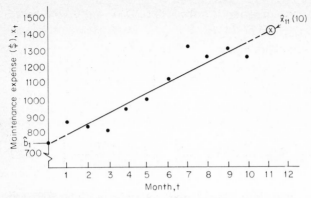

Fig. 2-1 Data and fitted model for Example 2-1.

(2-7) and (2-8) are

$$\hat{b}_1 = \frac{2(2T+1)}{T(T-1)} \sum_{t=1}^{T} x_t - \frac{6}{T(T-1)} \sum_{t=1}^{T} tx_t$$

$$= \frac{2(21)}{10(9)}(10,755) - \frac{6}{10(9)}(64,050) = 749$$

$$\hat{b}_2 = \frac{12}{T(T^2-1)} \sum_{t=1}^{T} tx_t - \frac{6}{T(T-1)} \sum_{t=1}^{T} x_t$$

$$= \frac{12}{10(99)}(64,050) - \frac{6}{10(9)}(10,755) = 59.36$$

As these parameters were estimated at the end of period 10, they could be denoted as $\hat{b}_1(10) = \hat{b}_1 = 749$ and $\hat{b}_2(10) = \hat{b}_2 = 59.36$. The forecasting equation for any future time period, say $10 + \tau$, is found from (2-9) as

$$\hat{x}_{10+\tau}(10) = 749 + 59.36(10 + \tau)$$

The forecast of total maintenance expense for the next month, that is, $\tau = 1$, is

$$\hat{x}_{11}(10) = 749 + 59.36(11) = \$1,401.96$$

A graph of the data and the fitted simple linear regression model is shown in Fig. 2-1. Notice that the forecast for period 11 is just a projection of the fitted model.

Confidence and prediction intervals In addition to point estimates of the model parameters, the analyst may be interested in obtaining confidence interval estimates of b_1 and b_2. If we assume that the random errors $\{\epsilon_t\}$ are normally distributed with mean 0 and variance σ_ϵ^2, then the $100(1 - \alpha)\%$ confidence intervals are

$$\hat{b}_1 - t_{\alpha/2, T-2} \left[\hat{\sigma}_\epsilon^2 \frac{2(2T + 1)}{T(T - 1)} \right]^{\frac{1}{2}} \leqslant b_1 \leqslant \hat{b}_1 + t_{\alpha/2, T-2} \left[\hat{\sigma}_\epsilon^2 \frac{2(2T + 1)}{T(T - 1)} \right]^{\frac{1}{2}} \quad (2\text{-}11)$$

and

$$\hat{b}_2 - t_{\alpha/2, T-2} \left[\sigma_\epsilon^2 \frac{12}{T(T - 1)} \right]^{\frac{1}{2}} \leqslant b_2 \leqslant \hat{b}_2 + t_{\alpha/2, T-2} \left[\hat{\sigma}_\epsilon^2 \frac{12}{T(T^2 - 1)} \right]^{\frac{1}{2}} \quad (2\text{-}12)$$

where $t_{\alpha/2, T-2}$ is the percentage point of the t distribution with $T - 2$ degrees of freedom such that the probability to the right of $t_{\alpha/2, T-2}$ is $\alpha/2$.

Another useful interval estimate is the prediction interval. This is actually an interval estimate for a future observation at some point in time, say $x_{T+\tau}$. A point estimate of $x_{T+\tau}$ is just the forecast $x_{T+\tau}(T)$, which is computed from Eq. (2-9). The $100(1 - \alpha)\%$ prediction interval is

$$\hat{x}_{t+\tau}(T) - t_{\alpha/2, T-2} \left\{ \hat{\sigma}_\epsilon^2 \left[1 + \frac{2}{T(T^2 - 1)} \left[(2T - 1)(T - 1) + 6\tau(T + \tau - 1) \right] \right] \right\}^{\frac{1}{2}}$$

$$\leqslant x_{T+\tau}$$

$$\leqslant \hat{x}_{T+\tau}(T) + t_{\alpha/2, T-2} \left\{ \hat{\sigma}_\epsilon^2 \left[1 + \frac{2}{T(T^2 - 1)} \left[(2T - 1)(T - 1) \right. \right. \right.$$

$$\left. \left. \left. + 6\tau(T + \tau - 1) \right] \right] \right\}^{\frac{1}{2}} \quad (2\text{-}13)$$

The probability is $1 - \alpha$ that the observation at time $T + \tau$ will fall in the interval given by Eq. (2-13). Prediction intervals will be discussed further in Chap. 6. Further information on confidence and prediction intervals may be found in Hines and Montgomery ([34], chap. 12) and Bowker and Lieberman ([4], chap. 9).

2-1.2 Multiple Linear Regression

Suppose that we desire to find a relationship between a dependent variable x and *several* independent variables, say $z_1, z_2, \ldots, z_k$. An appropriate model might be

$$x = b_1 z_1 + b_2 z_2 + \cdots + b_k z_k + \epsilon \quad (2\text{-}14)$$

where $b_1, b_2, \ldots, b_k$ are unknown parameters and ϵ is a random error component. If a constant term or intercept is used in the model, then $z_1 = 1$.

Equation (2-14) is often called a *multiple linear regression* model. There are k unknown parameters to be estimated, $b_1, b_2, \ldots, b_k$. Any functional relationship that is linear in the unknown parameters can be expressed in the form of Eq. (2-14).

For example, if the independent variable is a time series $\{x_t\}$ which is a quadratic function of time, say

$$x_t = b_1 + b_2 + b_3 t^2 + \epsilon_t \tag{2-15}$$

then we may write $z_1 \equiv 1$, $z_2 \equiv t$, and $z_3 \equiv t^2$, and it is easy to see that (2-15) can be expressed in the form of the multiple linear regression model (2-14). Certain types of time series may require that more complex functions of time be employed as independent variables, such as

$$x_t = b_1 + b_2 t + b_3 \sin \omega t + b_4 \cos \omega t + \epsilon_t \tag{2-16}$$

which might be a model for a *seasonal* demand process. Once again, since we may let $z_1 \equiv 1$, $z_2 \equiv t$, $z_3 \equiv \sin \omega t$, and $z_4 \equiv \cos \omega t$, this model is really a multiple linear regression model.

In many applications of regression to forecasting, the dependent variable x_t is a time series, and the independent variables are time series as well. For example, consider a problem in which we wish to forecast the net sales of a plastic products company. We believe that the net sales of the company are closely related to the annual automobile production and the net sales of the cosmetics industry, as these two industries are the major users of the plastics company's products. A logical regression model might be

$$x_t = b_1 + b_2 w_t + b_3 y_t + \epsilon_t$$

where x_t = net sales of the plastic products company in year t
$\quad w_t$ = automobile production in year t
and y_t = net cosmetic industry sales in year t
Notice that both $\{w_t\}$ and $\{y_t\}$ are time series, and by letting $z_{1t} \equiv 1$, $z_{2t} \equiv w_t$, and $z_{3t} \equiv y_t$, we may express this model in the form of a general linear regression model. We note that developing forecasting models in which some or all of the independent variables are time series can be a difficult problem. We shall discuss this point again later in more detail.

We shall assume that the general model is of the form of Eq. (2-14), and that there are n observations $(n \geqslant k)$ on the dependent variable available. The model, written in terms of the observations, is

$$x_j = b_1 + b_2 z_{2j} + b_3 z_{3j} + \cdots + b_k z_{kj} + \epsilon_j$$

$$= b_1 + \sum_{i=2}^{k} b_i z_{ij} + \epsilon_j, \qquad j = 1, 2, \ldots, n \tag{2-17}$$

where z_{ij} denotes the jth level or value taken on by the ith independent variable with $z_{1j} \equiv 1$. In time series models, such as Eqs. (2-14) and (2-15), the subscript j denotes the time period, and is usually written as t.

The unknown parameters in (2-17), that is, the $\{b_i\}$, may be estimated by least squares. This procedure requires certain assumptions about the model error component ϵ_j. Stated simply, we assume that the expected value of the errors is zero, their variance is σ_ϵ^2, and that the errors are uncorrelated. In general, if ϵ_i and ϵ_j are two uncorrelated errors, then their *covariance* is zero, where we define the covariance as

$$\text{Cov}(\epsilon_i, \epsilon_j) = E[\epsilon_i - E(\epsilon_i)][\epsilon_j - E(\epsilon_j)]$$

$$= E(\epsilon_i \cdot \epsilon_j) \tag{2-18}$$

The least-squares estimator of the $\{b_i\}$ minimizes the sum of squares of the errors, say

$$\text{SS}_E = \sum_{j=1}^{n} \epsilon_j^2$$

$$= \sum_{j=1}^{n} \left(x_j - b_1 - \sum_{i=2}^{k} b_i z_{ij} \right)^2 \tag{2-19}$$

It is necessary that the least-squares estimators satisfy the equations given by the k first partial derivatives $\partial \text{SS}_E / \partial b_i = 0,\ i = 1, 2, \ldots, k$. Therefore, differentiating (2-19) with respect to $\{b_i\}$ and equating the result to zero we obtain

$$n\hat{b}_1 + \left(\sum_{j=1}^{n} z_{2j} \right) \hat{b}_2 + \left(\sum_{j=1}^{n} z_{3j} \right) \hat{b}_3 + \cdots + \left(\sum_{j=1}^{n} z_{kj} \right) \hat{b}_k = \sum_{j=1}^{n} x_j$$

$$\left(\sum_{j=1}^{n} z_{2j} \right) \hat{b}_1 + \left(\sum_{j=1}^{n} z_{2j}^2 \right) \hat{b}_2 + \left(\sum_{j=1}^{n} z_{2j} z_{3j} \right) \hat{b}_3 + \cdots + \left(\sum_{j=1}^{n} z_{2j} z_{kj} \right) \hat{b}_k = \sum_{j=1}^{n} z_{2j} x_j$$

$$\left(\sum_{j=1}^{n} z_{3j} \right) \hat{b}_1 + \left(\sum_{j=1}^{n} z_{3j} z_{2j} \right) \hat{b}_2 + \left(\sum_{j=1}^{n} z_{3j}^2 \right) \hat{b}_3 + \cdots + \left(\sum_{j=1}^{n} z_{3j} z_{kj} \right) \hat{b}_k = \sum_{j=1}^{n} z_{3j} x_j$$

$$\cdots \cdots \cdots \cdots \cdots \cdots \cdots \cdots \cdots \cdots \cdots \cdots \cdots$$

$$\left(\sum_{j=1}^{n} z_{kj} \right) \hat{b}_1 + \left(\sum_{j=1}^{n} z_{kj} z_{2j} \right) \hat{b}_2 + \left(\sum_{j=1}^{n} z_{kj} z_{3j} \right) \hat{b}_3 + \cdots + \left(\sum_{j=1}^{n} z_{kj}^2 \right) \hat{b}_k = \sum_{j=1}^{n} z_{kj} x_j$$

$$\tag{2-20}$$

The equations (2-20) are called the least-squares normal equations.

The $\{\hat{b}_i\}$ found by solving the normal equations (2-20) are the least-squares estimators of the parameters $\{b_i\}$. The only convenient way to express the solution to the normal equations is in matrix notation. Note that the normal equations (2-20) are just a $k \times k$ set of simultaneous linear equations in k

unknowns (the $\{\hat{b}_i\}$). They may be written in matrix notation as

$$\mathbf{G}\hat{\mathbf{b}} = \mathbf{g} \tag{2-21}$$

where

$$\mathbf{G} = \begin{bmatrix} n & \sum z_{2j} & \sum z_{3j} & \cdots & \sum z_{kj} \\ \sum z_{2j} & \sum z_{2j}^2 & \sum z_{2j}z_{3j} & \cdots & \sum z_{2j}z_{kj} \\ \sum z_{3j} & \sum z_{3j}z_{2j} & \sum z_{3j}^2 & \cdots & \sum z_{3j}z_{kj} \\ \cdots & \cdots & \cdots & & \cdots \\ \sum z_{kj} & \sum z_{kj}z_{2j} & \sum z_{kj}z_{3j} & \cdots & \sum z_{kj}^2 \end{bmatrix}$$

$$\hat{\mathbf{b}} = \begin{bmatrix} \hat{b}_1 \\ \hat{b}_2 \\ \vdots \\ \hat{b}_k \end{bmatrix} \quad \text{and} \quad \mathbf{g} = \begin{bmatrix} \sum x_j \\ \sum z_{2j}x_j \\ \vdots \\ \sum z_{kj}x_j \end{bmatrix}$$

Thus, $\mathbf{G}$ is a $k \times k$ matrix, and $\hat{\mathbf{b}}$ and $\mathbf{g}$ are both $k \times 1$ column vectors. The solution to the least-squares normal equations is

$$\hat{\mathbf{b}} = \mathbf{G}^{-1}\mathbf{g} \tag{2-22}$$

where $\mathbf{G}^{-1}$ denotes the inverse of the matrix $\mathbf{G}$. For further details of the matrix approach to multiple linear regression, see Draper and Smith [23], Hines and Montgomery [34], and Appendix 2A.

Given a solution to the least-squares normal equations, the fitted multiple linear regression model is

$$\hat{x} = \hat{b}_1 + \sum_{i=2}^{k} \hat{b}_i z_i$$

The difference between the fitted model and the actual data is called a *residual*. Thus, if $\hat{x}_j$ is the fitted value corresponding to x_j, the jth residual is

$$e_j = x_j - \hat{x}_j$$

Properties of the least-squares estimators The least-squares estimators $\{\hat{b}_i\}$ from (2-22) are unbiased estimators of the true unknown parameters $\{b_i\}$; that is,

$$E\left(\hat{b}_i\right) = b_i \qquad i = 1, 2, \ldots, k \tag{2-23}$$

We may also find the variances and covariances of the least-squares estimators. If we let

$$\mathbf{C} = \mathbf{G}^{-1}$$

and denote the individual elements of the matrix $\mathbf{C}$ by C_{ij}, then the variance of $\hat{b}_i$ is

$$V(\hat{b}_i) = C_{ii}\sigma_\epsilon^2 \tag{2-24a}$$

That is, the variance of $\hat{b}_i$ is σ_ϵ^2 times the ith diagonal element of $\mathbf{G}^{-1}$. Furthermore, the covariance between any two regression coefficients $\hat{b}_i$ and $\hat{b}_j$ is

$$\text{Cov}(\hat{b}_i, \hat{b}_j) = C_{ij}\sigma_\epsilon^2 \tag{2-24b}$$

The properties in (2-23) and (2-24) are proved in Appendix 2A.

The variance of the errors is usually unknown and must be estimated from the data. If the true process is adequately described by the model, then we may estimate σ_ϵ^2 by

$$\hat{\sigma}_\epsilon^2 = \frac{\displaystyle\sum_{j=1}^{n} (x_j - \hat{x}_j)^2}{n - k} \tag{2-25}$$

Regression analysis forms the underlying basis for many forecasting procedures, and, as we have indicated, a regression model may occasionally be used as a forecasting technique. When the independent variables are functions of time, the forecast for a future time period $T + \tau$ is obtained by setting the index for time equal to $T + \tau$. In certain situations when the independent variables are simple mathematical functions of time, very efficient estimation and forecasting procedures can be derived. We shall discuss this in more detail in Chap. 4.

When some or all of the independent variables in the regression model are not simple mathematical functions of time, the forecasting problem is more complicated. Many economic forecasting models assume that the observed time series $\{x_t\}$ is related to other time series, say $\{z_{1t}\}, \ldots, \{z_{kt}\}$, and the forecasting equation consists of a regression model with the $\{z_{it}\}$ as independent variables. If at time T we wish to forecast $x_{T+\tau}$, then we must have available values of each of the independent time series $\{z_{it}\}$ at time $T + \tau$. As these values of the independent time series are not usually known, we must forecast them. If the forecasts of the independent time series are in error, then additional error is introduced into the forecast for $x_{T+\tau}$.

A further disadvantage of this approach is that in practice it is difficult to select an appropriate set of independent time series, since it is possible to obtain very high correlations between time series that are really completely unrelated. That is, historically it may appear that the sales of a product are highly correlated with the closing price of the company's stock, but eventually sales will turn in the opposite direction from the stock price. Apparent correlations between time series that are really unrelated are sometimes called "nonsense" correlations.

Prediction interval in multiple regression   Suppose we wish to obtain an interval estimate for some future observation at a particular set of levels of the independent variables. Let $z_{1u}, z_{2u}, z_{3u}, \ldots, z_{ku}$ denote the desired levels of the independent variables (note that in models containing a constant term b_1, we would define $z_{1u} \equiv 1$). A point estimate of x_u, the future observation, is

$$\hat{x}_u = \sum_{i=1}^{k} \hat{b}_i z_{iu} \tag{2-26}$$

If, in addition to our previous assumptions, we assume that the errors are normally distributed, then the $100(1 - \alpha)\%$ prediction interval for x_u is

$$\hat{x}_u \pm t_{\alpha/2,\, n-k} \left[\hat{\sigma}_\epsilon^2 \left(1 + \sum_{i=1}^{k} \sum_{j=1}^{k} z_{iu} z_{ju} C_{ij} \right) \right]^{1/2} \tag{2-27}$$

where $t_{\alpha/2,\, n-k}$ is the upper $\alpha/2$ percentage point of the t distribution with $n - k$ degrees of freedom.

Significance of the model parameters   Before a multiple regression model is used to generate forecasts, the analyst should be certain that all the parameters in the model are statistically significant. A parameter which is not significant is assumed to be zero, and would be eliminated from the model. If the errors are assumed to be normally distributed, there are several statistical tests that may be employed. The overall significance of the regression model is tested by computing the statistic

$$F_0 = \frac{\sum_{j=1}^{n} (\hat{x}_j - \bar{x})^2 / (k - 1)}{\hat{\sigma}_\epsilon^2} \tag{2-28}$$

where $\bar{x} = 1/n \sum_{j=1}^{n} x_j$ is the average of the x_j's, and comparing F_0 to the upper α percentage point of the F distribution with $k - 1$ and $n - k$ degrees of freedom, which is usually denoted by $F_{\alpha,\, k-1,\, n-k}$. If $F_0 > F_{\alpha,\, k-1,\, n-k}$, then at least one parameter in the model is significant, i.e., nonzero. On the other hand, if $F_0 < F_{\alpha,\, k-1,\, n-k}$, then all parameters in the model are zero and a very poor regression model has been constructed.

The significance of individual parameters may be investigated by performing t tests. Recall that $C_{11}, C_{22}, \ldots, C_{kk}$ are the k diagonal elements of the matrix $\mathbf{C} = \mathbf{G}^{-1}$. To test the significance of the model parameter b_i, compute the statistic

$$t_0 = \frac{\hat{b}_i}{\sqrt{\hat{\sigma}_\epsilon^2 C_{ii}}}$$ (2-29)

If $|t_0| > t_{\alpha/2,\,n-k}$, then the parameter b_i would be assumed to be nonzero. This test procedure can be misleading, however. In general, the $\hat{b}_i$ are not independent, and thus the t tests of Eq. (2-29) will not be independent. The results of this may be that b_i appears to be significant only because its estimator $\hat{b}_i$ is not independent of $\hat{b}_j$, and b_j really *is* significant. For a fuller discussion of this problem, refer to Draper and Smith [23].

The coefficient of determination

$$R^2 = \frac{\displaystyle\sum_{j=1}^{n} (\hat{x}_j - \bar{x})^2}{\displaystyle\sum_{j=1}^{n} (x_j - \bar{x})^2}$$ (2-30)

is sometimes proposed as a measure of the adequacy of a regression model. R^2 can take on values from 0 to 1, with the latter value indicating a situation in which all the variability in the data has been explained by the regression model. However, R^2 is by itself almost meaningless, as it contains no information about the model's predictive capability. It is possible to make $R^2 = 1$ by simply fitting a polynomial of degree $n - 1$ to the n data points. Such a model would almost certainly be a worthless predictor.

2-2 SIMPLE MOVING AVERAGES FOR A CONSTANT PROCESS

Suppose that a time series is generated by a constant process plus random error, such as

$$x_t = b + \epsilon_t$$ (2-31)

where ϵ_t is a random variable with mean 0 and variance σ_ϵ^2, and b is an unknown parameter. It is possible that in different widely separated parts of the sequence of observations the value of b will be different, but in any local segment of data b is a constant.

To forecast future values of the time series we must estimate the unknown parameter b in Eq. (2-31). Suppose that all observations from the origin of time through the current period, say $x_1, x_2, \ldots, x_T$, are available. If we consider all these observations to be equally important in estimating b, then they would be weighted equally, and the least-squares criterion is to choose b so as to minimize

$$\text{SS}_E = \sum_{t=1}^{T} (x_t - b)^2$$

From $\partial SS_E / \partial b = 0$ we obtain

$$\hat{b} = \frac{1}{T} \sum_{t=1}^{T} x_t \qquad (2\text{-}32)$$

which is just the arithmetic mean, or sample mean, of the T observations.

The arithmetic mean includes all past observations of the time series $\{x_t\}$. Since the value of the unknown parameter b can change slowly with time, it is reasonable to place more weight on the most current observations than on those observed a long time ago.   Suppose we decide to include only the most recent N observations in the estimation problems and to weight these observations equally (note that this is equivalent to assigning weight $1/N$ to x_T, x_{T-1}, $\ldots, x_{T-N+1}$ and weight 0 to observations $x_{T-N}, x_{T-N-1}, \ldots, x_1$).   The least-squares criterion becomes

$$SS_E = \sum_{t=T-N+1}^{T} (x_t - b)^2$$

and we obtain

$$\frac{\partial SS_E}{\partial b} \bigg|_{b=\hat{b}} = -2 \sum_{t=T-N+1}^{T} (x_t - \hat{b}) = 0$$

whose solution is

$$\hat{b} = \frac{1}{N} \sum_{t=T-N+1}^{T} x_t \equiv M_T \qquad (2\text{-}33)$$

We see that M_T is just the average of the most recent N observations, that is,

$$M_T = \frac{x_T + x_{T-1} + x_{T-2} + \cdots + x_{T-N+1}}{N} \qquad (2\text{-}34)$$

At each period the oldest observation is discarded and the newest one added to the set.   For this reason, M_T is called an N-period *simple moving average*. At the end of period T, the forecast for any future period $T + \tau$ is just

$$\hat{x}_{T+\tau}(T) = M_T \qquad (2\text{-}35)$$

An alternate equation for computing the simple moving average is occasionally more convenient.   From Eq. (2-34) and the definition of a moving average we see that

$$M_T = \frac{x_T + (x_{T-1} + x_{T-2} + \cdots + x_{T-N+1} + x_{T-N}) - x_{T-N}}{N}$$

but $M_{T-1} = (x_{T-1} + x_{T-2} + \cdots + x_{T-N+1} + x_{T-N})/N$, so that an alternate equation for computing the N-period simple moving average is

$$M_T = M_{T-1} + \frac{x_T - x_{T-N}}{N} \qquad (2\text{-}36)$$

Thus it is possible to obtain M_T directly from the previous value, M_{T-1}.

EXAMPLE 2-2 Five years of demand data for a thermostat are shown in Fig. 2-2 and listed in Table 2-2. Notice that each year has been divided into 13 four-week periods so that reporting intervals will be of equal length. Management wishes to develop a technique for forecasting demand for this thermostat. Examination of the data reveals no significant trend or cyclic behavior, so that the assumption of a constant process is probably appropriate, and a simple moving average could be used as the forecasting technique.

Suppose we decide to use a six-period moving average. Since the first six periods' demands are $x_1 = 158$, $x_2 = 222$, $x_3 = 248$, $x_4 = 216$, $x_5 = 226$, and $x_6 = 239$, we may compute from Eq. (2-34)

$$M_6 = \frac{158 + 222 + 248 + 216 + 226 + 239}{6} = 218.17$$

Therefore, the one-period-ahead forecast is $\hat{x}_7(6) = 218.17$. Moving ahead to

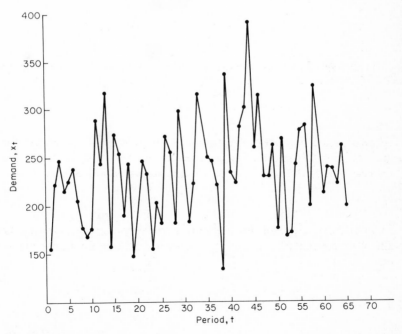

Fig. 2-2 Demand data for a thermostat.

TABLE 2-2   Six-Period Moving Average and Forecasts for the Thermostat Demand Data

Period, T	Demand, x_T	Six-period moving average, M_T	One-period-ahead forecast, $\hat{x}_T(T-1)$
1	158		
2	222		
3	248		
4	216		
5	226		
6	239	218.17	
7	206	226.17	218.17
8	178	218.83	226.17
9	169	205.67	218.83
10	177	199.17	205.67
11	290	209.83	199.17
12	245	210.83	209.83
13	318	229.50	210.83
14	158	226.17	229.50
15	274	243.67	226.17
16	255	256.67	243.67
17	191	240.17	256.67
18	244	240.00	240.17
19	149	211.83	240.00
20	195	218.00	211.83
21	247	213.50	218.00
22	233	209.83	213.50
23	156	204.00	209.83
24	203	197.17	204.00
25	182	202.67	197.17
26	272	215.50	202.67
27	256	217.00	215.50
28	184	208.83	217.00
29	299	232.67	208.83
30	246	239.83	232.67
31	184	240.17	239.83
32	224	232.17	240.17
33	316	242.17	232.17
34	285	259.00	242.17
35	251	251.00	259.00
36	248	251.33	251.00
37	222	257.67	251.33
38	135	242.83	257.67
39	337	246.33	242.83
40	235	238.00	246.33
41	225	233.67	238.00
42	282	239.33	233.67
43	302	252.67	239.33
44	391	295.33	252.67
45	261	282.67	295.33

TABLE 2-2 (Continued)

Period, T	Demand, x_T	Six-period moving average, M_T	One-period-ahead forecast, $\hat{x}_T(T-1)$
46	315	296.00	282.67
47	231	297.00	296.00
48	231	288.50	297.00
49	263	282.00	288.50
50	177	246.33	282.00
51	270	247.83	246.33
52	169	223.50	247.83
53	172	213.67	223.50
54	243	215.67	213.67
55	278	218.17	215.67
56	283	235.83	218.17
57	200	224.17	235.83
58	324	250.00	224.17
59	266	265.67	250.00
60	214	260.83	265.67
61	240	254.50	260.83
62	239	247.17	254.50
63	224	251.17	247.17
64	262	240.83	251.17
65	200	229.83	240.83

period 7, we find that $x_7 = 206$. Then to compute M_7 we drop x_1 and add x_7 to obtain

$$M_7 = \frac{222 + 248 + 216 + 226 + 239 + 206}{6} = 226.17$$

Alternatively, we may use Eq. (2-36) and obtain

$$M_7 = M_6 - \frac{x_7 - x_1}{6}$$

$$= 218.17 - \frac{206 - 158}{6} = 226.17$$

Table 2-2 shows the six-period moving average for the remaining periods, as well as the one-period-ahead forecast. The one-period-ahead forecast is plotted against the data in Fig. 2-3.

The properties of the simple-moving-average method depend on the number of past observations to be averaged. If N is large, the moving average will react

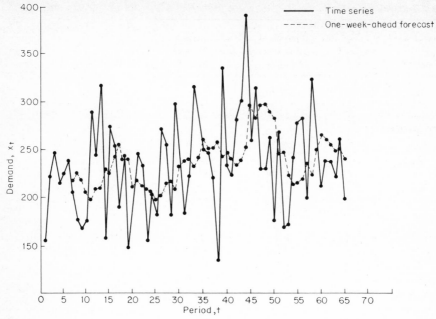

Fig. 2-3 Demand and one-week-ahead forecasts for the thermostat data.

slowly to changes in the parameter b, and when N is smaller, the moving average will react more quickly.   If the time series process has a value of $b = b_1$, say, and then suddenly shifts to a new value $b = b_2$, it will take N periods for the moving average to produce forecasts that are consistent with the new value of b. However, if the random errors are independent random variables, the variance of M_T (or $\hat{b}$) is σ_ϵ^2 / N, so that for small N the variance of M_T is relatively large. Therefore, when the process is really constant we would like to use a large value of N so that b can be estimated more precisely, and when the process is changing, we would like to use a small value of N so that M_T will be responsive to changes in b.

In many forecasting applications, it is difficult to change the number of observations averaged, as this may involve redesigning computer files or programs.   Often, this inflexibility is a major reason for using other forecasting methods.   Furthermore, an N-period moving average requires that all N observations must be saved.   For even a moderate number of different time series, a significant data storage problem could result.

2-3 MOVING AVERAGES FOR A LINEAR TREND PROCESS

The moving average approach may be used to forecast future observations from a time series which has a linear trend.   Suppose the time series model is

$$x_t = b_1 + b_2 t + \epsilon_t \tag{2-37}$$

where b_1 and b_2 are unknown parameters and ϵ_t is a random error component with mean 0 and variance σ_ϵ^2.

At time T, the N-period simple moving average is

$$M_T = \frac{x_T + x_{T-1} + \cdots + x_{T-N+1}}{N} \tag{2-38}$$

The expected value of M_T, assuming that observations come from the linear trend process (2-37), is

$$
\begin{aligned}
E(M_T) &= \frac{1}{N} E(x_T + x_{T-1} + \cdots + x_{T-N+1}) \\
&= \frac{1}{N} [E(x_T) + E(x_{T-1}) + \cdots + E(x_{T-N+1})] \\
&= \frac{1}{N} [b_1 + b_2 T + b_1 + b_2(T-1) + \cdots + b_1 + b_2(T-N+1)] \\
&= \frac{1}{N} \left[Nb_1 + Nb_2 T - \frac{N(N-1)}{2} b_2 \right] \\
&= b_1 + b_2 T - \frac{N-1}{2} b_2 \tag{2-39}
\end{aligned}
$$

or

$$E(M_T) = E(x_T) - \frac{N-1}{2} b_2 \tag{2-40}$$

That is, the simple moving average M_T lags behind the observation at time T by an amount equal to $[(N-1)/2]b_2$. Therefore some method must be devised to correct for this lag.

Consider a moving average *of* the moving averages, called a *double moving average*, say

$$M_T^{[2]} = \frac{M_T + M_{T-1} + \cdots + M_{T-N+1}}{N} \tag{2-41}$$

where the bracketed superscript [2] denotes a second-order statistic, not a squared quantity. An alternate way to compute $M_T^{[2]}$ is

$$M_T^{[2]} = M_{T-1}^{[2]} + \frac{M_T - M_{T-N}}{N} \tag{2-42}$$

which is analogous to Eq. (2-36) for the simple moving average. It can be shown that

$$
\begin{aligned}
E(M_T^{[2]}) &= E(x_T) - (N-1)b_2 \\
&= b_1 + b_2 T - (N-1)b_2 \tag{2-43}
\end{aligned}
$$

Solving Eqs. (2-40) and (2-43) for b_1 and b_2, we obtain

$$b_1 = 2E(M_T) - E(M_T^{[2]}) - b_2 T$$

$$b_2 = \frac{2}{N-1}[E(M_T) - E(M_T^{[2]})]$$

Therefore, it seems logical to estimate b_1 and b_2 by

$$\hat{b}_1 = 2M_T - M_T^{[2]} - \hat{b}_2 T \qquad (2\text{-}44)$$

$$\hat{b}_2 = \frac{2}{N-1}(M_T - M_T^{[2]}) \qquad (2\text{-}45)$$

The estimate of the observation in period T would be

$$\hat{x}_T = \hat{b}_1 + \hat{b}_2 T = 2M_T - M_T^{[2]} \qquad (2\text{-}46)$$

est of per t as of per t = cur amt value

The double-moving-average method may be used for forecasting τ periods into the future. The forecast for period $T + \tau$ is obtained by extrapolating the trend τ periods into the future according to

$$\hat{x}_{T+\tau}(T) = \hat{x}_T + \hat{b}_2 \tau$$

for integer T
for τ per into future

Thus, the forecasting equation is

$$\hat{x}_{T+\tau}(T) = 2M_T - M_T^{[2]} + \tau\left(\frac{2}{N-1}\right)(M_T - M_T^{[2]}) \qquad (2\text{-}47)$$

for 1 per into fut $\hat{x}_T + \hat{b}_2$

EXAMPLE 2-3 The weekly sales of a popular novelty item are shown in Fig. 2-4. The process generating this data would seem to be well approximated by a linear trend model, and a five-week double moving average is to be used to forecast sales one week ahead. The simple moving averages, M_T, can be computed for each week starting in period 5 and are shown in the third column of Table 2-3. As soon as five simple moving averages are available, the double moving average can be computed from Eq. (2-41). This yields the first double moving average in week 9, as shown in the fourth column of Table 2-3. Thereafter, the double moving average may be computed from either Eq. (2-41) or Eq. (2-42). The one-week-ahead forecasts made at the end of week T are computed from Eq. (2-47) with $\tau = 1$ and are shown in the last column of Table 2-3. For example,

cur smoot val plus trend

$$\hat{x}_{10}(9) = 2M_9 - M_9^{[2]} + \tau\left(\frac{2}{N-1}\right)(M_9 - M_9^{[2]})$$

$$= 2(45.60) - 46.84 + (1)\left(\frac{2}{4}\right)(45.60 - 46.84)$$

$$= 43.74$$

Figure 2-5 plots the one-week-ahead forecast against the actual time series.

TABLE 2-3 Weekly Sales and Double-Moving-Average Forecasts for a Novelty Item

Week, T	Sales, x_T	Simple moving average, M_T	Double moving average, $M_T^{[2]}$	One-week-ahead forecast, $\hat{x}_T(T-1)$
1	35			
2	46			
3	51			
4	46			
5	48	45.20		
6	51	48.40		
7	46	48.40		
8	42	46.60		
9	41	45.60	46.84	
10	43	44.60	46.72	43.74
11	61	46.60	46.36	41.42
12	55	48.40	46.36	46.96
13	67	53.40	47.72	51.46
14	42	53.60	49.32	61.92
15	61	57.20	51.84	60.02
16	58	56.60	53.84	65.24
17	49	55.40	55.24	60.74
18	58	53.60	55.28	55.64
19	43	53.80	55.32	51.08
20	51	51.80	54.24	51.52
21	60	52.20	53.36	48.14
22	58	54.00	53.08	50.46
23	46	51.60	52.68	55.38
24	54	53.80	52.68	49.98
25	51	53.80	53.08	55.48
26	66	55.00	53.64	54.88
27	64	56.20	54.08	57.04
28	53	57.60	55.28	59.38
29	72	61.20	56.76	61.08
30	64	63.80	58.76	67.86
31	54	61.40	60.04	71.36
32	61	60.80	60.96	63.44
33	77	65.60	62.56	60.56
34	72	65.60	63.44	70.16
35	67	66.20	63.92	68.84
36	67	68.80	65.40	69.62
37	64	69.40	67.12	73.90
38	50	64.00	66.80	72.82
39	83	66.20	66.92	59.80
40	67	66.20	66.92	65.12
41	66	66.00	66.36	65.12
42	76	68.40	66.16	65.46
43	79	74.20	68.20	71.76
44	94	76.40	70.24	83.20
45	74	77.80	72.56	85.64
46	83	81.20	75.60	85.66

TABLE 2-3 (Continued)

Week, T	Sales, x_T	Simple moving average, M_T	Double moving average, $M_T^{[2]}$	One-week-ahead forecast, $\hat{x}_T(T-1)$
47	70	80.00	77.92	89.60
48	70	78.20	78.72	83.12
49	76	74.60	78.36	77.42
50	63	72.40	77.28	68.96
51	78	71.40	75.32	65.08
52	63	70.00	73.32	65.52
53	64	68.80	71.44	65.02
54	76	68.80	70.28	64.84
55	82	72.60	70.32	66.58
56	83	73.60	70.76	76.02
57	70	75.00	71.76	77.86
58	90	80.20	74.04	79.86
59	82	81.40	76.56	89.44
60	74	79.80	78.00	88.66
61	79	79.00	79.08	82.50
62	79	80.80	80.24	78.88
63	77	78.20	79.84	81.64
64	84	78.60	79.28	75.74
65	74	78.60	79.04	77.58

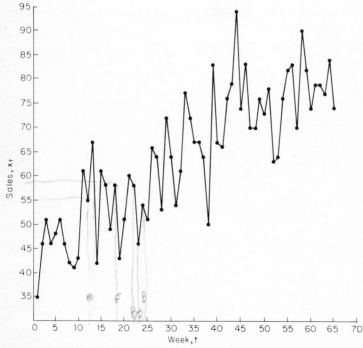

Fig. 2-4 Weekly sales of a novelty item.

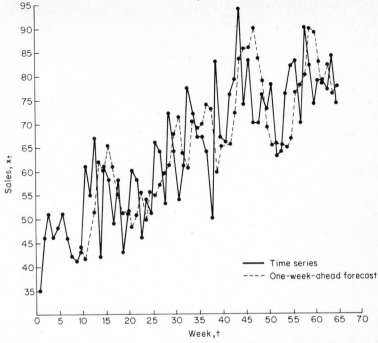

Fig. 2-5   Weekly sales and one-week-ahead forecasts for a novelty item.

The development of the double-moving-average method was *heuristic*; that is, the development was logical but not based on any optimality criterion such as least squares. It is possible to derive approximately equivalent procedures by applying the method of least squares to the linear trend model using only the most recent N observations.

The least-squares criterion to be minimized is

$$\mathrm{SS}_E = \sum_{t=T-N+1}^{T} (x_t - b_1 - b_2 t)^2 \tag{2-48}$$

where T is the time index of the latest period.   From $\partial\,\mathrm{SS}_E/\partial b_1 = \partial\,\mathrm{SS}_E/\partial b_2 = 0$ we obtain the normal equations

$$N\hat{b}_1 + \frac{N}{2}(2T+1-N)\hat{b}_2 = \sum_{t=T-N+1}^{T} x_t \tag{2-49}$$

$$\frac{N}{2}(2T+1-N)\hat{b}_1 + \frac{N}{6}[(N-1)(2N-1)+6T(T+1-N)]\hat{b}_2 = \sum_{t=T-N+1}^{T} tx_t \tag{2-50}$$

The solution to the normal equations is simplified if we shift the origin of time to the center of the data, that is, from $t = 0$ to $t = \bar{t}$, where

$$\bar{t} = \frac{1}{N} \sum_{t=T-N+1}^{T} t = T - \frac{N-1}{2}$$

Therefore, in the normal equations we make the transformation

$$t' = t - \left(T - \frac{N-1}{2} \right)$$

This results in the transformed normal equations

$$N\hat{b}_1' + (0)\hat{b}_2 = \sum_{t'=-(N-1)/2}^{(N-1)/2} x_{t'} \qquad (2\text{-}51)$$

$$(0)\hat{b}_1' + \frac{N(N^2-1)}{12} \hat{b}_2 = \sum_{t'=-(N-1)/2}^{(N-1)/2} t'x_{t'} \qquad (2\text{-}52)$$

Notice that $(N-1)/2$ is the new coded index for the current time period, that is, period T. Also, the transformation $t' = t - \bar{t}$ has not affected the slope $\hat{b}_2$, but has transformed the intercept into

$$\hat{b}_1' = \hat{b}_1 + \hat{b}_2\bar{t} \qquad (2\text{-}53)$$

Finally, we note that

$$\sum_{t'=-(N-1)/2}^{(N-1)/2} x_{t'} = \sum_{t=T-N+1}^{T} x_t$$

The solution to the transformed normal equations (2-51) and (2-52) is

$$\hat{b}_1' = \frac{1}{N} \sum_{t=T-N+1}^{T} x_t \equiv M_T \qquad (2\text{-}54)$$

and

$$\hat{b}_2 = \frac{12}{N(N^2-1)} \sum_{t'=-(N-1)/2}^{(N-1)/2} t'x_{t'}$$

$$= \frac{12}{N(N^2-1)} \left(\frac{N-1}{2} x_T + \frac{N-3}{2} x_{T-1} + \cdots - \frac{N-3}{2} x_{T-N+2} \right.$$

$$\left. - \frac{N-1}{2} x_{T-N+1} \right) \equiv U_T \qquad (2\text{-}55)$$

The transformed intercept $\hat{b}_1'$ is estimated by the simple moving average, M_T.

The slope $\hat{b}_2$ is estimated by a *weighted* moving average, U_T, in which the observation in each period is weighted by the number of periods from the center of the averaging interval. That is, we can estimate the transformed intercept and the slope at the end of period T as

$$\hat{b}_1'(T) = M_T \tag{2-56}$$

and

$$\hat{b}_2(T) = U_T \tag{2-57}$$

The original intercept at time T may be estimated by

$$\hat{b}_1(T) = M_T - U_T\left(T - \frac{N-1}{2}\right) \tag{2-58}$$

The estimates may be updated recursively as

$$\hat{b}_1'(T) \equiv M_T = M_{T-1} + \frac{x_T - x_{T-N}}{N} \tag{2-59}$$

and

$$\hat{b}_2(T) \equiv U_T = U_{T-1} + \frac{12}{N(N^2-1)}\left(\frac{N-1}{2}x_T + \frac{N+1}{2}x_{T-N} - NM_{T-1}\right) \tag{2-60}$$

To forecast τ periods into the future, we merely extrapolate the trend. The forecasting equation is

$$\hat{x}_{T+\tau}(T) = \hat{x}_T + \tau\hat{b}_2(T)$$

$$= \hat{b}_1(T) + \hat{b}_2(T)T + \tau\hat{b}_2(T)$$

$$= \hat{b}_1(T) + \hat{b}_2(T)(T + \tau)$$

$$= \hat{b}_1'(T) + \hat{b}_2(T)\left(\frac{N-1}{2} + \tau\right)$$

Using Eqs. (2-56) and (2-57), we obtain

$$x_{T+\tau}(T) = M_T + U_T\left(\frac{N-1}{2} + \tau\right) \tag{2-61}$$

The forecasting process is illustrated in Fig. 2-6. Note that the moving average lags behind the expected demand in the current period, T, by an amount $[(N-1)/2]\hat{b}_2$. Thus, to forecast for period $T + \tau$, we must first correct the moving average for the lag by adding $[(N-1)/2]\hat{b}_2(T)$ and then extrapolate the trend by adding $\tau\hat{b}_2(T)$. The numerical results obtained from this method

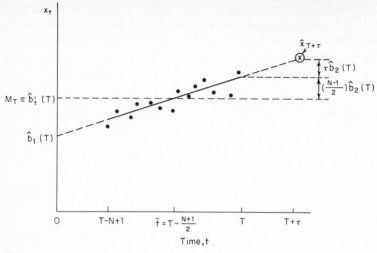

Fig. 2-6 Least-squares analysis of the last N observations.

will not agree exactly with those obtained from Eq. (2-47), that is, from the double-moving-average approach, because the double-moving-average procedure uses observations further back in time than period $T - N + 1$. These older observations are encountered in the statistics $M_T^{[2]}$, which use *simple* moving averages back to period $T - N + 1$, and M_{T-N+1} clearly is a function of observations older than $T - N + 1$.

2-4 EXERCISES

2-1   The weekly deliveries of a compact car to an automobile dealer are shown below. Fit the straight-line model $x_t = b_1 + b_2 t + \epsilon_t$ to these data. Estimate the error variance.

Week	1	2	3	4	5	6	7	8	9	10	11	12
Deliveries	75	74	79	83	69	78	71	80	77	85	81	70

2-2   An office supply firm sells file cabinets. The demand for a particular four-drawer file cabinet for the past 18 weeks is shown below. Fit the straight-line model $x_t = b_1 + b_2 t + \epsilon_t$ to the data. Estimate the error variance.

Month	1	2	3	4	5	6	7	8	9
Demand	12	4	16	9	10	15	6	8	10

Month	10	11	12	13	14	15	16	17	18
Demand	11	15	7	16	12	20	9	13	11

2-3   The data in Table B-12 (see Appendix B) represent the monthly demand for a plastic container. Fit the straight-line model $x_t = b_1 + b_2 t + \epsilon_t$ to these data. Use Eqs. (2-11) and (2-12) to construct a 95 percent prediction interval for the future observation in period 49.

2-4 The number of cases of soft drinks sold by a supermarket is thought to be linearly related to the daily high temperature. Data for the last 12 days are shown below. Fit a straight line to these data.

Sales	40	49	50	52	55	60	58	48	42	49	50	51
Temperature	79	83	84	85	86	88	87	83	78	81	82	85

2-5 Suppose we wish to fit the regression model

$$x_t = b_1 + b_2 t + b_3 t^2 + \epsilon_t$$

where ϵ_t is a random variable with $E(\epsilon_t) = 0$ and $V(\epsilon_t) = \sigma_\epsilon^2$. Find the least-squares estimators of b_1, b_2, and b_3.

2-6 Using the results of Exercise 2-5, fit the model $x_t = b_1 + b_2 + b_3 t^2 + \epsilon_t$ to the data shown below. Estimate the error variance.

t	1	2	3	4	5	6	7	8
x_t	3	5	9	14	20	26	35	44

2-7 *Weighted least squares.* Consider the simple linear regression model $x_t = b_1 + b_2 t + \epsilon_t$, and suppose that the variance of ϵ_t is no longer constant. Instead, suppose that $V(\epsilon_t) = \sigma_t^2 = \sigma^2 / w_t$, where the weights $\{w_t\}$ are known constants. Show that the least-squares normal equations are

$$\hat{b}_1 \sum_{t=1}^{T} w_t + \hat{b}_2 \sum_{t=1}^{T} t w_t = \sum_{t=1}^{T} w_t x_t$$

$$\hat{b}_1 \sum_{t=1}^{T} t w_t + \hat{b}_2 \sum_{t=1}^{T} t^2 w_t = \sum_{t=1}^{T} t w_t x_t$$

2-8 *Continuation of Exercise 2-7.* Suppose that in weighted least squares the variance of the ϵ_t are proportional to the index of time t such that $w_t = 1/t$. Simplify the normal equations, and, if possible, solve for closed-form estimators $\hat{b}_1$ and $\hat{b}_2$.

2-9 Show that for the straight-line model $x_t = b_1 + b_2 t + \epsilon_t$, with $E(\epsilon_t) = 0$, $V(\epsilon_t) = \sigma_\epsilon^2$, and $\text{Cov}(\epsilon_i, \epsilon_j) = 0$, the variances of the least-squares estimators of b_1 and b_2 are

$$V(\hat{b}_1) = \frac{2(2T+1)}{T(T-1)} \sigma_\epsilon^2$$

and

$$V(\hat{b}_2) = \frac{12}{T(T^2-1)} \sigma_\epsilon^2$$

respectively, where T periods of data are used to estimate b_1 and b_2.

2-10 Fit the regression model

$$x_t = b_1 + b_2 \sin \frac{\pi t}{3} + b_3 \cos \frac{\pi t}{3} + \epsilon_t$$

to the data in Exercise 2-1.

2-11   Consider the data in Table B-4, which represent the weekly demand for a journal bearing used in an engine crankshaft. Use a 12-week simple moving average to forecast bearing demand for a one-period lead time. Does the assumption of a constant model seem appropriate?

2-12   The data in Table B-2 represent the weekly sales of a cutting tool used in a numerical-controlled machine. Use a 10-week simple moving average to forecast sales for a one-week lead time.

2-13   Rework Exercise 2-12 using a 10-week double moving average. Does this seem to give better results than the simple moving average?

2-14   The monthly demand for a spare part is shown in Table B-5. Use an 8-week double moving average to forecast demand for a one-month lead time.

2-15   Rework Exercise 2-14 using Eq. (2-61) to generate the forecast. In computing M_T and U_T use $N = 8$. Compare the forecasts obtained from this procedure with those obtained from the 8-week double moving average.

2-16   Rework Example 2-2 using a 12-period simple moving average. Compare the forecasts obtained from this procedure with those obtained in the example based on a six-period simple moving average.

2-17   Apply a 10-period double moving average to the data in Example 2-3. Generate forecasts for both one-period and two-period lead times. Compare the one-period lead time forecasts with those obtained in the example.

APPENDIX 2A   THE MATRIX APPROACH TO MULTIPLE REGRESSION

We shall now present some of the results of Sec. 2-1.2 in matrix notation. The use of matrix algebra has many advantages, among them simplicity of expression and ease of calculation.

Assume that the general model is

$$x = b_1 + b_2 z_2 + b_3 z_3 + \cdots + b_k x_k + \epsilon \qquad (2A\text{-}1)$$

and that there are $n > k$ observations on the dependent variable, say $(x_j, z_{2j}, z_{3j}, \ldots, z_{kj})$ for $j = 1, 2, \ldots, n$. The model may be written in terms of the observations as

$$x_j = b_1 + \sum_{i=2}^{k} b_2 z_{ij} + \epsilon_j \qquad j = 1, 2, \ldots, n \qquad (2A\text{-}2)$$

Note that z_{ij} denotes the jth level of the ith independent variable.

It is convenient to express (2A-2) in matrix notation. Let $\mathbf{x}$ be an $n \times 1$ column vector of the observations, $\mathbf{Z}$ be an $n \times k$ matrix of the independent variables, $\mathbf{b}$ be a $k \times 1$ column vector of the unknown parameters, and $\boldsymbol{\epsilon}$ be an

$n \times 1$ column vector of the errors; that is,

$$
\mathbf{x} = \begin{bmatrix} x_1 \\ x_2 \\ \vdots \\ x_n \end{bmatrix}
\qquad
\mathbf{Z} = \begin{bmatrix} 1 & z_{21} & z_{31} & \cdots & z_{k1} \\ 1 & z_{22} & z_{32} & \cdots & z_{k2} \\ & \cdots & \cdots & \cdots & \\ 1 & z_{2n} & z_{3n} & \cdots & z_{kn} \end{bmatrix}
$$

$$
\mathbf{b} = \begin{bmatrix} b_1 \\ b_2 \\ \vdots \\ b_k \end{bmatrix}
\qquad \text{and} \qquad
\boldsymbol{\epsilon} = \begin{bmatrix} \epsilon_1 \\ \epsilon_2 \\ \vdots \\ \epsilon_n \end{bmatrix}
$$

Consequently, in matrix notation the model (2A-2) is

$$\mathbf{x} = \mathbf{Z}\mathbf{b} + \boldsymbol{\epsilon} \tag{2A-3}$$

Equation (2A-3) is often called the *general linear model*, as any functional relationship which is linear in the unknown parameters can be expressed in this form.

To estimate the vector of unknown parameters $\mathbf{b}$ by least squares, certain assumptions are required about the elements of the error vector $\boldsymbol{\epsilon}$. Specifically, we assume that the expected value of the errors is zero, their variance is σ_ϵ^2, and that the errors are uncorrelated. It is notationally convenient to express these assumptions in matrix form. We may write $E(\epsilon_t) = 0$ for $t = 1, 2, \ldots, n$, as

$$E(\boldsymbol{\epsilon}) = \mathbf{0}$$

where $\mathbf{0}$ represents an $n \times 1$ column vector of 0's. The variance and correlation assumptions on $\boldsymbol{\epsilon}$ may be summarized in the $n \times n$ *covariance matrix*

$$
\begin{bmatrix} \sigma_\epsilon^2 & 0 & 0 & \cdots & 0 \\ 0 & \sigma_\epsilon^2 & 0 & \cdots & 0 \\ & \cdots & \cdots & \cdots & \\ 0 & 0 & 0 & \cdots & \sigma_\epsilon^2 \end{bmatrix}
$$

The covariance matrix of $\boldsymbol{\epsilon}$ is an $n \times n$ matrix whose ith diagonal element is the variance of ϵ_i, and whose (i, j)th off-diagonal element is the *covariance* between ϵ_i and ϵ_j. It is easy to see that the covariance matrix of $\boldsymbol{\epsilon}$ may also be written as $\sigma_\epsilon^2 \mathbf{I}$, where $\mathbf{I}$ is an $n \times n$ identity matrix.

For a vector of estimates $\hat{\mathbf{b}}' = [\hat{b}_1, \hat{b}_2, \ldots, \hat{b}_k]$ the fitted model is

$$\hat{\mathbf{x}} = \mathbf{Z}\hat{\mathbf{b}} \tag{2A-4}$$

where the prime (') denotes the transpose of a vector or matrix. The difference between the fitted model and the actual data is called a residual. Here the vector of residuals is

$$\mathbf{e} = \mathbf{x} - \hat{\mathbf{x}}$$

$$= \mathbf{x} - \mathbf{Z}\hat{\mathbf{b}} \tag{2A-5}$$

The least-squares estimator of $\mathbf{b}$ minimizes the sum of squares of the errors,

$$SS_E = \sum_{j=1}^{n} \epsilon_j^2$$

which in matrix notation is

$$SS_E = \epsilon'\epsilon = (\mathbf{x} - \mathbf{Zb})'(\mathbf{x} - \mathbf{Zb}) \tag{2A-6}$$

The right-hand side of (2A-6) may be expanded as

$$SS_E = \mathbf{x}'\mathbf{x} - \mathbf{b}'\mathbf{Z}'\mathbf{x} - \mathbf{x}'\mathbf{Zb} + \mathbf{b}'\mathbf{Zb}$$

$$= \mathbf{x}'\mathbf{x} - 2\mathbf{b}'\mathbf{Z}'\mathbf{x} + \mathbf{b}'\mathbf{Z}'\mathbf{Zb} \tag{2A-7}$$

It is necessary that the least-squares estimator satisfy $\partial SS_E / \partial \mathbf{b} = \mathbf{0}$. Therefore, differentiating (2A-7) with respect to $\mathbf{b}$, we obtain

$$-2\mathbf{Z}'\mathbf{x} + 2\mathbf{Z}'\mathbf{Z}\hat{\mathbf{b}} = \mathbf{0}$$

and thus the least-squares normal equations are

$$\mathbf{Z}'\mathbf{Z}\hat{\mathbf{b}} = \mathbf{Z}'\mathbf{x} \tag{2A-8}$$

The solution to the normal equations, i.e., the least-squares estimator, is

$$\hat{\mathbf{b}} = (\mathbf{Z}'\mathbf{Z})^{-1}\mathbf{Z}'\mathbf{x} \tag{2A-9}$$

if $(\mathbf{Z}'\mathbf{Z})^{-1}$ exists. Note that (2A-8) and (2A-9) correspond to (2-21) and (2-22), respectively. We may easily verify the bias and variance properties of the least-squares estimator $\hat{\mathbf{b}}$. Consider first bias:

$$E(\hat{\mathbf{b}}) = E\left[(\mathbf{Z}'\mathbf{Z})^{-1}\mathbf{Z}'\mathbf{x}\right]$$

$$= (\mathbf{Z}'\mathbf{Z})^{-1}\mathbf{Z}'\, E(\mathbf{x})$$

$$= (\mathbf{Z}'\mathbf{Z})^{-1}\mathbf{Z}'\, E(\mathbf{Zb} + \epsilon)$$

$$= (\mathbf{Z}'\mathbf{Z})^{-1}\mathbf{Z}'\mathbf{Zb} + (\mathbf{Z}'\mathbf{Z})^{-1}\mathbf{Z}'\, E(\epsilon)$$

$$= \mathbf{b}$$

because $E(\epsilon) = 0$ and $(\mathbf{Z}'\mathbf{Z})^{-1}\mathbf{Z}'\mathbf{Z} = \mathbf{I}$. The covariance matrix of the least-squares estimator is, letting $\mathbf{G} = \mathbf{Z}'\mathbf{Z}$ for convenience,

$$
\begin{aligned}
\mathbf{V} &= E\left[(\hat{\mathbf{b}} - \mathbf{b})(\hat{\mathbf{b}} - \mathbf{b})'\right] \\
&= E\left\{[\mathbf{G}^{-1}\mathbf{Z}'\mathbf{x} - \mathbf{G}^{-1}\mathbf{Z}'E(\mathbf{x})][\mathbf{G}^{-1}\mathbf{Z}'\mathbf{x} - \mathbf{G}^{-1}\mathbf{Z}'E(\mathbf{x})]'\right\} \\
&= E\left\{\mathbf{G}^{-1}\mathbf{Z}'[\mathbf{x} - E(\mathbf{x})][\mathbf{x} - E(\mathbf{x})]'[\mathbf{G}^{-1}\mathbf{Z}']'\right\} \\
&= \mathbf{G}^{-1}\mathbf{Z}'E(\epsilon\epsilon')\mathbf{Z}\mathbf{G}^{-1} = \mathbf{G}^{-1}\sigma_\epsilon^2 \qquad\qquad (2A\text{-}10)
\end{aligned}
$$

since $E(\epsilon\epsilon') = \sigma_\epsilon^2\mathbf{I}$ and $\mathbf{G}^{-1}$ is a symmetric matrix.

The error variance may be estimated by

$$
\hat{\sigma}_\epsilon^2 = \frac{(\mathbf{x} - \hat{\mathbf{x}})'(\mathbf{x} - \hat{\mathbf{x}})}{n - k}
$$

$$
= \frac{\mathbf{e}'\mathbf{e}}{n - k} \qquad\qquad (2A\text{-}11)
$$

which is analogous to Eq. (2-25). We can show that $\hat{\sigma}_\epsilon^2$ is an unbiased estimator of σ_ϵ^2.

If we additionally assume that the errors ϵ are normally distributed, then we may develop confidence and prediction intervals, and test various hypotheses about the model parameters. Invoking this assumption, we now have $\epsilon \sim N(\mathbf{0}, \sigma_\epsilon^2\mathbf{I})$, and consequently, $\mathbf{x} \sim N(\mathbf{Zb}, \sigma_\epsilon^2\mathbf{I})$. Suppose we wish to find a $100(1-\alpha)\%$ prediction interval on a future observation at the point $\mathbf{z}_u' = (1, z_{2u}, z_{3u}, \ldots, z_{ku})$. The point estimate of the future observation is $\hat{x}_u = \mathbf{z}_u'\hat{\mathbf{b}}$, and the $100(1-\alpha)\%$ prediction interval is

$$
\hat{x}_u \pm t_{\alpha/2,\, n-k}\left[\hat{\sigma}_\epsilon^2\left(1 + \mathbf{z}_u'(\mathbf{Z}'\mathbf{Z})^{-1}\mathbf{z}_u\right)\right]^{1/2} \qquad\qquad (2A\text{-}12)
$$

Equation (2A-12) is the matrix counterpart of (2-27).

CHAPTER THREE

Exponential Smoothing Methods

In this chapter, we give a description of exponential smoothing methods for forecast generation. Exponential smoothing is probably the most widely used class of procedures for smoothing discrete time series in order to forecast the immediate future. As we shall see, this popularity can be attributed to its simplicity, its computational efficiency, the ease of adjusting its responsiveness to changes in the process being forecast, and its reasonable accuracy.

Initially, we shall present exponential smoothing methods for a constant process and a linear trend process, before giving a more general treatment for higher-ordered polynomial process models. In the first two cases, the estimation and forecasting equations can be developed heuristically, as well as through use of a weighted least-squares criterion. Both the intuitive and the mathematical development will be given.

3-1 EXPONENTIAL SMOOTHING FOR A CONSTANT PROCESS

3-1.1 Development of Simple Exponential Smoothing

Suppose we believe that the average level of demand is not changing over time, or, if it is changing, it is doing so very slowly. In this case we might model the process as

$$x_t = b + \epsilon_t$$

where b = expected demand in any period

    ϵ_t = random component having mean 0 and variance σ_ϵ^2

At the end of period T, we have available a demand history, $x_1, x_2, \ldots, x_T$, from which we wish to estimate b and σ_ϵ^2. We could use an N-period moving average, developed in Sec. 2-2, as an estimate of b; however, here we shall use an alternative method, called *simple exponential smoothing*.

Since our forecasting system involves reestimating the model parameters each period in order to incorporate the most recent period's demand, we can assume that at the end of period T we have available the estimate of b made at the end of the previous period, $\hat{b}(T-1)$, and the current period's actual demand, x_T. We want to use this information to calculate an updated estimate $\hat{b}(T)$. A reasonable way to obtain the new estimate is to modify the old estimate by some fraction of the forecast error resulting from using the old estimate to forecast demand in the current period. This forecast error is

$$e_1(T) = x_T - \hat{b}(T-1)$$

so that if α is the desired fraction, the new estimate of expected demand is

$$\hat{b}(T) = \hat{b}(T-1) + \alpha\left[x_T - \hat{b}(T-1)\right]$$

To simplify notation, define $\hat{b}(T) \equiv S_T$, and write the above as

$$S_T = S_{T-1} + \alpha[x_T - S_{T-1}]$$

or

$$S_T = \alpha x_T + (1-\alpha)S_{T-1} \qquad (3\text{-}1)$$

The operation defined by (3-1) is called *simple exponential smoothing*,[1] and S_T is called the smoothed value, or the smoothed statistic. The fraction α is called the *smoothing constant*. From the above development, we note that exponential smoothing is a procedure that adjusts the smoothed statistic by an amount that is proportional to the most recent forecast error.

Although the above development was heuristic, it turns out that the result (3-1) has some formal statistical respectability in that it can be obtained using a weighted least-squares criterion. To demonstrate this, suppose that we wish to estimate b such that the following sum of weighted squared errors is minimized:

$$SS_E = \sum_{t=1}^{T} \beta^{T-t}(x_t - b)^2 \qquad 0 < \beta < 1 \qquad (3\text{-}2)$$

The weight given to the tth squared error is β^{T-t}, so that the weights decrease geometrically with the age of the data. The estimate of b, made at the end of

---

[1] Other commonly used names are *basic exponential smoothing, first-order exponential smoothing,* and *single smoothing*.

period T and denoted by $\hat{b}(T)$, must satisfy

$$\frac{dSS_E}{db}\bigg|_{\hat{b}} = -2\sum_{t=1}^{T}\beta^{T-t}\left[x_t - \hat{b}(T)\right] = 0$$

or

$$\hat{b}(T)\sum_{t=1}^{T}\beta^{T-t} = \sum_{t=1}^{T}\beta^{T-t}x_t$$

This solution is

$$\hat{b}(T) = \frac{1-\beta}{1-\beta^{T}}\sum_{t=1}^{T}\beta^{T-t}x_t \tag{3-3}$$

Equation (3-3) expresses the estimator as a function of all prior historical data. However, it will be more convenient to have an equation that permits $\hat{b}(T)$ to be computed from x_T and $\hat{b}(T-1)$.   It is not difficult to show that

$$\hat{b}(T) = \frac{(1-\beta)x_T + \beta(1-\beta^{T-1})\hat{b}(T-1)}{1-\beta^{T}} \tag{3-4}$$

If T is large, then $\beta^{T} \approx 0$ and (3-4) becomes

$$\hat{b}(T) = (1-\beta)x_T + \beta\hat{b}(T-1)$$

Letting $\alpha = 1 - \beta$ and $S_T = \hat{b}(T)$, we obtain

$$S_T = \alpha x_T + (1-\alpha)S_{T-1}$$

which is identical to (3-1).

3-1.2 Properties of Simple Exponential Smoothing

The statistic S_T is a weighted average of all past observations.   To show this, we first demonstrate how S_T can be written as a linear combination of past data and then observe that the weights given to past observations are nonnegative and add to 1, thus making it possible to interpret S_T as a weighted average. Substituting for S_{T-1} in the right-hand side of Eq. (3-1), we obtain

$$S_T = \alpha x_T + (1-\alpha)[\alpha x_{T-1} + (1-\alpha)S_{T-2}]$$

$$= \alpha x_T + \alpha(1-\alpha)x_{T-1} + (1-\alpha)^2 S_{T-2}$$

Continuing to substitute recursively for S_{T-k}, $k = 2, 3, \ldots, T$, we finally obtain

$$S_T = \alpha \sum_{k=0}^{T-1}(1-\alpha)^k x_{T-k} + (1-\alpha)^T S_0 \tag{3-5}$$

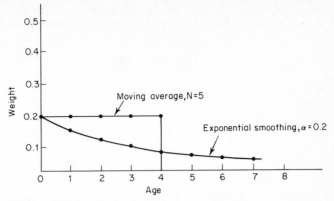

Fig. 3-1 Weights of past observations.

where S_0 is the initial estimate of b used to start the smoothing process. The weights sum to unity, since

$$\alpha \sum_{k=0}^{T-1} (1-\alpha)^k = \alpha \left[\frac{1-(1-\alpha)^T}{1-(1-\alpha)} \right] = 1-(1-\alpha)^T$$

With the exception of the coefficient of S_0, the weights decrease geometrically with the age of the observations. If the smoothing constant is 0.2, then the weight associated with the current observation is 0.2 and the weights assigned to previous observations are 0.16, 0.128, 0.1024, and so on. A comparison of these weights with those of a five-period moving average is shown in Fig. 3-1. Because these weights appear to decline exponentially when connected by a smooth curve, the name *exponential smoothing* has been applied to this procedure.

For T sufficiently large so that $(1-\alpha)^T S_0$ is close to zero, the exponential smoothing process yields an unbiased estimate of the true process average, b, since

$$E(S_T) = E\left[\alpha \sum_{k=0}^{\infty} (1-\alpha)^k x_{T-k} \right] = \alpha \sum_{k=0}^{\infty} (1-\alpha)^k E(x_{T-k})$$

$$= b\alpha \sum_{k=0}^{\infty} (1-\alpha)^k = b$$

Therefore, it seems reasonable to use S_T as an estimator of the unknown parameter b, that is, at time T,

$$\hat{b}(T) = S_T$$

and our forecast for demand in any future period $T + \tau$ would be

$$\hat{x}_{T+\tau}(T) = S_T \tag{3-6}$$

The choice of the smoothing constant α is important in determining the operating characteristics of exponential smoothing. Essentially the response of the forecast to changes in the parameter b is a function of the size of α. The smaller the value of α, the slower the response. Larger values of α cause the smoothed value to react quickly—not only to real changes but also to random fluctuations. The effect of α on responsiveness can be judged by comparing exponential smoothing and moving average methods. The average age of the data in an N-period moving average is

av age of data

$$\frac{1}{N}\sum_{k=0}^{N-1} k = \frac{N-1}{2}$$

In exponential smoothing, the weight given to data k periods ago is $\alpha(1-\alpha)^k$, so that the average age is

$\frac{1-.6}{.6}=\frac{2}{3}$ $\frac{1-.5}{.5}=1$ *$\frac{1-.2}{.2}=4$*

$$\alpha\sum_{k=0}^{\infty}(1-\alpha)^k k = \frac{1-\alpha}{\alpha}$$

Thus if we wish to define an exponential smoothing system that is equivalent to an N-period moving average, we set $(1-\alpha)/\alpha = (N-1)/2$ or

$\alpha=.5$
$\frac{2}{.5}-1=4-1=3$

$$\alpha = \frac{2}{N+1}$$ *$N+1=\frac{2}{\alpha}$*   (3-7)

$N=\frac{2}{\alpha}-1$

The same result can be obtained by equating the variance of S_T and the variance of the moving average M_T. Assuming independent demands,

$\frac{2}{.6}-1=3.33-1$
≈ 2.3

$$V(S_T)=V\left[\alpha\sum_{k=0}^{\infty}(1-\alpha)^k x_{T-k}\right]=\alpha^2\sum_{k=0}^{\infty}(1-\alpha)^{2k}V(x_{T-k})$$

$$=\frac{\alpha}{2-\alpha}\sigma_\epsilon^2 \tag{3-8}$$

and

$$V(M_T)=V\left[\frac{1}{N}\sum_{k=0}^{N-1}x_{T-k}\right]=\frac{\sigma_\epsilon^2}{N} \tag{3-9}$$

Setting (3-8) equal to (3-9), we obtain (3-7). In general, the value of α should lie between 0.01 and 0.30. We shall discuss the choice of a smoothing constant more thoroughly in Sec. 3-4.

Exponential smoothing requires a starting value S_0. If historical data are available, then one can use a simple average of the most recent N observations as S_0. If there are no reliable past data available, then some subjective prediction must be made. When T is small, S_T will be unbiased only if the initial estimate S_0 is also unbiased. If this prediction is likely to be inaccurate,

TABLE 3-1   Minimum Number of Periods for Weight
Given S_0 in Computing S_T To Be Less Than or Equal to δ

Smoothing constant, α	Weight given S_0, δ			
	0.50	0.20	0.10	0.05
0.01	70	161	230	299
0.05	14	32	45	59
0.10	7	16	22	29
0.15	5	10	15	19
0.20	4	8	11	14
0.30	2	5	7	9
0.40	2	4	5	6
0.50	1	3	4	5

$$\frac{N-1}{2} = \frac{a}{1-a}$$

$$(N-1)(1-a) = 2a$$

$$N-1 = \frac{2a}{1-a}$$

$$N = 1 + \frac{2a}{1-a} = \frac{1-a+2a}{1+a}$$

$$= \frac{1+a}{1-a}$$

a larger value of α may be used in the first few periods to allow early demand
history to rapidly modify the initial estimate. The weight given to S_0 is
$(1 - \alpha)^T$, which will be less than 0.10 if

$$N = \frac{2}{\alpha} - 1$$

$$T > \frac{\ln 0.10}{\ln (1 - \alpha)} \qquad N = \frac{2}{1-a} - 1 \qquad (3\text{-}10)$$

$$= 2 - (1-a)$$

For $\alpha = 0.05$, the minimum time for S_0 to have a weight less than 0.10 in
computing S_T is calculated from (3-10) to be 45 periods; for $\alpha = 0.3$, this drops
to 7 periods, and for $\alpha = 0.5$, 4 periods. Other values are given in Table 3-1.

$$1-a$$

$$= \frac{1+a}{1-a}$$

EXAMPLE 3-1   A manufacturer of office furniture wishes to forecast the monthly
sales of a certain model desk. This model has been in the product line for
several years and it is felt that the demand for this item is relatively stable. The
most recent two years of sales history are given in Table 3-2. A plot of these
data (see Fig. 3-2) confirms the choice of a constant process model. Simple
exponential smoothing is therefore chosen as the forecasting procedure, with
$\alpha = 0.10$ as the arbitrarily selected smoothing constant. The initial value,
$S_0 = 393.13$, is determined by averaging the demand over the past two years.
Letting the end of December 1976 be the origin of time, the forecast for period 1
(January 1977), computed at time 0, is

$$\hat{x}_1(0) = S_0 = 393$$

$$\frac{N-1}{2} = \frac{1-\alpha}{\alpha}$$

TABLE 3-2   Sales of Desks in 1975 and 1976

Year	Jan.	Feb.	Mar.	Apr.	May	June	July	Aug.	Sept.	Oct.	Nov.	Dec.
1975	423	403	474	451	465	445	459	325	365	331	376	331
1976	350	400	470	311	395	333	452	414	310	341	433	378

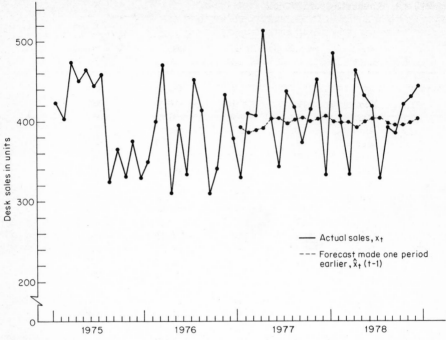

Fig. 3-2 Desk sales and one-period-ahead forecasts for Example 3-1.

after rounding. Since we are assuming a constant model, the forecast for any future month $0 + \tau$ would be

$$\hat{x}_{0+\tau}(0) = 393$$

Suppose the actual sales in January 1977 are 330 desks. Then at the end of January, the exponentially smoothed average is revised by

$$S_1 = (0.1)(330) + (0.9)(393.13) = 386.82$$

and the forecasting model becomes

$$\hat{x}_{1+\tau}(1) = 387$$

For each month in the following two years, the actual number of desks sold, the exponentially smoothed average computed at the end of the period, and the forecast made one month before for the current month are shown in Table 3-3. The results are plotted in Fig. 3-2.

The data used in this example were artificially generated using a table of random normal numbers to simulate a process having a mean $b = 400$ and a standard deviation $\sigma_\epsilon = 50$, with no serial correlation.

TABLE 3-3   Forecasting for 1977 and 1978

Year and month		Period number, T	Actual sales, x_T	Smoothed statistic, S_T	Forecast made last period, $\hat{x}_T(T-1)$
1977	Jan.	1	330	386.82	393
	Feb.	2	410	389.14	387
	Mar.	3	408	391.02	389
	Apr.	4	514	403.32	391
	May	5	402	403.19	403
	June	6	343	397.17	403
	July	7	438	401.25	397
	Aug.	8	419	403.03	401
	Sept.	9	374	400.12	403
	Oct.	10	415	401.61	400
	Nov.	11	451	406.55	402
	Dec.	12	333	399.19	407
1978	Jan.	13	386	397.87	399
	Feb.	14	408	398.89	398
	Mar.	15	333	392.30	399
	Apr.	16	463	399.37	392
	May	17	432	402.63	399
	June	18	419	404.27	403
	July	19	329	396.74	404
	Aug.	20	392	396.27	397
	Sept.	21	385	395.14	396
	Oct.	22	421	397.73	395
	Nov.	23	430	400.95	398
	Dec.	24	443	405.16	401

3-1.3 Estimation of Demand Variance

Examination of the results of Example 3-1 might cause one to wonder whether or not a better forecasting procedure could be found.   The forecast remained close to 400, while the actual sales varied from 325 to 514.   Thus, some rather large forecast errors were experienced.   It seems logical to ask whether or not there is any way to predict when sales will be below average and when they will be above average.   The answer is negative for the constant demand process under study.   This demand process is of the form

$$x_t = b + \epsilon_t$$

where b is the expected value of demand in any period and ϵ_t is the random deviation from the mean in period t.   The random component, ϵ_t, sometimes called the "noise" component in the data, is assumed to have mean 0 and variance σ_ϵ^2.   Further, it is assumed that the demands are not serially correlated; that is, $E(\epsilon_j \epsilon_k) = 0$, for all $j \neq k$.

The data for Example 3-1 were artificially generated to conform with these assumptions, using $b = 400$ and $\sigma_\epsilon = 50$. Thus, deviations of actual demand from the mean of 400 are pure random variation, and therefore by implication cannot be predicted with certainty. Exponential smoothing merely provides an estimate of the expected demand level, b, and in Example 3-1, we saw that it did a good job.

For many decision problems, however, an estimate of the expected demand is not sufficient. A measure of likely forecast error is also needed. The variance of forecast error, σ_e^2, is often used to describe uncertainty in forecasting. In Chap. 6, we shall discuss this measure in detail and show how it is related to the demand variance σ_ϵ^2. At this point, we give, without explanation, the following result for a constant demand process and simple exponential smoothing:

$$\sigma_e^2 = \frac{2}{2 - \alpha} \sigma_\epsilon^2 \tag{3-11}$$

Thus, if forecast errors are approximately normally distributed, we would expect most forecast errors to be within $\pm 2\sigma_e$.

One way to estimate the standard deviation of demand, σ_ϵ, for a constant process is to compute the sample standard deviation of a sequence of actual demand realizations. For instance, in Example 3-1, the sample standard deviation of the monthly sales in 1975 and 1976 is 55.2. This method is not satisfactory if the process mean or standard deviation is changing with time, and so other procedures, to be described in Chap. 6, are recommended.

3-2 EXPONENTIAL SMOOTHING FOR A LINEAR TREND PROCESS

The concept of exponential smoothing can be extended to certain cases where the demand process changes over time. One of these occurs where the process mean changes linearly with time according to the following model:

$$x_t = b_1 + b_2 t + \epsilon_t \tag{3-12}$$

where the expected demand at time t is a linear function of t

$$E(x_t \mid t) = b_1 + b_2 t$$

and ϵ_t is a random component having $E(\epsilon_t) = 0$ and $V(\epsilon_t) = \sigma_\epsilon^2$. Thus, the variance of demand is σ_ϵ^2, which is assumed to remain constant over time.

If simple exponential smoothing were applied to the observations from the linear process of Eq. (3-12), we would obtain at the end of period T

$$S_T = \alpha x_T + (1 - \alpha) S_{T-1} \tag{3-13}$$

By Eq. (3-5), letting $\beta = 1 - \alpha$ for convenience,

$$S_t = \alpha \sum_{k=0}^{T-1} \beta^k x_{T-k} + \beta^T S_0$$

Taking expected values,

$$E(S_T) = \alpha \sum_{k=0}^{T-1} \beta^k E(x_{T-k}) + \beta^T S_0$$

$$= \alpha \sum_{k=0}^{T-1} \beta^k [b_1 + b_2(T-k)] + \beta^T S_0$$

As $T \to \infty$, $\beta^T = 0$, and we obtain

$$E(S_T) = (b_1 + b_2 T)\alpha \sum_{k=0}^{\infty} \beta^k - b_2 \alpha \sum_{k=0}^{\infty} k\beta^k$$

$$= b_1 + b_2 T - \frac{\beta}{\alpha} b_2$$

Since $E(x_T) = b_1 + b_2 T$, we have

$$E(S_T) = E(x_T) - \frac{\beta}{\alpha} b_2 \qquad (3\text{-}14)$$

This shows that, for a linear model, the first-order exponentially smoothed statistic, S_T, will tend to lag behind the true signal by an amount equal to $(\beta/\alpha)b_2$.

Now suppose we apply the exponential smoothing operator to the output of Eq. (3-13). This results in

$$S_T^{[2]} = \alpha S_T + (1 - \alpha)S_{T-1}^{[2]} \qquad (3\text{-}15)$$

where the notation $S_T^{[2]}$ implies *double exponential smoothing*, or *second-order exponential smoothing*, not the square of the single smoothed statistic. By proceeding as above, we may show that

$$E(S_T^{[2]}) = E(S_T) - \frac{\beta}{\alpha} b_2 \qquad (3\text{-}16)$$

and therefore

$$b_2 = \frac{\alpha}{\beta} [E(S_T) - E(S_T^{[2]})] \qquad (3\text{-}17)$$

Thus, it seems logical to estimate b_2 at the end of period T by

$$\hat{b}_2(T) = \frac{\alpha}{\beta} (S_T - S_T^{[2]}) \qquad (3\text{-}18)$$

The expected demand at the end of period T may be obtained from Eqs. (3-14) and (3-17) as

$$E(x_T) = E(S_T) + \frac{\beta}{\alpha} \cdot \frac{\alpha}{\beta} [E(S_T) - E(S_T^{[2]})]$$

$$= 2E(S_T) - E(S_T^{[2]})$$

Again, a reasonable estimate of $E(x_T)$, made at the end of period T, would be

$$\hat{x}_T = 2S_T - S_T^{[2]} \tag{3-19}$$

$\widehat{x}_{T+0}(T)$

To forecast τ periods into the future using double exponential smoothing, we use the forecasting equation

$$\hat{x}_{T+\tau}(T) = \hat{x}_T + \tau \hat{b}_2(T)$$

$$= 2S_T - S_T^{[2]} + \tau \frac{\alpha}{\beta}\left(S_T - S_T^{[2]}\right)$$

$$= \left(2 + \frac{\alpha\tau}{\beta}\right)S_T - \left(1 + \frac{\alpha\tau}{\beta}\right)S_T^{[2]} \tag{3-20}$$

move into part

We have not estimated the intercept directly. However, if necessary, this can be done easily. At time T, we estimate the intercept at the original time origin as

$$\hat{b}_1(T) = \hat{x}_T - T\hat{b}_2(T)$$

$$= 2S_T - S_T^{[2]} - T\frac{\alpha}{\beta}\left(S_T - S_T^{[2]}\right) \tag{3-21}$$

If it is more convenient to think of the origin of time as shifted to the end of period T, then the intercept would be $E(x_T)$, which we denote by $a_1(T)$ to avoid confusion with b_1, the intercept on the "original-origin" basis. The estimate of the "current-origin" intercept is

$$\hat{a}_1(T) = \hat{x}_T$$

$$= 2S_T - S_T^{[2]} \tag{3-22}$$

Note that

$$a_1(T) = b_1 + Tb_2 \tag{3-23}$$

The forecasting equation based on the original origin is

$$\hat{x}_{T+\tau}(T) = \hat{b}_1(T) + (T + \tau)\hat{b}_2(T) \tag{3-24}$$

and based on the current origin is

$$\hat{x}_{T+\tau}(T) = \hat{a}_1(T) + \tau\hat{b}_2(T) \tag{3-25}$$

Both Eqs. (3-24) and (3-25) yield the same forecasts as Eq. (3-20). Finally, note that shifting the origin of time does not affect the slope, only the intercept.

In initiating double smoothing, values must be given to S_0 and $S_0^{[2]}$. Because of their lack of intuitive meaning, it is difficult to assign values directly to these quantities. Usually these initial conditions are obtained from estimates of the two coefficients b_1 and b_2, which may be developed through simple linear regression analysis of historical data. If no representative historical data are available, it is necessary to estimate b_1 and b_2 subjectively. Given initial estimates $\hat{b}_1(0)$ and $\hat{b}_2(0)$, Eqs. (3-18) and (3-21) may be solved, with $T = 0$, to yield the initial smoothed statistics:

$$S_0 = \hat{b}_1(0) - \frac{\beta}{\alpha}\,\hat{b}_2(0) \qquad\qquad (3\text{-}26)$$

$$S_0^{[2]} = \hat{b}_1(0) - 2\,\frac{\beta}{\alpha}\,\hat{b}_2(0) \qquad\qquad (3\text{-}27)$$

EXAMPLE 3-2 A manufacturer of oil filters for automobile engines markets a popular model filter that has experienced a steadily growing sales rate over the past few years. This trend is expected to continue in the future. A forecasting procedure, using double exponential smoothing, is to be established using the past two years to provide data for initializing the model. Sales in thousands of units are given by month in Table 3-4 and graphed in Fig. 3-3. The analyst, who is establishing the forecasting system at the end of 1976, fits a linear model to this historical data using simple linear regression (not discounted) methods, and calculates an intercept of 275.00 and a slope of 10.88, so that the model is

$$\hat{x}_t = 275.00 + 10.88t$$

where the origin of time is the start of 1975. This line is shown in Fig. 3-3.

The problem is to use this information to find initial values for double

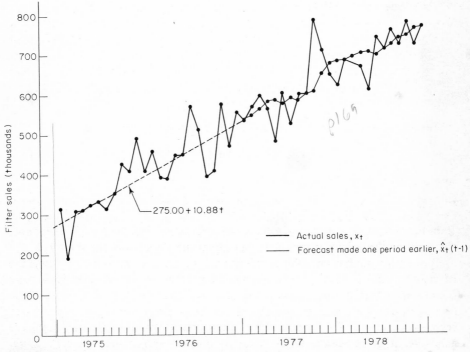

Fig. 3-3 Filter sales and one-period-ahead forecasts for Example 3-2.

TABLE 3-4   Filter Sales in Thousands, 1975 and 1976

Year	Jan.	Feb.	Mar.	Apr.	May	June	July	Aug.	Sept.	Oct.	Nov.	Dec.
1975	317	194	312	316	322	334	317	356	428	411	494	412
1976	460	395	392	447	452	571	517	397	410	579	473	558

smoothing, starting at the end of 1976. Two approaches occur to the analyst. The first is to redefine the origin of time as the end of 1976 and estimate the intercept at that point in time, which is period 24 in terms of the original origin. This intercept is just the expected demand at the end of 1976, which is estimated as $275.00 + (10.88)(24) = 536.12$. Thus, based on an intercept of 536.12 and a slope of 10.88, the initial values for double smoothing are, using Eqs. (3-26) and (3-27) and $\alpha = 0.10$,

$$S_0 = 536.12 - \frac{0.90}{0.10}(10.88) = 438.20$$

$$S_0^{[2]} = 536.12 - 2\frac{0.90}{0.10}(10.88) = 340.28$$

An alternative procedure is to convert the slope and original intercept estimates into values of the smoothed statistics as of the start of 1975, and then use the actual historical data to smooth these statistics repeatedly month-by-month, according to Eqs. (3-13) and (3-15), until values at the end of 1976 (the current time) are obtained. Doing this, the values at the original origin are computed using a slope of 10.88 and an intercept of 275.00 to be

$$S_0 = 275.00 - \frac{0.90}{0.10}(10.88) = 177.08$$

$$S_0^{[2]} = 275.00 - 2\frac{0.90}{0.10}(10.88) = 79.16$$

Smoothing these results sequentially for the 24 months of historical data yields

$$S_{24} = 436.09$$

$$S_{24}^{[2]} = 341.77$$

The subscript 24 is based on the original origin of time. It seems natural to shift to a current origin basis, so that we have as starting values for our forecasting system $S_0 = 436.09$ and $S_0^{[2]} = 341.77$. Noting that these results are very close to those obtained by the first method, the analyst uses them in Eq.

(3-20) to establish the following forecasting model at the end of 1976:

$$x_{0+\tau}(0) = \left(2 + \frac{0.10}{0.90}\tau\right)S_0 - \left(1 + \frac{0.10}{0.90}\tau\right)S_0^{[2]}$$

$$= (2 + 0.111\tau)(436.09) - (1 + 0.111\tau)(341.77)$$

$$= 530.41 + 10.48\tau$$

Forecasts for the first three months of 1977, made at the end of December 1976, are

January: $\hat{x}_1(0) = 530.41 + (10.48)(1) = 540.89 \approx 541$

February: $\hat{x}_2(0) = 530.41 + (10.48)(2) = 551.37 \approx 551$

March: $\hat{x}_3(0) = 530.41 + (10.48)(3) = 561.85 \approx 562$

Suppose that the actual sales in January 1977 were 538,000 filters. At the end of January, the smoothed statistics would be revised as follows:

$$S_1 = (0.10)(538) + (1 - 0.10)(436.09) = 446.28$$

$$S_1^{[2]} = (0.10)(446.28) + (1 - 0.10)(341.77) = 352.22$$

TABLE 3-5 Smoothing and Forecasting of Filter Sales, Example 3-2

Year and month	Period number, T	Actual sales, x_T	Smoothed Statistics S_T	$S_T^{[2]}$	Forecast made last period, $\hat{x}_T(T-1)$
1977 Jan.	1	538	446.28	352.22	541
Feb.	2	570	458.65	362.86	551
Mar.	3	600	472.79	373.85	565
Apr.	4	565	482.01	384.67	583
May	5	485	482.31	394.43	590
June	6	604	494.48	404.44	580
July	7	527	497.73	413.77	595
Aug.	8	603	508.26	423.22	591
Sept.	9	604	517.83	432.68	603
Oct.	10	790	545.05	443.91	612
Nov.	11	714	561.94	445.72	657
Dec.	12	653	571.05	467.25	680
1978 Jan.	13	626	576.54	478.18	686
Feb.	14	690	587.89	489.15	686
Mar.	15	680	597.10	499.95	698
Apr.	16	673	604.69	510.42	705
May	17	613	605.52	519.93	709
June	18	744	619.37	529.87	701
July	19	718	629.23	539.81	719
Aug.	20	767	643.01	550.13	729
Sept.	21	728	651.51	560.27	746
Oct.	22	793	665.66	570.81	753
Nov.	23	726	671.69	580.90	771
Dec.	24	777	682.22	591.03	773

The forecasts for future months would be computed from

$$\hat{x}_{1+\tau} = (2 + 0.111\tau)(446.28) - (1 + 0.111\tau)(352.22)$$
$$= 540.34 + 10.45\tau \qquad \text{new trend}$$

Thus, the forecast for February, made at the end of January, would be

$$\hat{x}_2(1) = 540.34 + (10.45)(1) = 550.79 \approx 551$$

The monthly sales for the next two years, the exponentially smoothed statistics, and the one-period-ahead forecast, $\hat{x}_T(T-1)$, are shown in Table 3-5.

The data for this example were artificially generated from a normally distributed process having a mean of $300 + 10t$, where t is measured from an origin at the end of 1974, and a standard deviation of 50. This is the type of demand process for which double smoothing is designed, and we note that it does a good job of estimating the expected demand.

3-3 HIGHER-ORDER SMOOTHING*

In general, exponential smoothing can be used to estimate the coefficients in polynomial models of any degree. To illustrate this, we consider the quadratic model[1]

$$x_t = b_1 + b_2 t + \tfrac{1}{2} b_3 t^2 + \epsilon_t \qquad (3\text{-}28)$$

where we require that $E(\epsilon_t) = 0$ and $V(\epsilon_t) = \sigma_\epsilon^2$. Assuming we have estimates of the model parameters based on the original origin of time, our forecasting equation at the end of period T would be

$$\hat{x}_{T+\tau}(T) = \hat{b}_1(T) + \hat{b}_2(T) \cdot (T + \tau) + \tfrac{1}{2} \hat{b}_3(T) \cdot (T + \tau)^2 \qquad (3\text{-}29)$$

However, if we define the origin of time at the end of period T, the coefficients will have different values and the forecasting equation will be

$$\hat{x}_{T+\tau}(T) = \hat{a}_1(T) + \hat{a}_2(T)\tau + \tfrac{1}{2} \hat{a}_3(T)\tau^2 \qquad (3\text{-}30)$$

For the latter case, we can use the first three exponentially smoothed statistics, computed at the end of period T,

$$S_T = \alpha x_T + (1 - \alpha)S_{T-1}$$
$$S_T^{[2]} = \alpha S_T + (1 - \alpha)S_{T-1}^{[2]} \qquad (3\text{-}31)$$
$$S_T^{[3]} = \alpha S_T^{[2]} + (1 - \alpha)S_{T-1}^{[3]}$$

---

* Some of the material in this section is of a more advanced nature than the rest of the book. It may be omitted on first reading without loss of continuity.

[1] The unusual way of writing the quadratic term results in somewhat simpler expressions for the estimating equations.

to estimate the coefficients in the model as

$$\hat{a}_1(T) = 3S_T - 3S_T^{[2]} + S_T^{[3]}$$

$$\hat{a}_2(T) = \frac{\alpha}{2\beta^2}\left[(6-5\alpha)S_T - 2(5-4\alpha)S_T^{[2]} + (4-3\alpha)S_T^{[3]}\right] \qquad (3\text{-}32)$$

$$\hat{a}_3(T) = \left(\frac{\alpha}{\beta}\right)^2 \left(S_T - 2S_T^{[2]} + S_T^{[3]}\right)$$

This procedure is usually called *triple exponential smoothing*.

Starting values must be provided for the three smoothed statistics. Equation (3-32) can be solved for the smoothed statistics in terms of estimates of the coefficients of the process model based on a current time origin at the end of period T:

$$S_T = \hat{a}_1(T) - \frac{\beta}{\alpha}\hat{a}_2(T) + \frac{\beta(2-\alpha)}{2\alpha^2}\hat{a}_3(T)$$

$$S_T^{[2]} = \hat{a}_1(T) - \frac{2\beta}{\alpha}\hat{a}_2(T) + \frac{2\beta(3-2\alpha)}{2\alpha^2}\hat{a}_3(T) \qquad (3\text{-}33)$$

$$S_T^{[3]} = \hat{a}_1(T) - \frac{3\beta}{\alpha}\hat{a}_2(T) + \frac{3\beta(4-3\alpha)}{2\alpha^2}\hat{a}_3(T)$$

Equation (3-33) can be used to determine the required initial values for the smoothed statistics, S_0, $S_0^{[2]}$, and $S_0^{[3]}$, from predictions (possibly least-squares estimates from historical data) of the model coefficients at $T=0$, $\hat{a}_1(0)$, $\hat{a}_2(0)$, and $\hat{a}_3(0)$.

These results may be generalized to the case of an nth degree polynomial model of the form

$$x_t = \mu_t + \epsilon_t = b_1 + b_2 t + \frac{b_3}{2!}t^2 + \cdots + \frac{b_{n+1}}{n!}t^n + \epsilon_t \qquad (3\text{-}34)$$

where μ_t is the expected value of demand at time t and, as usual, ϵ_t is a random variable having $E(\epsilon_t)=0$ and $V(\epsilon_t)=\sigma_\epsilon^2$. The first $n+1$ exponentially smoothed statistics will be used to estimate the coefficients in the model (3-34). Exponential smoothing of order p is defined as

$$S_T^{[p]} = \alpha S_T^{[p-1]} + (1-\alpha)S_{T-1}^{[p]} \qquad (3\text{-}35)$$

where, for convenience, we let $S_T^{[1]} = S_T = \alpha x_T + (1-\alpha)S_{T-1}$. Note that the partial derivatives of the noise-free process μ_t with respect to t are

$$\mu_t^{(k)} = \frac{\partial^k \mu_t}{\partial t^k} = \begin{cases} \displaystyle\sum_{j=k}^{n} \frac{b_{j+1}}{(j-k)!}t^{j-k} & \text{for } k = 1, 2, \ldots, n \\[2ex] 0 & \text{for } k = n+1, n+2, \ldots \end{cases} \qquad (3\text{-}36)$$

To obtain the coefficient b_{k+1}, we can evaluate $\mu_t^{(k)}$ at $t = 0$:

$$b_{k+1} = \frac{\partial^k \mu_t}{\partial t^k}\bigg|_{t=0}$$

Using the above, the following equivalent representation of the expected demand in period $T + \tau$ can be derived (the proof is omitted):

$$E(x_{T+\tau}) \equiv \mu_{T+\tau} = \sum_{k=0}^{n} \frac{b_{k+1}}{k!}(T+\tau)^k = \sum_{k=0}^{n} \frac{(T+\tau)^k}{k!}[\mu_t^{(k)}]_{t=0} = \sum_{k=0}^{n} \mu_T^{(k)} \frac{\tau^k}{k!}$$

(3-37)

Note that if we choose to define a current time origin at the end of period T, our model for the expected demand in period $T + \tau$ would be

$$E(x_{T+\tau}) = a_1(T) + a_2(T)\tau + a_3(T)\frac{\tau^2}{2!} + \cdots + a_{n+1}(T)\frac{\tau^n}{n!}$$

$$= \sum_{k=0}^{n} a_{k+1}(T)\frac{\tau^k}{k!}$$

(3-38)

where the a's are in general not equal to the b's in the original-origin model (3-34). By comparing (3-37) and (3-38), we observe that

$$a_{k+1}(T) = \mu_T^{(k)} \qquad k = 0, 1, \ldots, n$$

(3-39)

Brown [9] has shown the following relationship between the first $n + 1$ exponentially smoothed statistics and the coefficients in the current-origin model:

$$E(S_T^{[p]}) = \sum_{k=0}^{n} (-1)^k \frac{\mu_T^{(k)}}{k!} \frac{\alpha^p}{(p-1)!} \sum_{j=0}^{\infty} j^k \beta^j \frac{(p-1+j)!}{j!}$$

$$p = 1, 2, \ldots, n+1$$

(3-40)

where, by Eq. (3-39), $\mu_T^{(k)} = a_{k+1}(T)$. Equation (3-40) can be written in matrix form as

$$E(S_T) = \mathbf{M}a(T)$$

(3-41)

where $\mathbf{S}_T' = [S_T^{[1]}, S_T^{[2]}, \ldots, S_T^{[n+1]}]$, $\mathbf{a}'(T) = [a_1(T), a_2(T), \ldots, a_{n+1}(T)]$, and $\mathbf{M}$ is an $(n+1) \times (n+1)$ matrix with components

$$M_{pk} = \frac{(-1)^k}{k!} \frac{\alpha^p}{(p-1)!} \sum_{j=0}^{\infty} j^k \beta^j \frac{(p-1+j)!}{j!}$$

which can be written in closed form. Brown [9] gives $\mathbf{M}$ in closed form for $n = 4$ (page 65):

$$\mathbf{M} = \begin{bmatrix}
1 & -\dfrac{\beta}{\alpha} & \dfrac{\beta(1+\beta)}{2\alpha^2} & -\dfrac{\beta(1+4\beta+\beta^2)}{6\alpha^3} & \dfrac{\beta(1+11\beta+11\beta^2+\beta^3)}{24\alpha^4} \\[2.5ex]
1 & -\dfrac{2\beta}{\alpha} & \dfrac{2\beta(1+2\beta)}{2\alpha^2} & -\dfrac{2\beta(1+7\beta+4\beta^2)}{6\alpha^3} & \dfrac{2\beta(1+18\beta+33\beta^2+8\beta^3)}{24\alpha^4} \\[2.5ex]
1 & -\dfrac{3\beta}{\alpha} & \dfrac{3\beta(1+3\beta)}{2\alpha^2} & -\dfrac{3\beta(1+10\beta+9\beta^2)}{6\alpha^3} & \dfrac{3\beta(1+25\beta+67\beta^2+27\beta^3)}{24\alpha^4} \\[2.5ex]
1 & -\dfrac{4\beta}{\alpha} & \dfrac{4\beta(1+4\beta)}{2\alpha^2} & -\dfrac{4\beta(1+13\beta+16\beta^2)}{6\alpha^3} & \dfrac{4\beta(1+32\beta+113\beta^2+64\beta^3)}{24\alpha^4} \\[2.5ex]
1 & -\dfrac{5\beta}{\alpha} & \dfrac{5\beta(1+5\beta)}{2\alpha^2} & -\dfrac{5\beta(1+16\beta+25\beta^2)}{6\alpha^3} & \dfrac{5\beta(1+39\beta+171\beta^2+125\beta^3)}{24\alpha^4}
\end{bmatrix}$$

The solution to (3-41) is

$$\mathbf{a}(T) = \mathbf{M}^{-1}E(\mathbf{S}_T) \tag{3-42}$$

which expresses the model coefficients in terms of the expected values of the first $n + 1$ exponentially smoothed statistics. It is reasonable to estimate $E(\mathbf{S}_T)$ by $\mathbf{S}_T$, and hence to estimate $\mathbf{a}(T)$ by

$$\hat{\mathbf{a}}(T) = \mathbf{M}^{-1}\mathbf{S}_T \tag{3-43}$$

These estimates can be used in the forecasting equations:

$$\hat{x}_{T+\tau}(T) = \hat{a}_1(T) + \hat{a}_2(T)\tau + \hat{a}_3(T)\frac{\tau^2}{2!} + \cdots + \hat{a}_{n+1}(T)\frac{\tau^n}{n!} \tag{3-44}$$

For the polynomial model (3-34), D'Esopo [21] has shown that the estimates of the coefficients obtained by multiple exponential smoothing using Eq. (3-43) are optimal with regard to a minimum discounted squared errors criterion.

EXAMPLE 3-3 To demonstrate the general procedure, we shall derive the results for triple smoothing given at the start of this section. The model is given by Eq. (3-30), and since $n = 2$,

$$\mathbf{S}_T = \begin{bmatrix} S_T \\ S_T^{[2]} \\ S_T^{[3]} \end{bmatrix} \qquad \hat{\mathbf{a}} = \begin{bmatrix} \hat{a}_1(T) \\ \hat{a}_2(T) \\ \hat{a}_3(T) \end{bmatrix}$$

The matrix $\mathbf{M}$ is

$$\mathbf{M} = \begin{bmatrix} 1 & -\dfrac{\beta}{\alpha} & \dfrac{\beta(2-\alpha)}{2\alpha^2} \\ 1 & -\dfrac{2\beta}{\alpha} & \dfrac{2\beta(3-2\alpha)}{2\alpha^2} \\ 1 & -\dfrac{3\beta}{\alpha} & \dfrac{3\beta(4-3\alpha)}{2\alpha^2} \end{bmatrix}$$

It is clear that $\mathbf{S}_T = \mathbf{Ma}(T)$ is identical to Eq. (3-33). The inverse of $\mathbf{M}$ is

$$\mathbf{M}^{-1} = \begin{bmatrix} 3 & -3 & 1 \\ \dfrac{\alpha(6-5\alpha)}{2\beta^2} & \dfrac{-2\alpha(5-4\alpha)}{2\beta^2} & \dfrac{\alpha(4-3\alpha)}{2\beta^2} \\ \left(\dfrac{\alpha}{\beta}\right)^2 & -2\left(\dfrac{\alpha}{\beta}\right)^2 & \left(\dfrac{\alpha}{\beta}\right)^2 \end{bmatrix}$$

and $\hat{\mathbf{a}}(T) = \mathbf{M}^{-1}\mathbf{S}_T$ is easily seen to be Eq. (3-32).

3-4 CHOICE OF SMOOTHING CONSTANT

In any application of exponential smoothing, it is necessary to specify a value for the smoothing constant. In this section, we discuss some considerations and approaches in making a choice.

The smoothing constant controls the number of past realizations of the time series that influence the forecast. Small values of the smoothing constant give significant weight to many prior observations and result in a slow response of the forecasting system to changes in the parameters of the time series model. Larger values of the smoothing constant give weight to only the more recent historical data and cause the forecasting system to respond more rapidly to parameter shifts. However, a large smoothing constant may cause the system to respond to random variations in demand, when actually the model parameters have not changed. Such oversensitivity is not desirable. Brown [9] discusses the response characteristics of exponential smoothing to various standard demand inputs, such as impulse, step, and linear trend functions. A study of this material should give an analyst a better understanding of the effect of the smoothing constant on forecast system dynamics.

As a general rule, the smoothing constant for a constant model (Sec. 3-1) should be between 0.01 and 0.3. A widely used technique is to carry out a sequence of trials on a set of actual historical data using several different values for the smoothing constant, and then to select the value of α that optimizes some measure of effectiveness, such as minimum sum of squared errors. Of course, this approach may also be used for more complicated models. Various modifications of this concept are often employed. For example, if three years of historical data are available, one might use the first two years to optimize the smoothing constant and then simulate a forecast for each period of the remaining year to see how the "optimum" smoothing constant will react to new data.

If the results of a set of trials indicate an optimum value of α for a constant model that is greater than 0.3, then the validity of the model should be questioned. The data may be significantly autocorrelated, in which case the methods of Chap. 9 should be considered. Plotting the data may reveal unanticipated trends or cyclic patterns that will lead to a large smoothing constant, but should be dealt with by employing a more appropriate model.

The idea of an equivalent smoothing constant often is useful. For example, in Eq. (3-7) we gave a relationship between the number of periods, N, in a moving average and α, the smoothing constant in simple exponential smoothing. This equivalence was calculated to give both statistics the same sampling variance (also to yield the same average age of data included in their computation). Since it is usually easier to think about the consequences of choosing N, this may be a helpful relationship for evaluating a choice for α.

However, we shall use the term *equivalent smoothing constant* to refer to a comparison of simple exponential smoothing with higher-ordered polynomial models. It is possible to define smoothing constants for these models so that they all yield the same estimate of the constant term, $a_1(T)$. If α_1 is the smoothing constant for single smoothing, then the equivalent value of the smoothing constant for a model with k parameters to be estimated would be α_k, given by

$$(1 - \alpha_k)^k = 1 - \alpha_1$$

or

$$\alpha_k = 1 - \beta_1^{1/k} \tag{3-45}$$

EXAMPLE 3-4 Suppose we plan to use double smoothing and wish to use a smoothing constant equivalent to single smoothing with $\alpha = 0.10$. Since double smoothing estimates a linear model having two parameters, we compute

$$\alpha_2 = 1 - \sqrt{1 - 0.10} = 0.051$$

The equivalent smoothing constant for triple smoothing would be

$$\alpha_3 = 1 - (1 - 0.10)^{1/3} = 0.035$$

It is logical for the smoothing constant to be decreased as the number of parameters in the model increases. For example, each demand observation is smoothed by triple smoothing to affect estimates of three parameters in the forecasting model, and they in turn each contribute to a change in the forecast. To effect the same change in a single-parameter model would require a larger rate of smoothing. Equivalent smoothing constants are given in Table 3-6. Also shown is the equivalent N for a simple moving average.

Many practitioners prefer to have available several values of the smoothing

TABLE 3-6   Equivalent Smoothing Constants for k-Parameter Models

Numbers of parameters						Moving average, N
1	2	3	4	5	6	
0.010	0.005	0.003	0.003	0.002	0.002	199
0.050	0.025	0.017	0.013	0.010	0.009	39
0.100	0.051	0.035	0.026	0.021	0.017	19
0.150	0.078	0.053	0.040	0.032	0.027	12
0.200	0.106	0.072	0.054	0.044	0.037	9
0.250	0.134	0.091	0.069	0.056	0.047	7
0.300	0.163	0.112	0.085	0.069	0.058	6
0.400	0.225	0.157	0.120	0.097	0.082	4
0.500	0.293	0.206	0.159	0.129	0.109	3

constant, and use an appropriate value at different times. For example, a normal value for the α when the process seems stable may be 0.10; however, in addition, the value 0.25 may be used when the coefficients in the underlying process seem to be changing more rapidly. A number of procedures have been developed for maintaining control of the smoothing constant and shifting from one value to another. These *adaptive-control procedures*, as they are often called, are described in Chap. 8.

As discussed in Sec. 3-1.2, a high rate of smoothing may be used in the first few periods following the start of forecasting, before switching to the normal smoothing constant. This is especially desirable if there is considerable uncertainty about the values used to initialize the forecasting system.

3-5 EXERCISES

3-1 Repeat the analysis in Example 3-1 with $\alpha = 0.1$ and using the average sales in the last four months of 1976 as the starting value.

3-2 Repeat Example 3-1 using $\alpha = 0.3$. What is the effect of increasing the smoothing constant from 0.1 to 0.3?

3-3 Repeat Exercise 3-1 using $\alpha = 0.4$ for six periods and then switching to $\alpha = 0.10$ for the remainder of the computations. Does this improve the forecast?

3-4 In Example 3-1, suppose that the process mean, b, had increased by 200 units at the start of 1978, and that the actual demand realizations in that year were 200 units more than the values given in Table 3-3. Starting at the end of 1977, simulate forecasting for 1978, using $\alpha = 0.10$. Repeat using $\alpha = 0.30$. Plot the results, as in Fig. 3-1. What are your conclusions about the effect of the smoothing constant on the response of simple exponential smoothing to a step increase in expected demand?

3-5 In Example 3-1, suppose that because of a strike closing a competitor's plant, the expected sales in January 1978 were 200 units higher than the usual level and that the actual sales in January 1978 were 586 units instead of 386. In February and subsequent months, sales remain at their usual level. Starting at the end of 1977, simulate forecasting for 1978, using $\alpha = 0.10$. Repeat using $\alpha = 0.30$. Plot the results, as in Fig. 3-1. What are your conclusions regarding the effect of the smoothing constant on the response of simple exponential smoothing to a change in the expected demand for a single period (sometimes called an *impulse*, or *transient*, change)?

3-6 The weekly demand (in hundreds of yards) for a textile product is given in Table B-1 in the Appendix. Assume the first 40 weeks of data are available for use in initializing the forecasting process. Simulate forecasting for the next 20 weeks using simple exponential smoothing. Explain how you selected your smoothing constant. Plot the results. Does the constant model appear appropriate? If so, estimate σ_ϵ^2.

3-7   Use simple exponential smoothing to forecast the seasonal data in Table B-7 in the Appendix. Assume the 1972 data are available for model initialization. Use $\alpha = 0.10$ and then repeat for $\alpha = 0.30$. What are your conclusions about the use of simple exponential smoothing for cyclical (seasonal) data with a trend?

3-8   *Response of single smoothing to step change in expected demand.* Suppose simple exponential smoothing is being used to forecast the constant process, $x_t = b + \epsilon_t$. At the start of period t^*, the mean of the process shifts to a new level $b^* = b + \delta$, so that the expected demand in period t^* and all subsequent periods is b^*. Show that the expected value of the statistic S_T is the following:

$$E(S_T) = \begin{cases} b & T < t^* \\ b^* - \delta\beta^{T-t^*+1} & T \geqslant t^* \end{cases}$$

Note that as $T \to \infty$, $E(S_T) \to b^*$. Illustrate this graphically.

3-9   Using the results of Exercise 3-8, determine the number of periods following the step change in the process mean required for $E(S_T)$ to be within 0.10δ of b^*. Plot the number of periods as a function of the smoothing constant, α. What are your conclusions?

3-10 *Response of single smoothing to a transient (impulse) change in expected demand.* Suppose simple exponential smoothing is being used to forecast the constant process, $x_t = b + \epsilon_t$. At the start of period t^*, the mean of the process shifts to a new level $b^* = b + \delta$, but it reverts to its original level, b, at the start of period $t^* + 1$. Thus the expected demand in period t^* is b^*, while for all other periods it is b. Show that the expected value of the statistic S_T is the following:

$$E(S_T) = \begin{cases} b & T < t^* \\ b + \delta\alpha\beta^{T-t^*} & T \geqslant t^* \end{cases}$$

Note that as $T \to \infty$, $E(S_T) \to b$. Illustrate this graphically.

3-11 Using the results of Exercise 3-10, determine the number of periods following the impulse change required for $E(S_T)$ to be within 0.10δ of b. Plot the number of periods as a function of the smoothing constant, α. What are your conclusions?

3-12 The error in forecasting for period $T+1$ at the end of period T is defined as $e_1(T+1) = x_{T+1} - \hat{x}_{T+1}(T)$. If the observations are independent random variables, x_{T+1} will be independent of $\hat{x}_{T+1}(T)$. Assume single exponential smoothing is applied to the constant process $x_t = b + \epsilon_t$, where $V(x_t) = V(\epsilon_t) = \sigma_\epsilon^2$. Show that the variance of the forecast error is given by Eq. (3-11); that is

$$\sigma_e^2 = \frac{2}{2-\alpha}\sigma_\epsilon^2$$

Plot σ_e^2 versus α. What are your conclusions?

3-13 Suppose we have a noise-free process $x_t = 100 + 20t$; that is, $\sigma_\epsilon^2 = 0$. Use single exponential smoothing to forecast the first 20 periods. Use $\alpha = 0.10$ and $S_0 = 100$.

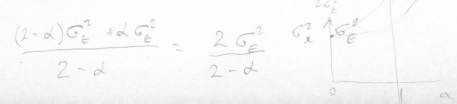

Repeat for $\alpha = 0.30$. Plot your results: x_t, S_t, and $\hat{x}_t(t-1)$. What are your conclusions about the ability of single smoothing to track a linear trend? What is the effect of increasing α?

3-14 Carry out Exercise 3-6 using double smoothing with $\alpha = 0.10$ instead of single smoothing. Are improved forecasts obtained? Which procedure would you recommend?

3-15 Use double exponential smoothing to forecast the demand for spare parts shown in Table B-5 in the Appendix. Assume the first two years of data are available for model initialization. Simulate forecasting for the next two years. Plot actual demand versus the one-period-ahead forecast, that is, x_t versus $\hat{x}_t(t-1)$.

3-16 Carry out Exercise 3-7 using double smoothing instead of single smoothing. Are improved forecasts obtained? Is this model satisfactory for seasonal data?

3-17 *Alternate procedure for linear trend.* There are several equivalent procedures for forecasting linear trend processes through exponential smoothing. One form often appearing in the literature involves the following:

$$\hat{x}_{T+\tau}(T) = S_T + \frac{1-\alpha}{\alpha}\hat{b}_2(T) + \tau\hat{b}_2(T)$$

where the estimate of the trend component is

$$\hat{b}_2(T) = \alpha(S_T - S_{T-1}) + (1-\alpha)\hat{b}_2(T-1)$$

and

$$S_T = \alpha x_T + (1-\alpha)S_{T-1}$$

Typically, this is called *exponential smoothing, corrected for trend.* Give an explanation for the development of these equations. Show that they are equivalent to the double-exponential-smoothing procedure of Sec. 3-2.

3-18 Show that the forecasting model of Exercise 3-17 yields an unbiased estimate of $E(x_{T+\tau})$.

3-19 *Direct smoothing of coefficients in the linear model.* Instead of computing the first two exponentially smoothed statistics and using them in the nonintuitive forecasting model of Eq. (3-20), we may elect to smooth directly the estimates of the current origin, $a_1(T)$, and the slope, b_2, and then use the more natural equation (3-25) for forecasting. The appropriate smoothing equations for use at the end of period T are

$$S_t = S_{t-1} + B_{t-1} + \alpha \ell_{t-1}$$

$$\hat{a}_1(T) = \hat{a}_1(T-1) + \hat{b}_2(T-1) + h_1 e_1(T)$$

$$\hat{b}_2(T) = \hat{b}_2(T-1) + h_2 e_1(T)$$

where $h_1 = 1 - \beta^2$ and $h_2 = (1-\beta)^2$ are smoothing constants, and $e_1(T) = x_T - \hat{x}_T(T-1)$ is the single-period-ahead forecast error. Show that this procedure is equivalent to double smoothing with $\alpha = 1 - \beta$. (Direct smoothing will be covered in detail in Chaps. 4 and 5.)

3-20 For a linear trend process, the original-origin model is

$$E(x_{T+\tau}) = b_1 + b_2(T + \tau)$$

and the current-origin model is

$$E(x_{T+\tau}) = a_1(T) + a_2(T)\tau$$

Verify that Eq. (3-39) holds for this case. Use Eq. (3-43) to derive Eqs. (3-18) and (3-22).

APPENDIX 3A DEVELOPMENT OF DOUBLE SMOOTHING BY LEAST-SQUARES CRITERION

Results equivalent to double smoothing can be obtained using a discounted least-squares criterion. At time T, we desire to find estimates $\hat{b}_1(T)$ and $\hat{b}_2(T)$ to minimize the weighted sum of squares

$$\text{SS}_E = \sum_{t=1}^{T} \beta^{T-t}(x_t - b_1 - b_2 t)^2 \tag{3A-1}$$

The normal equations are obtained from

$$\left.\frac{\partial \text{SS}_E}{\partial b_1}\right|_{\hat{b}_1, \hat{b}_2} = -2 \sum_{t=1}^{T} \beta^{T-t}\left[x_t - \hat{b}_1(T) - \hat{b}_2(T)t\right] = 0$$

$$\left.\frac{\partial \text{SS}_E}{\partial b_2}\right|_{\hat{b}_1, \hat{b}_2} = -2 \sum_{t=1}^{T} \beta^{T-t}\left[x_t - \hat{b}_1(T) - \hat{b}_2(T)t\right]t = 0$$

These equations are

$$\left(\sum_{t=1}^{T} \beta^{T-t}\right)\hat{b}_1(T) + \left(\sum_{t=1}^{T} \beta^{T-t}t\right)\hat{b}_2(T) = \sum_{t=1}^{T} \beta^{T-t}x_t \tag{3A-2a}$$

$$\left(\sum_{t=1}^{T} \beta^{T-t}t\right)\hat{b}_2(T) + \left(\sum_{t=1}^{T} \beta^{T-t}t^2\right)\hat{b}_2(T) = \sum_{t=1}^{T} \beta^{T-t}tx_t \tag{3A-2b}$$

or

$$c_{11}\hat{b}_1(T) + c_{12}\hat{b}_2(T) = \sum_{t=1}^{T} \beta^{T-t}x_t$$

$$c_{21}\hat{b}_1(T) + c_{22}\hat{b}_2(T) = \sum_{t=1}^{T} \beta^{T-t}tx_t$$

where the coefficients in closed form are

$$c_{11} = \frac{1 - \beta^T}{1 - \beta}$$

$$c_{12} = c_{21} = \frac{\beta^{T+1} - (T+1)\beta + T}{(1 - \beta)^2}$$

$$c_{22} = \frac{(T+1)^2 \beta^2 - (2T^2 + 2T - 1)\beta - (1 + \beta)\beta^{T+1}}{(1 - \beta)^3}$$

When T is large, $\beta^T \approx 0$ and we may use

$$c_{11} = \frac{1}{1 - \beta} = \frac{1}{\alpha}$$

$$c_{12} = c_{21} = \frac{T - (T+1)\beta}{(1 - \beta)^2} = \frac{\alpha T - \beta}{\alpha^2}$$

$$c_{22} = \frac{(T+1)^2 \beta^2 - (2T^2 + 2T - 1)\beta + T^2}{(1 - \beta)^3}$$

$$= \frac{(T+1)^2 \beta^2 - 2(T+1)T\beta + T^2 + \beta}{\alpha^3}$$

Also, since

$$S_T = \alpha \sum_{t=0}^{T-1} \beta^t x_{T-t} + \beta^T S_0 = \alpha \sum_{t=1}^{T} \beta^{T-t} x_t + \beta^T S_0$$

then for large T,

$$\sum_{t=1}^{T} \beta^{T-t} x_t = \frac{1}{\alpha} S_T \qquad (3A-3)$$

and, since

$$S_T^{[2]} = \alpha \sum_{t=0}^{T-1} \beta^t S_{T-t} + \beta^T S_0^{[2]} = \alpha \sum_{t=1}^{T} \beta^{T-t} S_t + \beta^T S_0^{[2]}$$

$$= \alpha \sum_{t=1}^{T} \beta^{T-t} \left[\alpha \sum_{k=1}^{t} \beta^{t-k} x_k + \beta^t S_0 \right] + \beta^T S_0^{[2]}$$

then for large T

$$S_T^{[2]} = \alpha^2 \sum_{t=1}^{T} \sum_{k=1}^{t} \beta^{T-k} x_k = \alpha^2 \sum_{k=1}^{T} (T - k + 1)\beta^{T-k} x_k$$

$$= \alpha^2 \left[(T+1) \sum_{k=1}^{T} \beta^{T-k} x_k - \sum_{k=1}^{T} \beta^{T-k} k x_k \right]$$

$$= \alpha^2 \left[(T+1) \frac{S_T}{\alpha} - \sum_{k=1}^{T} \beta^{T-k} k x_k \right]$$

or

$$\sum_{k=1}^{T} \beta^{T-k} k x_k = \frac{T+1}{\alpha} S_T - \frac{1}{\alpha^2} S_T^{[2]} \tag{3A-4}$$

The normal equations therefore imply the relationships

$$\frac{1}{\alpha} \hat{b}_1(T) + \frac{\alpha T - \beta}{\alpha^2} \hat{b}_2(T) = \frac{1}{\alpha} S_T \tag{3A-5a}$$

$$\frac{\alpha T - \beta}{\alpha^2} \hat{b}_1(T) + \frac{(T+1)^2 \beta^2 - 2(T+1)T\beta + T^2 + \beta}{\alpha^3} \hat{b}_2(T)$$

$$= \frac{T+1}{\alpha} S_T - \frac{1}{\alpha^2} S_T^{[2]} \tag{3A-5b}$$

Solving these equations, we obtain

$$\hat{b}_2(T) = \frac{\alpha}{\beta} [S_T - S_T^{[2]}] \tag{3A-6}$$

and

$$\hat{b}_1(T) = S_T + \left(\frac{\beta}{\alpha} - T \right) \hat{b}_2(T) \tag{3A-7}$$

which agree with the results obtained by the heuristic expected value argument given in Sec. 3-2.

The general use of the discounted least-squares criterion will be described in detail in Chap. 4.

CHAPTER FOUR

Discounted Least Squares
and Direct Smoothing*

A major disadvantage in the use of regression analysis as a forecasting technique is that the estimated model parameters $\{\hat{b}_i\}$ need to be updated at the end of each period to account for the most recent observation. The calculations associated with estimating the parameters in a multiple linear regression model have been described in Sec. 2-1.2. Clearly, these calculations would be prohibitively time-consuming if a large number of time series were analyzed every period. However, if the independent variables in the model are simple mathematical functions of time, a direct method of revising the model parameters is available. The method, in effect, smooths the old coefficients with the current period's forecast error to obtain the new coefficients. The procedure is called *direct smoothing*, and is very efficient computationally. It is developed using a weighted least-squares criterion, in which the squared errors are discounted with age. When the independent variables are polynomial functions of time, direct smoothing is equivalent to exponential smoothing. The use of trigonometric functions of time as independent variables leads to efficient models to represent seasonal time series. This chapter presents a detailed development of the general discounted least-squares process, and describes its application to polynomial and transcendental time series models.

* Some of the material in this chapter is of a more advanced nature than the rest of the book. It may be omitted on first reading without loss of continuity.

4-1 DISCOUNTED LEAST SQUARES

We shall assume that the time series $\{x_t\}$ can be represented by the general model

$$x_t = \sum_{i=1}^{k} b_i z_i(t) + \epsilon_t \qquad t = 1, 2, \ldots, T \tag{4-1}$$

where b_i is the coefficient of the ith term in the model and the independent variables $z_i(t)$, $i = 1, 2, \ldots, k$, are appropriate mathematical functions of time. The $\{\epsilon_t\}$ are random errors such that $E(\epsilon_t) = 0$, $V(\epsilon_t) = \sigma_\epsilon^2$, and $E(\epsilon_t \cdot \epsilon_{t+u}) = 0$. We must also require that there are at least as many observations as independent variables, that is, $T \geqslant k$.

It is convenient to express Eq. (4-1) in matrix notation. Let **b** denote the $k \times 1$ column vector whose ith element is b_i and let $\mathbf{z}(t)$ denote the $k \times 1$ column vector whose ith element is the ith independent variable $z_i(t)$. Then Eq. (4-1) may be written as

$$x_t = \mathbf{z}'(t)\mathbf{b} + \epsilon_t \qquad t = 1, 2, \ldots, T \tag{4-2}$$

If $\hat{\mathbf{b}}$ denotes the vector of estimates of **b**, then the fitted model is

$$\hat{x}_t = \mathbf{z}'(t)\hat{\mathbf{b}} = \sum_{i=1}^{k} \hat{b}_i z_i(t)$$

and the tth residual is

$$e_t = x_t - \hat{x}_t = x_t - \mathbf{z}'(t)\hat{\mathbf{b}} \tag{4-3}$$

Observations that are close to the current time period T may be of more importance in estimating **b** than observations realized in the distant past, as the recent data may be more indicative of the true behavior of the process. In such situations, it is customary to *discount* the errors away from the current time period so that older observations receive proportionally less weight. Therefore, we seek the estimator of **b** that minimizes the discounted, or weighted, sum of squares of the errors

$$SS_E = \sum_{t=1}^{T} W_{tt}^2 \epsilon_t^2 \tag{4-4}$$

where W_{tt} is the square root of the weight given to the tth error. The process of finding estimators **b** which minimize Eq. (4-4) is called the method of *discounted least squares*.

Let **x** be a $T \times 1$ column vector of the observations, $\boldsymbol{\epsilon}$ be a $T \times 1$ column vector of the model error components, and **Z** be a $T \times k$ matrix of the independent variables such that

$$
\mathbf{Z}(T) = \begin{bmatrix} z_1(1) & z_2(1) & \cdots & z_k(1) \\ z_1(2) & z_2(2) & \cdots & z_k(2) \\ \cdots\cdots\cdots\cdots\cdots\cdots\cdots\cdots \\ z_1(T) & z_2(T) & \cdots & z_k(T) \end{bmatrix}
$$

That is, the tth row of $\mathbf{Z}(T)$ represents the levels of the independent variables corresponding to the tth observation x_t. The model [Eq. (4-2)] can now be expressed as

$$
\mathbf{x} = \mathbf{Z}(T)\mathbf{b} + \boldsymbol{\epsilon} \tag{4-5}
$$

The weighted sum of squared errors is

$$
\begin{aligned}
\mathrm{SS}_E &= (\mathbf{W}\boldsymbol{\epsilon})'(\mathbf{W}\boldsymbol{\epsilon}) \\
&= \boldsymbol{\epsilon}'\mathbf{W}'\mathbf{W}\boldsymbol{\epsilon} \\
&= \boldsymbol{\epsilon}'\mathbf{W}^2\boldsymbol{\epsilon} \\
&= [\mathbf{x} - \mathbf{Z}(T)\mathbf{b}]'\mathbf{W}^2[\mathbf{x} - \mathbf{Z}(T)\mathbf{b}] \\
&= \mathbf{x}'\mathbf{W}^2\mathbf{x} - 2\mathbf{b}'\mathbf{Z}'(T)\mathbf{W}^2\mathbf{x} + \mathbf{b}'\mathbf{Z}'(T)\mathbf{W}^2\mathbf{Z}(T)\mathbf{b}
\end{aligned}
$$

where $\mathbf{W}$ is the $T \times T$ diagonal matrix of the square roots of the weights

$$
\mathbf{W} = \begin{bmatrix} W_{11} & 0 & \cdots & 0 \\ 0 & W_{22} & \cdots & 0 \\ \cdots\cdots\cdots\cdots\cdots\cdots\cdots \\ 0 & 0 & \cdots & W_{TT} \end{bmatrix}
$$

It is necessary that the discounted least-squares estimator computed at the end of period T, say $\hat{\mathbf{b}}(T)$, satisfy

$$
\frac{\partial\,\mathrm{SS}_E}{\partial \mathbf{b}}\bigg|_{\hat{\mathbf{b}}} = -2\mathbf{Z}'(T)\mathbf{W}^2\mathbf{x} + 2\mathbf{Z}'(T)\mathbf{W}^2\mathbf{Z}(T)\hat{\mathbf{b}}(T) = \mathbf{0}
$$

Therefore, the least-squares normal equations are

$$
\mathbf{Z}'(T)\mathbf{W}^2\mathbf{Z}(T)\mathbf{b}(T) = \mathbf{Z}'(T)\mathbf{W}^2\mathbf{x} \tag{4-6}
$$

or

$$G(T)\hat{b}(T) = g(T) \tag{4-7}$$

where $G(T) = [WZ(T)]'[WZ(T)]$ is a $k \times k$ matrix consisting of weighted sums of squares and cross products of the independent variables computed at time T and $g(T) = Z'(T)W^2x$ is a $k \times 1$ column vector of weighted sums of products of the independent variables computed at time T. In scalar notation, the elements of $G(T)$ are

$$G_{ij}(T) = \sum_{t=1}^{T} W_{tt}^2 z_i(t)z_j(t) \qquad i, j = 1, 2, \ldots, k$$

and the elements of $g(T)$ are

$$g_i(T) = \sum_{t=1}^{T} W_{tt}^2 x_t z_i(t) \qquad i = 1, 2, \ldots, k$$

The solution to the normal equations (4-7) is

$$\hat{b}(T) = G(T)^{-1}g(T) \tag{4-8}$$

if the matrix $G(T)^{-1}$ exists.

Discounted least-squares estimators have several useful statistical properties. It is relatively simple to show that $\hat{b}(T)$ is unbiased, that is,

$$E[\hat{b}(T)] = b$$

and that the covariance matrix of $\hat{b}(T)$ is

$$V \equiv E[\hat{b}(T) - b][\hat{b}(T) - b]'$$

$$= G(T)^{-1}F(T)G(T)^{-1}\sigma_\epsilon^2 \tag{4-9}$$

where the matrix $F(T)$ is defined as

$$F(T) = Z'(T)W^4Z(T)$$

Note that V is a function of T. These properties are generalizations of those presented in Sec. 2-1.2. Notice that if all past data are weighted equally, that is, if $W = I$, then Eq. (4-9) reduces to Eq. (2-24).

4-2 SHIFTING THE ORIGIN OF TIME

If we were to use the discounted least-squares approach for periodic forecasting, the estimates of the model parameters $\hat{b}$ would need to be revised at the end of each time period to take into account the new data. Solving Eq. (4-8) at the end of every time period would involve computing $G(T)^{-1}$ every period. The computations associated with finding $\mathbf{G}(T)^{-1}$ would be prohibitive if a large number of time series were being analyzed.

Direct smoothing is a very efficient method of updating the model coefficients that does not require $\mathbf{G}(T)^{-1}$ to be computed every time period, provided that the model utilizes certain types of independent variables and weights. The direct smoothing approach smooths the old estimates of the model parameters with the forecast error for the current period to obtain revised estimates. The procedure was first systematically presented by Brown [9].

It will be convenient to always have the origin of time for the model to be the end of the current period, say T. This will require that the origin of time be shifted each period. To accomplish this, let the discounted least-squares criterion at the end of any period T be

$$SS_E = \sum_{j=0}^{T-1} W^2_{T-j,\,T-j}\left[x_{T-j} - \mathbf{z}'(-j)\mathbf{a}(T)\right]^2$$

The subscript on the observation x denotes the calendar time period associated with the observation, the argument T in $\mathbf{a}(T)$ indicates the calendar time period considered to be the origin of time, and $\mathbf{z}(-j)$ indicates that the mathematical functions of time $\mathbf{z}$ are to be evaluated at $-j$. We shall also let the weights W^2_{tt} be defined as

$$W^2_{T-j,\,T-j} = \beta^j \qquad j = 0, 1, \ldots, T-1 \qquad (4\text{-}10)$$

where the *discount factor* β is chosen so that $0 < \beta < 1$. Notice that this is equivalent to choosing the matrix of weights in the discounted least-squares process to be the $T \times T$ diagonal matrix

$$\mathbf{W}^2 = \begin{bmatrix} \beta^{T-1} & 0 & \cdots & 0 & 0 \\ 0 & \beta^{T-2} & \cdots & 0 & 0 \\ \cdot & \cdot & \cdots & \cdot & \cdot \\ 0 & 0 & \cdots & \beta & 0 \\ 0 & 0 & \cdots & 0 & 1 \end{bmatrix}$$

Therefore, the regression equations to be solved at the end of each time period will be based on

$$SS_E = \sum_{j=0}^{T-1} \beta^j\left[x_{T-j} - \mathbf{z}'(-j)\mathbf{a}(T)\right]^2 \qquad (4\text{-}11)$$

We shall now assume that the independent variables $z_i(t)$ are mathematical functions of time such that their values at time period $t+1$ are simply linear combinations of the same functions evaluated at the previous time, t. Therefore,

$$z_i(t+1) = L_{i1}z_1(t) + L_{i2}z_2(t) + \cdots + L_{ik}z_k(t) \qquad i = 1, 2, \ldots, k \quad (4\text{-}12)$$

$1 \qquad = L_{11}(1) + L_{12}(t) \qquad ; L_{12} = 0, L_{11} = 1 \qquad z_1(t) = 1$

$1 + t \qquad = L_{21}(1) + L_{22}(t) \qquad ; L_{21} = 1, L_{22} = 1 \qquad z_2(t) = t$

$z_1(t+1) = 1$

$z_2(t+1) = 1 + t$

If we let $\mathbf{L}$ be the $k \times k$ matrix of the L_{ij}, we may write Eq. (4-12) as

$$\mathbf{z}(t+1) = \mathbf{L}\mathbf{z}(t) \qquad (4\text{-}13)$$

The only functions of time for which the transition property in Eq. (4-13) exists are polynomial, exponential, and trigonometric functions. Also, notice that given the matrix $\mathbf{L}$ and $\mathbf{z}(0)$, we may find $\mathbf{z}(t)$ as

$$\mathbf{z}(t) = \mathbf{L}^t\mathbf{z}(0) \qquad (4\text{-}14)$$

The transition matrix $\mathbf{L}$ can be written down from inspection of the terms in the model. For example, consider the linear trend model

$$x_t = b_1 + b_2 t + \epsilon_t$$

Then $z_1(t) \equiv 1$ and $z_2(t) \equiv t$, and it is easy to verify that

$$\mathbf{L} = \begin{bmatrix} 1 & 0 \\ 1 & 1 \end{bmatrix}$$

We shall discuss the development of the $\mathbf{L}$ matrix for various models in more detail in Sec. 4-3 and 4-4.

Consider the matrix $\mathbf{G}(T)$. Notice that

$$\mathbf{G}(T) = \sum_{j=0}^{T=1} \beta^j \mathbf{z}(-j)\mathbf{z}'(-j)$$

$$= \mathbf{G}(T-1) + \beta^{T-1}\mathbf{z}(-T+1)\mathbf{z}'(-T+1)$$

It can be shown that if the functions $\{z_i(t)\}$ do not decay too rapidly,[1] the matrix $\mathbf{G}(T)$ approaches a limit $\mathbf{G}$, where

$$\mathbf{G} \equiv \lim_{T \to \infty} \mathbf{G}(T) = \sum_{j=0}^{\infty} \beta^j \mathbf{z}(-j)\mathbf{z}'(-j) \qquad (4\text{-}15)$$

Therefore, $\mathbf{G}^{-1}$ need be computed only once.

The right-hand side of the normal equation (4-7) may be written as

$$\mathbf{g}(T) = \sum_{j=0}^{T-1} \beta^j x_{T-j}\mathbf{z}(-j)$$

$$= x_T\mathbf{z}(0) + \sum_{j=1}^{T-1} \beta^j x_{T-j}\mathbf{z}(-j)$$

$$= x_T\mathbf{z}(0) + \beta \sum_{j=1}^{T-1} \beta^{j-1} x_{T-j}\mathbf{L}^{-1}\mathbf{z}(-j+1)$$

$$= x_T\mathbf{z}(0) + \beta\mathbf{L}^{-1} \sum_{k=0}^{T-2} \beta^k x_{T-1-k}\mathbf{z}(-k)$$

[1] A steady-state $\mathbf{G}$ always exists if $z_i(t)$ are trigonometric or polynomial functions. If $z_i(t) = e^{-\theta t}$, then it is necessary that $\beta < e^{-2\theta}$.

or

$$g(T) = x_T z(0) + \beta L^{-1} g(T-1) \tag{4-16}$$

Therefore, it is possible to obtain $g(T)$ directly from $g(T-1)$.

Using the steady-state value for $G(T)$, we may write the estimator of $a(T)$ as

$$\hat{a}(T) = G^{-1} g(T)$$

$$= G^{-1}[x_T z(0) + \beta L^{-1} g(T-1)] \tag{4-17}$$

However, since $G\hat{a}(T-1) = g(T-1)$, Eq. (4-17) becomes

$$\hat{a}(T) = x_T G^{-1} z(0) + \beta G^{-1} L^{-1} G\hat{a}(T-1)$$

which may be written as

$$\hat{a}(T) = hx_T + H\hat{a}(T-1) \tag{4-18}$$

where

$$h = G^{-1} z(0) \tag{4-19}$$

and

$$H = \beta G^{-1} L^{-1} G \tag{4-20}$$

It is possible to further simplify Eq. (4-18). Notice that

$$L^{-1} G = L^{-1} G(L')^{-1} L'$$

$$= \sum_{j=0}^{\infty} \beta^j L^{-1} z(-j) z'(-j)(L')^{-1} L'$$

$$= \sum_{j=0}^{\infty} \beta^j [L^{-1} z(-j)][L^{-1} z(-j)]' L'$$

$$= \sum_{j=0}^{\infty} \beta^j z(-j+1) z'(-j+1) L'$$

If we let $p = j + 1$, we obtain

$$L^{-1} G = \beta^{-1} \sum_{p=1}^{\infty} \beta^p z(-p) z'(-p) L'$$

$$= \beta^{-1}[G - z(0)z'(0)]L'$$

Therefore, substituting for $L^{-1} G$ in (4-20),

$$H = \beta G^{-1} \beta^{-1}[G - z(0)z'(0)]L'$$

$$= G^{-1}[G - z(0)z'(0)]L'$$

$$= [I - G^{-1} z(0)z'(0)]L'$$

Since $\mathbf{h} = \mathbf{G}^{-1}\mathbf{z}(0)$, we obtain

$$\mathbf{H} = \mathbf{L}' - \mathbf{h}\mathbf{z}'(0)\mathbf{L}'$$

$$= \mathbf{L}' - \mathbf{h}[\mathbf{L}\mathbf{z}(0)]'$$

$$= \mathbf{L}' - \mathbf{h}\mathbf{z}'(1)$$

Now Eq. (4-18) becomes

$$\hat{\mathbf{a}}(T) = \mathbf{h}x_T + [\mathbf{L}' - \mathbf{h}\mathbf{z}'(1)]\hat{\mathbf{a}}(T-1)$$

$$= \mathbf{L}'\hat{\mathbf{a}}(T-1) + \mathbf{h}[x_T - \mathbf{z}'(1)]\hat{\mathbf{a}}(T-1) \qquad (4\text{-}21)$$

Let $\hat{x}_T(T-1)$ be the forecast for period T, made at the end of period $T-1$. Thus, since

$$\hat{x}_T(T-1) = \mathbf{z}'(1)\hat{\mathbf{a}}(T-1)$$

Eq. (4-21) becomes

$$\hat{\mathbf{a}}(T) = \mathbf{L}'\hat{\mathbf{a}}(T-1) + \mathbf{h}[x_T - \hat{x}_T(T-1)] \qquad (4\text{-}22)$$

The quantity in brackets in (4-22) is just the single-period forecast error, or

$$e_1(T) \equiv x_T - \mathbf{z}'(1)\hat{\mathbf{a}}(T-1)$$

We have shown that the discounted least-squares estimates of the model parameters at the end of period T are just linear combinations of the estimates made at the end of the previous period and the single-period forecast error, that is,

$$\hat{\mathbf{a}}(T) = \mathbf{L}'\hat{\mathbf{a}}(T-1) + \mathbf{h}e_1(T) \qquad (4\text{-}23)$$

This procedure is often called *direct smoothing* because the model parameters are updated directly instead of through the use of exponentially smoothed statistics. Brown [9] uses the term *adaptive smoothing*.

The estimates of the model parameters are modified each period for two reasons. The first is to shift the origin of time to the end of the current period, and the second is to update or modify the estimates according to the forecast error for the current period. These two purposes are accomplished by the first and second terms, respectively, of Eq. (4-23). The $k \times 1$ vector $\mathbf{h}$ is sometimes called the smoothing vector. Details of its calculation are discussed in Sec. 4-5.

The forecast for any future time period, say $T + \tau$, made at the end of period T would be

$$\hat{x}_{T+\tau}(T) = \mathbf{z}'(\tau)\hat{\mathbf{a}}(T) = \sum_{i=1}^{k} \hat{a}_i(T)z_i(\tau) \qquad (4\text{-}24)$$

To start the procedure, an initial estimate $\hat{\mathbf{a}}(0)$ is required. This could be a subjective estimate, or it could be obtained by least-squares analysis of historical data.

The variability of the estimator $\hat{\mathbf{a}}(T)$ is expressed by the covariance matrix

$$\mathbf{V} = \mathbf{G}^{-1}\mathbf{F}\mathbf{G}^{-1}\sigma_\epsilon^2 \tag{4-25}$$

where

$$\mathbf{F} = \sum_{j=0}^{\infty} \beta^{2j}\mathbf{z}(-j)\mathbf{z}'(-j)$$

It is also possible to express the variance of the forecast generated from Eq. (4-24) as

$$V[\hat{x}_{T+\tau}(T)] = V[\mathbf{z}'(\tau)\hat{\mathbf{a}}(T)]$$

$$= \sum_{i=1}^{k} \sum_{j=1}^{k} z_i(\tau)z_j(\tau)\text{Cov}[\hat{a}_i(T), \hat{a}_j(T)]$$

$$= \mathbf{z}'(\tau)\mathbf{V}\mathbf{z}'(\tau) \tag{4-26}$$

The variance of the τ-step-ahead forecast error is

$$V[e_\tau(T+\tau)] = V[x_{T+\tau} - \hat{x}_{T+\tau}(T)]$$

$$= \sigma_\epsilon^2 + V[\hat{x}_{T+\tau}(T)]$$

$$= \sigma_\epsilon^2 + \mathbf{z}'(\tau)\mathbf{V}\mathbf{z}'(\tau) \tag{4-27}$$

4-3 APPLICATION TO POLYNOMIAL MODELS

Consider a time series model where the independent variables $\{z_i(t)\}$ are polynomial functions of time. The direct smoothing approach, when applied to such a model, produces forecasts identical to multiple smoothing, except that the calculations are organized so that estimates of the model parameters are obtained directly instead of through linear combinations of the smoothed statistics.

To develop the direct smoothing equations for a particular polynomial model, the transition matrix $\mathbf{L}$ must be constructed. In general, for a polynomial of degree $k - 1$ the transition matrix is a $k \times k$ matrix with diagonal elements 1, the first element to the left of each diagonal 1, and all other elements 0. However, this requires a slightly modified definition of the polynomial model. Instead of writing the term of degree u (say) as $b_u t^u$, it must be written as $(1/u!)b_u t(t -$

1) $\cdots (t - u + 1)$.   This is equivalent to expressing the term of degree u as

$$b_u \binom{t}{u} = b_u \frac{t!}{(t-u)!u!}$$

As an example of these rules for constructing the transition matrix, consider the linear trend model

$$x_t = b_1 + b_2 t + \epsilon_t \tag{4-28}$$

The transition matrix would be

$$\mathbf{L} = \begin{bmatrix} 1 & 0 \\ 1 & 1 \end{bmatrix}$$

from a direct application of the above rules.   As a further example, the quadratic trend model is

$$x_t = b_1 + b_2 t + \tfrac{1}{2} b_3 t(t-1) + \epsilon_t \tag{4-29}$$

for which the transition matrix would be

$$\mathbf{L} = \begin{bmatrix} 1 & 0 & 0 \\ 1 & 1 & 0 \\ 0 & 1 & 1 \end{bmatrix}$$

To illustrate the direct smoothing approach for polynomial models, we shall develop the equations for updating the parameter estimates in the linear trend model (4-28).   For this model, note that $z_1(t) \equiv 1$ and $z_2(t) \equiv t$; therefore

$$\mathbf{z}(t) = \begin{bmatrix} 1 \\ t \end{bmatrix}$$

The updating equations are

$$\hat{\mathbf{a}}(T) = \mathbf{L}'\hat{\mathbf{a}}(T-1) + \mathbf{h} e_1(T)$$

or

$$\begin{bmatrix} \hat{a}_1(T) \\ \hat{a}_2(T) \end{bmatrix} = \begin{bmatrix} 1 & 1 \\ 0 & 1 \end{bmatrix} \begin{bmatrix} \hat{a}_1(T-1) \\ \hat{a}_2(T-1) \end{bmatrix} + \begin{bmatrix} h_1 \\ h_2 \end{bmatrix} e_1(T)$$

which in scalar notation is

$$\hat{a}_1(T) = \hat{a}_1(T-1) + \hat{a}_2(T-1) + h_1 e_1(T)$$

$$\hat{a}_2(T) = \hat{a}_2(T-1) + h_2 e_1(T) \tag{4-30}$$

The elements of the smoothing vector $\mathbf{h}$ are found from Eq. (4-19); that is,

$$\mathbf{h} = \mathbf{G}^{-1}\mathbf{z}(0)$$

Therefore, we must find the steady-state matrix $\mathbf{G}$. Notice that

$$\mathbf{G}(T) = \sum_{j=0}^{T-1} \beta^j \mathbf{z}(-j)\mathbf{z}'(-j)$$

$$= \sum_{j=0}^{T-1} \beta^j \begin{bmatrix} 1 \\ -j \end{bmatrix} [1, \quad -j]$$

$$= \sum_{j=0}^{T-1} \beta^j \begin{bmatrix} 1 & -j \\ -j & j^2 \end{bmatrix}$$

Since we know that

$$\sum_{j=0}^{T-1} \beta^j = \frac{1 - \beta^T}{1 - \beta}$$

$$\sum_{j=0}^{T-1} j\beta^j = \frac{-\beta(1 - \beta^T)}{(1 - \beta)^2}$$

and

$$\sum_{j=0}^{T-1} j^2\beta^j = \frac{\beta(1 + \beta)(1 - \beta^T)}{(1 - \beta)^3}$$

we may express $\mathbf{G}(T)$ in closed form as

$$\mathbf{G}(T) = (1 - \beta^T) \begin{bmatrix} \dfrac{1}{1 - \beta} & \dfrac{-\beta}{(1 - \beta)^2} \\ \dfrac{-\beta}{(1 - \beta)^2} & \dfrac{\beta(1 + \beta)}{(1 - \beta)^3} \end{bmatrix}$$

The steady-state value of $\mathbf{G}(T)$ is

$$\mathbf{G} \equiv \lim_{T \to \infty} \mathbf{G}(T) = \begin{bmatrix} \dfrac{1}{1-\beta} & \dfrac{-\beta}{(1-\beta)^2} \\ \dfrac{-\beta}{(1-\beta)^2} & \dfrac{\beta(1+\beta)}{(1-\beta)^3} \end{bmatrix}$$

and the inverse of $\mathbf{G}$ is

$$\mathbf{G}^{-1} = \begin{bmatrix} 1-\beta^2 & (1-\beta)^2 \\ (1-\beta)^2 & \dfrac{(1-\beta)^3}{\beta} \end{bmatrix}$$

The elements of the smoothing vector are found by substituting $\mathbf{G}^{-1}$ and $\mathbf{z}(0)$ into (4-19) as

$$\mathbf{h} = \begin{bmatrix} 1-\beta^2 & (1-\beta)^2 \\ (1-\beta)^2 & \dfrac{(1-\beta)^3}{\beta} \end{bmatrix} \begin{bmatrix} 1 \\ 0 \end{bmatrix} = \begin{bmatrix} 1-\beta^2 \\ (1-\beta)^2 \end{bmatrix}$$

Thus $h_1 = 1 - \beta^2$ and $h_2 = (1 - \beta)^2$, and the final form of the updating equations (4-30) are

$$\hat{a}_1(T) = \hat{a}_1(T-1) + \hat{a}_2(T-1) + (1-\beta^2)e_1(T)$$

$$\hat{a}_2(T) = \hat{a}_2(T-1) + (1-\beta^2)e_1(T)$$

$$(4\text{-}31)$$

As soon as we specify a value for the discount factor β, the direct smoothing equations for periodic updating of $\hat{a}_1(T)$ and $\hat{a}_2(T)$ are complete.

It can be shown (see Brown [9], pp. 172–173) that the parameter estimates obtained by Eq. (4-31) are identical to those found by double exponential smoothing with $\alpha = 1 - \beta$. In general, direct smoothing of a polynomial model of degree k is equivalent to multiple smoothing of order $k + 1$ with $\alpha = 1 - \beta$.

EXAMPLE 4-1 *Linear model.* We shall demonstrate the direct smoothing calculations for the linear trend model and show its equivalence to double smoothing. Consider the second column of Table 4-1, which shows the first six realizations of a time series. We assume that a linear trend model adequately

TABLE 4-1 Direct Smoothing for the Linear Trend Model and Comparison with Double Exponential Smoothing

Period, T	x_T	$\hat{a}_1(T)$	$\hat{a}_2(T)$	$\hat{x}_T(T-1)$, by direct smoothing	S_T	$S_T^{[2]}$	$\hat{x}_T(T-1)$, by double smoothing
0		90.00	1.00		81.00	72.00	
1	94	91.57	1.03	91.00	82.30	73.03	90.99
2	90	92.11	1.00	92.60	83.07	74.03	92.59
3	95	93.47	1.02	93.11	84.26	75.05	93.11
4	100	95.54	1.08	94.49	85.84	76.13	94.49
5	104	98.02	1.15	96.62	87.66	77.29	96.62
6	96	98.57	1.12	99.17	88.49	78.40	99.18

describes the process, and that preliminary subjective estimates of the model parameters are $\hat{a}_1(0) = 90.00$ and $\hat{a}_2(0) = 1.00$. The discount factor is $\beta = 0.90$. The forecast for period 1, made at time 0, is

$$\hat{x}_1(0) = \hat{a}_1(0) + \hat{a}_2(0)$$

$$= 90.00 + 1.00 = 91.00$$

The updating equations are, from (4-31),

$$\hat{a}_1(T) = \hat{a}_1(T-1) + \hat{a}_2(T-1) + (0.19)e_1(T)$$

$$\hat{a}_2(T) = \hat{a}_2(T-1) + (0.01)e_1(T)$$

since $1 - \beta^2 = 1 - (0.9)^2 = 0.19$ and $(1 - \beta)^2 = (1 - 0.90)^2 = 0.01$. The forecast error in period 1 is $e_1(1) = 94.00 - 91.00 = 3.00$. Thus, the new estimates of the model parameters are

$$\hat{a}_1(1) = \hat{a}_1(0) + \hat{a}_2(0) + (0.19)e_1(1)$$

$$= 90.00 + 1.00 + (0.19)(3.00) = 91.57$$

and

$$\hat{a}_2(1) = \hat{a}_2(0) + (0.01)e_1(1)$$

$$= 1.00 + (0.01)(3.00) = 1.03$$

Therefore the forecast for period 2, computed at the end of period 1, is

$$\hat{x}_2(1) = \hat{a}_1(1) + \hat{a}_2(1)$$

$$= 91.57 + 1.03 = 92.60$$

At this point, the model parameters may be revised again, using the period 2 forecast error $e_1(2) = 90.00 - 92.60 = -2.60$. The revised parameters and one-step-ahead forecasts for periods 2 to 6 are shown in columns 3 to 5, respectively, of Table 4-1.

Double exponential smoothing may also be applied to the data. The appropriate value of the smoothing constant is $\alpha = 1 - \beta = 1 - 0.90 = 0.10$, and starting values of the smoothed statistics can be obtained from $\hat{a}_1(0)$ and $\hat{a}_2(0)$ by using Eqs. (3-26) and (3-27), as

$$S_0 = \hat{a}_1(0) - \frac{\beta}{\alpha} \, \hat{a}_2(0) = 90.00 - \frac{0.90}{0.10} \, (1.00) = 81.00$$

$$S_0^{[2]} = \hat{a}_1(0) - 2 \, \frac{\beta}{\alpha} \, \hat{a}_2(0) = 90.00 - 2 \, \frac{0.90}{0.10} \, (1.00) = 72.00$$

Application of double smoothing as described in Sec. 3-2 yields the smoothed statistics shown in columns 6 and 7 of Table 4-1 and the forecasts shown in column 8. Comparing columns 5 and 8, we see that the direct smoothing and double smoothing procedures produce identical forecasts (apart from rounding), and thus the two procedures are equivalent.

4-4 APPLICATION TO TRANSCENDENTAL MODELS

Models which contain trigonometric or exponential terms are often called transcendental models. In particular, models with trigonometric components are very useful for modeling seasonal time series. Section 5-3 of the next chapter presents a detailed discussion of the application of trigonometric models to the analysis of time series. In this section we shall discuss the structure of the transition matrix for several important types of transcendental models.

Suppose the time series model contains a simple mixture of sine and cosine waves, such as

$$x_t = b_1 \sin \omega t + b_2 \cos \omega t + \epsilon_t \tag{4-32}$$

The transition matrix for the model (4-32) would be

$$L = \begin{bmatrix} \cos \omega & \sin \omega \\ -\sin \omega & \cos \omega \end{bmatrix}$$

This model would adequately represent a time series which exhibits a symmetric seasonal pattern. The height (amplitude), origin (phase angle), and length of the season are controlled by the parameters b_1, b_2, and ω. The direct smoothing equations for updating the estimates of the model parameters on a current-origin basis are found from Eq. (4-23) as

$$\hat{a}_1(T) = \cos \omega \, \hat{a}_1(T-1) - \sin \omega \, \hat{a}_2(T-1) + h_1 e_1(T)$$

$$\hat{a}_2(T) = \sin \omega \, \hat{a}_1(T-1) + \cos \omega \, \hat{a}_2(T-1) + h_2 e_1(T)$$

A model which would account for increasing heights or shifting origins in the seasonal pattern would include terms such as

$$x_t = b_1 \sin \omega t + b_2 \cos \omega t + b_3 t \sin \omega t + b_4 t \cos \omega t + \epsilon_t \qquad (4\text{-}33)$$

The transition matrix for this model would be

$$\mathbf{L} = \begin{bmatrix} \cos \omega & \sin \omega & 0 & 0 \\ -\sin \omega & \cos \omega & 0 & 0 \\ \cos \omega & \sin \omega & \cos \omega & \sin \omega \\ -\sin \omega & \cos \omega & -\sin \omega & \cos \omega \end{bmatrix}$$

Models with exponential functions as the independent variables are occasionally useful. A typical model containing exponential terms might be

$$x_t = b_1 e^{ut} + b_2 t e^{v(t-1)} = \epsilon_t \qquad (4\text{-}34)$$

where u and v are known constants. The transition matrix for the model (4-34) would be

$$\mathbf{L} = \begin{bmatrix} e^u & 0 \\ 1 & e^v \end{bmatrix}$$

A more general exponential model such as

$$x_t = b_1 u^t + b_2 t u^{t-1} v + \tfrac{1}{2} b_3 t(t-1) u^{t-2} v^2$$

$$+ \cdots + \frac{1}{k!} b_{k+1} t(t-1) \cdots (t-k+1) u^{t-k} v^k + \epsilon_t \qquad (4\text{-}35)$$

for $t > k$ would have a $(k+1) \times (k+1)$ transition matrix consisting of diagonal elements equal to u, elements immediately to the left of the diagonal equal to v, and all remaining elements equal to 0.

When we build a forecasting model for a specific time series, we may find that a combination of various polynomial, trigonometric, and exponential terms is required. In these cases, the transition matrix for the composite model consists of the simple matrices previously discussed placed along the main diagonal and

0's elsewhere.   For example, consider the model

$$x_t = b_1 + b_2 t + b_3 \sin \omega t + b_4 \cos \omega t + b_5 t \sin \omega t$$

$$+ b_6 t \cos \omega t + \epsilon_t \tag{4-36}$$

which contains a mixture of polynomial and trigonometric terms.   The transition matrix for this model is

$$
L = \begin{bmatrix}
1 & 0 & 0 & 0 & 0 & 0 \\
1 & 1 & 0 & 0 & 0 & 0 \\
0 & 0 & \cos\omega & \sin\omega & 0 & 0 \\
0 & 0 & -\sin\omega & \cos\omega & 0 & 0 \\
0 & 0 & \cos\omega & \sin\omega & \cos\omega & \sin\omega \\
0 & 0 & -\sin\omega & \cos\omega & -\sin\omega & \cos\omega
\end{bmatrix}
$$

We see that the transition matrix for the combined models has a *block diagonal* structure, with the matrices for the polynomial and trigonometric terms as the main diagonal submatrices.

The direct smoothing approach requires developing the transition matrix **L** and assigning numerical values to the elements of the smoothing vector **h**. Once **L** and **h** are specified, the direct smoothing equations for updating the estimates of the model parameters are obtained from Eq. (4-23).   However, computing the elements of the smoothing vector **h** is not always a simple problem.   We shall discuss this subject in more detail in Sec. 4-5.

4-5 DEVELOPMENT OF THE SMOOTHING VECTOR

The elements of the smoothing vector **h** are found from Eq. (4-19), which we repeat as

$$\mathbf{h} = \mathbf{G}^{-1}\mathbf{z}(0) \tag{4-37}$$

Notice that $\mathbf{z}(0)$ is a column vector of the independent variables $\mathbf{z}(t)$ evaluated at $t = 0$ and $\mathbf{G}^{-1}$ is the inverse of the steady-state matrix $\mathbf{G}$.   The problem essentially consists of finding the matrix $\mathbf{G}$.   In Sec. 4-3 we illustrated the development of the smoothing vector for a linear trend model.   However, when the model contains higher-order polynomial terms, or a mixture of polynomial and transcendental terms, the procedure for computing **h** is more complicated.

The elements of **G** are

$$G_{ij} = \sum_{n=0}^{\infty} \beta^n z_i(-n) z_j(-n) \qquad i, j = 1, 2, \ldots, k \tag{4-38}$$

TABLE 4-2 Infinite Sums Useful in Development of the Smoothing Vector

Form	Sum
$\displaystyle\sum_{k=0}^{\infty}\beta^k$	$\dfrac{1}{1-\beta}$
$\displaystyle\sum_{k=0}^{\infty}k\beta^k$	$\dfrac{\beta}{(1-\beta)^2}$
$\displaystyle\sum_{k=0}^{\infty}k^2\beta^k$	$\dfrac{\beta(1+\beta)}{(1-\beta)^3}$
$\displaystyle\sum_{k=0}^{\infty}k^3\beta^k$	$\dfrac{\beta(1+4\beta+\beta^2)}{(1-\beta)^4}$
$\displaystyle\sum_{k=0}^{\infty}k^4\beta^k$	$\dfrac{\beta(1+11\beta+11\beta^2+\beta^3)}{(1-\beta)^5}$
$\displaystyle\sum_{k=0}^{\infty}\beta^k\sin\omega k$	$\dfrac{\beta\sin\omega}{1-2\beta\cos\omega+\beta^2}$
$\displaystyle\sum_{k=0}^{\infty}\beta^k\cos\omega k$	$\dfrac{1-\beta\cos\omega}{1-2\beta\cos\omega+\beta^2}$
$\displaystyle\sum_{k=0}^{\infty}k\beta^k\sin\omega k$	$\dfrac{\beta(1-\beta^2)\sin\omega}{(1-2\beta\cos\omega+\beta^2)^2}$
$\displaystyle\sum_{k=0}^{\infty}k\beta^k\cos\omega k$	$\dfrac{2\beta^2-\beta(1+\beta^2)\cos\omega}{(1-2\beta\cos\omega+\beta^2)^2}$
$\displaystyle\sum_{k=0}^{\infty}\beta^k\sin\omega_1k\,\sin\omega_2k$	$\dfrac{1}{2}\left[\dfrac{1-\beta\cos(\omega_1+\omega_2)}{1-2\beta\cos(\omega_1+\omega_2)+\beta^2}-\dfrac{1-\beta\cos(\omega_1-\omega_2)}{1-2\beta\cos(\omega_1-\omega_2)+\beta^2}\right]$
$\displaystyle\sum_{k=0}^{\infty}\beta^k\sin\omega_1k\,\cos\omega_2k$	$\dfrac{1}{2}\left[\dfrac{\beta\sin(\omega_1+\omega_2)}{1-2\beta\cos(\omega_1+\omega_2)+\beta^2}+\dfrac{\beta\sin(\omega_1-\omega_2)}{1-2\beta\cos(\omega_1-\omega_2)+\beta^2}\right]$
$\displaystyle\sum_{k=0}^{\infty}\beta^k\cos\omega_1k\,\cos\omega_2k$	$\dfrac{1}{2}\left[\dfrac{1-\beta\cos(\omega_1+\omega_2)}{1-2\beta\cos(\omega_1+\omega_2)+\beta^2}+\dfrac{1-\beta\cos(\omega_1-\omega_2)}{1-2\beta\cos(\omega_1-\omega_2)+\beta^2}\right]$

Note that more complex forms can be obtained by successive differentiation of those given above. For example,

$$\beta\frac{\partial}{\partial\beta}\left(\sum_{k=0}^{\infty}k\beta^k\right)=\sum_{k=0}^{\infty}k^2\beta^k$$

which yields

$$\beta\frac{\partial}{\partial\beta}\left[\frac{\beta}{(1-\beta)^2}\right]=\frac{\beta(1+\beta)}{(1-\beta)^3}\equiv\sum_{k=0}^{\infty}k^2\beta^k$$

Similarly, we may evaluate

$$\sum_{k=0}^{\infty}k^2\beta^k\sin\omega k=-\frac{\partial}{\partial\omega}\left(\sum_{k=0}^{\infty}k\beta^k\cos\omega k\right)$$

TABLE 4-2   (Continued)

More complex forms may be factored and evaluated by use of the trigonometric identities

$$\sin a \sin b = -\tfrac{1}{2}[\cos(a+b) - \cos(a-b)]$$
$$\cos a \cos b = \tfrac{1}{2}[\cos(a+b) + \cos(a-b)]$$
$$\cos a \sin b = \tfrac{1}{2}[\sin(a+b) - \sin(a-b)]$$
$$\sin a \cos b = \tfrac{1}{2}[\sin(a+b) + \sin(a-b)]$$

where $z_i(-n)$ indicates that the mathematical function z_i is to be evaluated at $-n$ and $0 < \beta < 1$. Thus the elements of **G** are infinite, discounted sums of squares and cross products of the independent variables evaluated at $-n$. If the independent variables are either polynomial or certain transcendental functions, then closed-form expressions for these infinite sums may be found. Table 4-2 contains several of these infinite sums which frequently arise in the use of direct smoothing. In general, the infinite sum of functional forms not included in Table 4-2 may be found by the method of z transforms.

The value chosen for the discount factor β will affect the elements of the smoothing vector. As a general guide to the choice of β, it is possible to define an *equivalent discount factor* such that estimates of the constant term in a model with k parameters are the same as would be obtained when forecasting a constant process, i.e., a model with $k = 1$. This is equivalent to saying that if β_1 (say) is an appropriate discount factor for a model with only a constant component, then

$$\beta_k = \beta_1^{1/k} \tag{4-39}$$

would be the appropriate value of the discount factor for a model with k parameters. If we select the discount factor for a model which contains only polynomial terms, then h_1, the element of the smoothing vector that updates the permanent component, is always equal to $1 - \beta_1$. Since we know that in a constant model $\beta_1 = 1 - \alpha$, where α is the usual smoothing constant, and a reasonable range of values for α in a constant model is $0 < \alpha \le 0.30$, Eq. (4-39) can be used to generate a reasonable range of values for the discount factor for any k-parameter model. Such a tabulation is given in Table 3-6.

Once the matrix **G** has been structured, its inverse may be computed by any convenient method. After obtaining the inverse, the smoothing vector for the model may be computed from Eq. (4-37). The general computational procedure is illustrated in the following example.

EXAMPLE 4-2 Consider the six-parameter model

$$x_t = b_1 + b_2 t + b_3 \sin \frac{2\pi t}{12} + b_4 \cos \frac{2\pi t}{12} + b_5 \sin \frac{4\pi t}{12} + b_6 \cos \frac{4\pi t}{12} + \epsilon_t$$

This model contains a 12-point sine wave with one harmonic, superimposed on a linear trend. As we shall later see, it is capable of modeling a seasonal time series which is observed 12 times each season, such as the monthly demand for a product with a one-year season. The independent variables, current-time-origin model parameters in period T, and smoothing vector are

$$
\mathbf{z}(t) = \begin{bmatrix} 1 \\ t \\ \sin \dfrac{2\pi t}{12} \\ \cos \dfrac{2\pi t}{12} \\ \sin \dfrac{4\pi t}{12} \\ \cos \dfrac{4\pi t}{12} \end{bmatrix}
\qquad
\mathbf{a}(T) = \begin{bmatrix} a_1(T) \\ a_2(T) \\ a_3(T) \\ a_4(T) \\ a_5(T) \\ a_6(T) \end{bmatrix}
\quad \text{and} \quad
\mathbf{h} = \begin{bmatrix} h_1 \\ h_2 \\ h_3 \\ h_4 \\ h_5 \\ h_6 \end{bmatrix}
$$

Since $2\pi/12 = 30°$, we may write the transition matrix for this model as

$$
\mathbf{L} = \begin{bmatrix}
1 & 0 & 0 & 0 & 0 & 0 \\
1 & 1 & 0 & 0 & 0 & 0 \\
0 & 0 & \cos 30° & \sin 30° & 0 & 0 \\
0 & 0 & -\sin 30° & \cos 30° & 0 & 0 \\
0 & 0 & 0 & 0 & \cos 60° & \sin 60° \\
0 & 0 & 0 & 0 & -\sin 60° & \cos 60°
\end{bmatrix}
$$

or

$$
\mathbf{L} = \begin{bmatrix}
1 & 0 & 0 & 0 & 0 & 0 \\
1 & 1 & 0 & 0 & 0 & 0 \\
0 & 0 & 0.866 & 0.5 & 0 & 0 \\
0 & 0 & -0.5 & 0.866 & 0 & 0 \\
0 & 0 & 0 & 0 & 0.5 & 0.866 \\
0 & 0 & 0 & 0 & -0.866 & 0.5
\end{bmatrix}
$$

We shall compute the smoothing vector for $\beta = 0.90$. The steady-state $\mathbf{G}$ matrix for this model is found from Eq. (4-38) as

$$
G = \begin{bmatrix}
\sum \beta^k & -\sum \beta^k \sin \omega k & \sum \beta^k \cos \omega k & -\sum \beta^k \sin 2\omega k & \sum \beta^k \cos 2\omega k \\
-\sum k\beta^k & \sum k\beta^k \sin \omega k & -\sum k\beta^k \cos \omega k & \sum k\beta^k \sin 2\omega k & -\sum k\beta^k \cos 2\omega k \\
\sum k^2\beta^k & \sum \beta^k \sin \omega k \sin \omega k & -\sum \beta^k \sin \omega k \cos \omega k & \sum \beta^k \sin \omega k \sin 2\omega k & -\sum \beta^k \sin \omega k \cos 2\omega k \\
& & \sum \beta^k \cos \omega k \cos 2\omega k & -\sum \beta^k \sin \omega k \sin 2\omega k & \sum \beta^k \sin \omega k \cos 2\omega k \\
& & & \sum \beta^k \sin 2\omega k \sum \sin 2\omega k & -\sum \sin 2\omega k \cos 2\omega k
\end{bmatrix}
$$

where $\omega = 2\pi/12$ and all summations are from $k = 0$ to $k = \infty$. As $\mathbf{G}$ is symmetric (that is, $G_{ij} = G_{ji}$), we have written only the upper half.

Closed-form expressions for all the summations in $\mathbf{G}$ are found in Table 4-2. Replacing the summations with their closed-form expressions evaluated at $\beta = 0.90$ yields

$$\mathbf{G} = \begin{bmatrix} 20 & -380 & -1.84788 & 0.68965 & -0.86375 & 0.55118 \\ -380 & 14{,}820.00293 & 0.70090 & 3.62869 & 0.08842 & 0.99345 \\ -1.84788 & 0.70090 & 9.74935 & -0.43188 & -0.15517 & 0.67427 \\ 0.68965 & 3.62869 & -0.43188 & 10.27560 & -1.17361 & 0.60764 \\ -0.86375 & 0.08842 & -0.15517 & -1.17361 & 9.74146 & -0.14421 \\ 0.55118 & 0.99345 & 0.67427 & 9.60764 & -0.14421 & 10.25856 \end{bmatrix}$$

where we have shown the complete matrix.   The inverse of $\mathbf{G}$ is

$$\mathbf{G}^{-1} = \begin{bmatrix} 0.10252 & 0.00263 & 0.01959 & -0.00561 & 0.00860 & -0.00660 \\ 0.00263 & 0.00014 & 0.00050 & -0.00017 & 0.00022 & -0.00017 \\ 0.01959 & 0.00050 & 0.10706 & 0.00393 & 0.00379 & -0.00832 \\ -0.00561 & -0.00017 & 0.00393 & 0.09957 & 0.01148 & -0.00567 \\ 0.00860 & 0.00022 & 0.00379 & 0.01148 & 0.10486 & 0.00007 \\ -0.00660 & -0.00017 & -0.00832 & -0.00567 & 0.00007 & 0.09874 \end{bmatrix}$$

The vector $\mathbf{z}(0)$ is found by evaluating $\mathbf{z}(t)$ at $t = 0$ as

$$\mathbf{z}(0) = \begin{bmatrix} 1 \\ 0 \\ 0 \\ 1 \\ 0 \\ 1 \end{bmatrix}$$

Therefore, the smoothing vector for the six-parameter model for $\beta = 0.90$ is determined from (4-37) as

$$
\mathbf{h} = \mathbf{G}^{-1}\mathbf{z}(0) =
\begin{bmatrix}
0.09031 \\
0.00229 \\
0.01520 \\
0.08828 \\
0.02014 \\
0.08646
\end{bmatrix}
$$

4-6 EXERCISES

4-1 Show that the discounted least-squares estimator $\hat{\mathbf{b}}(T)$ is unbiased, and that the covariance matrix of $\hat{\mathbf{b}}(T)$ is $\mathbf{V}$, defined in Eq. (4-9).

4-2 Consider using direct smoothing for the quadratic trend model $x_t = b_1 + b_2 t + b_3 t^2 + \epsilon_t$. Can a transition matrix for this model be developed easily? Compare it with the transition matrix for the quadratic trend model in Sec. 4-3.

4-3 Write down the updating equations for the quadratic trend model $x_t = b_1 + b_2 t + \frac{1}{2} b_3 t(t-1) + \epsilon_t$. Develop the smoothing vector for $\beta = 0.95$.

4-4 Develop the smoothing vector for direct smoothing of a linear trend model using $\beta = 0.95$.

4-5 In Sec. 4-3 we state that direct smoothing of a polynomial of degree k is equivalent to $(k+1)$st-order exponential smoothing with $\alpha = 1 - \beta$. Offer a proof of this statement for the special case $k = 1$ (the linear trend model). An outline of the proof is as follows: First write down the steady-state matrix $\mathbf{G}$ and $\mathbf{G}^{-1}$. Next obtain the elements of the 2×1 data vector, $\mathbf{g}(T)$. Then, using the fact that the first two smoothed statistics can be written as

$$
S_T = \sum_{j=0}^{T-1} \beta^j x_{T-j} + \beta^T S_0
$$

and

$$
S_T^{[2]} = \alpha^2 \sum_{j=0}^{T-1} (j+1)\beta^j x_{T-j} + \beta^T (T+1) S_0^{[2]}
$$

substitute the expressions involving the smoothed statistics into the data vector. Finally, solve for the current-origin estimates of the model parameter using $\hat{\mathbf{a}}(T) = \mathbf{G}^{-1}(T)\mathbf{g}(T)$. The result should be estimates of the model parameters that are identical to those found from double smoothing, apart from transient terms involving β^T.

4-6   *Continuation of Exercise 4-5.*   Considering the transient terms in $\hat{a}(T)$ derived in Exercise 4-5, do you think that forecasts generated in the early history of the series are sensitive to the initial values of the smoothed statistics?   What do you think of initially using a small value of β until several periods have passed, and then switching to a larger value of β?

4-7   Suppose that an appropriate time series model is thought to be

$$x_t = b_1 + b_2 c^t + \epsilon_t$$

where c is an arbitrary constant.   Derive updating equations for b_1 and b_2 using adaptive smoothing with $\beta = 0.95$ and $c = 1.5$.

4-8   Consider the exponential model

$$x_t = b_1 e^{ut} + b_2 t e^{v(t-1)} + \epsilon_t$$

Derive updating equations for b_1 and b_2 for this model.   Find the smoothing vector for $\beta = 0.90$.

4-9   Consider the model

$$x_t = b_1 + b_2 t + b_3 e^{ut} + b_4 t e^{v(t-1)} + \epsilon_t$$

Develop the transition matrix and the updating equations for this model.   Find the smoothing vector for $\beta = 0.95$.

4-10   For the model

$$x_t = b_1 + b_2 t + b_3 \sin \omega t + b_4 \cos \omega t + \epsilon_t$$

develop the transition matrix and the parameter updating equations.   Find the elements of the smoothing vector for $\beta = 0.90$ and $\omega = 30°$.

4-11   For the model

$$x_t = b_1 + b_2 t + b_3 \sin \omega t + b_4 \cos \omega t + b_5 t \sin \omega t$$

$$+ b_6 t \cos \omega t + \epsilon_t$$

develop the transition matrix and the parameter updating equations.   Derive the elements of the smoothing vector for $\beta = 0.95$ and $\omega = 30°$.

4-12   The model

$$x_t = b_1 + b_2 t + b_3 \sin \omega_1 t + b_4 \cos \omega_1 t + b_5 \sin \omega_2 t$$

$$+ b_6 \cos \omega_2 t + \epsilon_t$$

with $\omega_1 \neq \omega_2$, is frequently useful. By proper selection of the frequencies ω_1 and ω_2 we can model seasonal patterns that are not symmetric. Write the transition matrix for this model. Develop the smoothing vector for $\beta = 0.90$, $\omega_1 = 60°$, and $\omega_2 = 30°$.

4-13   Consider the six-parameter model

$$x_t = b_1 + b_2 t + b_3 \sin \frac{2\pi t}{12} + b_4 \cos \frac{2\pi t}{12} + b_5 \sin \frac{4\pi t}{12}$$

$$+ b_6 \cos \frac{4\pi t}{12} + \epsilon_t$$

Derive the elements of the smoothing vector for $\beta = 0.99$.

4-14   *Autoregressive process of order p.* The stochastic process

$$x_t = \phi_1 x_{t-1} + \phi_2 x_{t-2} + \cdots + \phi_p x_{t-p} + \epsilon_t$$

is called a pth order autoregressive process, because the current observation x_t is regressed on the previous realizations x_{t-j}. Verify that the transition matrix is of the form

$$\mathbf{L} = \begin{bmatrix} \phi_1 & \phi_2 & \phi_3 & \cdots & \phi_{p-1} & \phi_p \\ 1 & 0 & 0 & \cdots & 0 & 0 \\ 0 & 1 & 0 & \cdots & 0 & 0 \\ \cdot & \cdot & \cdot & \cdot & \cdot & \cdot \\ 0 & 0 & 0 & \cdots & 1 & 0 \end{bmatrix}$$

and that

$$\mathbf{z}(0) = \begin{bmatrix} x_{-1} \\ x_{-2} \\ \vdots \\ x_{-p} \end{bmatrix}$$

We shall discuss models of this type extensively in Chap. 9.

4-15   *The second-order autoregressive process (continuation of Exercise 4-14).* The autoregressive process of order 2 is

$$x_t = \phi_1 x_{t-1} + \phi_2 x_{t-2} + \epsilon_t$$

Find the transition matrix for this model. Develop the updating equations for the model parameters ϕ_1 and ϕ_2. In finding the smoothing vector, note that

$$\mathbf{z}(0) = \begin{bmatrix} x_{-1} \\ x_{-2} \end{bmatrix}$$

Discuss how you would choose values for x_{-1} and x_{-2}. How sensitive to the choice of x_{-1} and x_{-2} are the elements of the smoothing vector?

CHAPTER FIVE

Smoothing Models for Seasonal Data

In previous chapters we have shown that exponential smoothing is an efficient technique for estimating the coefficients in a polynomial time series model, and that the fitted polynomial may be used to forecast future values of the time series. However, there are many time series that cannot be adequately modeled by a polynomial. For example, a time series with cyclical or *seasonal* variation could not be easily represented by a polynomial model. Many industrial time series exhibit seasonal behavior, such as the demand for apparel or toys, so that seasonal forecasting problems are of considerable importance.

There are several approaches to the analysis of seasonal time series data. This chapter will concentrate on smoothing methods, which are probably the most widely used in practice. Chapter 9 will present an alternate approach to seasonal models.

5-1 A MULTIPLICATIVE SEASONAL MODEL

This approach to forecasting a seasonal time series is due to Winters [64] and is frequently called *Winters' method*. We shall assume that the time series is adequately represented by the model

$$x_t = (b_1 + b_2 t)c_t + \epsilon_t \qquad (5\text{-}1)$$

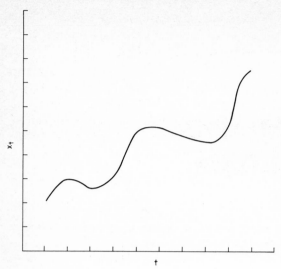

Fig. 5-1 Seasonal pattern with amplitude proportional to the average level of the series.

where b_1 = the base signal, usually called the *permanent component*
$\quad b_2$ = a linear trend component
$\quad c_t$ = a multiplicative seasonal factor
$\quad \epsilon_t$ = the usual random error component
The length of the season is L periods, and the seasonal factors are defined so that they sum to the length of the season, that is,

$$\sum_{t=1}^{L} c_t = L \tag{5-2}$$

This model incorporates both a linear trend and a seasonal effect. If we can assume that the trend component is unnecessary, then we may delete b_2 from the model. The multiplicative seasonal model is appropriate for the time series in which the amplitude (or height) of the seasonal pattern is proportional to the average level of the series. Figure 5-1 shows a time series for which the multiplicative seasonal model is probably appropriate. Notice that as the average level of the series, $b_1 + b_2 t$, increases, the amplitude of the seasonal pattern also increases.

Denote the estimates of the slope and seasonal component at the end of any time period, say T, as $\hat{b}_2(T)$ and $\hat{c}_T(T)$, respectively. The permanent component will be established on a current-origin basis, and following our usual convention, we shall denote its estimate at the end of period T by $\hat{a}_1(T)$. The procedure for periodically updating the estimates of the model parameters and for forecasting is relatively simple. At the end of the current period T, after observing the realization for that period, x_T, we would perform the following calculations:

1. Update the estimate of the permanent component:

$$\hat{a}_1(T) = \alpha \frac{x_T}{\hat{c}_T(T-L)} + (1-\alpha)\left[\hat{a}_1(T-1) + \hat{b}_2(T-1)\right] \qquad (5\text{-}3)$$

where $0 < \alpha < 1$ is a smoothing constant. Dividing x_T by $\hat{c}_T(T-L)$, which is the estimate of the seasonal factor for period T computed one season (L periods) ago, *deseasonalizes* the data so that only the trend component and the prior value of the permanent component enter into the updating process for $\hat{a}_1(T)$. This shifts the origin of time to the end of the current period.
  2. Update the estimate of the trend component:

$$\hat{b}_2(T) = \beta\left[\hat{a}_1(T) - \hat{a}_1(T-1)\right] + (1-\beta)\hat{b}_2(T-1) \qquad (5\text{-}4)$$

where $0 < \beta < 1$ is a second smoothing constant. We see that the estimate of the trend component is simply the smoothed difference between two successive estimates of the permanent component.
  3. Update the estimate of the seasonal factor for period T:

$$\hat{c}_T(T) = \gamma \frac{x_T}{\hat{a}_1(T)} + (1-\gamma)\hat{c}_T(T-L) \qquad (5\text{-}5)$$

where $0 < \gamma < 1$ is a third smoothing constant. Notice that the current *observed* seasonal variation [that is, $x_T/\hat{a}_1(T)$] is smoothed with the estimate of the seasonal factor for period T computed L periods ago, which was the last opportunity to observe this portion of the seasonal pattern, to obtain a new estimate of the seasonal effect in period T. Note that as we revise the estimates of the seasonal factors, they may not add to the length of the season. A possible modification of Winters' method is to "normalize" the seasonal factors at the end of every season.
  4. To forecast the observation in any future period $T + \tau$, compute

$$\hat{x}_{T+\tau}(T) = \left[\hat{a}_1(T) + \hat{b}_2(T)\tau\right]\hat{c}_{T+\tau}(T+\tau-L) \qquad (5\text{-}6)$$

Once again, remember that the quantity in parentheses for $\hat{a}_1(\cdot)$, $\hat{b}_2(\cdot)$, and $\hat{c}_t(\cdot)$ indicates the time of computation of the estimate. Thus, to forecast period $T + \tau$, we need the seasonal factor for period $T + \tau$ which was computed in period $T + \tau - L$. Forecasts for time periods more distant than L can be made by reusing the appropriate $\hat{c}_t(\cdot)$.
  The three equations (5-4) to (5-6) represent smoothing of an estimate based on information prior to the current period. They were developed heuristically, rather than formally through the use of a criterion such as least squares. Note that the technique uses three smoothing constants, which, in general, could be different. Also, because in estimating the permanent component the origin of time is shifted to the end of the current period T, we see that $\hat{x}_T = \hat{a}_1(T)\hat{c}_T(T)$.

The development of a forecasting system using Winters' method requires initial values of the parameters $\hat{a}_1(0)$, $\hat{b}_2(0)$, and $\hat{c}_t(0)$ for $t = 1, 2, \ldots, L$. Historical information, if available, can be used to provide some or all of the initial estimates. Several heuristic algorithms have been devised to utilize historical data for initial parameter estimation. We shall present an initialization procedure similar to the one proposed by Winters [64]. Suppose that the data for the last m seasons are available, and let $\bar{x}_j, j = 1, 2, \ldots, m$, denote the average of the observations during the jth season. Estimate the trend component by

$$\hat{b}_2(0) = \frac{\bar{x}_m - \bar{x}_1}{(m-1)L} \tag{5-7}$$

The permanent component at the start of the first period would be estimated by

$$\hat{a}_1(0) = \bar{x}_1 - \frac{L}{2} \hat{b}_2(0) \tag{5-8}$$

Seasonal factors are computed for each time period $t = 1, 2, \ldots, mL$, as the ratio of the actual observation to the average seasonally adjusted value for that season, further adjusted by the trend; that is,

$$\hat{c}_t = \frac{x_t}{\bar{x}_i - [(L+1)/2 - j]\hat{b}_2(0)} \qquad t = 1, 2, \ldots, mL \tag{5-9}$$

where $\bar{x}_i$ is the average for a season corresponding to the t index, and j is the position of period t *within* the season (for example, if $1 \leqslant t \leqslant L$, then $i = 1$, and if $L + 1 \leqslant t \leqslant 2L$, then $i = 2$; and when $t = 1$ to $t = L + 1$, then $j = 1$, etc.). Equation (5-9) will produce m estimates of the seasonal factor for each period. These should be averaged to produce a single estimate of the seasonal factor for each period within the season. This is accomplished by

$$\bar{c}_t = \frac{1}{m} \sum_{k=0}^{m-1} \hat{c}_{t+kL} \qquad t = 1, 2, \ldots, L \tag{5-10}$$

Finally, the seasonal factors should be normalized so that they add to L. This produces the initial estimates of the season factors as

$$c_t(0) = \bar{c}_t \frac{L}{\displaystyle\sum_{t=1}^{L} \bar{c}_t} \qquad t = 1, 2, \ldots, L \tag{5-11}$$

This procedure produces estimates $\hat{a}_1(0)$, $\hat{b}_2(0)$, and $\hat{c}_t(0)$ assuming that the origin of time is immediately prior to period 1. For forecasting future observations of the time series the analyst usually requires initial estimates of the parameters with period mL as the origin of time. Several approaches can be used. One possibility is to estimate the permanent component at that point in time by

$\bar{x}_m + (L/2)\hat{b}_2(0)$ instead of Eq. (5-8) and then use $\hat{b}_2(0)$ and $\hat{c}_t(0)$ as computed previously. Another approach is to repeatedly smooth $\hat{a}_1(0)$, $\hat{b}_2(0)$, and $\hat{c}_t(0)$ period by period according to Eqs. (5-3) to (5-5) until values at the end of period mL are obtained. Then the origin of time can be redefined as period mL. To emphasize the change in the origin of time, periods mL, $mL + 1$, $mL + 2, \ldots,$ can be renumbered as 0, 1, 2, $\ldots,$ if the analyst so desires.

Johnson and Montgomery [36] have also proposed a technique for obtaining initial estimates of the model parameters. Their method is very similar to the one discussed above, but involves an iterative calculation of the seasonal factors. A widely used scheme to estimate the initial values of the seasonal factors is simply to divide the observation in each period by the average for the season. This procedure may work quite well if *no trend component is present*. However, if the trend component is not zero, then estimates of the seasonal factors obtained by this method will contain trend effects, and the forecasting procedure may be adversely affected.

EXAMPLE 5-1 The demand for a popular soft drink packaged in a 48-oz. nonreturnable bottle is seasonal, with a large portion of the demand occurring during the summer and early fall months. Historical data for four years (1970–1973) are available and shown in Fig. 5-2. We would like to develop a forecasting procedure for this time series. From examining Fig. 5-2, it seems that the seasonal amplitude is growing with the average level of sales, and so Winters' method may be appropriate. We will use the first two years of data to estimate the model parameters and then simulate the forecast for the last two years.

The first two years of the time series are listed in column 2 of Table 5-1. We may compute the average demand in 1970 and 1971 to be $\bar{x}_1 = 352.75$ and $\bar{x}_2 = 478.58$, respectively. If the length of the season is $L = 12$ periods, we may estimate the trend component from (5-7) as

$$\hat{b}_2(0) = \frac{\bar{x}_2 - \bar{x}_1}{(m-1)L}$$

$$= \frac{478.58 - 352.75}{(2-1)12}$$

$$= 10.49$$

Using Eq. (5-8), the initial permanent component is

$$\hat{a}_1(0) = \bar{x}_1 - \frac{L}{2}\,\hat{b}_2(0)$$

$$= 352.75 - \frac{12}{2}\,(10.49)$$

$$= 289.81$$

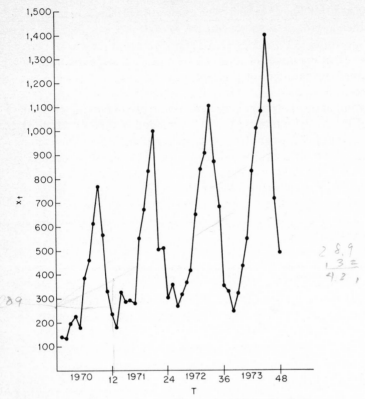

Fig. 5-2 Monthly demand for a 48-oz soft drink in hundreds of cases.

Initial estimates of the seasonal factors may be computed from Eqs. (5-9) to (5-11) as

$$\hat{c}_1(0) = 0.4762 \qquad \hat{c}_7(0) = 1.3574$$

$$\hat{c}_2(0) = 0.6158 \qquad \hat{c}_8(0) = 1.7088$$

$$\hat{c}_3(0) = 0.6483 \qquad \hat{c}_9(0) = 2.0468$$

$$\hat{c}_4(0) = 0.6818 \qquad \hat{c}_{10}(0) = 1.2356$$

$$\hat{c}_5(0) = 0.5723 \qquad \hat{c}_{11}(0) = 0.9137$$

$$\hat{c}_6(0) = 1.1658 \qquad \hat{c}_{12}(0) = 0.5774$$

We have now estimated $\hat{a}_1(0)$, $\hat{b}_2(0)$, and $\hat{c}_t(0)$ at time origin 0. These estimates can be updated to period 24 by smoothing $\hat{a}_1(0)$, $\hat{b}_2(0)$, and $\hat{c}_t(0)$ using Eqs. (5-3)

TABLE 5-1 Computation Results for Winters' Method in 1970 and 1971

Month, T	Observation	Permanent component	Trend	Seasonal factor	Forecast, $\hat{x}_T(T-1)$	Error
1970 1	143	300.30	10.49	0.4762	143	0
2	138	293.45	8.75	0.6013	191	−53
3	195	301.92	8.72	0.6481	196	−1
4	225	314.52	9.11	0.6852	212	13
5	175	320.06	8.75	0.5698	185	−10
6	389	329.78	8.85	1.1672	383	6
7	454	337.80	8.77	1.3561	460	−6
8	618	349.58	9.07	1.7147	592	26
9	564	362.16	9.42	2.0547	734	36
10	564	388.56	11.12	1.2572	459	105
11	327	391.31	10.28	0.9059	365	−38
12	235	402.68	10.39	0.5780	232	3
1971 13	189	409.83	10.07	0.4747	197	−7
14	326	444.35	12.51	0.6145	252	74
15	289	454.68	12.29	0.6468	296	−7
16	293	459.11	11.51	0.6805	320	−27
17	279	474.43	11.89	0.5716	268	11
18	552	483.64	11.62	1.1646	568	−16
19	674	495.61	11.66	1.3564	672	2
20	827	502.27	11.17	1.7079	870	−43
21	1,000	508.08	10.62	2.0461	1,055	−55
22	502	494.82	8.23	1.2329	652	−150
23	512	515.48	9.47	0.9147	456	56
24	300	523.76	9.36	0.5775	303	−3

to (5-5) until period 24 is reached. The values of the smoothing constants are specified arbitrarily as $\alpha = 0.20$, $\beta = 0.10$, and $\gamma = 0.10$.

To demonstrate these calculations, consider obtaining a forecast for month 1 (January 1970) at time 0. The desired forecast is

$$\hat{x}_1(0) = \left[\hat{a}_1(0) + \hat{b}_2(0) \right] \hat{c}_1(0)$$

$$= (289.81 + 10.49)(0.4762)$$

$$= 143$$

Notice that, by chance, $\hat{x}_1(0)$ is exactly equal to the observation x_1. Now advancing time to the end of month 1, we may revise the permanent component from Eq. (5-3) as

$$\hat{a}_1(1) = 0.2\left(\frac{143}{0.4762} \right) + 0.8(289.81 + 10.49)$$

$$= 300.30$$

The new estimate of the trend component is found from (5-4) as

$$\hat{b}_2(1) = 0.1(300.30 - 289.81) + 0.9(10.49)$$
$$= 10.49$$

The new estimate of the seasonal factor is computed from (5-5) as

$$\hat{c}_1(1) = 0.1\left(\frac{143}{300.30} \right) + 0.9(0.4762)$$

$$= 0.4762$$

Finally, we may forecast period 2 at the end of period 1 according to

$$\hat{x}_2(1) = \left[\hat{a}_1(1) + \hat{b}_2(1) \right]\hat{c}_2(0)$$

$$= (300.30 + 10.49)(0.6158)$$

$$= 191.38 \approx 191$$

TABLE 5-2   Forecast Simulation for 1972 and 1973 Using Winters' Method

Month, T		Observation	Permanent component	Trend	Seasonal factor	Forecast, $\hat{x}_T(T-1)$	Error
1972	25	359	577.75	13.82	0.4894	253	106
	26	264	559.18	10.58	0.6003	364	−100
	27	315	553.21	8.93	0.6391	369	−54
	28	361	555.81	8.29	0.6774	383	−22
	29	414	596.14	11.50	0.5839	322	92
	30	647	597.22	10.46	1.1565	708	−61
	31	836	609.40	10.63	1.3580	824	12
	32	901	601.54	8.78	1.6869	1,059	−158
	33	1,104	596.16	7.36	2.0267	1,249	−145
	34	874	624.60	9.47	1.2495	744	130
	35	683	656.60	11.72	0.9272	580	103
	36	352	656.57	10.55	0.5734	386	−34
1973	37	332	669.37	10.77	0.4900	326	6
	38	244	625.42	5.30	0.5792	408	−164
	39	320	604.72	2.70	0.6281	403	−83
	40	437	614.96	3.46	0.6807	411	26
	41	544	681.07	9.72	0.6054	361	183
	42	830	696.18	10.26	1.1600	799	31
	43	1,011	714.05	11.02	1.3638	959	52
	44	1,081	708.22	9.34	1.6708	1,223	−142
	45	1,400	712.20	8.80	2.0206	1,454	−54
	46	1,123	756.55	12.35	1.2730	901	222
	47	713	768.91	12.36	0.9272	713	0
	48	487	794.89	13.72	0.5773	448	39

The remaining updating calculations and one-step-ahead forecasts are shown in Table 5-1.

At the end of period 24, the estimates of the permanent component and trend are $\hat{a}_1(24) = 523.76$ and $\hat{b}_2(24) = 9.36$, respectively. The seasonal factors at the end of 24 are the last 12 entries in the seasonal factor column of Table 5-1. Using these values of the model parameters, a forecast simulation for 1972 and 1973 can be performed. For example, the forecast for period 25 (January 1972) would be computed according to

$$\hat{x}_{25}(24) = \left[\hat{a}_1(24) + \hat{b}_2(24)\right]\hat{c}_{13}(25)$$

$$= (523.76 + 9.36)(0.4747)$$

$$= 253.20 \approx 253$$

Using the previous values of the smoothing constants, we would update the model parameters as follows:

$$\hat{a}_1(25) = 0.2\left(\frac{359}{0.4747}\right) + 0.8(523.76 + 9.36)$$

$$= 577.75$$

$$\hat{b}_2(25) = 0.1(577.75 - 523.76) + 0.9(9.36)$$

$$= 13.82$$

$$\hat{c}_{25}(25) = 0.1\left(\frac{359}{577.75}\right) + 0.9(0.4747)$$

$$= 0.4894$$

The remaining calculations are shown in Table 5-2. Figure 5-3 gives a graphical display of the time series and the one-step-ahead forecast.

It is interesting to observe the effect of fresh data on the forecasting procedure. During the first 24 months, from which the model parameters were estimated, the forecasts are much closer to the actual observations than during the last 24 months. This can be seen qualitatively by inspection of Fig. 5-3. We may also compare the standard deviation of forecast errors during the two periods. For months 1 to 24 we find $\hat{\sigma}_e = 48.68$, while for months 25 to 48 we find $\hat{\sigma}_e = 105.73$. Of course it is natural to expect better results during months 1 to 24, as we have estimated the model parameters using these data, and the forecasts really represent the "fit" of the model to the data. The errors observed during months 25 to 48 are much more indicative of true model performance. This point is sometimes overlooked by designers of forecasting systems, who may erroneously expect a model to perform as well in forecasting

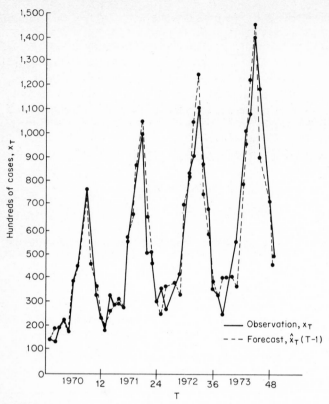

Fig. 5-3 Historical demand and one-step-ahead forecasts using Winters' method.

future observations as it did during the design stage, when the model may have been chosen on the basis of its fit to historical data.

5-2 AN ADDITIVE SEASONAL MODEL

Suppose that a seasonal time series can be described by

$$x_t = b_1 + b_2 t + c_t + \epsilon_t \tag{5-12}$$

where b_1 = the permanent component
b_2 = a linear trend component
c_t = an *additive* seasonal factor
ϵ_t = a random error component

We shall assume that the length of the season is L periods. This model would be appropriate for a time series in which the amplitude of the seasonal pattern is *independent* of the average level of the series. In light of the behavior of the time series, it seems reasonable to define the seasonal factors so that they sum to zero, that is,

$$\sum_{t=1}^{L} c_t = 0 \qquad\qquad (5\text{-}13)$$

If the trend component is unnecessary, it may be deleted from the model.

A time series for which the additive seasonal model is appropriate is shown in Fig. 5-4. Notice that even though the average level of the time series is increasing, the magnitude of the seasonal variation remains constant.

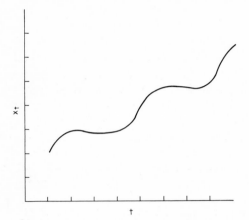

Fig. 5-4 Seasonal pattern with amplitude independent of the average level of the series.

Suppose the estimates of the trend component and the seasonal factor in the additive model (5-12) at the end of period T are denoted by $\hat{b}_2(T)$ and $\hat{c}_T(T)$. The permanent component will be estimated on a current-origin basis, and is denoted by $\hat{a}_1(T)$.   A simple procedure for periodically revising the estimates of these parameters and for forecasting may be devised.   At the end of the current period T, after observing x_T, we would perform the following calculations:

1. Update the estimate of the permanent component:

$$\hat{a}_1(T) = \alpha[x_T - \hat{c}_T(T-L)] + (1-\alpha)\big[\hat{a}_1(T-1) + \hat{b}_2(T-1)\big] \qquad (5\text{-}14)$$

where $0 < \alpha < 1$ is a smoothing constant.   Notice that subtracting $\hat{c}_T(T-L)$ from x_T *deseasonalizes* the current observation so that the updating process for the permanent component is based only on the previous estimate of the permanent component and trend.   As in the multiplicative model, we are shifting the origin of time to the end of the current period.

2. Update the estimate of the trend component:

$$\hat{b}_2(T) = \beta[\hat{a}_1(T) - \hat{a}_1(T-1)] + (1-\beta)\hat{b}_2(T-1) \qquad\qquad (5\text{-}15)$$

where $0 < \beta < 1$ is a second smoothing constant. This is identical to the updating for the trend component in the multiplicative model [see Eq. (5-4)].

3. Update the estimate of the seasonal factor for period T:

$$\hat{c}_T(T) = \gamma [x_T - \hat{a}_1(T)] + (1 - \gamma)\hat{c}_T(T - L) \qquad (5\text{-}16)$$

where $0 < \gamma < 1$ is a third smoothing constant. Here we see that the revision procedure smooths the current *observed* seasonal variation $[x_T - \hat{a}_1(T)]$ with the estimate of the seasonal factor for period T computed L periods ago to obtain an updated estimate of the seasonal factor for the current period.

4. To forecast the observation in any future time period $T + \tau$ we would compute

$$\hat{x}_{T+\tau}(T) = \hat{a}_1(T) + \hat{b}_2(T)\tau + \hat{c}_{T+\tau}(T + \tau - L) \qquad (5\text{-}17)$$

Notice that in forecasting for period $T + \tau$ we use the seasonal factor for that period which was computed L periods ago, which is the time of our most recent observation of that portion of the seasonal pattern. Forecasts for time periods further than one season away can be made by reusing the appropriate seasonal factors.

As in the case of the multiplicative seasonal model, the updating procedures for the additive seasonal model are heuristic; that is, they are logical and have intuitive appeal, but are not based on a sound criterion, such as least squares. The three smoothing constants in Eqs. (5-14) to (5-16) could, in general, be different.

The development of a forecasting system using the additive seasonal model requires that initial estimates of the parameters $\hat{a}_1(0)$, $\hat{b}_2(0)$, and $\hat{c}_t(0)$, $t = 1, 2, \ldots, L$, be determined. Least-squares estimates of the initial parameter values may be obtained through analysis of historical data. Suppose there are m complete seasons of historical data available, and that these mL observations are denoted $x_1, x_2, \ldots, x_{L-1}, x_L, x_{L+1}, \ldots, x_{mL}$. The initial estimates will be used for forecasting in time periods greater than period mL; that is, after the initial estimates are obtained, period mL will be the new origin of time.

Using the model (5-12), the mL observations may be written as

$$x_t = b_1 + b_2 t + c_t + \epsilon_t \qquad t = 1, 2, \ldots, mL \qquad (5\text{-}18)$$

However, there are only L distinct seasonal factors, since $c_t = c_{t+L} = c_{t+2L} = \cdots = c_{t+(m-1)L}$. This implies that the seasonal factors may be expressed as $c_{t-L[t/L]}$, where the square bracket notation means the largest integer less than t/L. Therefore, the model (5-18) becomes

$$x_t = b_1 + b_2 t + c_{t-L[t/L]} + \epsilon_t \qquad t = 1, 2, \ldots, mL$$

and the least-squares criterion to be minimized is

$$SS_E = \sum_{t=1}^{mL} (x_t - b_1 - b_2 t - c_{t-L[t/L]})^2 \qquad (5\text{-}19)$$

Letting the index $j = t - L[t/L]$, differentiating SS_E with respect to b_1, b_2, and c_t for $t = 1, 2, \ldots, L$, and equating the results to zero yield the normal equations

$$mL\hat{b}_1 + \hat{b}_2 \sum_{t=1}^{mL} t + m \sum_{t=1}^{L} \hat{c}_t = \sum_{t=1}^{mL} x_t \tag{5-20}$$

$$\hat{b}_1 \sum_{t=1}^{mL} t + \hat{b}_2 \sum_{t=1}^{mL} t^2 + \sum_{t=1}^{L} [mt + (m-1)L]\hat{c}_t = \sum_{t=1}^{mL} t x_t \tag{5-21}$$

$$m\hat{b}_1 + \hat{b}_2 \sum_{j=0}^{m-1} (t + jL) + m\hat{c}_t = \sum_{j=0}^{m-1} x_{t+jL} \qquad t = 1, 2, \ldots, L \tag{5-22}$$

The solution to (5-22) is

$$\hat{c}_t = \frac{\displaystyle\sum_{j=0}^{m-1} x_{t+jL} - m\hat{b}_1 - \hat{b}_2[mt + m(m-1)/2]}{m} \tag{5-23}$$

Substituting (5-23) into (5-21) and noting that $\sum_{t=1}^{L} [mt + (m-1)L]\hat{c}_t = (1/m) \sum_{t=1}^{mL} t(x_t - \hat{b}_1 - \hat{b}_2 t)$, we find the second normal equation reduces to

$$\hat{b}_1 \sum_{t=1}^{mL} t + \hat{b}_2 \sum_{t=1}^{mL} t^2 = \sum_{t=1}^{mL} t x_t \tag{5-24}$$

Also, from Eq. (5-23), it is easily seen that $\hat{c}_t$ is just the average of the residuals in periods $t + jL$ ($j = 0, 1, \ldots, m - 1$) from a straight-line regression. Since the residuals in any regression model sum to zero, we have $\sum_{t=1}^{L} \hat{c}_t = 0$, and the first normal equation (5-20) reduces to

$$mL\hat{b}_1 + \hat{b}_2 \frac{(mL + 1)mL}{2} = \sum_{t=1}^{mL} x_t \tag{5-25}$$

Equations (5-24) and (5-25) are the usual normal equations for a simple linear regression [see Sec. 2-1.1, Eqs. (2-5) and (2-6)]. They may be solved directly for $\hat{b}_1$ and $\hat{b}_2$. Therefore, the initial values of the model parameters are

$$\hat{b}_2(0) = \hat{b}_2 \tag{5-26}$$

$$\hat{a}_1(0) = \hat{b}_1 + mL\hat{b}_2 \tag{5-27}$$

$$\hat{c}_t(0) = \hat{c}_t \qquad t = 1, 2, \ldots, L \tag{5-28}$$

Notice that $\hat{a}_1(0)$ is the permanent component at the new origin of time, period mL.

5-3 DIRECT SMOOTHING MODELS

In Chap. 4 we developed the mathematical details underlying *direct smoothing*, which is a technique for updating parameters in a multiple linear regression model such as

$$x_t = \sum_{i=1}^{k} b_i z_i(t) + \epsilon_t \qquad t = 1, 2, \ldots, T \qquad (5\text{-}29)$$

where the $z_i(t)$ are certain mathematical functions of time. If the $z_i(t)$ are polynomial functions of time, then the direct smoothing approach produces forecasts which are identical to multiple exponential smoothing, except that the calculations are organized so that revised estimates of the b_i's are obtained directly instead of through the exponential smoothing statistics.

The most important use of direct smoothing is with trigonometric functions, such as sine and cosine, to model a seasonal demand process. For example, consider a seasonal time series that increases for the first six months, decreases for the next six months, and then repeats. This is a seasonal process with a period of 12 months. It could be described by a sine wave, such as

$$x_t = b_1 + b_2 \sin \frac{2\pi t}{12} + \epsilon_t \qquad (5\text{-}30)$$

The behavior of this model, without the error component ϵ_t, is depicted in Fig. 5-5. Notice that the seasonal pattern is symmetric about the mean b_1.

By appropriate choice of terms in the model, many different time series characteristics may be modeled. For example, a sine wave has three characteristics that may be controlled: the *amplitude*, or height; the *phase angle*, or

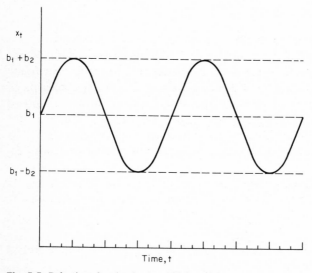

Fig. 5-5 Behavior of a simple sinusoidal model.

origin; and the *period*, or cycle length.   Thus

$$x = b \sin \omega t \qquad (5\text{-}31)$$

defines a sine wave with amplitude b and origin at $t = 0$.   A 12-period season is obtained by setting $\omega = 2\pi/12$, if ω is expressed in radians.   Other common seasonal patterns are a yearly cycle observed weekly ($\omega = 2\pi/52$), a yearly cycle observed quarterly ($\omega = 2\pi/4$), and a yearly cycle observed in four-week accounting periods rather than calendar months ($\omega = 2\pi/13$).   The origin of the sine wave may be shifted θ periods by setting

$$x = b \sin \omega(t + \theta) \qquad (5\text{-}32)$$

Thus, we may place the origin of time at any point in the cycle.

It is usually more convenient to express the sine wave with arbitrary origin (5-32) as a sine-cosine pair.   Using the trigonometric identity

$$\sin(u + v) = \cos u \sin v + \sin u \cos v$$

we may rewrite (5-32) as

$$x = b \sin \omega(t + \theta)$$
$$= b \cos \omega\theta \sin \omega t + b \sin \omega\theta \cos \omega t$$
$$= b_1 \sin \omega t + b_2 \cos \omega t$$

$$\theta = \frac{1}{\omega} \tan^{-1}\left(\frac{b_1}{b_2}\right)$$

say, with $b_1 = b \cos \omega\theta$ and $b_2 = b \sin \omega\theta$.   Thus a reasonable model for a simple, symmetric seasonal pattern that repeats every 12 periods might be

$$b = b_2 / \sin\left(\tan^{-1}\left(\frac{b_1}{b_2}\right)\right)$$

$$x_t = b_1 + b_2 \sin \frac{2\pi t}{12} + b_3 \cos \frac{2\pi t}{12} + \epsilon_t \qquad (5\text{-}33)$$

Note that (5-33) is equivalent to (5-30).

Suppose that an appropriate time series model of the general form (5-29) has been determined.   The initial estimates of the model parameters may be found using multiple linear regression, as discussed in Chap. 2.   Periodic revision of the model parameters is usually done in such a way that the origin of time is shifted to the end of the current period, since this greatly simplifies the forecasting procedure.   Following our usual convention, we shall let $\hat{a}_i(T)$, $i = 1, 2, \ldots, k$, be the estimates of the model parameters on a current-origin basis.   *a's*

This updating process is very simple computationally.   At the end of period T, after observing x_T, we may revise the estimates of the model parameters by using the following result from Chap. 4 [Eq. (4-23)]:

$$\hat{\mathbf{a}}(T) = \mathbf{L}'\hat{\mathbf{a}}(T - 1) + \mathbf{h}e_1(T) \qquad (5\text{-}34)$$

where $\mathbf{L}$ is a $k \times k$ matrix that depends on the particular model chosen, $e_1(T)$ is

est on cur. basis of a's

the single-period forecast error [that is, $e_1(T) = x_T - \hat{x}_T(T-1)$], $\mathbf{h}$ is a $k \times 1$ column vector of constants called the *smoothing vector*, and

$$\hat{\mathbf{a}}(T) = \begin{bmatrix} \hat{a}_1(T) \\ \hat{a}_2(T) \\ \vdots \\ \hat{a}_k(T) \end{bmatrix}$$

is a $k \times 1$ column vector of the current-origin estimates of the model parameters computed at time T.   Notice that the argument in parentheses denotes the time of computation of $\hat{\mathbf{a}}(T)$.   Once the model parameters have been revised, we may forecast the observation in period $T + \tau$ as

$$\hat{x}_{T+\tau}(T) = \sum_{i=1}^{k} \hat{a}_i(T) z_i(\tau) \tag{5-35}$$

where $z_i(\tau)$ represents the independent variables in the model evaluated at τ.

The complete derivation of Eq. (5-34) is given in Secs. 4-1 and 4-2 of Chap. 4. This updating process moves the origin of time to the end of the current period [accomplished by the term $\mathbf{L}'\hat{\mathbf{a}}(T-1)$ in (5-34)] and modifies the parameter estimates to reflect the information contained in the new observation [accomplished by the term $\mathbf{h}e_1(T)$ in (5-34)].   Rules for determining the $\mathbf{L}$ matrix for any direct smoothing model containing polynomial, exponential, or trigonometric functions are given in Secs. 4-3 and 4-4 of Chap. 4.   We shall give the $\mathbf{L}$ matrix for several useful direct smoothing models below.

The elements of the smoothing vector $\mathbf{h}$ are determined by a procedure described in Sec. 4-5. $\mathbf{h}$ is a function of a discount factor $\beta(0 < \beta < 1)$ that is related to the smoothing constant in exponential smoothing.   The appropriate value of β for any model is usually determined by experimentation.   Frequently, we select the discount factor for a model with k parameters according to

$$\beta_k = \beta_1^{1/k}$$

where $\beta_1 = 1 - \alpha_1$ would be a reasonable discount factor for a constant model (that is, a model with $k = 1$).   See page 92 for a further discussion of this approach to selecting the discount factor and its effect on the elements of $\mathbf{h}$. Brown ([9], pp. 184–193) tabulates the smoothing vectors for several useful models.

We have illustrated the behavior of the simple seasonal model

$$x_t = b_1 + b_2 \sin \frac{2\pi t}{12} + b_3 \cos \frac{2\pi t}{12} + \epsilon_t \tag{5-36}$$

in Fig. 5-5.   The transition matrix for this model is

$$L = \begin{bmatrix} 1 & 0 & 0 \\ 0 & 0.866 & 0.500 \\ 0 & -0.500 & 0.866 \end{bmatrix}$$

Therefore, the updating equations for the model parameters on a current-origin basis are found by substituting for L in Eq. (5-34) as

$$\hat{a}_1(T) = \hat{a}_1(T-1) + h_1 e_1(T)$$

$$\hat{a}_2(T) = 0.866\hat{a}_2(T-1) - 0.500\hat{a}_3(T-1) + h_2 e_1(T) \qquad (5\text{-}37)$$

$$\hat{a}_3(T) = 0.500\hat{a}_2(T-1) + 0.866\hat{a}_3(T-1) + h_3 e_1(T)$$

Brown ([9], p. 187) shows that if the discount factor $\beta = 0.96549$, then the elements of the smoothing vector are $h_1 = 0.03347$, $h_2 = 0.00640$, and $h_3 = 0.06654$.   Note that $\beta = 0.95649$ for this model corresponds to a simple smoothing constant of $\alpha = 0.10$, since $0.96549 = (1 - 0.10)^{1/3}$.   The forecasting equation for a future observation in period $T + \tau$ is

$$\hat{x}_{T+\tau}(T) = \hat{a}_1(T) + \hat{a}_2(T)\sin\frac{2\pi\tau}{12} + \hat{a}_3(T)\cos\frac{2\pi\tau}{12} \qquad (5\text{-}38)$$

Another useful direct smoothing model would consist of imposing the symmetric 12-period seasonal pattern on a linear trend, that is,

$$x_t = b_1 + b_2 t + b_2 \sin\frac{2\pi t}{12} + b_4 \cos\frac{2\pi t}{12} + \epsilon_t \qquad (5\text{-}39)$$

The transition matrix for this model is

$$L = \begin{bmatrix} 1 & 0 & 0 & 0 \\ 1 & 1 & 0 & 0 \\ 0 & 0 & 0.866 & 0.500 \\ 0 & 0 & -0.500 & 0.866 \end{bmatrix}$$

resulting in the parameter updating equations

$$\hat{a}_1(T) = \hat{a}_1(T-1) + \hat{a}_2(T-1) + h_1 e_1(T)$$

$$\hat{a}_2(T) = \hat{a}_2(T) + h_2 e_1(T)$$

$$\hat{a}_3(T) = 0.866\hat{a}_3(T-1) - 0.500\hat{a}_4(T-1) + h_3 e_1(T)$$

$$\hat{a}_4(T) = 0.500\hat{a}_3(T-1) + 0.866\hat{a}_4(T-1) + h_4 e_1(T)$$

$$(5\text{-}40)$$

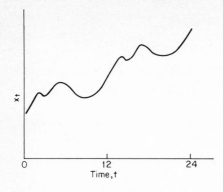

Fig. 5-6 Behavior of the harmonic model [Eq. (5-39)].

If we use $\beta = (1 - 0.10)^{1/4} = 0.9740$, then Brown ([9], p. 191) shows that the elements of the smoothing vector are $h_1 = 0.05024$, $h_2 = 0.00066$, $h_3 = 0.00605$, and $h_4 = 0.04977$. The forecasting equation for this model is

$$\hat{x}_{T+\tau}(T) = \hat{a}_1(T) + \hat{a}_2(T)\tau + \hat{a}_3(T)\sin\frac{2\pi\tau}{12} + \hat{a}_4(T)\cos\frac{2\pi\tau}{12} \qquad (5\text{-}41)$$

Frequently a seasonal pattern will exhibit a more irregular behavior than could be well modeled by a simple sine-cosine pair. The usual approach in these cases is to include a *second* sine-cosine pair chosen so as to introduce a higher frequency harmonic into the theoretical model waveform. For example, a 12-point sine wave with one harmonic superimposed on a linear trend would be

$$x_t = b_1 + b_2 t + b_3\sin\frac{2\pi t}{12} + b_4\cos\frac{2\pi t}{12}$$

$$+ b_5\sin\frac{4\pi t}{12} + b_6\cos\frac{4\pi t}{12} + \epsilon_t \qquad (5\text{-}42)$$

The behavior of this model is depicted in Fig. 5-6. In practice, this is a very useful model capable of representing a wide range of time series. The **L** matrix for this model is given in Chap. 4, page 93. Using this result, we may write the updating equations for the model parameters on a current-origin basis as

$$\hat{a}_1(T) = \hat{a}_1(T-1) + \hat{a}_2(T-1) + h_1 e_1(T)$$

$$\hat{a}_2(T) = \hat{a}_2(T-1) + h_2 e_1(T)$$

$$\hat{a}_3(T) = 0.866\hat{a}_3(T-1) - 0.500\hat{a}_4(T-1) + h_3 e_1(T)$$

$$\hat{a}_4(T) = 0.500\hat{a}_3(T-1) + 0.866\hat{a}_4(T-1) + h_4 e_1(T)$$

$$\hat{a}_5(T) = 0.500\hat{a}_5(T-1) - 0.866\hat{a}_6(T-1) + h_5 e_1(T)$$

$$\hat{a}_6(T) = 0.866\hat{a}_5(T-1) + 0.500\hat{a}_6(T-1) + h_6 e_1(T)$$

$$(5\text{-}43)$$

The elements of the smoothing vector for this model are shown in Sec. 4-5 to be $h_1 = 0.09031$, $h_2 = 0.00229$, $h_3 = 0.01520$, $h_4 = 0.08828$, $h_5 = 0.02014$, and $h_6 = 0.08646$, if $\beta = 0.90$. The forecasting equation for this model is

$$\hat{x}_{T+\tau}(T) = \hat{a}_1(T) + \hat{a}_2(T)\tau + \hat{a}_3(T)\sin \frac{2\pi\tau}{12} + \hat{a}_4(T)\cos \frac{2\pi\tau}{12}$$

$$+ \hat{a}_5(T)\sin \frac{4\pi\tau}{12} + \hat{a}_6(T)\cos \frac{4\pi\tau}{12} \qquad (5\text{-}44)$$

Models such as (5-39) and (5-43) are suitable for time series where the amplitude of the seasonal cycle is independent of the average level of the process. In many time series, we would find the amplitude of the seasonal cycle proportional to the trend. A model capable of representing such a process is

$$x_t = b_1 + b_2 t + (b_3 + b_5 t)\sin \frac{2\pi t}{12} + (b_4 + b_6 t)\cos \frac{2\pi t}{12} + \epsilon_t \qquad (5\text{-}45)$$

If appropriate, a harmonic could also be superimposed on this model by adding a second sine-cosine pair with a higher frequency. The **L** matrix for this model is

$$\mathbf{L} = \begin{bmatrix} 1 & 0 & 0 & 0 & 0 & 0 \\ 1 & 1 & 0 & 0 & 0 & 0 \\ 0 & 0 & 0.866 & 0.500 & 0 & 0 \\ 0 & 0 & -0.500 & 0.866 & 0 & 0 \\ 0 & 0 & 0.866 & 0.500 & 0.866 & 0.500 \\ 0 & 0 & -0.500 & 0.866 & -0.500 & 0.866 \end{bmatrix}$$

and the updating equations for the model parameters on a current-origin basis are

$$\hat{a}_1(T) = \hat{a}_1(T-1) + \hat{a}_2(T-1) + h_1 e_1(T)$$

$$\hat{a}_2(T) = \hat{a}_2(T-1) + h_2 e_1(T)$$

$$\hat{a}_3(T) = 0.866\hat{a}_3(T-1) - 0.500\hat{a}_4(T-1)$$

$$+ 0.866\hat{a}_5(T-1) - 0.500\hat{a}_6(T-1) + h_3 e_1(T)$$

$$\hat{a}_4(T) = 0.500\hat{a}_3(T-1) + 0.866\hat{a}_4(T-1)$$

$$+ 0.500\hat{a}_5(T-1) + 0.866\hat{a}_6(T-1) + h_4 e_1(T)$$

$$\hat{a}_5(T) = 0.866\hat{a}_5(T-1) - 0.500\hat{a}_6(T-1) + h_5 e_1(T)$$

$$\hat{a}_6(T) = 0.500\hat{a}_5(T-1) + 0.866\hat{a}_6(T-1) + h_6 e_1(T)$$

$$(5\text{-}46)$$

Brown ([9], p. 193) shows that if the discount factor $\beta = (1 - 0.10)^{1/6} = 0.98259$, then the elements of the smoothing vector are $h_1 = 0.03347$, $h_2 = 0.00029$, $h_3 = 0.00640$, $h_4 = 0.06656$, $h_5 = 0.00006$, and $h_6 = 0.00058$. The forecasting equation for this model is

$$x_{T+\tau}(T) = \hat{a}_1(T) + \hat{a}_2(T)\tau + [\hat{a}_3(T) + \hat{a}_5(T)\tau]\sin\frac{2\pi\tau}{12}$$

$$+ [\hat{a}_4(T) + \hat{a}_6(T)\tau]\cos\frac{2\pi\tau}{12} \tag{5-47}$$

In developing a direct smoothing model, one should remember that a better fit to the historical data can always be achieved by simply adding more terms (such as higher-frequency harmonics) to the model. However, such additional terms may improve the fit, yet the model may be no better for forecasting. As a general rule, a term should not be added to a model unless its coefficient $\hat{a}_i(T)$ is statistically significant.

EXAMPLE 5-2 We shall demonstrate direct smoothing by forecasting the soft drink demand data in Fig. 5-2 using the six-parameter model in Eq. (5-42). Assuming the length of the seasonal pattern is 12 months, the model is

$$x_t = b_1 + b_2 t + b_3 \sin\frac{2\pi t}{12} + b_4 \cos\frac{2\pi t}{12}$$

$$+ b_5 \sin\frac{4\pi t}{12} + b_6 \cos\frac{4\pi t}{12} + \epsilon_t$$

We shall use the first 24 months of data to estimate the model parameters, and then simulate a one-month-ahead forecast for the last 24 months.

The starting value of the model parameters at time origin 0, that is, the $\hat{a}_i(0)$ for $i = 1, 2, \ldots, 6$, may be estimated by least squares. In matrix notation we may write

$$
\begin{bmatrix} x_1 \\ x_2 \\ \vdots \\ x_{24} \end{bmatrix}
=
\begin{bmatrix}
1 & 1 & \sin\frac{2\pi}{12} & \cos\frac{2\pi}{12} & \sin\frac{4\pi}{12} & \cos\frac{4\pi}{12} \\
1 & 2 & \sin\frac{4\pi}{12} & \cos\frac{4\pi}{12} & \sin\frac{8\pi}{12} & \cos\frac{8\pi}{12} \\
& & & \cdots & & \\
1 & 24 & \sin\frac{48\pi}{12} & \cos\frac{48\pi}{12} & \sin\frac{96\pi}{12} & \cos\frac{96\pi}{12}
\end{bmatrix}
$$

$$
\times
\begin{bmatrix} a_1(0) \\ a_2(0) \\ \vdots \\ a_6(0) \end{bmatrix}
+
\begin{bmatrix} \epsilon_1 \\ \epsilon_2 \\ \vdots \\ \epsilon_{24} \end{bmatrix}
$$

or

$$\mathbf{x} = \mathbf{Za}(0) + \boldsymbol{\epsilon}$$

and we know from Chap. 2 that the least-squares estimators are

$$\hat{\mathbf{a}}(0) = (\mathbf{Z}'\mathbf{Z})^{-1}\mathbf{Z}'\mathbf{x}$$

It is easy to show that

$$\mathbf{Z}'\mathbf{Z} = \begin{bmatrix} 24 & 300 & 0 & 0 & 0 & 0 \\ 300 & 4900 & -44.785 & 12 & -20.785 & 12 \\ 0 & -44.785 & 12 & 0 & 0 & 0 \\ 0 & 12 & 0 & 12 & 0 & 0 \\ 0 & -20.785 & 0 & 0 & 12 & 0 \\ 0 & 12 & 0 & 0 & 0 & 12 \end{bmatrix}$$

and

$$\mathbf{Z}'\mathbf{x} = \begin{bmatrix} 10{,}021 \\ 144{,}010 \\ -3{,}239.385 \\ -9{,}947.573 \\ 445.137 \\ -1{,}164.000 \end{bmatrix}$$

The inverse of $\mathbf{Z}'\mathbf{Z}$ is

$$(\mathbf{Z}'\mathbf{Z})^{-1} = \begin{bmatrix} 0.21098 & -0.01354 & -0.05055 & 0.01354 & -0.02346 & 0.01354 \\ -0.01354 & 0.00108 & 0.00404 & -0.00108 & 0.00188 & -0.00108 \\ -0.05055 & 0.00404 & 0.09843 & -0.00404 & 0.00700 & -0.00404 \\ 0.01354 & -0.00108 & -0.00404 & 0.08442 & -0.00188 & 0.00108 \\ -0.02346 & 0.00188 & 0.00700 & -0.00188 & 0.08658 & -0.00188 \\ 0.01354 & -0.00108 & -0.00400 & 0.00108 & -0.00188 & 0.08442 \end{bmatrix}$$

Therefore the initial estimates of the model parameters at time origin 0 are

$$\hat{\mathbf{a}}(0) = \begin{bmatrix} \hat{a}_1(0) \\ \hat{a}_2(0) \\ \hat{a}_3(0) \\ \hat{a}_4(0) \\ \hat{a}_5(0) \\ \hat{a}_6(0) \end{bmatrix} = \begin{bmatrix} 287.6779 \\ 10.38910 \\ -231.1761 \\ -93.28553 \\ 55.08923 \\ -107.3891 \end{bmatrix}$$

TABLE 5-3　Statistical Significance of Model Parameters for Example 5-2

| Parameter | Estimate | Standard error | Approximate 95% confidence limits | |
			Lower limit	Upper limit
$a_1(0)$	287.6779	31.74	224.1979	351.1579
$a_2(0)$	10.38910	2.27	5.84910	14.92910
$a_3(0)$	-231.1761	21.68	-274.5361	-187.8161
$a_4(0)$	-93.28553	20.07	-133.42553	-53.14553
$a_5(0)$	55.08926	20.33	14.42923	95.74923
$a_6(0)$	-107.3891	20.07	-147.5591	-67.2191

To assess the adequacy of this fitted model, we will examine the statistical significance of the model parameters. An estimate of the error variance is given by

$$\hat{\sigma}_\epsilon^2 = \frac{\sum_{t=1}^{N}(x_t - \hat{x}_t)^2}{N - k} = \frac{\sum_{t=1}^{24}(x_t - \hat{x}_t)^2}{18} = 4{,}733.67$$

In Chap. 2 it is shown that the variance of the estimate of any parameter in a multiple linear regression model is just the error variance times the main diagonal element in the row of $(\mathbf{Z'Z})^{-1}$ corresponding to that parameter. The *standard error* (or sample standard deviation) of a parameter is just the square root of the estimate of the variance of that parameter. Therefore, the standard errors of the $\hat{a}_i(0)$ are the square roots of the main diagonal elements of $(\mathbf{Z'Z})^{-1}\hat{\sigma}_\epsilon^2$, and if $\hat{a}_i(0)$ is large relative to its standard error, we would conclude that the parameter is significant statistically and belongs in the model. Approximate 95% confidence intervals on the parameters $\hat{a}_i(0)$ are computed according to $\hat{a}_i(0) \pm [2 \times$ standard error of $\hat{a}_i(0)]$, and are shown in Table 5-3. If such a confidence interval includes zero, this would be equivalent to stating that the model parameter is not different statistically from zero. This is not the case here, as all six parameters are statistically significant. Thus all six parameters belong in the model.

To simulate a forecast for the last two years, 1972 and 1973, we must obtain estimates of the model parameters at time origin 24, that is, $\hat{a}_i(24)$. This can be done by successively updating the $\hat{a}_i(t)$ using Eq. (5-43). In choosing the smoothing vector, we shall specify $\beta = 0.90$. This yields the smoothing vector given on page 96. To illustrate the updating, consider month 1. The forecast for month 1 is obtained from Eq. (5-44) as follows:

$$\hat{x}_1(0) = 287.6779 + 10.38910(1) - 231.1761 \sin\frac{2\pi}{12}$$

$$- 93.28553 \cos\frac{2\pi}{12} + 55.08923 \sin\frac{4\pi}{12}$$

$$- 107.3891 \cos\frac{4\pi}{12}$$

$$= 95.71 \approx 96$$

and the one-step-ahead forecast error is

$$e_1(1) = 143 - 95.71$$
$$= 47.29 \approx 47$$

The revised estimates of the model parameters at the end of month 1 are found from Eq. (5-43) as

$$\hat{a}_1(1) = 287.6779 + 10.38910 + (0.09031)(47.29) = 302.34$$

$$\hat{a}_2(1) = 10.38910 + (0.00229)(47.29) = 10.50$$

$$\hat{a}_3(1) = (0.866)(-231.1761) - (0.500)(-93.28553) + (0.01520)(47.29)$$
$$= -152.84$$

$$\hat{a}_4(1) = (0.500)(-231.1716) + (0.866)(-96.28553) + (0.08828)(47.29)$$
$$= -192.20$$

$$\hat{a}_5(1) = (0.500)(55.08923) - (0.866)(-107.3891) + (0.02014)(47.29)$$
$$= 121.50$$

$$\hat{a}_6(1) = (0.866)(55.08923) + (0.500)(-107.3891) + (0.08646)(47.29)$$
$$= -1.90$$

TABLE 5-4 Computational Results for Direct Smoothing in 1970 and 1971

Month, T	Observation	$\hat{a}_1(T)$	$\hat{a}_2(T)$	$\hat{a}_3(T)$	$\hat{a}_4(T)$	$\hat{a}_5(T)$	$\hat{a}_6(T)$	Forecast, $\hat{x}_T(T-1)$	Error
1970 1	143	302.34	10.50	-152.84	-192.20	121.50	-1.90	96	47
2	138	309.56	10.41	-36.81	-246.06	61.66	101.13	174	-36
3	195	320.21	10.42	91.19	-231.27	-56.70	104.19	192	3
4	225	334.79	10.53	195.31	-150.61	-117.65	6.98	179	46
5	175	341.78	10.44	243.85	-36.23	-65.65	-101.78	214	-39
6	389	357.09	10.56	230.11	95.31	56.40	-103.08	335	54
7	454	357.85	10.31	149.97	188.01	115.28	-12.08	563	-109
8	618	360.78	10.12	34.62	230.59	66.45	86.72	670	-82
9	770	378.23	10.31	-84.07	224.17	-40.24	107.93	689	81
10	564	388.92	10.32	-184.83	152.47	-113.50	19.48	560	4
11	327	397.14	10.27	-236.65	37.56	-74.09	-90.57	350	-23
12	235	409.47	10.32	-223.37	-83.78	41.84	-107.47	212	23
1971 13	189	417.16	10.25	-151.99	-186.50	113.41	-20.01	218	-29
14	326	431.76	10.36	-37.49	-233.51	75.00	92.37	278	48
15	289	438.21	10.26	83.63	-224.79	-43.36	107.40	332	-43
16	293	446.78	10.22	184.53	-154.51	-115.06	14.53	312	-19
17	279	453.02	10.12	236.39	-45.43	-71.00	-96.19	323	-44
18	552	473.94	10.39	229.25	89.41	50.21	-99.24	432	120
19	664	483.77	10.38	153.73	191.50	110.92	-6.68	670	-6
20	827	493.92	10.37	37.34	242.48	61.19	92.50	830	-3
21	1000	519.44	10.76	-86.35	243.47	-46.13	113.75	832	168
22	502	510.98	10.27	-199.75	148.88	-125.86	-1.47	715	-213
23	512	527.70	10.43	-246.34	35.36	-60.22	-103.55	441	71
24	300	534.37	10.34	-231.64	-96.22	58.73	-107.53	342	-42

The remaining updating calculations, as well as the one-step-ahead forecast errors, are shown in Table 5-4.

The results of the one-step-ahead forecast simulation for the last 24 months of data are shown in Table 5-5. All four years of data and the one-step-ahead forecasts are plotted in Fig. 5-7. The overall impression from comparing Fig. 5-7 and Fig. 5-3 (Winters' method applied to the same data) is that Winters' method produces better forecasts. This is probably because the amplitude of the seasonal pattern in this data increases with the trend, and our direct smoothing model does not contain terms to account for this. Note in Fig. 5-7 that the forecast error at the low and high points of the season seems to be increasing over time. This implies that a direct smoothing model such as (5-45) should be used [or perhaps (5-45) with one harmonic]. The reader is asked to investigate this in Exercise 5-16.

TABLE 5-5   Forecast Simulation for 1972 and 1973 Using Direct Smoothing

Month, T		Observation	$\hat{a}_1(T)$	$\hat{a}_2(T)$	$\hat{a}_3(T)$	$\hat{a}_4(T)$	$\hat{a}_5(T)$	$\hat{a}_6(T)$	Forecast, $\hat{x}_T(T-1)$	Error
1972	25	359	546.19	10.38	-152.24	-197.71	122.81	-1.49	343	16
	26	264	542.94	10.03	-35.28	-260.65	59.66	92.57	415	-151
	27	315	544.61	9.82	98.37	-251.54	-52.20	89.95	408	-93
	28	361	552.21	9.76	210.58	-170.81	-104.49	-2.35	386	-25
	29	414	560.74	9.73	267.56	-43.84	-50.48	-92.84	428	-14
	30	647	576.87	9.89	254.71	102.07	56.59	-84.01	576	71
	31	836	589.15	9.95	169.94	218.08	101.58	9.29	810	26
	32	901	593.28	9.81	37.15	268.13	41.45	87.03	966	-65
	33	1,104	618.50	10.20	-99.30	265.85	-51.21	94.17	933	171
	34	874	634.30	10.34	-217.98	186.05	-105.91	8.10	812	62
	35	683	651.31	10.51	-280.67	58.65	-58.48	-81.28	609	74
	36	352	650.17	10.21	-274.34	-100.93	38.55	-102.43	481	-129
1973	37	332	652.62	10.02	-188.42	-232.17	106.25	-25.26	418	-86
	38	244	644.32	9.55	-50.17	-313.17	70.92	61.85	447	-203
	39	320	642.14	9.25	111.16	-307.76	-20.72	81.11	450	-130
	40	437	649.04	9.19	249.75	-213.24	-81.13	20.36	463	-26
	41	544	658.74	9.21	322.99	-59.29	-58.08	-59.59	538	6
	42	830	679.87	9.51	311.36	121.80	25.22	-68.68	698	132
	43	1,011	695.97	9.68	209.85	267.60	73.56	-6.19	938	73
	44	1,081	703.67	9.63	47.60	334.73	41.70	58.71	1,103	-22
	45	1,400	741.07	10.33	-121.47	340.82	-23.80	92.06	1,092	308
	46	1,123	761.49	10.59	-273.91	244.28	-89.37	35.08	1,011	112
	47	713	765.41	10.42	-360.47	68.08	-76.55	-66.24	787	-74
	48	487	769.67	10.26	-347.24	-127.29	17.71	-105.30	555	-68

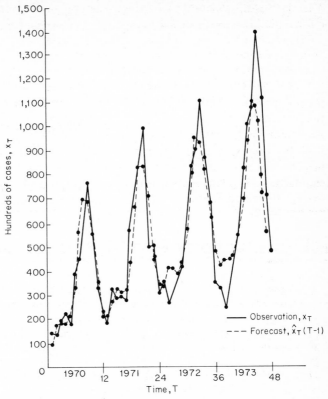

Fig. 5-7 Historical data and one-step-ahead forecasts using direct smoothing.

5-4 EXERCISES

5-1 The data in Table B-7 in the Appendix represent four years of monthly demand history for a 32-oz soft drink, in hundreds of cases. Use the first two years of this history to estimate the parameters in Winters' model. Simulate a forecast for each month of the last two years, using a one-month lead time. Use $\alpha = 0.20$, $\beta = 0.10$, and $\gamma = 0.2$. Repeat the forecast simulation using a two-month lead time, and compare the accuracy of the forecasts obtained with the accuracy of the one-month lead time forecasts.

5-2 The data in Table B-8 represent four years of monthly demand history for carpet. Use the additive trend and seasonal model described in Sec. 5-2 to forecast the last two years of data for a one-month lead time, with $\alpha = 0.1$, $\beta = 0.1$, and $\gamma = 0.15$. Use the first two years of data to determine appropriate starting values for the model.

5-3 The monthly champagne sales for a French wine company during the past eight years are shown in Table B-9. From an examination of this data, formulate an appropriate forecasting model.   Use the first three years of history to initialize the model, and simulate a one-month lead time forecast for the last five years.

5-4   The numbers of cases of Rubella in the east north-central United States reported by two-week intervals for three years are shown in Table B-11.   Suggest an appropriate forecasting model for these data.   Use the first two years of history to initialize the model, and simulate a one-period lead time forecast for the last year.

5-5   Rework Example 5-1 with $\alpha = 0.15$, $\beta = 0.05$, and $\gamma = 0.20$.   Compare your forecasts with those obtained in the example.   How sensitive to the choice of smoothing constants are the results?

5-6   Rework Example 5-1 using the additive trend model described in Sec. 5-3, with $\alpha = 0.20$, $\beta = 0.10$, and $\gamma = 0.10$.   Compare the results with the forecasts obtained in Example 5-1.

5-7   Consider the time series in Example 5-1.   Suppose initial estimates of the seasonal factors are obtained by dividing the observation in each period by the seasonal average, and averaging seasonal factors for corresponding months.   Using this procedure and the first two years of data, initialize Winters' model.   Then simulate a one-month lead time forecast for the last two years with $\alpha = 0.20$, $\beta = 0.10$, and $\gamma = 0.10$.   Compare the forecasts obtained with this method with the forecasts obtained in the example.   What do you think of this method of estimating the seasonal factors?

5-8   *An alternative seasonal model.*   Consider a model in which both the trend and seasonal factors are multiplicative, say

$$x_t = (b_1 \cdot b_2 t)c_t + \epsilon_t$$

Develop equations for periodic updating of the estimates of the model parameters which are similar to those in Secs. 5-1 and 5-2.   Give the τ-period-ahead forecasting equation.

5-9   *An alternative seasonal model.*   Suppose a time series contains a multiplicative trend effect and additive seasonals.   The appropriate time series model is

$$x_t = b_1 \cdot b_2 t + c_t + \epsilon_t$$

Develop equations for periodic updating of the estimates of the model parameters which are similar to those in Secs. 5-1 and 5-2.   Give the τ-period-ahead forecasting equation.

5-10   The data in Table B-7 represent four years of monthly demand history for a 32-oz soft drink.   Develop an appropriate adaptive smoothing model for this demand process, and simulate a one-month lead time forecast for the last two years.

5-11   Four years of monthly demand data for a carpet are given in Table B-8.   Develop an appropriate adaptive smoothing model for these data, and simulate a one-month lead time forecast for the last two years.

5-12   The monthly champagne sales for a French wine company during the past eight years are shown in Table B-9.   Develop an appropriate adaptive smoothing model for this process.   Simulate a one-month lead time forecast for the last four years.

5-13   Consider the irregular 12-point periodic function

$$x_t = b_0 + \sum_{j=1}^{4} \left(b_j \sin \frac{2\pi jt}{12} + b_j' \cos \frac{2\pi jt}{12} \right) + \epsilon_t$$

This model contains four harmonic frequencies and can describe almost any periodic process that is observed 12 times during the period of the lowest frequency.   Write down the transition matrix and the equations for updating the coefficients.   Describe how you would find the smoothing vector.

5-14   *A 13-point periodic function.*   Consider the model

$$x_t = b_0 + \sum_{j=1}^{4} \left(b_j \sin \frac{2\pi jt}{13} + b_j' \cos \frac{2\pi jt}{13} \right) + \epsilon_t$$

In this model, there are 13 observations during the period of the lowest frequency.   Thus, this model would be applicable to situations in which the company observes sales in four-week accounting periods rather than calendar months.   Write down the transition matrix and the equations for updating the coefficients.   Describe how you would find the smoothing vector.

5-15   *Determining the frequencies in adaptive smoothing of trigonometric models.*   The autocorrelation function of a time series $\{x_t\}$ is

$$\rho_k = \frac{E[(x_t - \mu)(x_{t+k} - \mu)]}{\sigma^2} \qquad k = 0, 1, \ldots$$

and it is a measure of the degree of association of any pair of observations that are k periods apart.   Clearly $-1 \leqslant \rho_k \leqslant 1$ and $\rho_0 = 1$.   A satisfactory estimate of ρ_k is the *sample* autocorrelation function

$$\hat{\rho}_k = \frac{[1/(N-k)] \sum_{t=1}^{N-k} (x_t - \bar{x})(x_{t+k} - \bar{x})}{(1/N) \sum_{t=1}^{N} (x_t - \bar{x})^2} \qquad k = 0, 1, \ldots, K$$

Discuss how the sample autocorrelation function could be used to select the appropriate frequencies for an adaptive smoothing model with trignometric terms.

5-16   Rework Example 5-2 using an adaptive smoothing model with one harmonic.   Compare the results with the forecasts obtained in the example.   Does the addition of the harmonic frequency improve the forecast accuracy?

5-17   *A hybrid exponential smoothing model.*   A soft drink bottler is interested in forecasting the number of cases of product sold each day.   He or she decides to smooth the daily demand x_t in the usual fashion, assuming Winters' method.   The bottler knows that the daily temperature has a pronounced effect on soft drink sales.   Let $\hat{F}_{T+1}$ be the estimate of the maximum temperature for tomorrow, made at the end of the current day.   The bottler decides to use the decision rule that the following number of cases of soft drink will be added to the forecast of demand for the three given temperature forecast ranges:

$$
\begin{aligned}
\beta(\hat{F}_{T+1} - 85°), &\qquad \hat{F}_{T+1} > 85° \\
0, &\qquad 65° \leqslant \hat{F}_{T+1} \leqslant 85° \\
\beta(65° - \hat{F}_{T+1}), &\qquad \hat{F}_{T+1} < 65°
\end{aligned}
$$

where $\beta = 100$.   Write a single forecasting equation to incorporate both the smoothed statistics and the temperature effect.   Show how the smoothed statistics would be updated.

5-18   *Continuation of Exercise 5-17.*   Suppose that, in Exercise 5-17, the coefficient β is unknown.   How could it be estimated, and how could that estimate be periodically revised?

CHAPTER SIX

Forecasting

To this point, we have concentrated on development of efficient computational procedures for periodically revising estimates of the parameters in a time series model. We have said little about the use of the fitted model in forecasting, except to give an equation that can be used to estimate the expected demand in a time period τ periods in the future. In this chapter, we shall discuss the problem of forecasting with a time series model in more detail.

Typically, the decision problem at hand requires a forecast over a number of future periods. That is, we must forecast over some *lead time* or *planning horizon*. The length of the planning horizon depends upon the nature of the decision problem, particularly the time required for the decision to be implemented or become effective, and the method of analysis being applied to the problem. These considerations also determine whether a forecast is required for each period in the planning horizon or whether a forecast of the total demand over all periods in the horizon will be adequate. The former will be called a *period-by-period* forecast, and the latter, a *cumulative* forecast.

Forecasting yields a prediction about future events. If our forecast is made by extrapolating a time series model, we are assuming that, over the forecast horizon, the process will behave as it did in the recent past. Specifically, we are assuming that the model form is correct and that the true parameter values do not change. In that case, the estimates of model parameters computed from historical data would yield accurate forecasts. In most situations, these assumptions are not exactly correct; the underlying process is changing with time.

Therefore, we would expect forecast accuracy to decrease as the planning lead time increases. A forecast of March sales, made at the end of February, will likely be more accurate than a forecast of October sales, also made at the end of February.

The accuracy of a forecasting procedure can be quantitatively described by the variance of the forecast error. Even if the process does not change over time, the forecast will differ from the actual demand because of random variation in the demand process and errors in estimating the parameters in the model. Even if the true parameter values were known, there would be forecast errors because of the random variation. Thus, the variance of the forecast error is a function of the variance of the demand process and the sampling variances of the statistics used to estimate model parameters. As we shall see in Sec. 6-2, the forecast error variance also depends upon the forecast lead time τ. As a practical matter, it is always desirable to have an estimate of the forecast error variance in order to quantify the uncertainty, or risk, associated with the forecast.

Usually, a time series model is used to provide an estimate of the expected value of the process at some future period. By adding and subtracting a multiple of the standard deviation of forecast error, this point estimate can be converted into a *prediction interval*. In some cases, the probability that the actual time series realization will fall in the interval can be stated. Prediction intervals can be very useful in describing the uncertainty associated with a forecast. Their construction is described in Sec. 6-3.

In some cases, it will be desirable to forecast the probability distribution of demand directly. A smoothing procedure for estimating the percentiles of a stationary demand process is given in Sec. 6-4.

Finally, in Sec. 6-5 we discuss the effect of uncertainty about the lead time length on the forecast of total demand during the lead time. Variable-length lead times are common in many procurement and inventory processes.

6-1 PERIOD AND CUMULATIVE FORECASTS

Assume that our time series model has the form considered in Chaps. 4 and 5, that is,

$$x_t = b_1 z_1(t) + b_2 z_2(t) + \cdots + b_k z_k(t) + \epsilon_t \tag{6-1}$$

where the $\{b_i\}$ are constants, the $\{z_i(t)\}$ are mathematical functions of time t, and ϵ_t is the random component having mean 0 and variance σ_ϵ^2. At time T, we have estimated the coefficients $\{b_i\}$ from historical data using, say, discounted least squares and have the following forecasting equation in terms of the original time origin:

$$\hat{x}_{T+\tau}(T) = \sum_{i=1}^{k} \hat{b}_i(T) z_i(T + \tau) \tag{6-2}$$

or, if a current time origin is used,

$$\hat{x}_{T+\tau}(T) = \sum_{i=1}^{k} \hat{a}_i(T) z_i(\tau) \tag{6-3}$$

The forecasting equation provides a point estimate of the expected demand in period $T + \tau$. If we desire a period-by-period forecast over a forecast horizon of L periods, we evaluate the forecasting equation successively for $\tau = 1, 2, \ldots, L$, to obtain $\hat{x}_{T+1}, \hat{x}_{T+2}, \ldots, \hat{x}_{T+L}$.

The cumulative demand over a horizon of L periods, starting with period $T + 1$, will be denoted by $X_L(T)$ and is defined by

$$X_L(T) = \sum_{\tau=1}^{L} x_{T+\tau} \tag{6-4}$$

The cumulative forecast computed at time T is

$$\hat{X}_L(T) = \sum_{\tau=1}^{L} \hat{x}_{T+\tau}(T) \tag{6-5}$$

Depending upon the nature of the $\{z_i(t)\}$, it may be possible to calculate the cumulative forecast directly, rather than first calculating each of the L individual forecasts and then adding. This is illustrated in Examples 6-1 and 6-2.

EXAMPLE 6-1 Suppose a process follows the linear trend model

$$x_t = b_1 + b_2 t + \epsilon_t$$

The forecasting equation at time T is

$$\hat{x}_{T+\tau}(T) = \hat{b}_1(T) + \hat{b}_2(T)(T + \tau)$$

The L-period cumulative forecast is

$$\hat{X}_L(T) = \sum_{\tau=1}^{L} \left[\hat{b}_1(T) + \hat{b}_2(T)(T + \tau) \right]$$

$$= L\hat{b}_1(T) + \left[LT + \frac{L(L+1)}{2} \right] \hat{b}_2(T)$$

If the origin of time had been at the end of period T, these results would have been

$$\hat{x}_{T+\tau}(T) = \hat{a}_1(T) + \hat{a}_2(T)\tau$$

and

$$\hat{X}_L(T) = \sum_{\tau=1}^{L} [\hat{a}_1(T) + \hat{a}_2(T)\tau]$$

$$= L\hat{a}_1(T) + \frac{L(L+1)}{2} \hat{a}_2(T)$$

We can verify that both forecasting equations lead to the same result, if we remember that for a linear model $\hat{a}_1(T) = \hat{b}_1(T) + T\hat{b}_2(T)$ and $\hat{a}_2(T) = \hat{b}_2(T)$.

EXAMPLE 6-2 The following model describes a time series with a linear trend and a stable seasonal pattern:

$$x_t = b_1 + b_2 t + b_3 \sin \omega_1 t + b_4 \cos \omega_1 t + b_5 \sin \omega_2 t + b_6 \cos \omega_2 t + \epsilon_t$$

Assume that the frequencies ω_1 and ω_2 have been selected to be representative of the periodicity of the process and that direct smoothing has been used to estimate the coefficients on a current-origin basis. At the end of period T, the forecasting equation is

$$\hat{x}_{T+\tau}(T) = \hat{a}_1(T) + \hat{a}_2(T)\tau + \hat{a}_3(T)\sin \omega_1\tau + \hat{a}_4(T)\cos \omega_1\tau$$

$$+ \hat{a}_5(T)\sin \omega_2\tau + \hat{a}_6(T)\cos \omega_2\tau$$

The cumulative forecast over the next L periods would be

$$\hat{X}_L(T) = \sum_{\tau=1}^{L} \hat{x}_{T+\tau}(T)$$

$$= c_1\hat{a}_1(T) + c_2\hat{a}_2(T) + c_3\hat{a}_3(T) + c_4\hat{a}_4(T)$$

$$+ c_5\hat{a}_5(T) + c_6\hat{a}_6(T)$$

where the constants are

$$c_1 = \sum_{\tau=1}^{L} 1 = L$$

$$c_2 = \sum_{\tau=1}^{L} \tau = \frac{L(L+1)}{2}$$

$$c_3 = \sum_{\tau=1}^{L} \sin \omega_1\tau = \frac{\sin(L\omega_1/2)\sin[(L+1)\omega_1/2]}{\sin(\omega_1/2)}$$

$$c_4 = \sum_{\tau=1}^{L} \cos \omega_1\tau = \frac{\cos(L\omega_1/2)\sin[(L+1)\omega_1/2]}{\sin(\omega_1/2)} - 1$$

$$c_5 = \sum_{\tau=1}^{L} \sin \omega_2\tau = \frac{\sin(L\omega_2/2)\sin[(L+1)\omega_2/2]}{\sin(\omega_2/2)}$$

$$c_6 = \sum_{\tau=1}^{L} \cos \omega_2\tau = \frac{\cos(L\omega_2/2)\sin[(L+1)\omega_2/2]}{\sin(\omega_2/2)} - 1$$

For example, if $\omega_1 = 2\pi/12$, $\omega_2 = 2\pi/6$, and $L = 4$, the cumulative forecast can be computed from

$$\hat{X}_4(T) = 4\hat{a}_1(T) + 10\hat{a}_2(T) + 3.2321\hat{a}_3(T) + 0.8660\hat{a}_4(T)$$

$$+ 0.8660\hat{a}_5(T) - 1.5000\hat{a}_6(T)$$

TABLE 6-1   Summations Useful in Forecasting Cumulative Demand

$$\sum_{\tau=1}^{L} (1) = L$$

$$\sum_{\tau=1}^{L} \tau = \frac{L(L+1)}{2}$$

$$\sum_{\tau=1}^{L} \tau^2 = \frac{L(L+1)(2L+1)}{6}$$

$$\sum_{\tau=1}^{L} \tau^3 = \frac{L^2(L+1)^2}{4}$$

$$\sum_{\tau=1}^{L} \tau^4 = \frac{L(L+1)(2L+1)(3L^2+3L-1)}{30}$$

$$\sum_{\tau=1}^{L} \sin \omega\tau = \frac{\sin(L\omega/2)\sin[(L+1)\omega/2]}{\sin(\omega/2)}$$

$$\sum_{\tau=1}^{L} \cos \omega\tau = \frac{\cos(L\omega/2)\sin[(L+1)\omega/2]}{\sin(\omega/2)} - 1$$

$$\sum_{\tau=1}^{L} \tau \sin \omega\tau = \frac{\sin[(L+1)\omega]}{4\sin^2(\omega/2)} - \frac{(L+1)\cos[(2L+1)\omega/2]}{2\sin(\omega/2)}$$

$$\sum_{\tau=1}^{L} \tau \cos \omega\tau = \frac{(L+1)\sin[2(L+1)\omega/2]}{2\sin(\omega/2)} - \frac{1-\cos[(L+1)\omega]}{4\sin^2(\omega/2)}$$

$$\sum_{\tau=0}^{L} x^\tau = \frac{1-x^{L+1}}{1-x} \qquad x \neq 1$$

$$\sum_{\tau=0}^{L} \tau x^\tau = \frac{x[1-(L+1)x^L+Lx^{L+1}]}{(1-x)^2} \qquad x \neq 1$$

$$\sum_{\tau=0}^{L} \tau^2 x^\tau = \frac{x^{L+1}[(2L^2+2L-1)x-L^2x^2-(L+1)^2]+x(1+x)}{(1-x)^3} \qquad x \neq 1$$

Table 6-1 contains closed-form expressions for selected finite summations that are useful in developing a cumulative forecasting model.

6-2 VARIANCE OF FORECAST ERRORS

6-2.1 Definition of Forecast Error

There are a number of possible definitions of the forecast error experienced in a period, depending upon the prior point in time at which the forecast was made. For example, the forecast error for October could be computed based on a forecast made at the end of September, or it might be calculated based upon a forecast made at the end of July. In the former case, we would be calculating the *one-period-ahead* forecast error, and in the latter, the *three-period-ahead* forecast error. Naturally, other possibilities exist for different forecast lead times. In general, the τ-*period-ahead* forecast error computed for period T is the actual demand in period T less the forecast for period T made at the end of period $T - \tau$, or

$$e_\tau(T) = x_T - \hat{x}_T(T - \tau) \tag{6-6}$$

The circumstances of the particular decision problem for which the forecast is required will dictate the value, or values, of the forecast lead time τ that are of interest in monitoring forecast performance. For statistical purposes, the analysis of forecast error in Chap. 7 will generally require computation of only $e_1(T)$, and there, for convenience, we shall sometimes refer to this as "the forecast error," without stating $\tau = 1$.

We shall define the *L-period cumulative forecast error*, computed at time T, as the total actual demand in periods $T - L + 1, T - L + 2, \ldots, T$, less the cumulative forecast for these periods made at time $T - L$; that is,

$$
\begin{aligned}
E_L(T) &= X_L(T - L) - \hat{X}_L(T - L) \\
&= \sum_{\tau=1}^{L} x_{T-L+\tau} - \sum_{\tau=1}^{L} \hat{x}_{T-L+\tau}(T - L) \\
&= \sum_{\tau=1}^{L} e_\tau(T - L + \tau) \tag{6-7}
\end{aligned}
$$

This notation is somewhat complicated, but it is consistent with previous definitions. The concept, however, is simple, as the following example demonstrates.

EXAMPLE 6-3 In Example 3-2, we illustrated the application of double exponential smoothing to forecast a linear trend process. Table 3-5 contains the results of using the model during a two-year period to forecast each month for the next month. This information is repeated in Table 6-2, which also contains results from using the model each period to forecast two and three periods ahead. Each month, Eq. (3-20) was evaluated for $\tau = 1$, 2, and 3 to obtain $\hat{x}_{T+1}(T)$, $\hat{x}_{T+2}(T)$, and $\hat{x}_{T+3}(T)$. Thus, for example, in August 1977 the forecasts for September, October, and November were computed to be 603, 612, and 622, respectively. Also, at the end of August it was possible to calculate the errors associated with prior forecasts made for that month. At the end of May, the forecast for August was $\hat{x}_8(5) = 599$. The actual demand in August was $x_8 = 603$, so that the three-period-ahead error was

$$e_3(8) = x_8 - \hat{x}_8(5) = 603 - 599 = 4$$

Similarly, the errors in forecasts for August made at the end of June and July were found to be

$$e_2(8) = x_8 - \hat{x}_8(6) = 603 - 605 = -2$$

$$e_1(8) = x_8 - \hat{x}_8(7) = 603 - 591 = 12$$

TABLE 6-2 Forecasts and Forecast Errors, Example 6-3

Year and month	Period number, T	Actual sales, x_T	Forecasts for the next three periods			Errors in last three forecasts for period t			Cumulative error, $E_3(T)$
			$\hat{x}_{T+1}(T)$	$\hat{x}_{T+2}(T)$	$\hat{x}_{T+3}(T)$	$e_1(T)$	$e_2(T)$	$e_3(T)$	
1977 Jan.	1	538	551	561	572	-3			
Feb.	2	570	565	576	586	19	19		
Mar.	3	600	583	594	605	35	39	38	
Apr.	4	565	590	601	612	-18	-9	-7	51
May	5	485	580	590	599	-105	-109	-101	-75
June	6	604	595	605	615	24	3	-1	-128
July	7	527	591	600	610	-68	-63	-85	-187
Aug.	8	603	603	612	622	12	-2	4	-35
Sept.	9	604	612	622	631	1	4	11	-59
Oct.	10	790	657	669	680	178	178	180	196
Nov.	11	714	680	692	704	57	92	92	271
Dec.	12	653	686	698	709	-27	-16	22	292
1978 Jan.	13	626	686	697	708	-60	-66	-54	-13
Feb.	14	690	698	709	720	4	-8	-14	-107
Mar.	15	680	705	716	727	-18	-17	-29	-97
Apr.	16	673	709	720	730	-32	-36	-35	-48
May	17	613	701	710	720	-96	-103	-107	-161
June	18	744	719	729	739	43	24	17	-118
July	19	718	729	739	748	-1	8	-12	-84
Aug.	20	767	746	757	767	38	38	47	98
Sept.	21	728	753	763	773	-18	-11	-11	26
Oct.	22	793	771	782	792	40	36	45	72
Nov.	23	726	773	783	793	-45	-37	-41	-23
Dec.	24	777	784	794	804	4	-5	4	7

respectively.   Similar computations were made for each month in the 24-month simulation.

It also was possible to obtain measures of the error in forecasting cumulative demand over a three-month horizon.   Again using August 1977 to illustrate the concept, we observe that the actual demand in the most recent three months was

$$X_3(5) = x_6 + x_7 + x_8$$

$$= 604 + 527 + 603 = 1{,}734$$

The cumulative forecast for June, July, and August, made at the end of May, was

$$\hat{X}_3(5) = \hat{x}_6(5) + \hat{x}_7(5) + \hat{x}_8(5)$$

$$= 580 + 590 + 599 = 1{,}769$$

Therefore, the cumulative forecast error was

$$E_3(8) = X_3(5) - \hat{X}_3(5)$$

$$= 1734 - 1769 = -35$$

Similar calculations were made for each month, starting with March 1977 ($T = 3$).

6-2.2 Variance of Period Forecast Errors

From Eq. (6-6) we can observe that the τ-period forecast error is the difference of two random variables, the demand in period T and the forecast made τ periods before. These random variables are independent, since the forecast is based on demand values prior to period T and we assume the demands are independent. Therefore, the forecast error variance is the sum of the variance of the demand process, σ_ϵ^2, and the variance of the forecast; that is,

$$\text{Var}[e_\tau(T)] = \text{Var}(x_T) + \text{Var}[\hat{x}_T(T - \tau)] \tag{6-8}$$

The variance of the forecast is a function of the variances and covariances describing the uncertainty in using estimates of the model parameters in the forecasting equation. The sampling variances of the estimators are defined as

$$\text{Var}(\hat{b}_i) \equiv E\left\{\left[\hat{b}_i - E(\hat{b}_i)\right]^2\right\} \equiv V_{ii} \tag{6-9}$$

and the covariance between $\hat{b}_i$ and $\hat{b}_j$ is defined as

$$\text{Cov}(\hat{b}_i, \hat{b}_j) = E\left\{\left[\hat{b}_i - E(\hat{b}_i)\right]\left[\hat{b}_j - E(\hat{b}_j)\right]\right\} \equiv V_{ij} \tag{6-10}$$

where E is the expected value operator.

If the forecasting equation is (6-2), then the variance of the forecast is

$$\text{Var}[\hat{x}_{T+\tau}(T)] = \text{Var}\left[\sum_{i=1}^{k} \hat{b}_i(T)z_i(T + \tau)\right]$$

$$= \sum_{i=1}^{k}\sum_{j=1}^{k} z_i(T + \tau)z_j(T + \tau)V_{ij} \tag{6-11}$$

In matrix notation, (6-11) becomes

$$\text{Var}[\hat{x}_{T+\tau}(T)] = \mathbf{z}'(T + \tau)\mathbf{V}\mathbf{z}(T + \tau) \tag{6-12}$$

where $\mathbf{z}(T + \tau)$ is a k-component column vector of the independent variables evaluated at $T + \tau$, and $\mathbf{V}$ is the variance-covariance matrix having elements V_{ij}. Procedures for developing $\mathbf{V}$ are given in Appendix 2A and Sec. 4-1, and are illustrated in Examples 6-4 and 6-5.

Should a current-origin forecasting equation of the form (6-3) be used, then

$$\text{Var}[\hat{x}_{T+\tau}(T)] = \mathbf{z}'(\tau)\mathbf{V}\mathbf{z}(\tau) \tag{6-13}$$

where $\mathbf{V}$ now must be the variance-covariance matrix of the $\{\hat{a}_i(T)\}$.

EXAMPLE 6-4 *Linear trend model, conventional least-squares analysis.* Assume, as in Sec. 2-1.1, we apply simple linear regression methods to estimate the parameters in the model

$$x_t = b_1 + b_2 t + \epsilon_t$$

from a time series history $x_1, x_2, \ldots, x_T$. Application of the least-squares criterion to minimize

$$\mathrm{SS}_E = \sum_{t=1}^{T} (x_t - b_1 - b_2 t)^2$$

results in the following normal equations [Eq. (2-22)]:

$$\mathbf{Z'Zb} = \mathbf{Z'x}$$

where $\mathbf{Z}$ is a $T \times 2$ matrix of values of the independent variables and $\mathbf{x}$ is a column vector of the dependent variable realizations; that is,

$$\mathbf{Z} = \begin{bmatrix} 1 & 1 \\ 1 & 2 \\ \vdots & \vdots \\ 1 & T \end{bmatrix} \qquad \mathbf{x} = \begin{bmatrix} x_1 \\ x_2 \\ \vdots \\ x_T \end{bmatrix} \qquad \hat{b} = \begin{bmatrix} \hat{b}_1 \\ \hat{b}_2 \end{bmatrix}$$

The 2×2 matrix $\mathbf{Z'Z}$, which we shall denote by $\mathbf{G}(T)$ for convenience, is composed of sums of squares and cross products of the independent variables:

$$\mathbf{G}(T) = \begin{bmatrix} \sum_{t=1}^{T} (1)^2 & \sum_{t=1}^{T} t \\ \sum_{t=1}^{T} t & \sum_{t=1}^{T} t^2 \end{bmatrix} = \begin{bmatrix} T & \dfrac{T(T+1)}{2} \\ \dfrac{T(T+1)}{2} & \dfrac{T(T+1)(2T+1)}{6} \end{bmatrix} \qquad (6\text{-}14)$$

The vector $\mathbf{Z'x}$ contains sums of cross products of the independent variables with the dependent variable. Calling this vector $\mathbf{g}(T)$, we have

$$\mathbf{g}(T) = \begin{bmatrix} \sum_{t=1}^{T} x_t \\ \sum_{t=1}^{T} t x_t \end{bmatrix}$$

The solution to the normal equations is

$$\hat{\mathbf{b}}(T) = \mathbf{G}^{-1}(T)\mathbf{g}(T)$$

where the inverse of $\mathbf{G}(T)$ can be shown to be

$$\mathbf{G}^{-1}(T) = \begin{bmatrix} \dfrac{2(2T+1)}{T(T-1)} & \dfrac{-6}{T(T-1)} \\[3mm] \dfrac{-6}{T(T-1)} & \dfrac{12}{T(T^2-1)} \end{bmatrix} \qquad (6\text{-}15)$$

The least-squares estimators computed at the end of period T are then

$$\hat{b}_1(T) = \frac{2(2T+1)}{T(T-1)} \sum_{t=1}^{T} x_t - \frac{6}{T(T-1)} \sum_{t=1}^{T} t x_t$$

$$\hat{b}_2(T) = \frac{12}{T(T^2-1)} \sum_{t=1}^{T} t x_t - \frac{6}{T(T-1)} \sum_{t=1}^{T} x_t$$

The $\hat{b}$'s are random variables with variance-covariance matrix $\mathbf{V}$ determined from Eq. (2A-10):

$$\mathbf{V}(T) = \mathbf{G}^{-1}(T)\sigma_\epsilon^2$$

Computing $\mathbf{V}(T)$, we find

$$\text{Var}(\hat{b}_1) = \frac{2(2T+1)}{T(T-1)} \sigma_\epsilon^2 \qquad (6\text{-}16)$$

$$\text{Var}(\hat{b}_2) = \frac{12}{T(T^2-1)} \sigma_\epsilon^2 \qquad (6\text{-}17)$$

$$\text{Cov}(\hat{b}_1, \hat{b}_2) = \frac{-6}{T(T-1)} \sigma_\epsilon^2 \qquad (6\text{-}18)$$

With this information, we can use Eq. (6-12) to calculate the variance of a τ-period-ahead forecast made at time T:

$$\text{Var}[\hat{x}_{T+\tau}(T)] = \text{Var}(\hat{b}_1) + (T+\tau)^2 \text{Var}(\hat{b}_2) + 2(T+\tau)\text{Cov}(\hat{b}_1, \hat{b}_2)$$

$$= \frac{2}{T(T^2-1)} [(2T-1)(T-1) + 6\tau(T+\tau-1)]\sigma_\epsilon^2 \quad (6\text{-}19)$$

Finally, the variance of the error in forecasting demand in period $T+\tau$ is given by

$$\text{Var}[e_\tau(T+\tau)] = \text{Var}(x_{T+\tau}) + \text{Var}[\hat{x}_{T+\tau}(T)] \qquad (6\text{-}20)$$

where

$$\text{Var}(x_{T+\tau}) = \sigma_\epsilon^2$$

Note that $\mathbf{V}$ is a function of T and must be recomputed each period along with $\mathbf{b}$, if the most recent data are to be incorporated into the estimates.

EXAMPLE 6-5 *Linear trend model, direct smoothing.* In Sec. 4-3, direct smoothing methods were applied to develop forecasting procedures for the linear process

$$x_t = b_1 + b_2 t + \epsilon_t$$

In direct smoothing, the origin of time is assumed to be at the end of the current period, T, so that the forecasting equation is

$$\hat{x}_{T+\tau}(T) = \hat{a}_1(T) + \hat{a}_2(T)\tau$$

A discounted least-squares criterion is used; that is, minimize

$$\sum_{j=0}^{T-1} \beta^j \left[x_{T-j} - a_1(T) - a_2(T) \cdot (-j) \right]^2$$

This leads to the least-squares normal equations

$$\mathbf{G}(T)\hat{\mathbf{a}}(T) = \mathbf{g}(T)$$

where, as shown in Sec. 4-3,

$$\mathbf{G}(T) = \begin{bmatrix} \dfrac{1}{1-\beta} & \dfrac{-\beta}{(1-\beta)^2} \\[2ex] \dfrac{-\beta}{(1-\beta)^2} & \dfrac{\beta(1+\beta)}{(1-\beta)^3} \end{bmatrix} (1-\beta^T)$$

and

$$\mathbf{g}(t) = \begin{bmatrix} \displaystyle\sum_{j=0}^{T-1} \beta^j x_{T-j} \\[3ex] \displaystyle\sum_{j=0}^{T-1} \beta^j (-j) x_{T-j} \end{bmatrix}$$

The solution is

$$\hat{\mathbf{a}}(T) = \mathbf{G}^{-1}(T)\mathbf{g}(T)$$

In Sec. 4-3, this solution is developed to allow easy recursive calculation of $\hat{\mathbf{a}}(T)$ from $\hat{\mathbf{a}}(T-1)$ and x_T, making use of the stationary property of $\mathbf{G}(T)$ for large T; that is, as $T \to \infty$,

$$\mathbf{G}(T) \to \mathbf{G} = \begin{bmatrix} \dfrac{1}{1-\beta} & \dfrac{-\beta}{(1-\beta)^2} \\[2ex] \dfrac{-\beta}{(1-\beta)^2} & \dfrac{\beta(1+\beta)}{(1-\beta)^3} \end{bmatrix}$$

which has the following inverse, also independent of T:

$$G^{-1} = \begin{bmatrix} 1 - \beta^2 & (1-\beta)^2 \\ (1-\beta)^2 & \dfrac{(1-\beta)^3}{\beta} \end{bmatrix} \qquad (6\text{-}21)$$

Our interest here is in the computation of the covariance matrix for $\hat{\mathbf{a}}(T)$. By Eq. (4-9),

$$\mathbf{V}(T) = \mathbf{G}^{-1}(T)\mathbf{F}(T)\mathbf{G}^{-1}(T)\sigma_\epsilon^2 \qquad (6\text{-}22)$$

where

$$\mathbf{F}(T) = \sum_{j=0}^{T-1} \beta^{2j}\mathbf{z}(-j)\mathbf{z}'(-j) = \sum_{j=0}^{T-1} \beta^{2j} \begin{bmatrix} 1 \\ -j \end{bmatrix} [1, \ -j]$$

$$= \begin{bmatrix} \displaystyle\sum_{j=0}^{T-1} \beta^{2j} & \displaystyle\sum_{j=0}^{T-1} (-j)\beta^{2j} \\ \displaystyle\sum_{j=0}^{T-1} (-j)\beta^{2j} & \displaystyle\sum_{j=0}^{T-1} j^2\beta^{2j} \end{bmatrix}$$

If T is large, terms in β^T are near zero, so that $\mathbf{F}(T)$ is approximately

$$\mathbf{F} = \sum_{j=0}^{\infty} \beta^{2j}\mathbf{z}(-j)\mathbf{z}'(-j) = \begin{bmatrix} \dfrac{1}{1-\beta^2} & \dfrac{-\beta^2}{(1-\beta^2)^2} \\ \dfrac{-\beta^2}{(1-\beta^2)^2} & \dfrac{\beta^2(1+\beta^2)}{(1-\beta^2)^3} \end{bmatrix} \qquad (6\text{-}23)$$

Then for large T, $\mathbf{V}(T)$ becomes stationary at

$$\mathbf{V} = \mathbf{G}^{-1}\mathbf{F}\mathbf{G}^{-1}\sigma_\epsilon^2 = \frac{\alpha}{(1+\beta)^3} \begin{bmatrix} 1 + 4\beta + 5\beta^2 & \alpha(1+3\beta) \\ \alpha(1+3\beta) & 2\alpha^2 \end{bmatrix} \sigma_\epsilon^2 \qquad (6\text{-}24)$$

where $\alpha = 1 - \beta$.   Therefore we have

$$\text{Var}(\hat{a}_1) = \frac{\alpha(1+4\beta+5\beta^2)}{(1+\beta)^3}\,\sigma_\epsilon^2 \qquad (6\text{-}25)$$

$$\text{Var}(\hat{a}_2) = \frac{2\alpha^3}{(1+\beta)^3}\,\sigma_\epsilon^2 \qquad (6\text{-}26)$$

$$\text{Cov}(\hat{a}_1, \hat{a}_2) = \frac{\alpha^2(1+3\beta)}{(1+\beta)^3}\,\sigma_\epsilon^2 \qquad (6\text{-}27)$$

The variance of the forecast for period $T + \tau$ computed at the end of period T is,

TABLE 6-3   Steady-State Variance of τ-Period-Ahead Forecast and Forecast Error as a Multiple of σ_ϵ^2, When Direct Smoothing Is Used for a Linear Model

	Forecast variance					
τ	$\beta=0.70$	$\beta=0.75$	$\beta=0.80$	$\beta=0.85$	$\beta=0.90$	$\beta=0.95$
1	0.5062	0.3994	0.3032	0.2161	0.1372	0.0654
2	0.6528	0.4927	0.3580	0.2445	0.1489	0.0681
3	0.8213	0.5977	0.4184	0.2751	0.1611	0.0709
4	1.0118	0.7143	0.4842	0.3078	0.1739	0.0737
5	1.2243	0.8426	0.5556	0.3426	0.1873	0.0766
6	1.4588	0.9825	0.6324	0.3796	0.2013	0.0796
7	1.7152	1.1341	0.7147	0.4187	0.2159	0.0826
8	1.9937	1.2974	0.8025	0.4599	0.2311	0.0857
9	2.2941	1.4723	0.8957	0.5032	0.2468	0.0889
10	2.6165	1.6589	0.9945	0.5487	0.2632	0.0921
11	2.9609	1.8571	1.0988	0.5964	0.2801	0.0954
12	3.3273	2.0671	1.2085	0.6461	0.2976	0.0988

	Forecast error variance					
τ	$\beta=0.70$	$\beta=0.75$	$\beta=0.80$	$\beta=0.85$	$\beta=0.90$	$\beta=0.95$
1	1.5062	1.3994	1.3032	1.2161	1.1372	1.0654
2	1.6528	1.4927	1.3580	1.2445	1.1489	1.0681
3	1.8213	1.5977	1.4184	1.2751	1.1611	1.0709
4	2.0118	1.7143	1.4842	1.3078	1.1739	1.0737
5	2.2243	1.8426	1.5556	1.3426	1.1873	1.0766
6	2.4588	1.9825	1.6324	1.3796	1.2013	1.0796
7	2.7152	2.1341	1.7147	1.4187	1.2159	1.0826
8	2.9937	2.2974	1.8025	1.4599	1.2311	1.0857
9	3.2941	2.4723	1.8957	1.5032	1.2468	1.0889
10	3.6165	2.6589	1.9945	1.5487	1.2632	1.0921
11	3.9609	2.8571	2.0988	1.5964	1.2801	1.0954
12	4.3273	3.0671	2.2085	1.6461	1.2976	1.0988

from (6-13) with $\mathbf{z}'(\tau) = [1, \tau]$,

$$\mathrm{Var}[\hat{x}_{T+\tau}(T)] = \mathbf{z}'(\tau)\mathbf{V}\mathbf{z}(\tau)$$

$$= \mathrm{Var}[\hat{a}_1(T)] + \tau^2\mathrm{Var}[\hat{a}_2(T)] + 2\tau\,\mathrm{Cov}[\hat{a}_1(T),\,\hat{a}_2(T)]$$

$$= \frac{\alpha}{(1+\beta)^3}\,[(1+4\beta+5\beta^2) + 2\alpha(1+3\beta)\tau + 2\alpha^2\tau^2]\sigma_\epsilon^2 \quad (6\text{-}28)$$

The variance of the error in forecasting for period $T + \tau$ at the end of period T is

$$\mathrm{Var}[e_\tau(T+\tau)] = \sigma_\epsilon^2 + \mathrm{Var}[\hat{x}_{T+\tau}(T)] \quad (6\text{-}29)$$

For selected values of β and τ, Table 6-3 contains the forecast variance and forecast error variance as a multiple of σ_ϵ^2 for the linear trend model.

6-2.3 Variance of Cumulative Forecast Errors

The cumulative forecast over an L-period horizon and the associated cumulative forecast error were defined by Eqs. (6-5) and (6-7), respectively. From the latter equation, we see that the cumulative forecast error is the difference between the cumulative demand actually experienced and the cumulative forecast. Assuming that the period demands are mutually independent random variables, these two quantities are uncorrelated, so that the variance of the forecast error is the sum of the variance of the cumulative demand and the variance of the forecast.

The results can be stated symbolically by assuming that we are at the end of period T and wish a cumulative forecast for the next L periods. The forecast is, for an original-origin model,

$$\hat{X}_L(T) = \sum_{\tau=1}^{L} \hat{x}_{T+\tau}(T)$$

$$= \sum_{\tau=1}^{L} \sum_{i=1}^{k} \hat{b}_i(T) z_i(T+\tau)$$

$$= \sum_{\tau=1}^{L} \hat{\mathbf{b}}'(T)\mathbf{z}(T+\tau) = \hat{\mathbf{b}}'(T) \sum_{\tau=1}^{L} \mathbf{z}(T+\tau) \qquad (6\text{-}30)$$

where $\mathbf{z}'(T+\tau) = [z_1(T+\tau), z_2(T+\tau), \ldots, z_k(T+\tau)]$ is the vector of independent variables evaluated at $T+\tau$. The variance of the forecast is the following function of the variances of the $\{\hat{b}_i(T)\}$:

$$\text{Var}\left[\hat{X}_L(T)\right] = \text{Var}\left[\sum_{\tau=1}^{L} \sum_{i=1}^{k} \hat{b}_i(T) z_i(T+\tau)\right]$$

$$= \sum_{i=1}^{k} \sum_{j=1}^{k} \left[\sum_{\tau=1}^{L} z_i(T+\tau)\right]\left[\sum_{\tau=1}^{L} z_j(T+\tau)\right] V_{ij}$$

$$= \left[\sum_{\tau=1}^{L} \mathbf{z}(T+\tau)\right]' \mathbf{V}\left[\sum_{\tau=1}^{L} \mathbf{z}(T+\tau)\right] \qquad (6\text{-}31)$$

where $\mathbf{V}$ is the variance-covariance matrix having elements $V_{ij} = \text{Cov}(\hat{b}_i, \hat{b}_j)$.

For a current-origin forecasting model, the forecast variance is

$$\text{Var}\left[\hat{X}_L(T)\right] = \left[\sum_{\tau=1}^{L} \mathbf{z}(\tau)\right]' \mathbf{V}\left[\sum_{\tau=1}^{L} \mathbf{z}(\tau)\right] \qquad (6\text{-}32)$$

where now $V_{ij} = \text{Cov}(\hat{a}_i, \hat{a}_j)$.

We should observe that even though the forecast is the sum of L period forecasts, the forecast variance is not the sum of the period forecast variances.

This is because all of the period forecasts in the cumulative forecast are based upon the same $\hat{\mathbf{b}}(T)$ [or $\hat{\mathbf{a}}(T)$] and therefore are correlated.

The variance of the cumulative error in forecasting for periods $T + \tau, T + \tau + 1, \ldots, T + L$ is

$$\text{Var}[E_L(T + L)] = \text{Var}[X_L(T)] + \text{Var}\left[\hat{X}_L(T)\right]$$

$$= L\sigma_\epsilon^2 + \text{Var}\left[\hat{X}_L(T)\right] \tag{6-33}$$

EXAMPLE 6-6 *Linear trend model, conventional least-squares analysis.* In Example 6-4, we developed the period forecast error variance for this process and estimation procedure. Now we consider the cumulative forecast error variance. At time T, the L-period cumulative forecast is

$$\hat{X}_L(T) = \sum_{\tau=1}^{L} \left[\hat{b}_1(T) + \hat{b}_2(T)(T + \tau)\right]$$

$$= L\hat{b}_1(T) + \left[LT + \frac{L(L+1)}{2}\right]\hat{b}_2(T) \tag{6-34}$$

The cumulative forecast variance is, using Eqs. (6-16), (6-17), and (6-18),

$$\text{Var}\left[\hat{X}_L(T)\right] = L^2\text{Var}(\hat{b}_1) + \left[\frac{L(2T + L + 1)}{2}\right]^2 \text{Var}(\hat{b}_2)$$

$$+ 2L\left[\frac{L(2T + L + 1)}{2}\right]\text{Cov}(\hat{b}_1, \hat{b}_2)$$

$$= \frac{L^2}{T(T^2 - 1)}(4T^2 + 6TL + 3L^2 - 1)\sigma_\epsilon^2 \tag{6-35}$$

The cumulative forecast error variance is then given by Eq. (6-33).

EXAMPLE 6-7 *Linear trend model, direct smoothing.* Using the results from Example 6-5, we will compute the variance of the cumulative forecast error using direct smoothing. At time T, the L-period cumulative forecast is

$$\hat{X}_L(T) = \sum_{\tau=1}^{L} \left[\hat{a}_1(T) + \hat{a}_2(T)\tau\right]$$

$$= L\hat{a}_1(T) + \frac{L(L+1)}{2}\hat{a}_2(T) \tag{6-36}$$

TABLE 6-4   Steady-State Variance of L-Period Cumulative Forecast and Forecast Error as a Multiple of σ_ϵ^2, When Direct Smoothing Is Used for a Linear Model

	Cumulative forecast					
L	$\beta=0.70$	$\beta=0.75$	$\beta=0.80$	$\beta=0.85$	$\beta=0.90$	$\beta=0.95$
1	0.5062	0.3994	0.3032	0.2161	0.1372	0.0654
2	2.3069	1.7784	1.3196	0.9203	0.5718	0.2671
3	5.8748	4.4344	3.2222	2.2009	1.3397	0.6131
4	11.7484	8.6997	6.2003	4.1530	2.4785	1.1120
5	20.5323	14.9417	10.4595	6.8777	4.0276	1.7722
6	32.8968	23.5627	16.2222	10.4827	6.0280	2.6026
7	49.5785	35.0000	23.7270	15.0822	8.5227	3.6123
8	71.3796	49.7259	33.2291	20.7966	11.5562	4.8103
9	99.1685	68.2478	45.0000	27.7527	15.1750	6.2062
10	133.8795	91.1079	59.3278	36.0837	19.4270	7.8095
11	176.5127	118.8834	76.5171	45.9295	24.3623	9.6300
12	228.1343	152.1866	96.8889	57.4360	30.0324	11.6777

	Cumulative forecast error					
L	$\beta=0.70$	$\beta=0.75$	$\beta=0.80$	$\beta=0.85$	$\beta=0.90$	$\beta=0.95$
1	1.5062	1.3994	1.3032	1.2161	1.1372	1.0654
2	4.3069	3.7784	3.3196	2.9203	2.5718	2.2671
3	8.8748	7.4344	6.2222	5.2009	4.3397	3.6131
4	15.7484	12.6997	10.2003	8.1530	6.4785	5.1120
5	25.5323	19.9417	15.4595	11.8777	9.0276	6.7722
6	38.8968	29.5627	22.2222	16.4827	12.0280	8.6026
7	56.5785	42.0000	30.7270	22.0822	15.5227	10.6123
8	79.3796	57.7259	41.2291	28.7966	19.5562	12.8103
9	108.1685	77.2478	54.0000	36.7527	24.1750	15.2062
10	143.8795	101.1079	69.3278	46.0837	29.4270	17.8095
11	187.5127	129.8834	87.5171	56.9295	35.3623	20.6300
12	240.1343	164.1866	108.8889	69.4360	42.0324	23.6777

The cumulative forecast variance is

$$\mathrm{Var}\left[\hat{X}_L(T)\right] = L^2\mathrm{Var}[\hat{a}_1(T)] + \left[\frac{L(L+1)}{2}\right]^2 \mathrm{Var}[\hat{a}_2(T)]$$

$$+ 2L\left[\frac{L(L+1)}{2}\right]\mathrm{Cov}[\hat{a}_1(T),\,\hat{a}_2(T)]$$

$$= \frac{\alpha L^2}{2(1+\beta)^3}\,[5(1+2\beta+\beta^2) + 4(1-\beta^2)L + \alpha^2 L^2]\sigma_\epsilon^2 \qquad (6\text{-}37)$$

where the covariance terms were obtained from Eqs. (6-25) to (6-27).   The variance of the cumulative forecast error is then given by Eq. (6-33).

Table 6-4 contains the forecast variance and forecast error variance as a multiple of σ_ϵ^2 for selected values of L and β.

6-3 PREDICTION INTERVALS

Having developed expressions for the variance of forecast error in terms of the variance of the demand process, σ_ϵ^2, we now turn to the problem of using this information to make probability statements about forecast errors, and, in so doing, quantitatively describe the risks we take when we use an estimate of the expected demand as a forecast.

Our basic time series model has been

$$X_t = \sum_{i=1}^{k} b_i z_i(t) + \epsilon_t$$

where the expected value of demand at time t is

$$E(x_t) = \sum_{i=1}^{k} b_i z_i(t)$$

and the random component ϵ_t has mean $E(\epsilon_t) = 0$ and variance σ_ϵ^2. We further assumed that the $\{\epsilon_t\}$ are independently distributed random variables.

Using one of the estimation techniques described in earlier chapters, we can develop a forecasting equation, such as

$$\hat{x}_{T+\tau}(T) = \sum_{i=1}^{k} \hat{b}_i(T) z_i(T+\tau)$$

to provide an estimate of the expected demand in period $T + \tau$, which we will compute at the end of period T. For procedures based on the least-squares criterion, these forecasts have been shown (in Chap. 4) to be unbiased; that is,

$$E[\hat{x}_{T+\tau}(T)] = E(x_{T+\tau})$$

For many applications, however, it is not sufficient to have only an unbiased estimate of the expected demand in a period. Some measure of the extent by which the actual demand might differ from the forecast is desired. This is provided by the variance of forecast error, $\text{Var}[e_\tau(T+\tau)]$, which is the expected squared forecast error, assuming the forecast is unbiased. Of the other variances we have defined, note that σ_ϵ^2 is a measure of the deviation of the actual demand, $x_{T+\tau}$, from the true expected demand, $E(x_{T+\tau})$, and that the forecast variance, $\text{Var}[\hat{x}_{T+\tau}(T)]$, measures the deviation of the forecast, $\hat{x}_{T+\tau}(T)$, from the expected demand, $E(x_{T+\tau})$. The latter variance is used in many applications of regression analysis to provide confidence-interval estimates of the true regression function. However, in forecasting time series, confidence-interval estimates of expected demand are of little value, because only one realization of the random variable will occur in any period, and the decision maker is concerned with its magnitude rather than that of its expected value. The decision maker will take action based on the forecast; thus, it is the forecast error that is of concern.

A *prediction interval* for demand in a period is based on a probability statement about the forecast error. For example, if we believe forecast error is normally distributed with mean 0 and variance $\text{Var}[e_\tau(T + \tau)]$, which we shall denote $\sigma_{e_\tau}^2$ for convenience, the probability is 0.95 that the error in forecasting for period $T + \tau$ will lie between $\pm 1.96 \sigma_{e_\tau}$. We then can say that the probability is 0.95 that the actual demand in period $T + \tau$ will lie between $\hat{x}_{T+\tau}(T) \pm 1.96 \sigma_{e_\tau}$. We shall call this interval estimate a prediction interval.

To develop a general form for a prediction interval estimate of demand, we assume that forecast errors are normally distributed and introduce the notation u_γ to represent a value of the standard normal random variable such that

$$\int_{-\infty}^{u_\gamma} \frac{1}{\sqrt{2\pi}} e^{-\frac{1}{2}v^2} \, dv = \gamma$$

Thus u_γ is the 100γ percentile of the standard normal distribution. Values of u_γ are given in Appendix Table A-1. If the forecasting procedure is unbiased, that is, if $E(e_\tau) = 0$, the following probability statement is correct:

$$P\{u_{\gamma/2}\sigma_{e_\tau} < e_\tau < u_{1-\gamma/2}\sigma_{e_\tau}\} = 1 - \gamma$$

Since $e_\tau \equiv e_\tau(T + \tau) = x_{T+\tau} - \hat{x}_{T+\tau}(T)$ and $u_{1-\gamma/2} = -u_{\gamma/2}$,

$$P\{u_{\gamma/2}\sigma_{e_\tau} < x_{T+\tau} - \hat{x}_{T+\tau}(T) < -u_{\gamma/2}\sigma_{e_\tau}\} = 1 - \gamma$$

or, equivalently,

$$P\{\hat{x}_{T+\tau}(T) + u_{\gamma/2}\sigma_{e_\tau} < x_{T+\tau} < \hat{x}_{T+\tau}(T) - u_{\gamma/2}\sigma_{e_\tau}\} = 1 - \gamma \qquad (6\text{-}38)$$

The interval

$$\hat{x}_{T+\tau}(T) \pm u_{\gamma/2}\sigma_{e_\tau} \qquad (6\text{-}39)$$

which has probability $1 - \gamma$ of containing the actual demand in period $T + \tau$, is called a *100(1 - γ)% prediction interval* for $x_{T+\tau}$.

In effect the above procedure provides estimates of the $100(\gamma/2)$ and $100(1 - \gamma/2)$ percentiles of the probability distribution of demand in period $T + \tau$. A one-sided prediction interval would require estimation of only one percentile; for example, we would estimate the $100(1 - \gamma)$ percentile as

$$\hat{x}_{T+\tau}(T) + u_{1-\gamma}\sigma_{e_\tau} \qquad (6\text{-}40)$$

The probability of demand being less than or equal to this value is $1 - \gamma$.

Equation (6-38) is strictly correct only if the forecast is unbiased and the forecast errors are normally distributed. The first requirement is satisfied for models developed by least squares, including exponential smoothing and direct smoothing procedures, provided the correct model form has been chosen to represent the time-varying behavior of the process mean. The normality assumption is often reasonable. If the $\{x_t\}$ are normally distributed, then, for forecasts based upon parameter estimates that are linear combinations of past demand, the forecast errors also will be normally distributed. The forecasting procedures we have studied are in this category. Even if the demand is nonnormal, these procedures yield forecast errors that are approximately normal for a wide range of demand patterns. (See Brown [9], chap. 19.) Thus, if the forecast is unbiased, we may use (6-39) or (6-40) to generate prediction intervals that are approximately correct.

We must know or have an estimate of the standard deviation of forecast error, $\sigma_{e_\tau}^2$, in order to compute a prediction interval. In Sec. 6-2.2 this variance was shown to be a function of the variance in the demand process, σ_ϵ^2, which generally is not known. Therefore, we use an estimate of $\sigma_{e_\tau}^2$ in computing prediction intervals. Then strictly speaking, we should use a somewhat larger multiplier than the standard normal values of $u_{\gamma/2}$ and $u_{1-\gamma}$ in Eqs. (6-39) and (6-40), respectively. However, as a practical matter, most analysts do not worry about this, assuming that the error in the probability statement will decrease as the amount of data smoothed increases and, more importantly, that they will not adversely affect decisions based on the probability statement. In Chap. 7, we shall describe procedures for efficiently estimating $\sigma_{e_\tau}^2$ and σ_ϵ^2 from historical data.

Prediction intervals can also be developed for cumulative forecasts. Using the same arguments as for the period forecast case, we find that the $100(1-\gamma)\%$ two-sided prediction interval for an L-period cumulative forecast made at time T is given by

$$\hat{X}_L(T) \pm u_{\gamma/2}\sigma_{E_L} \qquad (6\text{-}41)$$

where $\sigma_{E_L}^2$ is the variance of the cumulative forecast error and is defined by (6-33). An estimate of the $100(1-\gamma)$ percentile of the distribution of $X_L(T)$ is

$$\hat{X}_L(T) + u_{1-\gamma}\sigma_{E_L} \qquad (6\text{-}42)$$

Methods for estimating σ_{E_L} will be given in Chap. 7.

EXAMPLE 6-8 Suppose, as in Example 3-2, we are using exponential smoothing to forecast a linear trend process having $\sigma_\epsilon = 50$. Since double exponential smoothing is equivalent to direct smoothing for this process model, we can use the results of Examples 6-5 and 6-7 to establish prediction intervals. With $\alpha = 0.1$, the variance-covariance matrix of the $\{\hat{a}_i(T)\}$ is, by Eq. (6-24),

$$\mathbf{V} = \begin{bmatrix} 315.3 & 13.49 \\ 13.49 & 0.7290 \end{bmatrix}$$

Using Tables 6-3 and 6-4, we can compute the following standard deviations of forecast errors:

τ	$\sqrt{\mathrm{Var}[e_{\tau}(T+\tau)]}$	L	$\sqrt{\mathrm{Var}[E_L(T+L)]}$
1	53.32	1	53.32
2	53.59	2	80.18
3	53.88	3	104.16
4	54.17	4	127.26
5	54.48	5	150.23
6	54.80	6	173.41

If the lead time were three periods, we might want to compute prediction intervals for each period, as well as a prediction interval for the cumulative demand over all three periods. For a 90% prediction interval, we use $u_{0.95} = - u_{0.05} = 1.645$ from the standard normal table (A-1). This would give the following intervals:

$$\hat{x}_1(T) \pm (1.645)(53.32) = \hat{x}_1(T) \pm 87.71$$

$$\hat{x}_2(T) \pm (1.645)(53.59) = \hat{x}_2(T) \pm 88.16$$

$$\hat{x}_3(T) \pm (1.645)(53.88) = \hat{x}_3(T) \pm 88.63$$

$$\hat{X}_3(T) \pm (1.645)(104.16) = \hat{X}_3(T) \pm 171.34$$

Referring to Table 6-2, Example 6-3, we see that at the end of May 1977 the 90% prediction interval for demand in June would be 580 ± 87.71, or [492.29, 667.71], and the 90% prediction interval for cumulative demand in June, July, and August would be $1,769 \pm 171.34$, or [1,597.66, 1,940.34]. The forecasts made at the end of May could be consolidated as shown in Table 6-5, where the upper and lower prediction limits are based on $1 - \gamma = 0.90$.

TABLE 6-5   June, July, and August Forecasts

Month	Period forecast			Cumulative forecast		
	Lower	Expected	Upper	Lower	Expected	Upper
June	492	580	668	492	580	688
July	502	590	678	1,038	1,170	1,302
August	510	599	688	1,598	1,769	1,940

Note that the prediction-interval limits on the cumulative forecast are *not* simply the sum of the prediction limits on the period forecasts.

6-4 DIRECT ESTIMATION OF PERCENTILES OF THE DEMAND DISTRIBUTION

As explained in the previous section, prediction intervals provide information about the probability distribution of demand in a period. In effect, they are estimates of percentiles of the demand distribution computed by first estimating the mean and then adding proper multiples of the standard deviation of forecast error. When the demand process is constant, that is,

$$x_t = b + \epsilon_t$$

there is a simpler procedure available that directly forecasts the percentiles. It is a form of exponential smoothing and we describe it in this section.

Suppose that x_t has probability distribution function F; that is, $P\{x_t \leqslant \theta\} = F(\theta)$. Usually, the exact form of F is unknown and must be estimated. We require that F be stationary or changing very slowly with time. The forecasting problem is, for a given γ, $0 < \gamma < 1$, to find $\hat{\theta}_{1-\gamma}$, an estimate of $\theta_{1-\gamma}$, such that $F(\theta_{1-\gamma}) = 1 - \gamma$. That is, we wish to find an estimate of $\theta_{1-\gamma}$ such that the probability is $1 - \gamma$ of observing a demand in period t smaller than $\theta_{1-\gamma}$. Note that $\theta_{1-\gamma}$ is the $100(1 - \gamma)$ percentile of F.

Assume that the observations of demand are measured on a scale with n class limits, say

$$N_0 < N_1 < N_2 < \cdots < N_n$$

The class limits must be defined so that each observation x_t is assigned to one and only one class. That is, there is only one k such that

$$N_{k-1} < x_t \leqslant N_k$$

The class limits N_0 and N_n should be finite, so that interpolation can be carried out to estimate percentiles in the tail of the distribution, if desired. Ideally, there should be between 10 and 20 classes. They do not have to be of the same width, but may be defined to obtain more information about certain percentile ranges.

Let p_k be the probability that the random variable x_t falls in the interval from N_{k-1} to N_k; that is,

$$p_k = P\{N_{k-1} < x_t \leqslant N_k\} \qquad k = 1, 2, \ldots, n \qquad (6\text{-}43)$$

We see that $\sum_{k=1}^{n} p_k = 1$. Furthermore since

$$\sum_{j=1}^{k} p_j = P\{x_t \leqslant N_k\} = F(N_k)$$

we may estimate the unknown distribution function F by estimating the n unknown probabilities $p_1, p_2, \ldots, p_n$. We shall write these probabilities as an

$n \times 1$ column vector **p**, where

$$\mathbf{p} = \begin{bmatrix} p_1 \\ p_2 \\ \vdots \\ p_n \end{bmatrix}$$

and denote the estimates of these probabilities at time T as

$$\hat{\mathbf{p}}(T) = \begin{bmatrix} \hat{p}_1(T) \\ \hat{p}_2(T) \\ \vdots \\ \hat{p}_n(T) \end{bmatrix}$$

The estimate of $F(N_k)$ is $\hat{F}(N_k) = \sum_{j=1}^{k} \hat{p}_j(T)$.

To develop a procedure for computing the estimate of p_k, we define the random variable $v_k(T)$ as follows:

$$v_k(T) = \begin{cases} 1 & \text{if } N_{k-1} < x_T \leqslant N_K \\ 0 & \text{otherwise} \end{cases} \tag{6-44}$$

That is, $v_k(T) = 1$, if the demand in period T falls in the kth class interval. Note that $\sum_{t=1}^{T} v_k(t)$ is the total number of observations falling in interval k during the T periods. Let $\mathbf{v}(T)$ be the vector

$$\mathbf{v}(T) = \begin{bmatrix} v_1(T) \\ v_2(T) \\ \vdots \\ v_n(T) \end{bmatrix}$$

having $n-1$ elements equal to 0 and one element equal to 1.

Exponential smoothing is applied to revise $\hat{p}_k(T-1)$ in light of the current information $v_k(T)$:

$$\hat{p}_k(T) = \alpha v_k(T) + (1-\alpha)\hat{p}_k(T-1) \tag{6-45}$$

where $0 < \alpha < 1$ is the smoothing constant. This is done each period for all n

probabilities, so that we may describe the procedure in vector form by

$$\hat{\mathbf{p}}(T) = \alpha \mathbf{v}(T) + (1 - \alpha)\hat{\mathbf{p}}(T) \tag{6-46}$$

Brown [9] has referred to (6-46) as *vector smoothing*.

It may be shown that $\hat{p}_k(T)$ is an unbiased estimator; that is,

$$E[\hat{p}_k(T)] = p_k$$

and has variance

$$\mathrm{Var}[\hat{p}_k(T)] = \frac{\alpha}{2 - \alpha} p_k(1 - p_k) \tag{6-47}$$

This follows from the fact that $v_k(T)$ is a Bernoulli variable with parameter p_k.

An initial estimate of the probabilities $\hat{\mathbf{p}}(0)$ is required. This may be a subjective estimate, or it may be obtained through an analysis of historical data.

The results of smoothing are used generally to obtain estimates of certain desirable percentiles of the distribution F. From $\hat{\mathbf{p}}(T)$, we can compute the following:

$$\hat{F}(x) = \begin{cases} 0 & \text{if } x \leqslant N_0 \\ \sum_{j=1}^{k} \hat{p}_j(T) & \text{if } x = N_k, \, k = 1, 2, \ldots, n \\ 1 & \text{if } x \geqslant N_n \end{cases}$$

These values could be plotted on a graph and connected by a smooth curve to form the estimated cumulative probability distribution, $\hat{F}$. Then, if it is desired to estimate $\theta_{1-\gamma}$, where $F(\theta_{1-\gamma}) = 1 - \gamma$, $\hat{\theta}_{1-\gamma}$ could be determined graphically by reading the abscissa value corresponding to an ordinate value of $\hat{F} = 1 - \gamma$. Alternatively, this estimate could be obtained mathematically. If $1 - \gamma$ is such that one of the class limits exactly satisfies $\hat{F}(N_k) = 1 - \gamma$, the estimate is $\hat{\theta}_{1-\gamma} = N_k$. However, if

$$\hat{F}(N_{k-1}) < 1 - \gamma < \hat{F}(N_k)$$

we may estimate $\theta_{1-\gamma}$ by linear interpolation as

$$\hat{\theta}_{1-\gamma} = \frac{\left[\hat{F}(N_k) - (1 - \gamma)\right]N_{k-1} + \left[(1 - \gamma) - \hat{F}(N_{k-1})\right]N_k}{\hat{F}(N_k) - \hat{F}(N_{k-1})} \tag{6-48}$$

It may be desirable to use nonlinear interpolation schemes[1] near the tails of the distribution or if the class limits in the region of interest are widely spaced.

---

[1] A reference is Milne [39].

TABLE 6-6   Spare-Part Demand Distribution

k	Class limits N_{k-1}	N_k	Probability $\hat{p}_k(T-1)$	Cumulative $\hat{F}(N_k)$
1	0	20	0.10	0.10
2	20	40	0.20	0.30
3	40	50	0.40	0.70
4	50	60	0.20	0.90
5	60	80	0.10	1.00

EXAMPLE 6-9 At the end of period $T-1$, the data in Table 6-6 are available concerning the weekly usage of a certain spare part at an aircraft maintenance facility.   Suppose that the usage in week T is $x_T = 54$ units.   Thus the current observation vector is $\mathbf{v}'(T) = [0, 0, 0, 1, 0]$.   Using $\alpha = 0.1$, we update the probabilities by smoothing according to Eq. (6-46) to obtain

$$
\hat{\mathbf{p}}(T) = (0.1)\begin{bmatrix} 0 \\ 0 \\ 0 \\ 1 \\ 0 \end{bmatrix} + (0.9)\begin{bmatrix} 0.10 \\ 0.20 \\ 0.40 \\ 0.20 \\ 0.10 \end{bmatrix} = \begin{bmatrix} 0.09 \\ 0.18 \\ 0.36 \\ 0.28 \\ 0.09 \end{bmatrix}
$$

The new estimated distribution function is $\hat{F}(0) = 0$, $\hat{F}(20) = 0.09$, $\hat{F}(40) = 0.27$, $\hat{F}(50) = 0.63$, $\hat{F}(60) = 0.91$, and $\hat{F}(80) = 1.00$. If we wish to find the 85th percentile, we use Eq. (6-48) to interpolate as follows:

$$
\hat{\theta}_{0.85} = \frac{(0.91 - 0.85)(50) + (0.85 - 0.63)(60)}{0.91 - 0.63} = 57.9
$$

Based on this estimate, we would say that the probability of spare-part demand in a week being less than 58 units is 0.85.   Information of this nature would be useful in managing inventories.

6-5   EXERCISES

6-1   Using the closed-form expressions in Table 6-1, one can develop an equation of the form

$$
\hat{X}_L(T) = \sum_{i=1}^{k} c_i \hat{a}_i(T)
$$

to compute the forecast of cumulative demand in periods $T+1$ through $T+L$.

The $\{c_i\}$ will be functions of L, as in Examples 6-1 and 6-2. Do this for each of the following process models:

a. $x_t = b_1 + b_2 t + b_3 \dfrac{t^2}{2} + \epsilon_t$

b. $x_t = b_1 + b_2 t \sin \dfrac{2\pi}{12} t + b_3 \cos \dfrac{2\pi}{12} t + \epsilon_t$

c. $x_t = b_1 + b_2 e^t + \epsilon_t$

6-2 Suppose an N-period moving average is used to forecast demand from a constant process, $x_t = b + \epsilon_t$, where $V(x_t) = \sigma_\epsilon^2$. Find the variance of the following:
a. The forecast for period $T + \tau$, $\hat{x}_{T+\tau} = M_T$.
b. The cumulative forecast, $\hat{X}_L(T) = \sum_{\tau=1}^{L} \hat{x}_{T+\tau}$.
c. The forecast error, $e_1(T + 1) = x_{T+1} - \hat{x}_{T+1}(T)$.
d. The cumulative forecast error $= X_L(T) - \hat{X}_L(T)$.

6-3 Using the results of Exercise 6-2, write expressions for $100(1 - \gamma)$ percent prediction intervals for period and cumulative forecasts. How are these intervals affected by increasing τ and L?

6-4 Assume direct smoothing is used to forecast a constant process, $x_t = b + \epsilon_t$, where $V(x_t) = \sigma_\epsilon^2$. For this forecasting procedure, find the variances and prediction intervals required by Exercises 6-2 and 6-3.

6-5 Suppose direct smoothing is used to forecast the process

$$x_t = b_1 + b_2 t + b_3 \sin \omega t + b_4 \cos \omega t + \epsilon_t$$

where $\omega = \pi/6$ and $\sigma_\epsilon = 40$.
a. Calculate the variance-covariance matrix **V**.
b. Calculate a 95 percent prediction interval for x_{T+4}.
c. Calculate a 95 percent prediction interval for $X_4(T)$.

6-6 Suppose direct smoothing is used to forecast the process

$$x_t = b_1 + b_2 t + b_3 \dfrac{t^2}{2} + \epsilon_t$$

where $\sigma_\epsilon = 50$.
a. Calculate the variance-covariance matrix **V**.
b. Calculate a 90 percent prediction interval for x_{T+3}.
c. Calculate a 90 percent prediction interval for $X_3(T)$.

6-7 Suppose direct smoothing is used to forecast the linear trend process

$$x_t = b_1 + b_2 t + \epsilon_t$$

where $\sigma_\epsilon = 100$. At time T, estimates of the parameters on a current basis are $\hat{a}_1(T) = 2,000$ and $\hat{a}_2(T) = -40$. Use Tables 6-3 and 6-4 to aid in the following:
a. Compute 80 and 95 percent prediction intervals for demand in each of the next 10 periods. Do this for $\alpha = 0.10$ and $\alpha = 0.30$. Plot the results on a graph so that the effect of varying γ and α can be seen readily.

b. Compute 80 and 95 percent prediction intervals for cumulative demand for $L = 1, 2, \ldots, 10$. Do this for $\alpha = 0.10$ and $\alpha = 0.30$. Plot the results.

6-8 *Forecasting over variable-length lead times.* Suppose a forecast of cumulative demand over a decision lead time is required, but that there is considerable uncertainty about the required lead time length. An example would be the delivery lead time required in reordering from a vendor in an inventory control decision. If L is the lead time length in periods (that is, L is an integer multiple of the basic forecasting interval), and $g(L)$ is a probability distribution defined on L to express the uncertainty about lead time length, the expected cumulative demand is

$$E[X_L(T)] = \sum_{L=0}^{\infty} X_L(T)g(L)$$

where $X_L(T)$ is given by Eq. (6-4).
a. How would a forecast of cumulative demand be obtained?
b. In the situation of Example 6-3, suppose

$$g(L) = \begin{cases} 0.3 & \text{for } L = 1 \\ 0.5 & \text{for } L = 2 \\ 0.2 & \text{for } L = 3 \\ 0 & \text{otherwise} \end{cases}$$

What would be the estimate of expected lead time demand made at the end of July 1977?

6-9 The following result is sometimes useful when lead time length is a random variable. Let x_t be the demand in period t and assume a constant process, so that $E(x_t) = b$ and $V(x_t) = \sigma_\epsilon^2$. Let L be the lead time over which a cumulative forecast is required. Assume L is measured as an integer multiple of the forecasting period. Then the cumulative demand is

$$X_L(T) = x_{T+1} + x_{T+2} + \cdots + x_{T+L}$$

If the $\{x_t\}$ and L are independent random variables, it can be shown that

$$E[X_L(T)] = bE(L)$$

$$V[X_L(T)] = b^2 V(L) + E(L)\sigma_\epsilon^2$$

a. Verify these results.
b. What do the above reduce to when L is known with certainty?

6-10 When the lead time L is a random variable, as described in Exercise 6-8, how would a prediction interval for cumulative demand be developed?

6-11 In the situation of Exercise 6-8, how could the probability distribution of lead time length be developed? Could the smoothing method described in Sec. 6-4 be used to revise this distribution each time an observation on lead time length is obtained? Explain.

6-12   Show that the smoothing procedure given by Eq. (6-45) yields unbiased estimates. Also show that the variance of the estimator $\hat{p}_k$ is

$$\frac{\alpha}{2 - \alpha} \, p_k(1 - p_k)$$

6-13   Give an expression for an approximate $100(1 - \delta)$ percent confidence interval for elements of the probability vector $\hat{p}(T)$, defined in Eq. (6-46), where δ is the confidence level.

6-14   It is desired to forecast the probability distribution of the weekly demand for spare 10-horsepower electric motors used in the maintenance of a large chemical plant. The initial estimate of this distribution is as shown below:

Class, k	Upper class limit, N_k	Initial probability, $\hat{p}_k(0)$	Initial cumulative probability
1	4	0.10	0.10
2	8	0.15	0.25
3	12	0.25	0.50
4	16	0.25	0.75
5	20	0.20	0.95
6	24	0.04	0.99
7	30	0.01	1.00

The actual requirements for the first five weeks are 17, 22, 25, 18, and 21. For each week, find the revised probabilities using the smoothing procedure of Eq. (6-46) with $\alpha = 0.20$. Also compute $\hat{\theta}_{0.90}$, an estimate of the 90th percentile of the demand distribution, for each week. How could this type of forecast be used in establishing an inventory policy for control of spare motors?

6-15   The smoothing procedure described in Sec. 6-4 is being used to directly forecast percentiles of the distribution of weekly demand for a certain type of battery at a warehouse supplying a number of retail automotive supply stores. The results to date are the following:

Class	Upper class limit	Probability	Cumulative probability
1	10	0.02	0.02
2	20	0.07	0.09
3	30	0.12	0.21
4	40	0.24	0.45
5	50	0.22	0.67
6	60	0.18	0.85
7	70	0.12	0.97
8	80	0.03	1.00

    a. If demand in the next week is 24 batteries, what would be the revised estimate of the probability distribution?   Use $\alpha = 0.10$.

    b. Calculate an approximate 95 percent confidence interval for p_8.

    c. Estimate the 80th percentile, $\theta_{0.80}$.

6-16 A hotel has records showing the number of rooms occupied each day over a long interval.   These data are to be used to develop a probability distribution for the number of rooms demanded on a day.   The problem is that many nights the hotel has been full and no record of unfilled demand on those nights is available.   How would you proceed to use the historical data?   How would you proceed if it were desired to update the model periodically in the future?   Does the use for the probability model affect your choice of a forecasting procedure?

CHAPTER SEVEN

Analysis of Forecast Errors

No forecasting system will produce perfect forecasts of future observations. There will always be some difference between the forecast for period $T + \tau$, $\hat{x}_{T+\tau}(T)$, and the actual realization for that period, $x_{T+\tau}$. As in Chap. 6, we define the τ-period-ahead forecast error to be

$$e_\tau(T + \tau) = x_{T+\tau} - \hat{x}_{T+\tau}(T) \qquad (7\text{-}1)$$

where T is the point in time when the forecast was made.

Analysis of forecast errors can provide useful information about both the time series and the forecasting system. In this chapter, we describe methods for estimating properties of the distribution of forecast errors and for making inferences about the accuracy of the forecasting system. The former will be useful in establishing prediction interval forecasts (see Sec. 6-3) and the latter for monitoring and control of the forecasting process.

7-1 ESTIMATION OF EXPECTED FORECAST ERROR

The forecasting procedures described in previous chapters have involved (1) choosing a time series model to represent the demand process, (2) estimating the parameters of this model, and (3) extrapolating the estimated model into the future. We have assumed that the time series model is of the general form

$$x_t = \mu(t) + \epsilon_t \qquad (7\text{-}2)$$

where the expected value of x_t is $\mu(t)$, some mathematical function of t, and ϵ_t is a random component having mean 0 and variance σ_ϵ^2. Thus, in choosing a time series model, we are assuming the expected value of demand changes over time according to the mathematical model $\mu(t)$. If we have chosen the correct model, that is, if the process mean is changing with t in the assumed manner, and if the statistical procedure used to estimate parameters in the model yields unbiased estimates, then the expected forecast error will be zero. We can examine forecast errors to evaluate the adequacy of the model. If it does satisfactorily represent the process, we would expect the average value of the forecast errors to be near zero.

Given that we have a history of, say, single-period-ahead forecast errors, $e_1(1), e_1(2), \ldots, e_1(T)$, we have a choice of several statistics that could be used to estimate the expected forecast error. We could average all past errors to obtain

$$\overline{Y}_T = \frac{\sum_{t=1}^{T} e_1(t)}{T} \equiv \frac{Y(T)}{T} \tag{7-3}$$

where $Y(T)$ is defined implicitly as the sum of the forecast errors, or *cumulative error*. Often $Y(T)$ is used for forecast evaluation, rather than $\overline{Y}_T$, because one does not have to keep up with the value T to compute the cumulative error each period by

$$Y(T) = Y(T-1) + e_1(T) \tag{7-4}$$

Since we are primarily interested in the representativeness of the forecasting model in the near future, we logically might wish to give more weight to recent forecast errors than to older data. We could adopt the moving average concept and use only the last N errors in an average:

$$\frac{1}{N} \sum_{t=T-N+1}^{T} e_1(t) \tag{7-5}$$

or we could apply the exponential smoothing concept to obtain

$$Q(T) = \alpha e_1(T) + (1-\alpha)Q(T-1) \tag{7-6}$$

where $0 < \alpha < 1$ is the smoothing constant. We shall call $Q(T)$ the *smoothed error*. By the same argument used in Chap. 3 for simple exponential smoothing, we can show that $Q(T)$ is a weighted average of all past errors, where the weights decrease geometrically with age; that is,

$$Q(T) = \alpha \sum_{t=0}^{T-1} (1-\alpha)^t e_1(T-t) + (1-\alpha)^T Q(0)$$

where $Q(0) \equiv 0$. The larger the smoothing constant, the more relative weight is given to the more recent errors.

All of these statistics are linear combinations of past errors with weights adding to one. Therefore, each has an expected value of zero, if the expected forecast error is zero. Because of noise (σ_ϵ^2) in the time series, these statistics will be random variables, distributed about their means. At any time T, a statistic, such as $Q(T)$, could differ from zero, even though the expected forecast error is zero. Thus, to evaluate possible bias in the forecasting procedure, we would have to know something about the sampling variance of the random variable $Q(T)$.

In the next sections, we discuss estimation of the variance of forecast error and the variances of the statistics $Y(T)$ and $Q(T)$. The latter are commonly used in forecast control schemes, because of their limited data storage requirements and ease of computation.

7-2 ESTIMATION OF VARIANCES

7-2.1 Single-Period Forecast Error Variance

To estimate the variance of the single-period-ahead forecast error, $\mathrm{Var}[e_1(T)] \equiv \sigma_e^2$, we could compute the sample variance of the last N forecast errors:

$$\hat{\sigma}_e^2(T) = \frac{\displaystyle\sum_{t=T-N+1}^{T} [e_1(t) - \bar{e}_1(T)]^2}{N-1} \tag{7-7}$$

where $\bar{e}_1(T)$ is the average of the last N errors and is defined by Eq. (7-5); or, if we assume $E[e] = 0$,

$$\hat{\sigma}_e^2(T) = \frac{\displaystyle\sum_{t=T-N+1}^{T} [e_1(t)]^2}{N} \tag{7-8}$$

The amount of computation and data storage required to evaluate (7-7) or (7-8) each period makes this statistic less attractive than one based on the mean absolute deviation of forecast error.

Suppose that forecast error is normally distributed with mean ν, possibly different from zero, and variance σ_e^2. The *mean absolute deviation*, Δ, is

$$\Delta = E[|e - E(e)|]$$

$$= 2\int_\nu^\infty (e-\nu)(2\pi\sigma_e^2)^{-1/2} \exp\left(\frac{e-\nu}{\sigma_e}\right)^2 de$$

$$= \sqrt{\frac{2}{\pi}}\; \sigma_e \approx 0.8\sigma_e \tag{7-9}$$

This approximation also holds well for nonnormal errors. Thus, at the end of period T, if we had an estimate of Δ, we could estimate σ_e as

$$\hat{\sigma}_e(T) = 1.25\,\hat{\Delta}\,(T)$$

To estimate the mean absolute deviation, we could use statistics such as

$$\hat{\Delta}\,(T) = \frac{\displaystyle\sum_{t=T-N+1}^{T} |e_1(t) - \bar{e}_1(T)|}{N} \tag{7-10}$$

or

$$\hat{\Delta}\,(T) = \alpha|e_1(T) - Q(T)| + (1-\alpha)\,\hat{\Delta}\,(T-1) \tag{7-11}$$

since $\bar{e}_1(T)$ and $Q(T)$ estimate $E[e]$.   However, *under the hypothesis that $E[e]$* $= 0$, we can use

$$\hat{\Delta}\,(T) = \frac{\displaystyle\sum_{t=T-N+1}^{T} |e_1(t)|}{N} \tag{7-12}$$

or

$$\hat{\Delta}\,(T) = \alpha|e_1(T)| + (1-\alpha)\,\hat{\Delta}\,(T-1) \tag{7-13}$$

Equation (7-13) is more efficient and is the one generally used in practice.

7-2.2 Variance of the Demand Process

Given that we have an estimate of σ_e^2, we can estimate the variance of the observations, σ_ϵ^2, provided we know the mathematical relationship between σ_e^2 and σ_ϵ^2.   For example, using the results of Sec. 6-2.2, we can show that for simple exponential smoothing

$$\sigma_e^2 = \frac{2}{2-\alpha}\,\sigma_\epsilon^2 \tag{7-14}$$

Thus, for this model,

$$\hat{\sigma}_\epsilon^2 = \frac{2-\alpha}{2}\,\hat{\sigma}_e^2 = \frac{2-\alpha}{2}\,(1.25\,\hat{\Delta})^2 \tag{7-15}$$

As a second illustration, consider the analysis of direct smoothing of a linear trend process given in Example 6-5.   Equations (6-28) and (6-29), evaluated for $\tau = 1$, can be solved to express σ_e^2 in terms of σ_ϵ^2.

In general, for direct smoothing forecasting procedures it will be possible to determine a constant c_1 such that

$$\sigma_e^2 = c_1\sigma_\epsilon^2 \tag{7-16}$$

and, hence,

$$\hat{\sigma}_\epsilon^2 = \frac{\hat{\sigma}_e}{c_1} = \frac{(1.25\,\hat{\Delta})^2}{c_1} \tag{7-17}$$

To find a general form for c_1, we observe from Eqs. (6-8) and (6-13) that

$$\sigma_e^2 \equiv \mathrm{Var}[e_1(T+1)] = \sigma_\epsilon^2 + \mathbf{z}'(1)\mathbf{V}\mathbf{z}(1) \tag{7-18}$$

where $\mathbf{V}$ is given by Eq. (4-25) as

$$\mathbf{V} = \mathbf{G}^{-1}\mathbf{F}\mathbf{G}^{-1}\sigma_\epsilon^2 \tag{7-19}$$

The matrices $\mathbf{G}$ and $\mathbf{F}$ are defined in terms of the independent variables $\{z_i(t)\}$ and the discount factor β as

$$\mathbf{G} = \sum_{j=0}^{\infty} \beta^j \mathbf{z}(-j)\mathbf{z}'(-j)$$

and

$$\mathbf{F} = \sum_{j=0}^{\infty} \beta^{2j} \mathbf{z}(-j)\mathbf{z}'(-j)$$

Thus,

$$\sigma_e^2 = \left[1 + \mathbf{z}'(1)\mathbf{G}^{-1}\mathbf{F}\mathbf{G}^{-1}\mathbf{z}(1)\right]\sigma_\epsilon^2 \tag{7-20}$$

which is of the form (7-16). The constant c_1, which depends only on β, is

$$c_1 = 1 + \mathbf{z}'(1)\mathbf{G}^{-1}\mathbf{F}\mathbf{G}^{-1}\mathbf{z}(1) \tag{7-21}$$

For convenience in notation, we shall define the matrix

$$\mathbf{V}^* \equiv \frac{\mathbf{V}}{\sigma_\epsilon^2} = \mathbf{G}^{-1}\mathbf{F}\mathbf{G}^{-1} \tag{7-22}$$

Then

$$c_1 = 1 + \mathbf{z}'(1)\mathbf{V}^*\mathbf{z}(1) \tag{7-23}$$

7-2.3 Variance of τ-Period-Ahead Forecast Error

For direct smoothing, Eqs. (6-8) and (6-13) give

$$\sigma_{e_\tau}^2 \equiv \mathrm{Var}[e_\tau(T+\tau)] = \left[1 + \mathbf{z}'(\tau)\mathbf{V}^*\mathbf{z}(\tau)\right]\sigma_\epsilon^2$$

$$\equiv c_\tau \sigma_\epsilon^2 \tag{7-24}$$

where c_τ is a constant depending upon τ and β. Using Eq. (7-24), we can estimate the variance of the τ-period-ahead forecast as $c_\tau \hat{\sigma}_\epsilon^2$, provided we have an estimate of the variance of the demand process.

In most forecasting systems, however, the estimate of the mean absolute deviation of the single-period forecast error $\hat{\Delta}$ will be routinely computed, and it will be desirable to use this statistic as the basis for estimating $\text{Var}(e_\tau)$. We note that

$$\frac{\text{Var}(e_\tau)}{\text{Var}(e_1)} = \frac{c_\tau}{c_1} \equiv d_\tau \tag{7-25}$$

where d_τ is a constant for given τ and β. Our estimate is then

$$\hat{\sigma}_{e_\tau}^2 = d_\tau \hat{\sigma}_e^2 = d_\tau (1.25\hat{\Delta})^2 \tag{7-26}$$

We can use this result in Eq. (6-39) to compute a $100(1-\gamma)\%$ prediction interval estimate for $x_{T+\tau}$ as

$$\hat{x}_{T+\tau}(T) \pm u_{\gamma/2}\left[1.25\sqrt{d_\tau}\,\hat{\Delta}(T)\right] \tag{7-27}$$

Table 7-1 of Example 7-1 contains values of c_τ, d_τ, and $1.25\sqrt{d_\tau}$ for the linear model.

7-2.4 Cumulative Forecast Error Variance

For direct smoothing, Eqs. (6-32) and (6-33) define the variance of the L-period cumulative forecast error as the following function of σ_ϵ^2:

$$\sigma_{E_L}^2 \equiv \text{Var}[E_L(T+L)] = \left\{ L + \left[\sum_{\tau=1}^{L} \mathbf{z}(\tau) \right]' \mathbf{V}^* \left[\sum_{\tau=1}^{L} \mathbf{z}(\tau) \right] \right\} \sigma_\epsilon^2$$

$$\equiv p_L \sigma_\epsilon^2 \tag{7-28}$$

where p_L is a constant whose value depends upon β and L. For $L = 1$, we note that $p_1 = c_1$, where c_1 is defined by Eq. (7-23). Therefore,

$$\frac{\text{Var}(E_L)}{\text{Var}(E_1)} = \frac{p_L}{p_1} = \frac{p_L}{c_1} \equiv q_L \tag{7-29}$$

and we can estimate the cumulative forecast error variance by

$$\hat{\sigma}_{E_L}^2 = q_L \hat{\sigma}_{E_1}^2 = q_L \hat{\sigma}_e^2 = q_L (1.25\hat{\Delta})^2 \tag{7-30}$$

This result can be used in Eq. (6-41) to compute a $100(1-\gamma)\%$ prediction

TABLE 7-1   Factors for Computing Prediction Intervals for τ-Period-Ahead Forecasts from $\hat{\Delta}$, When Direct Smoothing Is Used for a Linear Model

	$\beta = 0.70$			$\beta = 0.75$		
τ	c_τ	d_τ	$1.25\sqrt{d_\tau}$	c_τ	d_τ	$1.25\sqrt{d_\tau}$
1	1.5062	1.2500	1.0000	1.3994	1.0000	1.2600
2	1.6528	1.3094	1.0973	1.4927	1.0667	1.2910
3	1.8213	1.3745	1.2092	1.5977	1.1417	1.3356
4	2.0118	1.4446	1.3357	1.7143	1.2250	1.3835
5	2.2243	1.5190	1.4768	1.8426	1.3167	1.4343
6	2.4588	1.5971	1.6324	1.9825	1.4167	1.4878
7	2.7152	1.6783	1.8027	2.1341	1.5250	1.5436
8	2.9937	1.7623	1.9876	2.2974	1.6417	1.6016
9	3.2941	1.8486	2.1870	2.4723	1.7667	1.6615
10	3.6165	1.9369	2.4011	2.6589	1.9000	1.7230
11	3.9809	2.0271	2.6297	2.8571	2.0417	1.7861
12	4.3273	2.1187	2.8730	3.0671	2.1917	1.8505

	$\beta = 0.80$			$\beta = 0.85$		
τ	c_τ	d_τ	$1.25\sqrt{d_\tau}$	c_τ	d_τ	$1.25\sqrt{d_\tau}$
1	1.3032	1.0000	1.2500	1.2161	1.0000	1.2500
2	1.3580	1.0421	1.2760	1.2445	1.0234	1.2645
3	1.4184	1.0884	1.3041	1.2751	1.0485	1.2800
4	1.4842	1.1389	1.3340	1.3078	1.0754	1.2963
5	1.5556	1.1937	1.3657	1.3426	1.1040	1.3134
6	1.6324	1.2526	1.3990	1.3796	1.1344	1.3314
7	1.7147	1.3158	1.4338	1.4187	1.1666	1.3501
8	1.8025	1.3832	1.4701	1.4599	1.2005	1.3696
9	1.8957	1.4547	1.5077	1.5032	1.2361	1.3898
10	1.9945	1.5305	1.5464	1.5487	1.2735	1.4106
11	2.0988	1.6105	1.5863	1.5964	1.3127	1.4321
12	2.2085	1.6947	1.6273	1.6461	1.3536	1.4543

	$\beta = 0.90$			$\beta = 0.95$		
τ	c_τ	d_τ	$1.25\sqrt{d_\tau}$	c_τ	d_τ	$1.25\sqrt{d_\tau}$
1	1.1372	1.0000	1.2500	1.0654	1.0000	1.2500
2	1.1489	1.0103	1.2564	1.0681	1.0025	1.2516
3	1.1611	1.0210	1.2631	1.0709	1.0051	1.2532
4	1.1739	1.0323	1.2700	1.0737	1.0078	1.2549
5	1.1873	1.0441	1.2773	1.0766	1.0105	1.2565
6	1.2013	1.0564	1.2848	1.0796	1.0133	1.2583
7	1.2159	1.0692	1.2925	1.0826	1.0161	1.2600
8	1.2311	1.0826	1.3006	1.0857	1.0191	1.2619
9	1.2468	1.0964	1.3089	1.0889	1.0220	1.2637
10	1.2632	1.1108	1.3174	1.0921	1.0251	1.2656
11	1.2801	1.1256	1.3262	1.0954	1.0282	1.2675
12	1.2976	1.1410	1.3353	1.0988	1.0313	1.2694

TABLE 7-2 Factors for Computing Prediction Intervals for Cumulative Forecasts from $\hat{\Delta}$, When Direct Smoothing Is Used for a Linear Model

L	$\beta=0.70$			$\beta=0.75$		
	p_L	q_L	$1.25\sqrt{q_L}$	p_L	q_L	$1.25\sqrt{q_L}$
1	1.5062	1.0000	1.2500	1.3994	1.0000	1.2500
2	4.3069	2.8595	2.1137	3.7784	2.7000	2.0540
3	8.8748	5.8922	3.0342	7.4344	5.3125	2.8811
4	15.7484	10.4557	4.0419	12.6997	9.0750	3.7656
5	25.5323	16.9514	5.1465	19.9417	14.2500	4.7186
6	38.8968	25.8243	6.3522	29.5627	21.1250	5.7452
7	56.5785	37.5635	7.6611	42.0000	30.0125	6.8480
8	79.3796	52.7016	9.0745	57.7259	41.2500	8.0283
9	108.1685	71.8151	10.5930	77.2478	55.2000	9.2871
10	143.8795	95.5243	12.2171	101.1079	72.2500	10.6250
11	187.5127	124.4932	13.9471	129.8834	92.8125	12.0424
12	240.1343	159.4297	15.7832	164.1866	117.3250	13.5396

L	$\beta=0.80$			$\beta=0.85$		
	p_L	q_L	$1.25\sqrt{q_L}$	p_L	q_L	$1.25\sqrt{q_L}$
1	1.3032	1.0000	1.2500	1.2161	1.0000	1.2500
2	3.3196	2.5474	1.9951	2.9203	2.4013	1.9370
3	6.2222	4.7747	2.7314	5.2009	4.2767	2.5850
4	10.2003	7.8274	3.4972	8.1530	6.7041	3.2365
5	15.4595	11.8632	4.3054	11.8777	9.7669	3.9065
6	22.2222	17.0526	5.1619	16.4827	13.5536	4.6019
7	30.7270	23.5789	6.0698	22.0822	18.1580	5.3265
8	41.2291	31.6379	7.0309	28.7966	23.6791	6.0826
9	54.0000	41.4379	8.0465	36.7527	30.2213	6.8717
10	69.3278	53.2000	9.1173	46.0837	37.8942	7.6948
11	87.5171	67.1579	10.2437	56.9295	46.8125	8.5525
12	108.8889	83.5579	11.4263	69.4360	57.0964	9.4453

L	$\beta=0.90$			$\beta=0.95$		
	p_L	q_L	$1.25\sqrt{q_L}$	p_L	q_L	$1.25\sqrt{q_L}$
1	1.1372	1.0000	1.2500	1.0654	1.0000	1.2500
2	2.5718	2.2615	1.8798	2.2671	2.1278	1.8234
3	4.3397	3.8162	2.4419	3.6131	3.3912	2.3019
4	6.4785	5.6969	2.9835	5.1120	4.7980	2.7381
5	9.0276	7.9385	3.5219	6.7722	6.3563	3.1515
6	12.0280	10.5769	4.0653	8.6026	8.0744	3.5519
7	15.5227	13.6500	4.6182	10.6123	9.9606	3.9451
8	19.5562	17.1969	5.1836	12.8103	12.0237	4.3344
9	24.1750	21.2585	5.7634	15.2062	14.2724	4.7224
10	29.4270	25.8769	6.3587	17.8095	16.7158	5.1106
11	35.3623	31.0962	6.9705	20.6300	19.3631	5.5004
12	42.0324	36.9615	7.5995	23.6777	22.2237	5.8928

interval for the cumulative demand, $X_L(T)$, as

$$\hat{X}_L(T) \pm u_{\gamma/2}\left[1.25\sqrt{q_T}\,\hat{\Delta}(T)\right] \qquad (7\text{-}31)$$

Table 7-2 of Example 7-1 contains values of p_L, q_L, and $1.25\sqrt{q_L}$ for the linear model.

EXAMPLE 7-1 *Linear trend model.* In direct smoothing of a linear model, we may wish to compute prediction intervals based on an estimate, $\hat{\Delta}(T)$, of the mean absolute deviation. It will be helpful to have tables of factors, such as c_τ, d_τ, p_L, and q_L, to facilitate these calculations. From Example 6-5,

$$c_\tau = 1 + \frac{\alpha}{(1+\beta)^3}\left[(1+4\beta+5\beta^2)+2\alpha(1+3\beta)\tau+2\alpha^2\tau^2\right]$$

and from Example 6-7,

$$p_L = L + \frac{\alpha L^2}{2(1+\beta)^3}\left[5(1+2\beta+\beta^2)+4(1-\beta^2)L+\alpha^2L^2\right]$$

Tables 7-1 and 7-2 were computed based on these relationships to give factors for period forecasts and cumulative forecasts, respectively.

7-3 TRACKING SIGNAL TESTS

Having developed statistics for estimating the mean and variance of forecast errors, we now turn to the problem of using these results to periodically monitor and control the forecasting process. Generally, a major concern is that the forecasts be unbiased, i.e., that the expected value of forecast error be zero. To test this hypothesis, we can measure the deviation of our estimate of expected forecast error from zero, relative to a measure of the natural variability of this statistic about its true mean. If this deviation is large, we would reject the hypothesis.

7-3.1 Tests Based on the Cumulative Forecast Error

Suppose we use the sum of forecast errors $Y(T)$, defined by Eq. (7-4), as our estimate of $E[e_1]$. At any time T, $Y(T)$ will undoubtedly differ from zero. There are two possible explanations: (1) The forecasts are unbiased and the deviation from zero is due to random variation; and (2) the forecasts are biased and the deviation is due to a combination of bias and random variation. To distinguish between the two cases, we need a measure of the natural random variation in the statistic $Y(T)$ about its mean. The standard deviation of $Y(T)$, σ_Y, provides this information. Assuming we can estimate σ_Y, we will conclude that the forecast is biased if $|Y(T)|$ is greater than some multiple, K_1, of $\hat{\sigma}_Y$, that is, if

$$\left| \frac{Y(T)}{\hat{\sigma}_Y} \right| > K_1 \qquad (7\text{-}32)$$

To estimate σ_Y, we seek a relationship between σ_Y^2 and σ_ϵ^2 in which we can use $\hat{\sigma}_\epsilon^2$ to obtain $\hat{\sigma}_Y^2$. Brown ([9], pp. 288–289) gives the following results for direct smoothing of constant and linear processes:

$$\sigma_Y^2 = \frac{1}{1 - \beta^2} \sigma_\epsilon^2 \qquad \text{constant} \qquad (7\text{-}33)$$

$$\sigma_Y^2 = \frac{2 - 2\alpha^3 + \alpha^4}{4 - \alpha - 4\alpha^2 + 2\alpha^3} \frac{1}{1 - \beta^2} \sigma_\epsilon^2 \qquad \text{linear} \qquad (7\text{-}34)$$

In general, for direct smoothing with an n-parameter forecasting model, Brown found through simulation studies that the following relationship is approximately correct:

$$\sigma_Y^2 = \frac{1}{1 - \beta^{2n}} \sigma_\epsilon^2 \qquad (7\text{-}35)$$

Normally, the decision rule given by Eq. (7-32) is operated using the mean absolute deviation $\hat{\Delta}$, rather than $\hat{\sigma}_Y$. Equation (7-17) expresses the relationship between $\hat{\sigma}_\epsilon^2$ and $\hat{\Delta}$, so that we can substitute (7-17) into (7-35), and then the result into (7-32) to obtain

$$\hat{\sigma}_Y \approx [c_1(1 - \beta^{2n})]^{-1/2}(1.25\hat{\Delta}) \qquad (7\text{-}36)$$

and

$$\left| \frac{Y(T)}{\hat{\Delta}(T)} \right| > \frac{1.25 K_1}{[c_1(1 - \beta^{2n})]^{1/2}} \equiv K_2 \qquad (7\text{-}37)$$

The ratio $Y(T)/\hat{\Delta}(T)$ is called the *tracking signal*, computed at time T. Each period the absolute value of the tracking signal is compared with the constant K_2 to test the hypothesis that the expected forecast error is zero. Since K_1 is usually chosen to be 2 or 3, it turns out that K_2 is typically between 4 and 6. Often, especially when dealing with models other than the constant model, one will choose K_2 directly, rather than computing it from c_1, K_1, and β, as indicated in Eq. (7-37).

EXAMPLE 7-2 *Constant model.* A tracking signal test for simple exponential smoothing can be developed if we recall that for the constant model

$$\sigma_e^2 = \frac{2}{2 - \alpha} \sigma_\epsilon^2$$

so that $c_1 = 2/(2 - \alpha)$.   Then, since $n = 1$,

$$K_2 = 1.25 K_1 \sqrt{\frac{2 - \alpha}{2(1 - \beta^2)}} = \frac{0.884}{\sqrt{\alpha}} K_1 \qquad (7\text{-}38)$$

If $\alpha = 0.10$ and $K_1 = 2$, the tracking signal limit is $K_2 = 5.59$, while if $\alpha = 0.30$ and $K_1 = 2$, then $K_2 = 3.23$.

EXAMPLE 7-3 *Linear model.*   If we are using double exponential smoothing or, equivalently, direct smoothing of a linear model, the tracking signal limit is computed from (7-37), using $n = 2$, and c_1 from Table 7-1, for the given β. Suppose $\alpha = 0.1$, so that $\beta = 0.9$.   We read $c_1 = 1.1372$ from Table 7-1, and calculate

$$K_2 = \frac{1.25 K_1}{\sqrt{(1.1372)\left[1 - (0.9)^4\right]}} = 2.00 K_1$$

If $K_1 = 2$ is selected, we conclude the forecast is biased if

$$\left| \frac{Y(T)}{\hat{\Delta}(T)} \right| > 4.00$$

7-3.2 Tests Based on the Smoothed Forecast Error

It is also possible to develop a tracking signal test based on the smoothed error statistic, $Q(T)$.   We would reject the hypothesis of an unbiased forecast if

$$\left| \frac{Q(T)}{\hat{\Delta}(T)} \right| > K_3 \qquad (7\text{-}39)$$

It is clear that the ratio $|Q(T)/\hat{\Delta}(T)|$ can never exceed 1.0.   The proper value of K_3 is usually between 0.2 and 0.5.

EXAMPLE 7-4 *Constant model.*   For a constant model, where the level of demand is estimated by exponential smoothing, Brown ([10], p. 165) has shown that

$$\sigma_Q^2 = \frac{\alpha}{(1 + \beta)^2} \sigma_e^2 \qquad (7\text{-}40)$$

If the tracking signal test is of the form $|Q(T)/\hat{\sigma}_Q| > K_1$, where K_1 is usually between 2 and 5, we can substitute to obtain the following equivalent forms:

$$\left| \frac{Q(T)}{\hat{\sigma}_e} \right| > \frac{\sqrt{\alpha}\, K_1}{1 + \beta}$$

or

$$\left| \frac{Q(T)}{\hat{\Delta}(T)} \right| > \frac{1.25\alpha}{1 + \beta} K_1 \equiv K_3 \qquad (7\text{-}41)$$

If $\alpha = 0.1$ and $K_1 = 2$, the tracking signal limit is $K_3 = 0.42$. If $\alpha = 0.3$ and $K_1 = 2$, then $K_3 = 0.81$.

Although the result given in Eq. (7-40) is for a constant model, it appears to be a reasonable approximation for other models. From simulation runs using a seasonal model similar to (5-42), Brown ([10], p. 161) found that $\sigma_Q \approx 0.55\sqrt{\alpha}\, \Delta$. Using this result in (7-41), we would obtain $K_3 = 0.35$, for $\alpha = 0.1$ and $K_1 = 2$, and $K_3 = 0.60$, for $\alpha = 0.3$ and $K_1 = 2$. These are large values for α when a six-parameter model is being used. (The concept of an equivalent smoothing constant was described in Sec. 3-4.) For a more reasonable value, such as $\alpha = 1 - (1 - 0.1)^{1/6} = 0.0174$, the approximation would give $K_3 = 0.15$, for $K_1 = 2$, and $K_3 = 0.22$, for $K_1 = 3$.

The smoothed error form of the tracking signal appears to have several advantages relative to the cumulative error version. Suppose that there was a large, but random, error in the forecast for a particular time period. This would increase both the smoothed error and the cumulative error, but assume that the increase is not quite enough to generate an out-of-control signal. Now suppose that several periods go by with small errors averaging zero. The cumulative error remains at its large value, but the smoothed error decreases toward zero. At some point in time, a second large, random error with the same sign as the previous one occurs. The cumulative error tracking signal would incorrectly generate an out-of-control signal, but the smoothed error version would not.

As a second example, suppose the cumulative error tracking signal was just less than the control limit, and a period having zero forecast error occurs. The cumulative error would not change, but the mean absolute deviation estimate would become smaller. The net effect would be to increase the value of the tracking signal, perhaps above the control limit. If the smoothed error tracking signal had been employed, the perfect forecast would have caused the smoothed error to decrease along with the mean absolute deviation, resulting in little change in the tracking signal.

Finally, some adaptive methods for automatically responding to out-of-control signals make use of the smoothed error statistic $Q(T)$. An example is the method of Trigg and Leach, discussed in Sec. 8-1.

7-3.3 Forecast Control

When the tracking signal exceeds the control limit for two or more successive periods, this is a strong indication that something is wrong with the forecasting system and that corrective action is called for. In some procedures, particularly if the constant K_1 is large, a single out-of-control point will trigger action. The action to be taken depends upon the likely cause of the out-of-control condition. Several possibilities exist:

1. The out-of-control point is caused by random variation alone. In this case, no action should be taken. However, the tracking signal test was made specifically to evaluate this possibility. Values outside the limits are assumed to be the result of other than chance causes. Naturally, a mistake can be made, but its likelihood can be made small by choosing a large value for K_1.

2. The parameter estimates used in the forecasting model are not accurate because the true parameter values have changed with time. The model form is still correct, but improved estimates of the model parameters are required. This can be done by increasing the smoothing constant for a number of periods, so that more weight is given to current data and the parameter estimates are smoothed more rapidly. When the forecast appears to be back in control, the smoothing constant can be returned to its normal value. Alternatively, one could use one of several schemes that continually modify the smoothing constant, as a function of forecast error, and thereby correct, or adapt, the model to slow changes in the process parameters. Some of these procedures are described in Chap. 8. If the process parameters change rapidly, direct management intervention to reset parameter estimates may be required.

3. The model may not accurately describe the time series process. Terms may be added or deleted to obtain a better representation of how the process mean changes with time. The demand process may be highly autocorrelated, in which case models of the type described in Chap. 9 should be employed.

4. The variance of the demand process may have increased. If so, a higher smoothing constant can be used in computing $\hat{\Delta}$. This would affect both the tracking signal value and the control limits, since the latter are functions of $\hat{\Delta}$.

When the tracking signal goes out of control and after corrective action has been effected, the quantity $Q(T)$, or $Y(T)$, should be reset to zero to prevent a false out-of-control signal in the future.

7-4 INITIAL VALUES

When starting the forecasting procedure, initial values must be supplied for $\hat{\Delta}$ and Q, or Y. It is reasonable to assume that the model is correct and that the initial parameter estimates are unbiased. Therefore, $Q(0) = 0$, or $Y(0) = 0$, is the starting value. The choice of $\hat{\Delta}(0)$ is not so easy. Since we believe that there is some random variation in the process, that is, that $\sigma_\epsilon^2 > 0$, we believe that $\sigma_e^2 > 0$ and hence that $\Delta > 0$; therefore, we should *never* set $\hat{\Delta}(0) = 0$. There are three commonly used objective methods for estimating Δ initially:

1. If least-squares methods are used to fit the model to historical data, the variance of the residuals [see Eq. (2-25)] provides an estimate of σ_ϵ^2. Knowing the relationship between σ_ϵ^2, σ_e^2, and Δ, one can convert $\hat{\sigma}_\epsilon^2$ into $\hat{\Delta}(0)$.

2. If the model is used in a retrospective simulation with actual historical data, the single-period forecast errors can be analyzed to obtain an estimate of Δ directly, or alternatively, σ_e^2, from which $\hat{\Delta}(0)$ can be computed.

3. Often there is a relationship between the mean absolute deviation and the average level of demand. Brown ([9], chap. 20) reports a study, involving several thousand product items, in which the following well-defined relation between the standard deviation of forecast error, σ_e, and the average demand rate, a, was found:

$$\sigma_e = 0.82 a^{0.75}$$

Using $\Delta = 0.8\sigma_e$, this is equivalent to $\Delta = 0.66 a^{0.75}$. Thus, in this situation, a new product having an estimated initial expected demand of $\hat{\mu}(0)$ would use a starting mean absolute deviation of

$$\hat{\Delta}(0) = 0.66 [\, \hat{\mu}(0)]^{0.75}$$

Naturally, to determine such a relationship for specific product families will require analysis of considerable historical data.

EXAMPLE 7-5 In Example 3-2, double exponential smoothing was applied to forecast a linear trend process. To determine the initial estimates of the slope and intercept, simple linear regression methods were used to fit a linear model to two years of historical data. The fitted model was

$$\hat{x}_t = 275.00 + 10.88 t$$

where t is based on the original origin. For $t = 1, 2, \ldots, 24$, the residuals $x_t - \hat{x}_t$ were computed. The historical data, the fitted model, and the residuals are shown in Table 7-3. The sum of the residuals is, of course, zero, and the sum of squared residuals is 68,215.44. The demand variance is estimated by

$$\hat{\sigma}_\epsilon^2 = \frac{\sum_{t=1}^{n} (x_t - \hat{x}_t)^2}{n - 2} = \frac{68,215.44}{24 - 2} = 3,100.70$$

so that $\hat{\sigma}_\epsilon = 55.68$. Since $\sigma_e^2 = c_1 \sigma_\epsilon^2$ and $\Delta = 0.8\sigma_e$, we take as the initial value for the mean absolute deviation

$$\hat{\Delta}(0) = 0.8\sqrt{c_1}\, \hat{\sigma}_\epsilon$$

$$= 0.8\sqrt{1.1372}\,(55.68) = 47.50$$

TABLE 7-3   Results of Fitting Linear Model to Filter Sales Data

Year and month		Period, t	Sales, x_t	Fitted model, $\hat{x}_t$	Residual, $x_t - \hat{x}_t$
1975	Jan.	1	317	285.88	31.12
	Feb.	2	194	296.76	− 102.76
	Mar.	3	312	307.64	4.36
	Apr.	4	316	318.52	−2.52
	May	5	322	329.40	−7.40
	June	6	334	340.28	−6.28
	July	7	317	351.16	− 34.16
	Aug.	8	356	362.04	− 6.04
	Sept.	9	428	372.92	55.08
	Oct.	10	411	383.80	27.20
	Nov.	11	494	394.68	99.32
	Dec.	12	412	405.56	6.44
1976	Jan.	13	460	416.44	43.56
	Feb.	14	395	427.32	− 32.32
	Mar.	15	392	438.20	− 46.20
	Apr.	16	447	449.08	−2.08
	May	17	452	459.96	−7.96
	June	18	571	470.84	100.16
	July	19	517	481.72	35.28
	Aug.	20	397	492.60	−95.60
	Sept.	21	410	503.48	− 93.48
	Oct.	22	579	514.36	64.64
	Nov.	23	473	525.24	− 52.24
	Dec.	24	558	536.12	21.88

The model was used in Example 3-2 to simulate forecasting for the next two years, 1977 and 1978. Results are displayed in Tables 3-5 and 6-2. Some of this information is repeated in Table 7-4, where we show computation of the tracking signal. Both the cumulative error and the smoothed error tests are shown, although in practice only one of them would be applied. At the end of January (now month $T = 1$), the calculations are

$$e_1(1) = x_1 - \hat{x}_1(0) = 538 - 541 = -3$$

$$\hat{\Delta}(1) = \alpha|e_1(1)| + (1 - \alpha)\hat{\Delta}(0)$$

$$= (0.1)(3) + (0.9)(47.50) = 43.05$$

$$Y(1) = Y(0) + e_1(1) = 0 + (-3) = -3$$

$$Q(1) = \alpha e_1(1) + (1 - \alpha)Q(0)$$

$$= (0.1)(-3) + (0.9)(0) = -0.3$$

TABLE 7-4   Tracking Signal Computation for Example 7-5

		T	$e_1(T)$	$\hat{\Delta}(T)$	$Y(T)$	$Q(T)$	$Y(T)/\hat{\Delta}(T)$	$Q(T)/\Delta(T)$
1977	Jan.	1	-3	43.05	-3	-0.30	-0.07	-0.01
	Feb.	2	19	40.65	16	1.63	0.39	0.04
	Mar.	3	35	40.08	51	4.97	1.27	0.12
	Apr.	4	-18	37.87	33	2.67	0.87	0.07
	May	5	-105	44.59	-72	-8.10	-1.61	-0.18
	June	6	24	42.53	-48	-4.89	-1.13	-0.11
	July	7	-68	45.08	-116	-11.20	-2.57	-0.25
	Aug.	8	12	41.77	-104	-8.88	-2.49	-0.21
	Sept.	9	1	37.69	-103	-7.89	-2.73	-0.21
	Oct.	10	178	51.72	75	10.70	1.45	0.21
	Nov.	11	57	52.25	132	15.33	2.53	0.29
	Dec.	12	-27	49.73	105	11.10	2.11	0.22
1978	Jan.	13	-60	50.75	45	3.99	0.89	0.08
	Feb.	14	4	46.08	49	3.99	1.06	0.09
	Mar.	15	-18	43.27	31	1.79	0.72	0.04
	Apr.	16	-32	42.14	-1	-1.59	-0.02	-0.04
	May	17	-96	47.53	-97	-11.03	-2.04	-0.23
	June	18	43	47.08	-54	-5.63	-1.15	-0.12
	July	19	-1	42.47	-55	-5.17	-1.30	-0.12
	Aug.	20	38	42.02	-17	-0.85	-0.40	-0.02
	Sept.	21	-18	39.62	-35	-2.56	-0.88	-0.06
	Oct.	22	40	39.66	5	1.69	0.13	0.04
	Nov.	23	-45	40.19	-50	-2.98	-1.24	-0.07
	Dec.	24	4	36.57	-46	-2.28	-1.26	-0.06

where $\alpha = 0.1$ is the chosen smoothing constant. Similar computations are made for each period, once the error for that period is known.

Examining the tracking signal values, we observe that both types remained well in control during the simulation. This was to be expected, since the demand data were generated from a stationary normal process having a linear trend with slope $a_2 = 10$ and standard deviation $\sigma_\epsilon = 50$. Time series encountered in practice are not this well behaved.

7-5 SCREENING OF OBSERVATIONS

An implied assumption in using the regression and direct smoothing approaches to time series forecasting is that the model parameters do not change over time. Actually, however, in the discounting procedure of direct smoothing, we allow for slow drifts in these parameters and assume that the smoothing will be rapid enough to obtain a satisfactory tracking of the process. The use of a tracking signal test, such as those described in Sec. 7-3, allows detection of any changes in the process that require additional action to modify the forecasting model so that it will be more representative of the process in the future.

However, in many situations there will be *short* intervals of time when the demand process is distinctly different from its usual form.   Use of demand data observed during these periods in the smoothing of parameter estimates may seriously bias future forecasts.   For example, a soft drink bottler may promote a particular flavor and package size by offering a price discount during a two-week period.   Sales of this product during the promotional period would undoubtedly follow a different probability distribution than during a normal period.   These sales figures should not be used in smoothing and tracking signal computations.   (Such data would, however, be valuable in attempting to predict the effect of future price promotions on sales.)

Observations can be excluded by direct action of a manager who feels that they are biased by some temporary condition that he or she is aware of, such as the price promotion mentioned above, or a strike at a competitor's plant, or heavy sales because customers expect a price increase.   Also, in addition to providing for data exclusion through management initiative, it may be desirable to automatically screen all current observations to identify those that appear unusual, or *outliers*, as a statistician might refer to them.   Each outlier could be called to the attention of an appropriate management person, who would then decide whether or not to include the observation in the forecasting process.

Outliers can be identified by analyzing the forecast error $e_1(T) = x_T - \hat{x}_T(T-1)$.   If this error is large, it may be concluded that the observation x_T came from a different process.   The test for outliers might logically take the form

$$\left| \frac{e_1(T)}{\hat{\sigma}_e} \right| > K$$

where K is 4 or 5, or more conveniently,

$$\left| \frac{e_1(T)}{\hat{\Delta}(T)} \right| > 1.25 K \qquad (7\text{-}42)$$

If the inequality holds, x_T is considered an outlier.

Automatic exclusion of outliers is not desirable, because they may be the result of a permanent change in process characteristics.   It is better to present them to an informed person and let that person make the decision.

The same approach can be used in analyzing historical data in order to select the model form and develop initial values for model parameters.   Some of the data may be nontypical and should be excluded from the analysis.

7-6 EXERCISES

7-1   What is the probability that a normally distributed random variable will differ from its mean by more than twice its mean absolute deviation?

7-2   In Eq. (7-9), the mean absolute deviation of a normally distributed random variable is shown to be $\sqrt{2/\pi} \approx 0.798$ times its standard deviation. Consider a uniformly distributed random variable having probability density

$$f(x) = \begin{cases} \dfrac{1}{R} & M < x < M + R \\ 0 & \text{otherwise} \end{cases}$$

Show that this variable has variance $\sigma^2 = R^2/12$ and mean absolute deviation $\Delta = R/4$. Thus $\Delta = (\sqrt{3}/2)\sigma \approx 0.866\sigma$, which is close to the result for a normal distribution.

7-3 In Eq. (7-17), a scheme for estimating the variance of the demand process, σ_ϵ^2, from the estimated mean absolute deviation of the forecast error is given. Consider the following alternative methods that also make use of the demand history available at time T:

a. $\hat{\sigma}_\epsilon^2(T) = \sum_{t=1}^{T} \dfrac{(x_t - \bar{x})^2}{T-1}$ where $\bar{x} = \dfrac{1}{T}\sum_{t=1}^{T} x_t$

b. $\hat{\sigma}_\epsilon^2(T) = \dfrac{1.25}{T}\sum_{t=1}^{T} |x_t - \bar{x}|$

c. $\hat{\sigma}_\epsilon^2(T) = \alpha(x_T - \hat{x}_T)^2 + (1-\alpha)\hat{\sigma}_\epsilon^2(T-1)$ where $\hat{x}_T = \hat{x}_T(T-1)$

What can you say about the appropriateness, accuracy, and efficiency of these methods? What procedure would you recommend for estimating σ_ϵ^2?

7-4 Suppose the demand for a spare part over its replenishment lead time is thought to be Poisson distributed. Denote total lead time demand by X_L and average lead time demand (based on a number of observations) by $\bar{X}_L$. Consider using as an estimator of the standard deviation of demand the statistic

$$\hat{\sigma}_x = \sqrt{\bar{X}_L}$$

Do you think that this is a reasonable estimator? Explain.

7-5 What role, if any, do goodness-of-fit procedures such as the Kolmogorov-Smirnov test and the chi-square test play in developing forecasts?

7-6 Direct smoothing with $\beta = 0.9$ is being used to forecast the linear trend process $x_t = b_1 + b_2 t + \epsilon_t$. Assume that at time T, the smoothed statistics are $\hat{a}_1(T) = 100$, $\hat{a}_2(T) = 10$, and $\hat{\Delta}(T) = 4$.
a. Estimate σ_e and σ_ϵ.
b. Calculate a 95 percent confidence interval estimate for the trend component, b_2.
c. Compute a 90 percent prediction interval for the cumulative demand in periods $T+1$ and $T+2$.
d. In period $T+1$, the actual demand is 106. What are the new values of the smoothed statistics?
e. What is the equivalent smoothing constant for single smoothing?

7-7 For the situation of Exercise 7-6, develop a tracking signal test based on the sum of the forecast errors, $Y(T)$, to test the hypothesis that the forecast is unbiased.

7-8   Repeat Exercise 7-6 using the smoothed error, $Q(T)$, instead of $Y(T)$.

7-9   First-order exponential smoothing is used to forecast demand from a constant process, $x_t = b + \epsilon_t$, where $V(x_t) = \sigma_\epsilon^2$. The tracking signal has as its numerator the following estimator of the expected forecast error:

$$Y(T) = Y(T-1) + e_1(T)$$

where $e_1(T) = x_T - \hat{x}_T(T-1)$.   Show that

$$Y(T) = \sum_{t=1}^{T} \beta^{T-t} x_t - \frac{1 - \beta^T}{1 - \beta} S_0$$

and then, assuming the $\{x_t\}$ are mutually independent random variables, that

$$\sigma_Y^2 = \frac{1 - \beta^{2T}}{1 - \beta^2} \sigma_\epsilon^2$$

Thus, for large T,

$$\sigma_Y^2 = \frac{1}{1 - \beta^2} \sigma_\epsilon^2$$

7-10   You are forecasting the process

$$x_t = b_1 z_1(t) + b_2 z_2(t) + \epsilon_t$$

using direct smoothing.   At the end of period T, you have estimates $\hat{a}_1(T)$, $\hat{a}_2(T)$, and $\hat{\Delta}(T)$.   Also you have computed the matrix $\mathbf{V}^* = \mathbf{G}^{-1}\mathbf{FG}$.   Write an equation in terms of the elements $\{V_{ij}^*\}$ of $\mathbf{V}^*$ for estimating σ_ϵ^2 from $\hat{\Delta}(T)$.

7-11   Develop a general form, similar to Eq. (7-37), for a tracking signal test for direct smoothing applied to a linear trend model using the cumulative error $Y(T)$ and the exact expression for σ_Y^2 given in Eq. (7-34).   Calculate the control limits for $\beta = 0.9$ and compare with the results of Example 7-3.

7-12   Suppose a seasonal time series process can be represented by the model

$$x_t = b_1 + b_2 \sin \frac{2\pi}{12} t + b_3 \cos \frac{2\pi}{12} t + \epsilon_t$$

Direct smoothing with $\beta = 0.9$ is used to estimate the parameters in the current-origin forecasting equation

$$\hat{x}_{T+\tau}(T) = \hat{a}_1(T) + \hat{a}_2(T)\sin \frac{2\pi}{12} \tau + \hat{a}_3(T)\cos \frac{2\pi}{12} \tau$$

Assume that at time T, the smoothed statistics are $\hat{a}_1(T) = 1{,}000$, $\hat{a}_2(T) = -100$, $\hat{a}_3(T) = 20$, and $\hat{\Delta}(T) = 40$.
a. Estimate σ_e and σ_ϵ.
b. Calculate a 95 percent confidence interval estimate for the constant term, $a_1(T)$.

c. Calculate a 95 percent prediction interval for the cumulative demand in the next six periods.

d. In period $T + 1$, the actual demand is 900. What are the new values of the smoothed statistics?

e. What is the equivalent smoothing constant for single smoothing?

7-13 For the situation of Exercise 7-12, develop a procedure to test the hypothesis that the forecast is unbiased using (*a*) the sum of the forecast errors, $Y(T)$, and (*b*) the smoothed forecast error, $Q(T)$.

7-14 Develop a tracking signal test for use with Winters' model for seasonal processes, described in Sec. 5-1.

7-15 Consider the time series process represented by the model

$$x_t = b_1 + b_2 t \sin \frac{2\pi}{12} t + b_3 t \cos \frac{2\pi}{12} t + \epsilon_t$$

Suppose direct smoothing with $\beta = 0.9$ is used to estimate the parameters on a current-origin basis. At time T, the smoothed statistics are $\hat{a}_1(T) = 600$, $\hat{a}_2(T) = 30$, $\hat{a}_3(T) = -70$, and $\hat{\Delta}(T) = 20$.

a. Estimate σ_e and σ_ϵ.

b. Calculate a 95 percent confidence interval estimate for the constant term, $a_1(T)$.

c. Compute a 90 percent prediction interval for the cumulative demand in the next four periods.

d. In period $T + 1$, the actual demand is 900. What are the new values of the smoothed statistics?

e. What is the equivalent smoothing constant for single smoothing?

7-16 Assuming σ_ϵ^2 is known, how can one test for the significance of a coefficient b_i in the model? Propose a procedure to test the null hypothesis $H_0: b_i = 0$ versus the alternative $H_1: b_i \neq 0$. How would you proceed if σ_ϵ^2 were unknown and only $\hat{\Delta}$ were available?

CHAPTER EIGHT

Adaptive-Control Forecasting Methods

Forecasting systems that employ exponential smoothing assume that the time series of interest arises from some underlying stable process which depends only on time, and that successive observations consist of this deterministic component plus a random error or noise component. Regardless of the type of exponential smoothing technique chosen, the ability of the forecasting system to follow, or track, changes in the underlying time series model depends mainly on the value of the smoothing constant. If the smoothing constant is relatively small, more weight is given to the historical data. On the other hand, if the smoothing constant is large, more weight is placed on the current observation.

A major drawback of exponential smoothing is that it is difficult to select an "optimum" value of the smoothing constant without making some restrictive assumptions about the behavior of the time series. This problem is compounded when the form of the underlying time series model is changing. If the smoothing constant is left unchanged during these periods, it may take an unacceptably long time for the smoothing technique to react to, or track, the new process. Tracking signals, as discussed in Chap. 7, can be used to detect situations in which the process is changing. Forecast control procedures based on the tracking signal usually require direct management action as part of the control procedure. That is, the control procedures are not automatic; someone must personally intervene and change the value of the smoothing constant. However, when forecasts are being made regularly for a large number of time series, it may be quite time-consuming for management to examine effectively all series for which the tracking signal indicates an out-of-control condition. In these situations, it is usually desirable to treat the smoothing constant (or constants) as a *parameter*, and control its value automatically.

Several techniques have been developed to monitor and modify automatically the value of the smoothing constant in exponential smoothing. These techniques are usually called *adaptive-control* smoothing methods, because the smoothing parameter modifies or *adapts* itself to changes in the underlying time series. The decision rules employed in these adaptive-control methods are usually quite simple, and are easily executed by a computer without management intervention.

In this chapter, we shall present two methods for the automatic control of a single smoothing parameter, and two methods suitable for a smoothing technique using several parameters.

8-1 SINGLE-PARAMETER METHODS

Trigg and Leach [59] have described a procedure for adaptive control of a single exponential smoothing constant. Thus, their method would be applicable to any form of exponential smoothing that utilizes only one smoothing constant, such as, for example, simple smoothing

$$S_T = \alpha x_T + (1 - \alpha)S_{T-1}$$

for a constant process. The Trigg and Leach method is based on the smoothed error tracking signal

$$\frac{Q(T)}{\hat{\Delta}(T)} \tag{8-1}$$

where $Q(T)$ is the smoothed forecast error and $\hat{\Delta}(T)$ is the smoothed mean absolute deviation, both computed at the end of period T. The smoothed error is computed according to

$$Q(T) = \gamma e_1(T) + (1 - \gamma)Q(T - 1) \tag{8-2}$$

and the smoothed mean absolute deviation is

$$\hat{\Delta}(T) = \gamma |e_1(T)| + (1 - \gamma)\hat{\Delta}(T - 1) \tag{8-3}$$

where $e_1(T)$ is the forecast error in period T and γ is a smoothing constant such that $0 < \gamma < 1$.

The smoothed error tracking signal is discussed in Sec. 7-3.2. It is clear from Eq. (8-1) that the smoothed error tracking signal always lies in the interval $[-1, +1]$. If the forecasting system is performing adequately, the value of the tracking signal will be small, near zero, and we say that the forecasting system is "in control." If the underlying form of the time series changes, the forecasting

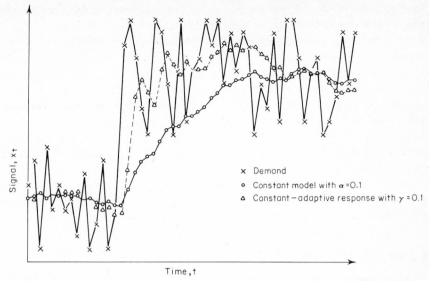

Signal, x_t

Time, t

× Demand

o Constant model with $\alpha = 0.1$

△ Constant-adaptive response with $\gamma = 0.1$

Fig. 8-1 Performance of the Trigg and Leach method for a constant model. (*Adapted from D. W. Trigg and A. G. Leach, "Exponential Smoothing with an Adaptive Response Rate,"* Operational Research Quarterly, *vol. 18, no. 1, 1967. By permission of the publisher.*)

system will eventually begin to generate large errors and the tracking signal will move towards either plus or minus unity.   That is, the forecasting system is "out of control."

A simple forecast control strategy is to increase the smoothing constant when the tracking signal indicates an out-of-control condition so as to give more weight to the recent data and allow the system to more rapidly track the new signal.   When the system has stabilized, however, the value of the smoothing constant should be reduced.   Trigg and Leach automatically adjust the value of the smoothing constant by setting

$$\alpha(T) = \left| \frac{Q(T)}{\hat{\Delta}(T)} \right| \tag{8-4}$$

That is, the value of the smoothing constant in period T, $\alpha(T)$, is set equal to the absolute value of the smoothed error tracking signal in period T.

The performance of the Trigg and Leach adaptive-control technique is illustrated in Fig. 8-1.   In Fig. 8-1, the line (×) represents a signal generated from a constant model, with a step function occurring after the 15th realization. The line (O) depicts the response of simple exponential smoothing with $\alpha = 0.1$. The dashed line represents the response of simple smoothing with adaptive control of the smoothing constant $\alpha(T)$; that is, $\alpha(T)$ is determined from Eq. (8-4).   The adaptive-control scheme uses $\gamma = 0.1$ in computing the tracking signal.   We see that the adaptive-control system reacts much more quickly to the step function than does conventional, or nonadaptive, smoothing.   The performance of the adaptive method before and after the step is the same as conventional smoothing.

Trigg and Leach also applied their adaptive control method to the direct smoothing models discussed in Chap. 4 and Sec. 5-3. These models utilize a smoothing vector **h** which depends on the discount factor β, where $0 < \beta < 1$. They experimented with making the entire **h** vector a function of the tracking signal by defining the discount factor in period t for a model with k components as

$$\beta(T) = \left(1 - \left|\frac{Q(T)}{\hat{\Delta}(T)}\right|\right)^{1/k} \tag{8-5}$$

Numerical experiments indicated that this approach caused overshoot and instability. Most direct smoothing models contain a constant as the first term, and the first element of the smoothing vector, say $h_1(T)$, operates on the constant term. If the adaptive-control scheme is applied only to $h_1(T)$, that is, if we set

$$h_1(T) = \left|\frac{Q(T)}{\hat{\Delta}(T)}\right| \tag{8-6}$$

then a stable forecasting system that has improved dynamic response characteristics will result.

While the Trigg and Leach method works quite well for the case of a single smoothing constant, it is not clear how the procedure would be extended to a smoothing technique that utilizes *several* smoothing constants, such as Winters' method (Sec. 5-1). Chow [15] has described a procedure for adaptive control of a single exponential smoothing constant which can be easily extended to the multiple-parameter case.

Chow's method requires that three equally spaced values for the smoothing constant be selected: a nominal value (α_0), an upper value (α_u), and a lower value (α_l). Thus

$$\alpha_u = \alpha_0 + \delta$$
$$\alpha_l = \alpha_0 - \delta \tag{8-7}$$

where δ is some suitable constant. Chow used values of δ of 0.05. The method requires maintaining three parallel smoothing operations, one for each value of the smoothing constant. Thus in each time period, three forecasts are computed, one using each value of the smoothing constant. The forecast associated with the nominal value α_0 is reported to management as the actual forecast. The mean absolute deviation is computed every period for each of the three forecasts. These mean absolute deviations are denoted by $\Delta(\alpha_0)$, $\Delta(\alpha_u)$, and $\Delta(\alpha_l)$ to indicate the smoothing constant employed. The decision rule for changing the value of the smoothing constant is based on the mean absolute

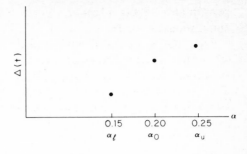

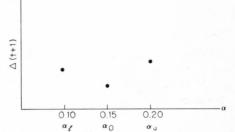

Fig. 8-2 Chow's adaptive control method.

deviation.   If $\Delta(\alpha_0)$ is less than both $\Delta(\alpha_u)$ and $\Delta(\alpha_l)$, then this indicates that the forecast errors associated with α_0 are less than the forecast errors associated with either α_u or α_l, and no change is made.   If $\Delta(\alpha_u) < \Delta(\alpha_0)$, we would like to shift the nominal value of the smoothing constant in the positive direction; therefore we set $\alpha_0 = \alpha_u$ and determine new upper and lower values of the smoothing constant from Eq. (8-7) using the new α_0.   If $\Delta(\alpha_l) < \Delta(\alpha_0)$, we would revise the nominal value of the smoothing constant downward by setting $\alpha_0 = \alpha_l$, and choosing new upper and lower values as before.   Should $\Delta(\alpha_0)$ exceed both $\Delta(\alpha_u)$ and $\Delta(\alpha_l)$, we would revise α_0 in the direction of the smallest mean absolute deviation.   After each revision of the smoothing constant, the mean absolute deviations are set equal to zero and the process begun anew.   The procedure is illustrated in Fig. 8-2 for $\Delta(\alpha_l) < \Delta(\alpha_0)$ at time t.

Chow reported several numerical experiments with his method in an inventory control setting with good results.   The number of items indicated out of control by the tracking signal was substantially reduced.   The major disadvantage of this procedure is that three forecasts must be computed each period, and the amount of data that must be carried by the information processing system is greatly increased.

8-2 METHODS FOR SEVERAL SMOOTHING PARAMETERS*

Roberts and Reed [54] have proposed an adaptive-control technique for monitoring several exponential smoothing parameters.   Essentially, their technique is

* Some of the material in this section is of a more advanced nature than the rest of the book.   It may be omitted on first reading without loss of continuity.

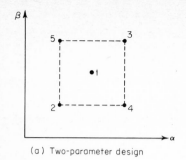

(a) Two-parameter design

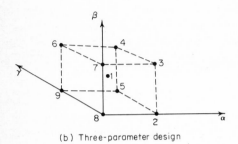

(b) Three-parameter design

Fig. 8-3 (*a*) and (*b*) Designs for Roberts and Reed's adaptive control method (SAFT).

an extension of Chow's method to an exponential smoothing model with several smoothing constants (for example, the seasonal models described in Secs. 5-1 and 5-2).   Their procedure is based on Evolutionary Operation, which is described in a more general setting by Box and Draper [5].   Roberts and Reed have called their technique SAFT, an acronym for Self Adaptive Forecasting Technique.

The SAFT procedure treats each smoothing parameter as one of the factors in a two-level factorial experimental design, that is, a 2^k factorial design.   Each smoothing constant is assigned a high and a low level.   The factorial design requires that all possible combinations of the high and low levels be investigated. Additionally, the combination of smoothing constants at the design's center is investigated.   The designs for a two-parameter and a three-parameter smoothing method are shown in Fig. 8-3*a* and *b*, respectively.   Notice that the two-parameter design is a 2^2 factorial plus center point and the three-parameter design is a 2^3 factorial plus center point.   Further results on factorial designs may be found in Hicks ([33] chaps. 6 and 13) and Hines and Montgomery ([34] chap. 13).

A complete replication of each design point is called a *cycle*.   Every time period, as a new observation becomes available, a cycle is run.   Thus, if k smoothing parameters are being controlled, then $2^k + 1$ forecasts are computed each period.   The forecast reported to management is the one computed from the combination of smoothing parameters at the center of the design.

The square of the forecast error is used as the measure of effectiveness.   Let SE_{ij} be the square of the forecast error at the ith design point in the jth cycle.

After n cycles, the average squared forecast error at the ith design point is

$$\overline{SE}_i = \frac{1}{n} \sum_{j=1}^{n} SE_{ij} \tag{8-8}$$

The SAFT control procedure consists of estimating the effects of each smoothing parameter in the same fashion as the effects of the factors in an analysis of variance for the 2^k design would be estimated, and adjusting the smoothing parameters (that is, *shifting* the design) if the effect of one or more of these parameters is significant.

Consider the two-parameter case. Define the effect of α as the effect on the average squared error of changing from the high to the low value of α, averaged over the levels of β. Thus the effect of α is

$$E_\alpha = \tfrac{1}{2}\left[\left(\overline{SE}_3 + \overline{SE}_4\right) - \left(\overline{SE}_2 + \overline{SE}_5\right)\right]$$
$$= \tfrac{1}{2}\left(\overline{SE}_3 + \overline{SE}_4 - \overline{SE}_2 - \overline{SE}_5\right) \tag{8-9}$$

Similarly, the effect of β is

$$E_\beta = \tfrac{1}{2}\left(\overline{SE}_3 + \overline{SE}_5 - \overline{SE}_2 - \overline{SE}_4\right) \tag{8-10}$$

The smoothing parameters should be changed if either E_α, E_β, or both exceed the approximate 99 percent error limits given by

$$\pm 3\hat{\sigma}_e\sqrt{\frac{1}{n}}$$

where $\hat{\sigma}_e$ is an estimate of the standard deviation of the forecast errors. A range method, which is described in Box and Draper ([5], app. 1), is used to compute $\hat{\sigma}_e$. Probability statements associated with the error limits are only approximate, because the squared errors within a cycle are not independent random variables. That is, the same data point is used in computing all $2^k + 1$ forecast errors.

To illustrate the SAFT technique, suppose E_β was below the lower error limit for a particular cycle, that is, $E_\beta < -3\hat{\sigma}_e\sqrt{1/n}$. This indicates that $\overline{SE}_2 + \overline{SE}_4$ is considerably larger than $\overline{SE}_3 + \overline{SE}_5$, and so we should shift the entire design upward, adopting the high value of β as the new center point and leaving the value of α unchanged. Following such a shift of the design, the old values of $\overline{SE}_i$ must be discarded and new ones computed over several cycles.

For the three-parameter case, the estimates of the effects are

$$E_\alpha = \tfrac{1}{4}\left(\overline{SE}_2 + \overline{SE}_3 + \overline{SE}_4 + \overline{SE}_5 - \overline{SE}_6 - \overline{SE}_7 - \overline{SE}_8 - \overline{SE}_9\right) \tag{8-11}$$

$$E_\beta = \tfrac{1}{4}\left(\overline{SE}_3 + \overline{SE}_4 + \overline{SE}_6 + \overline{SE}_7 - \overline{SE}_2 - \overline{SE}_3 - \overline{SE}_8 - \overline{SE}_9\right) \tag{8-12}$$

and

$$E_\gamma = \tfrac{1}{4} \left(\overline{SE}_4 + \overline{SE}_5 + \overline{SE}_6 + \overline{SE}_9 - \overline{SE}_2 - \overline{SE}_3 - \overline{SE}_7 - \overline{SE}_8 \right) \quad (8\text{-}13)$$

and the approximate 99 percent error limits are

$$\pm 3\hat{\sigma}_e \sqrt{\frac{1}{2n}}$$

The operation of the three-parameter control procedure is similar to the two-parameter case.

Roberts and Reed tested the SAFT procedure with several artificially generated time series. The test series contained impulse, ramp, step, or seasonal variation so that dynamic performance characteristics could be studied. The analysis also compared SAFT with Chow's method and Winters' method without the adaptive-control feature. The response to a step function for both uncorrelated and autocorrelated data is shown in Fig. 8-4. Both SAFT and Chow's method react to the step function more quickly, but SAFT settles down to the new level much more rapidly. These results are typical of their numerical experiments. They also report that SAFT can improve forecasting accuracy when dealing with highly autocorrelated data. The principal disadvantage of SAFT is the relatively large number of forecasts $(2^k + 1)$ that must be computed each period.

Another multiple-parameter adaptive-control technique has been reported by Montgomery [41]. His scheme is similar to the Roberts and Reed method, in that it is based on the *simplex*, which, like the two-version factorial, is an orthogonal first-order experimental design. However, the simplex requires only one more observation than the number of factors under investigation. Thus, if the smoothing technique requires k smoothing parameters, then the number of points in the design is $N = k + 1$. The N points correspond to the vertices of a regular-sided simplex, which for a two-parameter smoothing method $(k = 2)$ is an equilateral triangle and for a three-parameter smoothing method $(k = 3)$ is a tetrahedron. These designs are illustrated in Fig. 8-5.

Simplex designs can be constructed quite easily. Let $\mathbf{D}$ be a design matrix, that is, an $(N \times k)$ matrix whose rows correspond to the N runs or observations and whose columns correspond to the k factors. The design matrix for a simplex design with arbitrary origin can be written as the sum of two $(N \times k)$ matrices, that is,

$$\mathbf{D} = \theta \begin{bmatrix} 0 & 0 & 0 & \cdots & 0 \\ r & q & q & \cdots & q \\ q & r & q & \cdots & q \\ \multicolumn{5}{c}{\cdots\cdots\cdots\cdots\cdots\cdots} \\ q & q & q & \cdots & r \end{bmatrix} + \begin{bmatrix} O_1 & O_2 & \cdots & O_k \\ O_1 & O_2 & \cdots & O_k \\ O_1 & O_2 & \cdots & O_k \\ \multicolumn{4}{c}{\cdots\cdots\cdots\cdots\cdots} \\ O_1 & O_2 & \cdots & O_k \end{bmatrix} \quad (8\text{-}14)$$

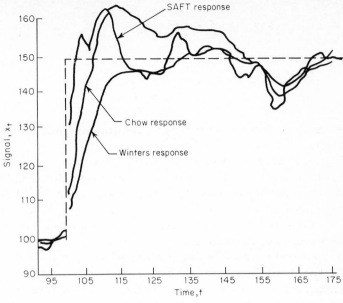

(a) Response to uncorrelated data

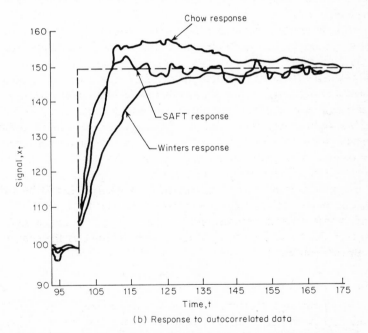

(b) Response to autocorrelated data

Fig. 8-4 (*a*) and (*b*) Roberts and Reed test results. (*Adapted from S. D. Roberts and R. Reed, "The Development of a Self-Adaptive Forecasting Technique," AIIE Transactions, vol. 1, no. 4, 1969. By permission of the publisher*).

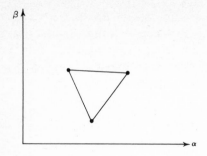

(a) Simplex design in two dimensions

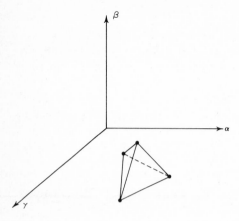

(b) Simplex design in three dimensions

Fig. 8-5 (a) and (b)   Designs for the simplex adaptive control method.

where $r = \dfrac{k - 1 + \sqrt{k + 1}}{k\sqrt{2}}$

$q = \dfrac{\sqrt{k + 1} - 1}{k\sqrt{2}}$

θ = the desired edge length

O_i = the coordinates of the chosen origin, $i = 1, 2, \ldots, k$

Equation (8-14) may be expressed in matrix form as

$$\mathbf{D} = \theta \mathbf{D}_0 + \mathbf{O} \tag{8-15}$$

with an obvious notation.   The design generated by Eq. (8-15) has an initial orientation in the parameter space of approximately 15 degrees.   Numerical experiments have indicated that the design orientation has little effect on performance.   The edge length, however, is an important consideration. Montgomery used an edge length of $\theta = 0.07$ in his experiments.   Edge lengths between 0.05 and 0.10 are probably appropriate for most applications.

We shall illustrate the construction of a simplex design matrix for a two-parameter smoothing method. Let the starting or origin values for the two smoothing constants be $\alpha = 0.10$ and $\beta = 0.075$ and the edge length be 0.07. If the first and second columns of the design matrix correspond to α and β, respectively, we can use Eq. (8-14) to write the design matrix as

$$
\mathbf{D} = (0.07)\begin{bmatrix} 0 & 0 \\ 0.971 & 0.257 \\ 0.757 & 0.971 \end{bmatrix} + \begin{bmatrix} 0.100 & 0.075 \\ 0.100 & 0.075 \\ 0.100 & 0.075 \end{bmatrix} = \begin{matrix} \alpha & \beta \\ \begin{bmatrix} 0.100 & 0.075 \\ 0.168 & 0.093 \\ 0.118 & 0.143 \end{bmatrix} \end{matrix}
$$

In the final $\mathbf{D}$ matrix, we have labeled the columns associated with α and β for clarity.

To use this adaptive-control technique, $k + 1$ forecasts are computed every period, one for each combination of smoothing parameters represented by the vertices of the simplex. Then the smoothing parameters are adjusted according to the following rules:

1. Denote by $|e_1^i(T)|$ the current absolute forecast error at the ith design point, $i = 1, 2, \ldots, N$. Also, let the ith row of the design matrix be denoted by the row vector $\mathbf{d}_i'$. Suppose the maximum value of the current absolute error occurs at the design point $\mathbf{d}_j'$. Form a new simplex by deleting $\mathbf{d}_j'$ from the design matrix $\mathbf{D}$ and replacing it by its "mirror image" point

$$
\mathbf{d}_{j*}' = \frac{2}{k} (\mathbf{d}_1' + \mathbf{d}_2' + \cdots + \mathbf{d}_{j-1}' + \mathbf{d}_{j+1}' + \cdots + \mathbf{d}_N') - \mathbf{d}_j' \qquad (8\text{-}16)
$$

Calculate the forecast for the next period using the smoothing parameters which are the elements of the row vector $\mathbf{d}_{j*}'$.

2. Apply rule 1 unless a design point has occurred in N successive simplexes without being eliminated. Should this situation apply for the ith design point, discard $|e_1^i(T)|$ and calculate the forecast for next period using the smoothing parameters in $\mathbf{d}_i'$. Then apply rule 1.

3. Should $|e_1^i(T)|$ be the maximum absolute current error in the Tth simplex and $|e_1^{i*}(T+1)|$ be the maximum absolute current error in the $(T+1)$st simplex, do not return to the previous design. Instead, move from the $(T+1)$st design by discarding the second largest absolute current error. This rule is designed to prevent oscillation.

Montgomery tested this technique for several artificially generated time series and found it to be superior to conventional, or nonadaptive, exponential smoothing. From a computational viewpoint this scheme is more efficient than the Roberts and Reed method, as it requires only k forecasts (versus $2^k + 1$) each period. Thus for two parameters there are 2 fewer forecasts each period, and for 3 parameters there are 5 fewer forecasts each period. This would seem to reduce substantially the amount of data to be carried by an information processing system. Some limited comparison of the forecast accuracy and dynamic response characteristics of these two methods has been made.   When the signal-to-noise ratio of the time series is relatively small, the Roberts and Reed method seems to yield better results.   However, the simplex adaptive-control method generally has superior trend-following characteristics.

8-3 EXERCISES

8-1   The minutes of usage per day for a computer terminal are shown in Table B-3 in the Appendix.   Simulate a one-day-ahead forecast for this data using simple exponential smoothing with $\alpha = 0.10$.   The first ten days' data may be used to initialize the system.   Then repeat the procedure, using Chow's method with $\delta = 0.05$.   Compare the accuracy of the procedures.

8-2   Rework Exercise 8-1 using the Trigg and Leach method instead of Chow's method.

8-3   The weekly sales of a cutting tool are shown in Table B-2.   Simulate a one-week-ahead forecast for these data using simple exponential smoothing with $\alpha = 0.10$.   Data from the first 20 days may be used to initialize the forecasting system.   Repeat the forecasting procedure, using the Trigg and Leach method.   Compare the results obtained with the forecasts obtained from conventional exponential smoothing.

8-4   Rework Exercise 8-3 using Chow's method instead of the Trigg and Leach method.

8-5   Appendix C-1 contains a listing of a computer program for multiple exponential smoothing.   Modify the first-order smoothing segment of this program to incorporate automatically the Trigg and Leach method.

8-6   Consider the following adaptive-control scheme for simple exponential smoothing. The smoothing constant in period T is $\alpha(T) = 1/r(T)$, where $l \leqslant r(T) \leqslant u$ and $l \geqslant 1$.   Thus if $r(T) = 10$, say, then $\alpha(T) = 0.1$.   If the tracking signal in period T is out of control, we set $r(T+1) = r(T) - 1$.   If the tracking signal is in control in period T, we set $r(T+1) = r(T) + 1$.   If $r(T) = l$ or if $r(T) = u$ and the tracking signal is out of control, we set $r(T+1) = r(T)$.   Discuss the potential performance of this adaptive-control method.

8-7   *Continuation of Exercise 8-6.*   Rework Exercise 8-3 using the adaptive-control scheme discussed in Exercise 8-6.   Compare its performance with that of the Trigg and Leach method.

8-8   Consider the following modification to the Trigg and Leach method.   If the tracking signal in period T is in control, the value of $\alpha(T)$ is not changed. However, if the tracking signal is out of control, then the new value of $\alpha(T)$ is determined from Eq. (8-4).   Test this method by using it in Exercise 8-3 instead of the conventional Trigg and Leach method.   Compare the results obtained from this method with the results of Exercise 8-3.

8-9   The monthly demand for a plastic container for four years is shown in Table B-12. Perform a one-month-ahead forecast simulation for the last two years of these data.   Assume that a linear trend model is appropriate, and use the trend model obtained from Winters' method without seasonality.   Use $\alpha = 0.15$ and $\beta = 0.10$, and initialize the model parameters from the first two years of history.   Repeat the analysis using the Roberts and Reed method.   Compare the results obtained from the two methods.

8-10 Rework Exercise 8-9 using the simplex adaptive-control method.   Compare the results obtained with those from Exercise 8-9.

8-11 Explain why Eqs. (8-9) and (8-10) are used to estimate the effects of α and β.

8-12 Prove that $\hat{\sigma}_e\sqrt{1/n}$ is the standard error of an effect in the two-parameter version of the Roberts and Reed method.   Also prove that $\hat{\sigma}_e\sqrt{1/(2n)}$ is the corresponding standard error in the three-parameter case.

8-13 Construct a simplex design in three dimensions about the point ($O_1 = 0.10$, $O_2 = 0.15$, $O_3 = 0.10$) with edge length 0.05.

8-14 A simplex design in k dimensions can always be constructed by considering only the last k columns of $N^{1/2}\mathbf{H}$, where $\mathbf{H}$ is any $N \times N$ orthogonal matrix having elements in the first column equal, and $N = k + 1$.   Construct designs using this procedure for $k = 2$ and $k = 3$.   Compare them graphically with the designs that would be obtained using Eq. (8-14) for $k = 2$ and $k = 3$.

CHAPTER NINE

The Box-Jenkins Models*

In previous chapters we have discussed forecasting techniques which are, in general, based on some variant of exponential smoothing. Some of these techniques, such as multiple smoothing for polynomial models and direct smoothing for transcendental models, are derived from the discounted least-squares criterion, while others, such as Winters' method, are developed heuristically. The discounted least-squares approach assumes that the mean of the time series is a deterministic function of time, and the observation in any time period consists of the mean plus a random error component. The random errors are generally assumed to be independent random variables. For example, in the development of double exponential smoothing we postulated the time series model

$$x_t = b_0 + b_1 t + \epsilon_t$$

or

$$x_t = \mu_t + \epsilon_t$$

where $\mu_t = b_0 + b_1 t$ is the deterministic mean of the process at time t and ϵ_t is a random error component. Notice that if the random errors $\{\epsilon_t\}$ are independent random variables, then the observations $\{x_t\}$ are also independent random

* Some of the material in this chapter is of a more advanced nature than the rest of the book. It may be omitted on first reading without loss of continuity.

variables.   Heuristic developments of exponential smoothing methods also usually assume independence of the $\{\epsilon_t\}$.

The assumption of independent errors, and hence independent observations,
is frequently unwarranted.   That is, there are many time series in which
successive observations are highly *dependent*.   If this is the case, forecasting
methods based on exponential smoothing may be inappropriate because they do
not take advantage of the dependency in the observations in the most effective
way.   Now, in practice, exponential smoothing methods are frequently applied
to time series in which observations are dependent with reasonably good results;
however, there are available forecasting techniques which are designed to exploit
this dependency and which will generally produce superior results.   Many of
these forecasting techniques are based on recent developments in time series
analysis recently consolidated and presented by Box and Jenkins [6], and are
called *Box-Jenkins models*.   In this chapter we shall present their approach to
forecasting.

9-1 A CLASS OF TIME SERIES MODELS

Consider a time series in which successive observations can be represented by a
linear combination of independent random variables, say $\epsilon_t, \epsilon_{t-1}, \epsilon_{t-2}, \ldots,$ that
are drawn from a stable probability distribution with mean 0 and variance σ_ϵ^2.
We also usually assume that the distribution of the $\{\epsilon_i\}$ is normal, and then the
sequence of random variables $\epsilon_t, \epsilon_{t-1}, \epsilon_{t-2}, \ldots,$ is called a *white noise process*.
The linear combination of the $\{\epsilon_i\}$ could be written as

$$x_t = \mu + \psi_0\epsilon_t + \psi_1\epsilon_{t-1} + \psi_2\epsilon_{t-2} + \cdots \tag{9-1}$$

or

$$x_t = \mu + \sum_{j=0}^{\infty} \psi_j\epsilon_{t-j}$$

where the constants $\psi_j (j = 0, 1, \ldots)$ are usually called *weights* and μ is a
constant that determines the level of the process.   Usually, $\psi_0 = 1$.   An alternate way of writing (9-1) is in terms of the backward shift operator, B, defined
such that

$$B\epsilon_t = \epsilon_{t-1} \; = \; B'\epsilon_t$$

In general, this implies that

$$B^j\epsilon_t = \epsilon_{t-j} \tag{9-2}$$

Using this notation, Eq. (9-1) can be written as

$$x_t = \mu + (\psi_0 B^0 + \psi_1 B^1 + \psi_2 B^2 + \cdots)\epsilon_t$$

or

$$x_t = \mu + \Psi(B)\epsilon_t \tag{9-3}$$

where $\Psi(B) = \psi_0 B^0 + \psi_1 B^1 + \psi_2 B^2 + \cdots$, and $\psi_0 = 1$.

Equation (9-1) is usually called a linear filter. It is clear that successive observations in the time series $\{x_t\}$ are dependent, because they are determined from the same previous realizations of $\{\epsilon_i\}$. Furthermore, if the $\{\epsilon_i\}$ are normally distributed, then the $\{x_t\}$ are normally distributed. In view of the linear filter model, we may define a time series model as *a function that transforms a white noise process into a time series*. As we shall see, it is possible to generate many different time series models from the linear filter (9-1). Box and Jenkins unified and extended these models and evolved a philosophy for their use. Thus, time series models derived from the linear filter are usually called Box-Jenkins models.

Models derived from (9-1) are capable of representing both *stationary* and *nonstationary* time series. If a time series is stationary, we mean that it fluctuates randomly about a constant mean, and if a time series is nonstationary, we imply that it has no natural mean. In general, if the sequence of weights $\{\psi_j\}$ in the linear filter is finite or infinite and convergent, the time series $\{x_t\}$ is stationary with mean μ. If the sequence $\{\psi_j\}$ is infinite and diverges, the time series is nonstationary and μ is only a reference point for the origin of the process.

Later in this section we shall discuss Box-Jenkins models in detail. First, however, we shall present some fundamental concepts in time series analysis.

9-1.1 Autocovariance, Autocorrelation, and Partial Autocorrelation

Suppose that the time series generated from the linear filter (9-1) is stationary. An important implication of this is that the statistical properties of the time series are unaffected by a shift of the time origin. That is, the statistical properties of n observations at origin t, say $x_t, x_{t+1}, \ldots, x_{t+n-1}$, are identical to those of n observations at origin $t + k$, say $x_{t+k}, x_{t+k+1}, \ldots, x_{t+k+n-1}$.

For a stationary time series the mean is just

$$E(x_t) = E\left(\mu + \sum_{j=0}^{\infty} \psi_j \epsilon_{t-j}\right) = \mu + E \sum_{j=0}^{\infty} \psi_j \epsilon_{t-j}$$

and since the sum $\sum_{j=0}^{\infty} \psi_j$ converges, we take expectation of $\sum_{j=0}^{\infty} \psi_j \epsilon_{t-j}$ term by term, yielding $\sum_{j=0}^{\infty} \psi_j E(\epsilon_{t-j}) = 0$. Thus the mean of the stationary series is

$$E(x_t) = \mu \qquad (9\text{-}4)$$

The variance of the time series process is

$$\gamma_0 = V(x_t) = E[x_t - E(x_t)]^2$$

$$= E\left[\sum_{j=0}^{\infty} \psi_j \epsilon_{t-j}\right]^2$$

$$= E\left[\sum_{j=0}^{\infty} \psi_j^2 \epsilon_{t-j}^2 + \text{cross products}\right]$$

and since the $\{\epsilon_i\}$ are independent, the cross products have zero expectation, yielding

$$\gamma_0 = \sigma_\epsilon^2 \sum_{j=0}^{\infty} \psi_j^2 \qquad (9\text{-}5)$$

The variance exists only if $\sum_{j=0}^{\infty}\psi_j^2$ converges.

The covariance between x_t and another observation separated by k units of time x_{t+k} is called *autocovariance* at lag k, and is defined as

$$\gamma_k = \text{Cov}(x_t, x_{t+k}) = E[x_t - E(x_t)][x_{t+k} - E(x_{t+k})]$$

Thus the autocovariance is just like the covariance of two random variables; the prefix *auto* merely implies that we are referring to the covariance of any two observations in a time series that are k time periods apart. It is not difficult to show that the autocovariance at lag k is

$$\gamma_k = \sigma_\epsilon^2 \sum_{j=0}^{\infty} \psi_j \psi_{j+k} \qquad (9\text{-}6)$$

Within the framework of the Box-Jenkins methodology, time series models are characterized by their autocorrelation functions. The correlation between two random variables, say W and Z, is defined as

$$\rho_{WZ} = \frac{\text{Cov}(W, Z)}{\sqrt{V(W)V(Z)}}$$

Thus the autocorrelation at lag k refers to the correlation between any two observations in a time series that are k periods apart. That is,

$$\rho_k = \frac{\text{Cov}(x_t, x_{t+k})}{\sqrt{V(x_t)\cdot V(x_{t+k})}} = \frac{\gamma_0}{\gamma_0} \qquad (9\text{-}7)$$

is the autocorrelation at lag k. A graphical display of ρ_k versus the lag k is called the autocorrelation function $\{\rho_k\}$ of the process. Notice that the auto-correlation function is dimensionless and that $-1 \leqslant \rho_k \leqslant 1$. Furthermore, $\rho_k = \rho_{-k}$; that is, the autocorrelation function is symmetric, so that it is necessary to consider only positive lags. In general, when observations k lags apart are close together in value, we would find ρ_k close to 1.0. When a large observation at time t is followed by a small observation at time $t + k$, we would find ρ_k close to -1.0. If there is little relationship between observations k lags apart, we would find ρ_k approximately zero.

Another useful concept in the description of time series models is partial correlation. Consider the three random variables W, Y, and Z. If we let the joint density function of W, Y, and Z be $f(w, y, z)$, then the conditional distribution of W and Y given Z is

$$h(w, y \mid z) = \frac{f(w, y, z)}{\int_{-\infty}^{\infty} \int_{-\infty}^{\infty} f(w, y, z)\, dw\, dy}$$

The correlation coefficient between W and Y in the conditional distribution $h(w, y \mid z)$ is called the partial (or conditional) correlation coefficient. That is, the partial correlation between W and Y is just the simple correlation between W and Y with the effect of their correlation with Z removed. In terms of a time series, it is convenient to think of the *partial autocorrelation* at lag k as the correlation between x_t and x_{t+k} with the effects of the intervening observations $(x_{t+1}, x_{t+2}, \ldots, x_{t+k-1})$ removed. Notationally, we shall refer to the kth partial autocorrelation coefficient as ϕ_{kk}. (The reason for this choice of notation will become apparent later.) A plot of ϕ_{kk} versus the lag k is called the *partial autocorrelation function* $\{\phi_{kk}\}$. Note that $\phi_{00} = \rho_0 = 1$ and $\phi_{11} = \rho_1$.

9-1.2 Autoregressive Processes

The linear filter (9-1) would not be a very useful time series model, since it contains an infinite number of unknown parameters (the ψ weights). Our approach will be to develop *parsimonious* models, that is, models which adequately describe the time series yet contain relatively few parameters.

An important special case of (9-1) is the model

$$x_t = \xi + \phi_1 x_{t-1} + \phi_2 x_{t-2} + \cdots + \phi_p x_{t-p} + \epsilon_t \qquad (9\text{-}8)$$

Equation (9-8) is called an *autoregressive* process because the current observation x_t is "regressed" on previous realizations $x_{t-1}, x_{t-2}, \ldots, x_{t-p}$ of the same time series. The process contains p unknown parameters $\phi_1, \phi_2, \ldots, \phi_p$ (apart from ξ and the unknown variance σ_ϵ^2), and as a result we refer to (9-8) as an autoregressive process of order p, abbreviated AR(p).

It is easy to show that the autoregressive process is a special case of the linear filter, as we can eliminate x_{t-1} from the right-hand side of (9-8) by substituting

$$x_{t-1} = \xi + \phi_1 x_{t-2} + \phi_2 x_{t-3} + \cdots + \phi_p x_{t-p-1} + \epsilon_{t-1}$$

Similarly, we could substitute for x_{t-2}, x_{t-3}, etc., to eventually obtain an infinite series in the ϵ_t.

The AR(p) process can be written in terms of the backward-shift operator as

$$x_t = \xi + \left(\phi_1 B^1 + \phi_2 B^2 + \cdots + \phi_p B^p\right) x_t + \epsilon_t$$

or

$$\left(1 - \phi_1 B^1 - \phi_2 B^2 - \cdots - \phi_p B^p\right) x_t = \xi + \epsilon_t \qquad (9\text{-}9)$$

If we let

$$\Phi_p(B) = 1 - \phi_1 B^1 - \phi_2 B^2 - \cdots - \phi_p B^p$$

we may write Eq. (9-9) as

$$\Phi_p(B) x_t = \xi + \epsilon_t \qquad (9\text{-}10)$$

Frequently it is convenient to work with the time series defined in terms of deviations from the mean μ. Therefore, let $\tilde{x}_t = x_t - \mu$ for all t. Then the AR(p) process (9-10) becomes

$$\Phi_p(B)\tilde{x}_t = \epsilon_t \qquad (9\text{-}11)$$

Comparing (9-10) and (9-11), we see that the mean of the AR(p) process is $\mu = \xi/(1 - \sum_{j=1}^{p}\phi_j)$.

The autoregressive model may be used to represent both stationary and nonstationary time series. Box and Jenkins show that if the roots of the polynomial $\Phi_p(B) = 0$ lie *outside* the unit circle, the process is stationary. This condition is derived from the fact that $\sum_{j=0}^{\infty}\psi_j$ must converge for the process $\{x_t\}$ to be stationary. Later we shall show what the condition implies in terms of admissible values for the $\{\phi_j\}$ in the AR(p) process. While it is theoretically possible to model a nonstationary time series by an appropriately chosen autoregressive process, this is not usually done, because more effective approaches are available.

We shall now briefly discuss two very important special cases of the AR(p) process.

The first-order autoregressive process   If $p = 1$, then Eq. (9-8) becomes the first-order autoregressive, or AR(1), process

$$x_t = \xi + \phi_1 x_{t-1} + \epsilon_t \qquad (9\text{-}12)$$

The AR(1) process is often called the Markov process because the observation at time t depends only on the observation at time $t - 1$. For the process to be stationary, we must require that the roots of $\Phi_1(B) = 1 - \phi_1 B^1 = 0$ lie outside the unit circle. This is equivalent to saying that we must have

$$|\phi_1| < 1$$

for stationarity.

The mean, variance, and autocovariance of the AR(1) process may be easily determined. The mean is just

$$\mu \equiv E(x_t) = E(\xi + \phi_1 x_{t-1} + \epsilon_t)$$

$$= \xi + \phi_1 E(x_{t-1})$$

$$= \xi + \phi_1[\mu + \phi_1 E(x_{t-2})]$$

$$= \xi \sum_{j=0}^{\infty} \phi_1^j$$

$$= \frac{\xi}{1 - \phi_1}$$

The variance and autocovariances of the AR(1) process can be shown to be

$$\gamma_k = \phi_1^k \frac{\sigma_\epsilon^2}{1 - \phi_1^2} \qquad k = 0, 1, \ldots \qquad (9\text{-}13)$$

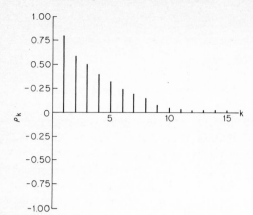

Fig. 9-1 Autocorrelation function for the AR(1) process $x_t = 5 + 0.8x_{t-1} + \epsilon_t$.

Therefore, the autocorrelation function is easily found from (9-13) as

$$\rho_k = \phi_1^k \qquad k = 0, 1, \ldots \tag{9-14}$$

We see that the autocorrelation function for AR(1) process decays exponentially when ϕ_1 is positive, and decays exponentially but oscillates in sign when ϕ_1 is negative.

The autocorrelation function for the process

$$x_t = 5 + 0.8x_{t-1} + \epsilon_t$$

with $\sigma_\epsilon^2 = 4$ is shown in Fig. 9-1 and a realization of the time series is pictured in Fig. 9-2. Note the exponential decay of the autocorrelation function. From examining the autocorrelation function, we would expect successive observations in the series to be positively correlated; that is, a high observation tends to be followed by another high observation. The realization in Fig. 9-2 confirms this

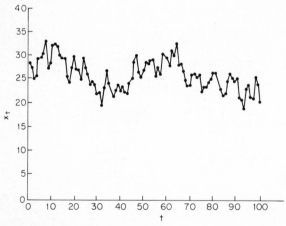

Fig. 9-2 Realization of the AR(1) process $x_t = 5 + 0.8x_{t-1} + \epsilon_t$.

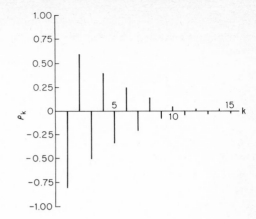

Fig. 9-3 Autocorrelation function of the AR(1) process $x_t = 5 - 0.8x_{t-1} + \epsilon_t$.

expected behavior. As a second illustration, the autocorrelation function for the process

$$x_t = 5 - 0.8x_{t-1} + \epsilon_t$$

with $\sigma_\epsilon^2 = 4$ is shown in Fig. 9-3 and a realization is shown in Fig. 9-4. The autocorrelation function still exhibits exponential decay, but the autocorrelations are positive for even lags and negative for odd lags, resulting in a series which oscillates rapidly.

The second-order autoregressive process If $p = 2$ in Eq. (9-8) we obtain the second-order autoregressive process

$$x_t = \xi + \phi_1 x_{t-1} + \phi_2 x_{t-2} + \epsilon_t \qquad (9\text{-}15)$$

For the AR(2) process to be stationary, we must require that the roots of

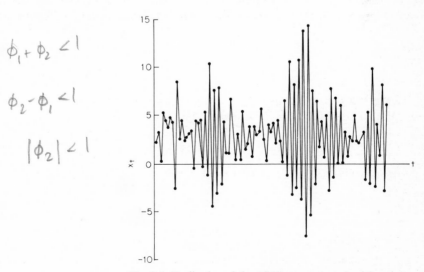

$\phi_1 + \phi_2 < 1$

$\phi_2 - \phi_1 < 1$

$|\phi_2| < 1$

Fig. 9-4 Realization of the AR(1) process $x_t = 5 - 0.8x_{t-1} + \epsilon_t$.

$(1 - \phi_1 B^1 - \phi_2 B^2) = 0$ lie outside the unit circle.   This is equivalent to requiring that the parameters ϕ_1 and ϕ_2 be chosen so that

$$\phi_1 + \phi_2 < 1$$

$$\phi_2 - \phi_1 < 1 \tag{9-16}$$

$$|\phi_2| < 1$$

If conditions (9-16) are satisfied, it is not difficult to show that the mean of the AR(2) process is

$$\mu \equiv E(x_t) = \frac{\xi}{1 - \phi_1 - \phi_2} \tag{9-17}$$

The variance and autocovariances of the AR(2) process obey an interesting relationship.   Consider the AR(2) process corrected for the mean, that is, $\tilde{x}_t = x_t - \mu = x_t - \xi/(1 - \phi_1 - \phi_2)$ for all t, or

$$\tilde{x}_t = \phi_1 \tilde{x}_{t-1} + \phi_2 \tilde{x}_{t-2} + \epsilon_t \tag{9-18}$$

Clearly the variance and autocovariances of (9-18) are identical to those of (9-15).   Multiplying both sides of (9-18) by $\tilde{x}_{t-k}$ yields

$$\tilde{x}_t \tilde{x}_{t-k} = \phi_1 \tilde{x}_{t-1} \tilde{x}_{t-k} + \phi_2 \tilde{x}_{t-2} \tilde{x}_{t-k} + \epsilon_t \tilde{x}_{t-k} \tag{9-19}$$

and upon taking expectation of (9-19), we obtain

$$\gamma_k = \phi_1 \gamma_{k-1} + \phi_2 \gamma_{k-2} \quad k > 0 \tag{9-20}$$

because $E(\epsilon_t \tilde{x}_{t-k})$ vanishes when $k > 0$, since $\tilde{x}_{t-k}$ is uncorrelated with ϵ_t.   If $k = 0$, we would obtain

$$\gamma_0 = \phi_1 \gamma_1 + \phi_2 \gamma_2 + \sigma_\epsilon^2 \tag{9-21}$$

because $\gamma_{-k} = \gamma_k$.

If we divide each term in (9-20) by γ_0, we obtain a recursive relationship for the autocorrelation function, namely,

$$\rho_k = \phi_1 \rho_{k-1} + \phi_2 \rho_{k-2} \quad k > 0 \tag{9-22}$$

Notice that if we write out (9-22) for $k = 1, 2$, we obtain

$$\rho_1 = \phi_1 + \phi_2 \rho_1$$

$$\rho_2 = \phi_1 \rho_1 + \phi_2 \tag{9-23}$$

which are usually called the *Yule-Walker* equations.   If we are given values of ϕ_1 and ϕ_2, (9-23) can be solved for ρ_1 and ρ_2.   Higher-order autocorrelations can then be found from (9-22).

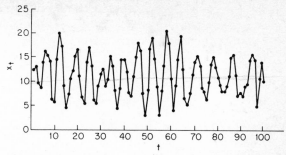

Fig. 9-5 Realization of the AR(2) process $x_t = 10 + 0.9x_{t-1} - 0.8x_{t-2} + \epsilon_t$.

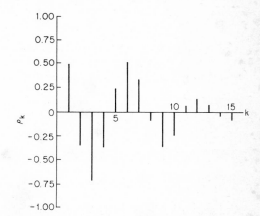

Fig. 9-6 Autocorrelation function of the AR(2) process $x_t + 10 + 0.9x_{t-1} - 0.8x_{t-2} + \epsilon_t$.

It is clear from examining (9-22) and (9-23) that the autocorrelation function for an AR(2) process is complex. Box and Jenkins ([6], pp. 58–60) show that if $\phi_1^2 + 4\phi_2 \geqslant 0$, the autocorrelation function is a mixture of damped exponentials, and if $\phi_1^2 + 4\phi_2 < 0$, the autocorrelation function is a damped sine wave.

Figure 9-5 shows a realization of the AR(2) process

$$x_t = 10 + 0.9x_{t-1} - 0.8x_{t-2} + \epsilon_t$$

with $\sigma_\epsilon^2 = 4$. The corresponding autocorrelation function is shown in Fig. 9-6. We see that the autocorrelation function decays as a damped sine wave, since $\phi_1^2 + 4\phi_2 = (0.9)^2 + 4(-0.8) = -2.39 < 0$. This pseudoperiodic behavior is also evident in the series.

9-1.3 Moving Average Processes

Consider the special case of the linear filter (9-1) with only the first q weights nonzero. The process would be

$$x_t = \mu + \epsilon_t - \theta_1\epsilon_{t-1} - \theta_2\epsilon_{t-2} - \cdots - \theta_q\epsilon_{t-q} \tag{9-24}$$

say, where $-\theta_1, -\theta_2, \ldots, -\theta_q$ are a *finite* set of weights from (9-1). The minus signs on the weights are introduced by convention. The model (9-24) is called a *moving average process* of order q, abbreviated MA(q). In terms of the backward-shift operator, the MA(q) process is

$$x_t = \mu + \left(1 - \theta_1 B^1 - \theta_2 B^2 - \cdots - \theta_q B^q\right)\epsilon_t$$

$$= \mu + \Theta_q(B)\epsilon_t \tag{9-25}$$

where $\Theta_q(B) = (1 - \theta_1 B^1 - \theta_2 B^2 - \cdots - \theta_q B^q)$. The name *moving average* may be somewhat misleading, as the weights $\{\theta_i\}$ need not sum to unity or be positive.

Since there are only a finite number of nonzero weights in the MA(q) process, any MA(q) process will be stationary regardless of the values chosen for the weights. Furthermore, the mean of the MA(q) process is simply

$$E(x_t) = E\left(\mu + \epsilon_t - \theta_1\epsilon_{t-1} - \theta_2\epsilon_{t-2} - \cdots - \theta_q\epsilon_{t-q}\right)$$

$$= \mu \tag{9-26}$$

The variance of the MA(q) process is

$$\gamma_0 = V(x_t) = V\left(\mu + \epsilon_t - \theta_1\epsilon_{t-1} - \theta_2\epsilon_{t-2} - \cdots - \theta_q\epsilon_{t-q}\right)$$

$$= \sigma_\epsilon^2 \sum_{i=0}^{q} \theta_i^2 \tag{9-27}$$

with the convention $\theta_0 = 1$. The autocovariance at lag k is found from

$$\gamma_k = E\Big[\left(\epsilon_t - \theta_1\epsilon_{t-1} - \theta_2\epsilon_{t-2} - \cdots - \theta_q\epsilon_{t-q}\right)$$

$$\times \left(\epsilon_{t-k} - \theta_1\epsilon_{t-k-1} - \theta_2\epsilon_{t-k-2} - \cdots - \theta_q\epsilon_{t-k-q}\right)\Big]$$

which simplifies to

$$\gamma_k = \begin{cases} \sigma_\epsilon^2\left(-\theta_k + \theta_1\theta_{k+1} + \theta_2\theta_{k+2} + \cdots + \theta_{q-k}\theta_q\right) & k = 1, 2, \ldots, q \\ 0 & k > q \end{cases} \tag{9-28}$$

Using (9-27) and (9-28), we see that the autocorrelation function of the MA(q) process is

$$\rho_k = \begin{cases} \dfrac{-\theta_k + \theta_1\theta_{k+1} + \theta_2\theta_{k+2} + \cdots + \theta_{q-k}\theta_q}{1 + \theta_1^2 + \theta_2^2 + \cdots + \theta_q^2} & k = 1, 2, \ldots, q \\ 0 & k > q \end{cases} \tag{9-29}$$

Therefore the autocorrelation function in MA(q) consists of nonzero spikes at lags $1, 2, \ldots, q$ and 0 thereafter. We say that the autocorrelation function *cuts off* at lag q.

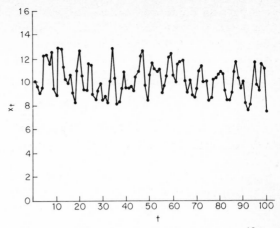

Fig. 9-7   A realization of the MA(1) process $x_t = 10 + \epsilon_t + 0.9\epsilon_{t-1}$.

The first-order moving average process   A very important special case of MA(q) is the first-order moving average process

$$x_t = \mu + \epsilon_t - \theta_1\epsilon_{t-1} \tag{9-30}$$

Using (9-26), (9-27), and (9-29), we find the mean, variance, and autocorrelation function of the MA(1) process as

$$E(x_t) = \mu$$

$$\gamma_0 = \sigma_\epsilon^2(1 + \theta_1^2)$$

$$\rho_k = \begin{cases} \dfrac{-\theta_1}{1 + \theta_1^2} & k = 1 \\[2mm] 0 & k > 1 \end{cases}$$

respectively.   Thus the autocorrelation function cuts off at lag 1.   The process is stationary for any value of θ_1.

A realization of the MA(1) process

$$x_t = 10 + \epsilon_t + 0.9\epsilon_{t-1}$$

with $\sigma_\epsilon^2 = 1$ is shown in Fig. 9-7 and the autocorrelation function is shown in Fig. 9-8.   As we would expect from the autocorrelation function, a high (low) observation in the series tends to be followed by another high (low) observation, although there is no tendency to find long "runs" on either side of the mean.

The second-order moving average process   Another useful process is

$$x_t = \mu + \epsilon_t - \theta_1\epsilon_{t-1} - \theta_2\epsilon_{t-2} \tag{9-31}$$

which is, of course, MA(2).   The MA(2) process is stationary for all values of θ_1

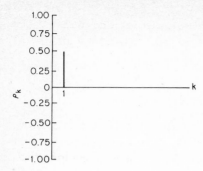

Fig. 9-8 Autocorrelation function of the MA(1) process $x_t = 10 + \epsilon_t + 0.9\epsilon_{t-1}$.

and θ_2.   It is easy to see that the mean, variance, and autocorrelation function of the MA(2) process are

$$E(x_t) = \mu$$

$$\gamma_0 = \sigma_\epsilon^2 (1 + \theta_1^2 + \theta_2^2)$$

$$\rho_1 = \frac{-\theta_1(1 - \theta_1)}{1 + \theta_1^2 + \theta_2^2}$$

$$\rho_2 = \frac{-\theta_2}{1 + \theta_1^2 + \theta_2^2}$$

$$\rho_k = 0 \qquad k > 2$$

respectively.   Therefore the autocorrelation function cuts off after lag 2.

   Invertibility of moving average processes   There is an interesting duality between the moving average and autoregressive processes.   For example, consider the MA(1) process

$$\tilde{x}_t = \epsilon_t - \theta_1 \epsilon_{t-1}$$

$$= (1 - \theta_1 B)\epsilon_t$$

which, when solved for ϵ_t, yields

$$\epsilon_t = (1 - \theta_1 B)^{-1} \tilde{x}_t$$

Now if $|\theta_1| < 1$, we may write the last equation as

$$\epsilon_t = \left(\sum_{j=0}^{\infty} \theta_j B^j \right) \tilde{x}_t$$

or

$$\epsilon_t = (1 + \theta_1 B^1 + \theta_2^2 B^2 + \cdots)\tilde{x}_t$$

which we recognize as an infinite-order autoregressive process with weights $\phi_j = \theta_1^j$. Notice that we have inverted the MA(1) process to obtain an AR(∞) process. The condition

$$|\theta_1| < 1$$

is called the *invertibility* condition for an MA(1) process.

In general, for any MA(q) process to be invertible to an AR(∞) process, we must require that the roots of the polynomial $\Theta_q(B) = 0$ lie outside the unit circle. For the AR(2) process, for example, this is equivalent to requiring that

$$\theta_1 + \theta_2 < 1$$

$$\theta_2 - \theta_1 < 1$$

$$|\theta_2| < 1 \tag{9-32}$$

The invertibility conditions for the parameters in the MA(q) process are identical to the stationary conditions for an AR(q) process. For example, compare (9-32) with (9-16). This duality holds for autoregressive processes as well; that is, the finite AR(p) process can be inverted to give an infinite-order moving average process. To sum up:

1. The MA(q) process is stationary regardless of the values of the weights $\{\theta_i\}$, but is *invertible* only if the roots of $\Theta_q(B) = 0$ lie outside the unit circle.

2. The AR(p) process is *stationary* only if the roots of $\Phi_p(B) = 0$ lie outside the unit circle, but is *invertible* for all values of the weights $\{\phi_i\}$.

9-1.4 Mixed Autoregressive-Moving Average Processes

In building an empirical model of an actual time series, we occasionally find that inclusion of both autoregressive *and* moving average terms leads to a more parsimonious model than could be achieved with either the pure autoregressive or pure moving average forms. This results in the mixed autoregressive–moving average model of order (p, q):

$$x_t = \xi + \phi_1 x_{t-1} + \phi_2 x_{t-2} + \cdots + \phi_p x_{t-p} - \theta_1 \epsilon_{t-1}$$

$$- \theta_2 \epsilon_{t-2} - \cdots - \theta_q \epsilon_{t-q} + \epsilon_t$$

or

$$\Phi_p(B)x_t = \xi + \Theta_q(B)\epsilon_t \tag{9-33}$$

which would be abbreviated ARMA(p, q). The stationarity and invertibility conditions for the AR(p) and MA(q) processes establish these properties for the ARMA(p, q) process. That is, ARMA(p, q) is *stationary* if the roots of $\Phi_p(B) = 0$ lie outside the unit circle, and *invertible* if the roots of $\Theta_q(B) = 0$ lie outside the unit circle.

A very useful special case of (9-33) is the ARMA(1, 1) process

$$x_t = \xi + \phi_1 x_{t-1} + \epsilon_t - \theta_1 \epsilon_{t-1} \tag{9-34}$$

The process is stationary if $|\phi_1| < 1$, and invertible if $|\theta_1| < 1$. It may be shown that the mean, variance, and autocovariances of ARMA(1, 1) are

$$\mu \equiv E(x_t) = \frac{\xi}{1 - \phi_1} \tag{9-35}$$

$$\gamma_0 = \phi_1 \gamma_1 + \sigma_\epsilon^2 [1 - \theta_1(\phi_1 - \theta_1)]$$

$$\gamma_1 = \phi_1 \gamma_0 - \theta_1 \sigma_\epsilon^2 \tag{9-36}$$

and

$$\gamma_k = \phi_1 \gamma_{k-1} \qquad k \geqslant 2$$

respectively. Note that the mean of the ARMA(1, 1) process is identical to the mean of AR(1). Also, the autocovariances for lags greater than one are identical to those for AR(1) because the moving average component of ARMA(1, 1) extends back only one period.

The autocorrelation function of the ARMA(1, 1) process is

$$\rho_1 = \frac{(1 - \phi_1 \theta_1)(\phi_1 - \theta_1)}{1 + \theta_1^2 - 2\theta_1 \phi_1}$$

$$\rho_k = \phi_1 \rho_{k-1} \qquad k \geqslant 2 \tag{9-37}$$

We see that the moving average component enters only into the determination of ρ_1, and thereafter the autocorrelation function decays exponentially from ρ_1. In contrast, recall that the autocorrelation function for AR(1) decays exponentially from $\rho_0 = 1$. For the general ARMA(p, q) process, the first q lags of the autocorrelation function will be affected by the moving average parameters, and lags greater than q will be affected only by the autoregressive parameters.

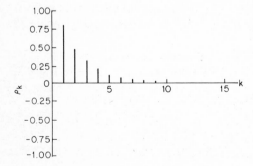

Fig. 9-9 Autocorrelation function of the ARMA(1, 1) process $x_t = 10 + 0.6 x_{t-1} + \epsilon_t + 0.9 \epsilon_{t-1}$.

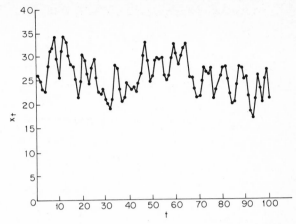

Fig. 9-10 Realization of the ARMA(1, 1) process $x_t = 10 + 0.6x_{t-1} + \epsilon_t + 0.9\epsilon_{t-1}$.

For example, the autocorrelation function of the ARMA(1, 1) process

$$x_t = 10 + 0.6x_{t-1} + \epsilon_t + 0.9\epsilon_{t-1}$$

with $\sigma_\epsilon^2 = 4$ is shown in Fig. 9-9, and a realization is shown in Fig. 9-10. Notice that the effect of the moving average term is to alter the value of ρ_1, after which the autocorrelation function decays just as if it were AR(1) with $\phi_1 = 0.6$.

9-1.5 Nonstationary Processes

The autoregressive-moving average processes discussed above are a powerful class of stationary time series models useful for describing a wide variety of time series. They may also be extended to the analysis of nonstationary time series by a simple operation which we shall describe in this section.

Many time series behave as if they have no constant mean; that is, in any local segment of time the observations look like those in any other segment, apart from their average. Such a time series is called *nonstationary in the mean*. Similarly, it is possible for a time series to exhibit nonstationary behavior in *both mean and slope*; that is, apart from the mean and slope, observations in different segments of time look very much alike. Examples of nonstationary time series are shown in Fig. 9-11.

To see how this type of nonstationary behavior can be incorporated into a time series model, consider the discrete, deterministic signals shown in Fig. 9-12. The time series in Fig. 9-12a exhibits nonstationary behavior in both mean and slope. However, its first difference (that is, $x_t - x_{t-1}$), shown in Fig. 9-12b, is nonstationary in the mean only. Finally, its second difference $[(x_t - x_{t-1}) - (x_{t-1} - x_{t-2}) = x_t - 2x_{t-1} + x_{t-2}]$, shown in Fig. 9-12c, is stationary. Therefore, it seems reasonable to use successive differencing to reduce a nonstationary

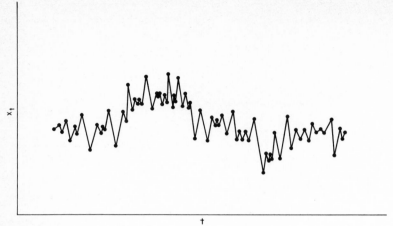

(a) Time series that is nonstationary in the mean

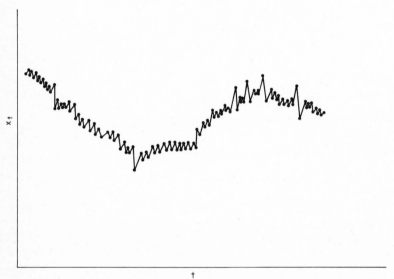

(b) Time series that is nonstationary in mean and slope

Fig. 9-11 (a) and (b)   Two nonstationary time series.

stochastic time series to a stationary series.   If a nonstationary time series can be reduced to a stationary series by applying a suitable degree of differencing, we say the original series is *homogeneously nonstationary*.

We may define the (backward) difference operator ∇ as

$$\nabla x_t = x_t - x_{t-1} \tag{9-38}$$

It is possible to express ∇ in terms of the backward-shift operator B as $\nabla = 1 - B$. Thus, higher-order differencing can be expressed as $\nabla^2 = (1 - B)^2$,

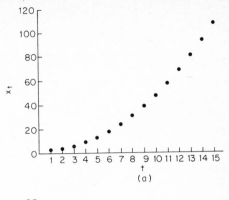

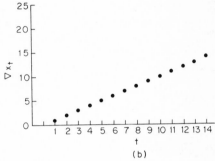

Fig. 9-12 Reducing a discrete, nonstationary signal to a stationary signal by successive differencing.

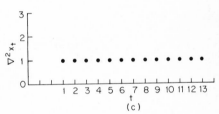

$\nabla^3 = (1 - B)^3, \ldots, \nabla^d = (1 - B)^d$. As an example, the second difference is

$$\nabla^2 x_t = (1 - B)^2 x_t = (1 - 2B + B^2)x_t = x_t - 2x_{t-1} + x_{t-2}$$

Differencing a time series $\{x_t\}$ of length n produces a new time series $\{w_t\}$ $= \{\nabla^d x_t\}$ of length $n - d$. Also, the difference operator acts as if it always operates on the original observations; that is, $w_t = \nabla^d x_t = \nabla^d \tilde{x}_t$. Thus it is immaterial whether or not the observations are corrected for the mean. However, note that in general the new series $\{w_t\}$ may have a nonzero mean.

A general model capable of representing a wide class of nonstationary time series is the *autoregressive integrated moving average* process of order (p, d, q), abbreviated ARIMA(p, d, q), which is

$$\Phi_p(B) \nabla^d x_t = \Theta_q(B)\epsilon_t \qquad (9\text{-}39)$$

or

$$\Phi_p(B)w_t = \Theta_q(B)\epsilon_t \tag{9-40}$$

Thus, the model represents the dth difference of the original series as a process containing p autoregressive and q moving average parameters.

If the differenced series $\{w_t\}$ has a nonzero mean, say μ_w, then the ARIMA(p, d, q) process would be

$$\Phi_p(B)w_t = \mu_w + \Theta_q(B)\epsilon_t \tag{9-41}$$

The effect of allowing μ_w to be nonzero is to introduce a deterministic polynomial of degree d into the eventual forecast function. For example, if $d = 1$ and the polynomial had positive slope, the forecasts would always increase regardless of the behavior of the series. Thus, for this reason we usually assume that $\mu_w = 0$ unless the data indicate otherwise. We shall discuss this point again in Sec. 9-2.1. Also refer to Box and Jenkins ([6], pp. 91–94, 193–195).

Most time series found in practice can usually be adequately modeled by an ARIMA(p, d, q) process in which p, d, and q do not exceed 2. For example, two important processes are the ARIMA(1, 1, 1) process

$$(1 - \phi_1 B)\nabla x_t = (1 - \theta_1 B)\epsilon_t$$

which simplifies to

$$x_t = (1 + \phi_1)x_{t-1} - \phi_1 x_{t-2} + \epsilon_t - \theta_1 \epsilon_{t-1}$$

and the ARIMA(2, 1, 0) process

$$(1 - \phi_1 B^1 - \phi_2 B^2)\nabla x_t = \epsilon_t$$

which can be written as

$$x_t = x_{t-1} + \phi_1(x_{t-1} - x_{t-2}) + \phi_2(x_{t-2} - x_{t-3}) + \epsilon_t$$

It is clear that if $d = 0$, the ARIMA process includes the autoregressive, moving average, and mixed processes discussed previously.

Occasionally, transformations other than differencing are useful in reducing a nonstationary time series to a stationary one. For example, in many economic time series the variability of the observations increases as the average level of the process increases; however, the percentage of change in the observations is relatively independent of level. Therefore, taking the logarithm of the original series will be useful in achieving stationarity.

9-1.6 Relationship to Exponential Smoothing

In certain special cases, exponential smoothing is equivalent to the Box-Jenkins models. For example, consider the ARIMA(0, 1, 1) process

$$\nabla x_t = (1 - \theta B)\epsilon_t$$

which is more conveniently expressed as

$$x_t = x_{t-1} + \epsilon_t - \theta\epsilon_{t-1}$$

Because this nonstationary process contains only a moving average parameter, it is sometimes called an *integrated moving average process*, or IMA(1, 1). We may invert the IMA(1, 1) process to obtain an infinite-order autoregressive process by substituting successively for ϵ_{t-1}, ϵ_{t-2}, etc. This leads to

$$
\begin{aligned}
x_t &= x_{t-1} + \epsilon_t - \theta\epsilon_{t-1} \\
&= x_{t-1} + \epsilon_t - \theta[(x_{t-1} - x_{t-2}) + \theta\epsilon_{t-2}] \\
&= \epsilon_t + (1 - \theta)x_{t-1} + \theta x_{t-2} + \theta^2[(x_{t-2} - x_{t-2}) + \theta\epsilon_{t-3}]
\end{aligned}
$$

and eventually,

$$x_t = (1 - \theta)\sum_{j=1}^{\infty}\theta^{j-1}x_{t-j} + \epsilon_t \qquad\qquad (9\text{-}42)$$

If we let $\alpha = 1 - \theta$, one sees an obvious resemblance to first-order exponential smoothing in (9-42). Note that the invertibility condition $-1 < \theta < 1$ is satisfied for $0 < \alpha < 2$, although, in practice, exponential smoothing is usually restricted to values of α between 0 and 1. Thus, first-order exponential smoothing is the optimal forecasting technique for the IMA(1, 1) process. One approach to selecting the appropriate smoothing constant for first-order exponential smoothing is to fit an IMA(1, 1) process to the data and set $\alpha = 1 - \theta$. This result seems to have first been noted by Muth [44].

Recently, Cogger [16] and Goodman [25] have shown that kth-order exponential smoothing is equivalent to forecasting an IMA(k, k) process. Other relationships between exponential smoothing and the Box-Jenkins models are given in Box and Jenkins ([5], pp. 103–108) and Pandit and Wu [47].

9-2 TIME SERIES MODELING

In their 1970 book, Box and Jenkins present a general methodology for developing an appropriate ARIMA time series model and using the model in forecasting. Their approach consists of a three-step iterative procedure. First a tentative model of the ARIMA class is identified through analysis of historical data. Then the unknown parameters of the model are estimated. Finally, diagnostic checks are performed to determine the adequacy of the model, or to indicate potential improvements. We shall now discuss each of these steps in more detail.

9-2.1 Identification

Tentative identification of an ARIMA time series model is done through analysis of actual historical data. In general, we must have at least 50 observations available to identify the appropriate model satisfactorily. The primary tool used in the identification process is the autocorrelation function. Actually, the *theoretical* autocorrelation function, defined in Eq. (9-7), is unknown and must be estimated by the *sample* autocorrelation function

$$\rho_k = \frac{\dfrac{1}{N-k}\displaystyle\sum_{t=1}^{N-k}(x_t - \bar{x})(x_{t+k} - \bar{x})}{\dfrac{1}{N}\displaystyle\sum_{t=1}^{N}(x_t - \bar{x})^2} \qquad k = 0, 1, \ldots, K \qquad (9\text{-}43)$$

where N is the length of the time series under study. As a general rule, we would compute the first $K \leqslant N/4$ sample autocorrelations.

The partial autocorrelation function also proves useful in the identification process. In Sec. 9-1.1 we defined the partial autocorrelation function in terms of the simple autocorrelation between two random variables in a conditional distribution. It is also possible to show that the partial autocorrelation coefficient ϕ_{kk} is the kth coefficient in an autoregressive process of order k. Therefore, using (9-22), we see that the partial autocorrelation coefficients satisfy the following *Yule-Walker equations*:

$$\rho_j = \phi_{k1}\rho_{j-1} + \phi_{k2}\rho_{j-2} + \cdots + \phi_{kk}\rho_{j-k} \qquad j = 1, 2, \ldots, k \qquad (9\text{-}44)$$

We may estimate the partial autocorrelation coefficients by substituting $\hat{\rho}_j$ for ρ_j in Eq. (9-44), obtaining

$$\hat{\rho}_j = \phi_{k1}\hat{\rho}_{j-1} + \phi_{k2}\hat{\rho}_{j-2} + \cdots + \phi_{kk}\hat{\rho}_{j-k} \qquad j = 1, 2, \ldots, k \qquad (9\text{-}45)$$

and solving (9-45) for $k = 1, 2, \ldots, K$, to obtain $\hat{\phi}_{11}, \hat{\phi}_{22}, \ldots, \hat{\phi}_{KK}$, the sample partial autocorrelation function. Box and Jenkins ([6], app. A3.2) give a simple recursive method for doing this; however, in some instances the sample partial autocorrelations obtained in this manner are sensitive to round-off errors.

Once the sample autocorrelation and partial autocorrelation functions have been computed, they may be exhibited on a graph and a tentative model identified by comparing the *observed* patterns with the *theoretical* autocorrelation function patterns. These theoretical patterns are shown in Table 9-1.

The expression *tails off* in Table 9-1 means that the function decays in an exponential, sinusoidal, or geometric fashion, approximately, with a relatively

TABLE 9-1   Behavior of Theoretical Autocorrelation and Partial Autocorrelation Functions for Stationary Models

Model	Autocorrelation function	Partial autocorrelation function
AR(p)	Tails off	Cuts off after lag p
MA(q)	Cuts off after lag q	Tails off
ARMA(p, q)	Tails off	Tails off

large number of nonzero values. Conversely, *cuts off* implies that the function truncates abruptly with only a very few nonzero values. The duality between the autoregressive and moving average processes referred to earlier is also apparent in Table 9-1. That is, the autocorrelation function for an autoregressive process tails off and the autocorrelation function for a moving average process cuts off, while the partial autocorrelation function for an autoregressive process cuts off and the partial autocorrelation function for a moving average process tails off.

The standard errors of the sample autocorrelation and partial autocorrelation functions are useful in identifying nonzero values. Barlett [2] has shown that the standard error of the kth sample autocorrelation coefficient is

$$S(\hat{\rho}_k) = N^{-\frac{1}{2}} \left[1 + 2 \sum_{j=1}^{k-1} r_j \right] \tag{9-46}$$

where

$$r_j = \begin{cases} \hat{\rho}_j & \text{for } \rho_j \neq 0 \\ 0 & \text{for } \rho_j = 0 \end{cases}$$

and Quenouille [52] has shown that the standard error of the kth sample partial autocorrelation coefficient is

$$S(\hat{\phi}_{kk}) \approx N^{-\frac{1}{2}} \tag{9-47}$$

As a general rule, we would assume an autocorrelation or partial autocorrelation coefficient to be zero if the absolute value of its estimate is less than twice its standard error. It is useful to plot the limits $\pm 2S(\hat{\rho}_k)$ and $\pm 2S(\hat{\phi}_{kk})$ directly on the graphs of these functions.

If the time series is nonstationary, the sample autocorrelation function will die down extremely slowly. This is because in any realization of a nonstationary series the observations will tend to be on the same side of the sample mean for many periods, and, as a result, large sample autocorrelations at very long lags are produced. If this type of behavior is exhibited, the usual approach is to compute the sample autocorrelation and partial autocorrelation function for the first difference of the series. If these functions behave according to the theoretical patterns in Table 9-1, then one difference is necessary to produce stationarity. If not, we must try successively higher orders of differencing until stationary behavior is achieved.

We have said that the differenced series $\{w_t\}$ may have a nonzero mean, say μ_w. At the identification stage we may obtain an indication of whether or not a nonzero value of μ_w is needed by comparing the *sample* mean of the differenced series, say $\bar{w} = \sum_{t=1}^{n-d} w_t / (n-d)$, with its approximate standard error. Box and Jenkins ([6], p. 195) give the approximate standard error of $\bar{w}$ for several useful ARIMA(p, d, q) models.

Identification of the appropriate ARIMA model requires skill obtained by experience. Several excellent examples of the identification process are given in Box and Jenkins ([6], chap. 6) and Nelson [45].

9-2.2 Estimation

After an appropriate time series model has been tentatively identified, the least-squares estimates of the model parameters are obtained. Recall that a *linear* model is a model which is linear in the unknown parameters. It is easy to see that this implies that if a model is linear, then the partial derivative of the ϵ_t with respect to any parameter is not a function of the model parameters.

For example, consider the AR(p) process

$$x_t = \xi + \phi_1 x_{t-1} + \phi_1 x_{t-2} + \cdots + \phi_p x_{t-p} + \epsilon_t$$

or

$$\epsilon_t = x_t - \xi - \phi_1 x_{t-1} - \phi_2 x_{t-2} - \cdots - \phi_p x_{t-p}$$

Now

$$\frac{\partial \epsilon_t}{\partial \phi_i} = -x_{t-i} \qquad \frac{\partial \epsilon_t}{\partial \xi} = -1$$

and since the partial derivatives are not functions of ϕ_i or ξ, we may estimate the parameters in the AR(p) process by linear least squares.

We shall illustrate this idea for the AR(2) process

$$x_t = \xi + \phi_1 x_{t-1} + \phi_2 x_{t-2} + \epsilon_t$$

Assuming that there are N observations available, the AR(2) model may be written in matrix form as

$$
\begin{bmatrix}
x_3 \\
x_4 \\
\vdots \\
x_{n-1} \\
x_n
\end{bmatrix}
=
\begin{bmatrix}
1 & x_2 & x_1 \\
1 & x_3 & x_2 \\
\cdots & \cdots & \cdots \\
1 & x_{n-2} & x_{n-3} \\
1 & x_{n-1} & x_{n-2}
\end{bmatrix}
\begin{bmatrix}
\xi \\
\phi_1 \\
\phi_2
\end{bmatrix}
+
\begin{bmatrix}
\epsilon_3 \\
\epsilon_4 \\
\vdots \\
\epsilon_{n-1} \\
\epsilon_n
\end{bmatrix}
$$

or, with an obvious notation,

$$\mathbf{x} = \mathbf{Z}\boldsymbol{\phi} + \boldsymbol{\epsilon}$$

Therefore, the least-squares estimates of the autoregressive parameters are

$$\hat{\boldsymbol{\phi}} = (\mathbf{Z}'\mathbf{Z})^{-1}\mathbf{Z}'\mathbf{x}$$

For the general AR(p) process, the $\mathbf{Z}$ matrix will be $(N-p)\times(p+1)$. Notice that this procedure uses only the last $N-2$ observations, because the quantities x_0 and x_{-1}, required by the AR(2) process at times $t=1$ and $t=2$, do not exist. An alternate solution to this problem of starting values is to set $x_0=x_{-1}=0$. Box and Jenkins ([6], chap. 7) discuss other approaches to the starting-value problem. In general, for moderately long time series, the choice of starting values will have little effect on the least-squares estimates $\hat{\phi}$.

Unfortunately, estimation of the parameters in moving average and mixed processes is not so simple. For example, consider the MA(1) process

$$x_t = \epsilon_t - \theta_1 \epsilon_{t-1}$$

or

$$\epsilon_t = (1 - B\theta_1)^{-1} x_t$$

The first derivative is

$$\frac{\partial \epsilon_t}{\partial \theta_1} = B(1 - B\theta_1)^{-2}$$

which is a function of the unknown parameter θ_1. Thus models with moving average terms cannot be treated by ordinary linear least squares. A discussion of least squares in the nonlinear case, or *nonlinear least squares*, is given in Box and Jenkins ([6], chap. 7) and Draper and Smith [23].

There are no closed-form solutions for the least-squares estimates of the parameters in nonlinear models. The usual approach is to apply an iterative search procedure directly to the residual sum of squares function. Any non-linear regression algorithm requires initial estimates of the model parameters. These *preliminary estimates* of parameters, as they are called by Box and Jenkins, are obtained through the relationships that link model parameters and auto-correlations. The procedure consists of replacing the autocorrelations by their estimates and solving for the unknown model parameters. For example, in the AR(1) process, we know that the theoretical autocorrelations obey the relationship $\rho_k = \phi_1^k$. Thus, if we had an estimate $\hat{\rho}_1$ of ρ_1, a logical preliminary estimate of ϕ_1 would be $\hat{\phi}_1 = \hat{\rho}_1$.

In addition to providing a starting point for a nonlinear regression algorithm, preliminary parameter estimates also give the analyst an idea of how the final model will look. One should exercise caution in drawing inferences from such models, however, as the final least-squares estimates of the model parameters may differ considerably from the preliminary estimates.

9-2.3 Diagnostic Checking

After a tentative model has been fit to the data, we must examine its adequacy, and, if necessary, suggest potential improvements. If the fitted model is adequate, it should transform the observations to a white noise process. Thus, a logical method of diagnostic checking is to compute the residuals, say

$e_t = x_t - \hat{x}_t$, and then estimate and examine their autocorrelation function. Let the sample autocorrelation function of the residuals be denoted by $\{\hat{\rho}_k(e)\}$. If the model is appropriate, then the residual sample autocorrelation function should have no structure to identify; that is, the autocorrelation should not differ significantly from zero for all lags greater than one. If the form of the model were *correct* and if we knew the *true* parameter values, then the standard error of the residual autocorrelations would be $N^{-1/2}$. However, at low lags, the standard error of $\hat{\rho}_k(e)$ may be substantially less than $N^{-1/2}$, and thus one must be careful in concluding that low-lag residual autocorrelations are not significantly different from zero.

If any of the residual autocorrelations are nonzero, we would incorporate the apparent structure into the original model and refit the series. This process is continued until the residual autocorrelations resemble those of a white noise process.

Rather than consider the $\hat{\rho}_k(e)$'s individually, we may obtain an indication of whether the first K residual autocorrelations *considered together* indicate adequacy of the model. This indication may be obtained through an approximate chi-square test of model adequacy. The test statistic is

$$Q = (N - d) \sum_{k=1}^{K} \hat{\rho}_k^2(e)$$

which is approximately distributed as chi-square with $K - p - q$ degrees of freedom if the model is appropriate. If the model is inadequate, the calculated value of Q will be too large. Thus we should reject the hypothesis of model adequacy if Q exceeds an appropriately small upper tail point of the chi-square distribution with $K - p - q$ degrees of freedom. Further details of this test are in Box and Pierce [7].

9-2.4 Examples of the Modeling Process

In this section we shall present two examples of the identification, estimation, and diagnostic checking process. One example presents the analysis for a stationary time series, while the other is an example of modeling a nonstationary series.

EXAMPLE 9-1 A chemical process yields a product whose viscosity is an important quality characteristic. The last 100 viscosity readings are available, and are listed in Table 9-2 and shown in Fig. 9-13. We would like to develop a time series model for this process so that a control scheme for the process output can be developed.

The sample autocorrelation and partial autocorrelation functions for the series are shown in Table 9-3 and Fig. 9-14. For assistance in interpreting these functions, two-standard-error limits computed from (9-46) and (9-47) are plotted on the graphs as dashed lines. We see from Fig. 9-14 that the sample auto-

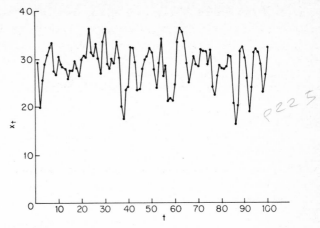

Fig. 9-13 Viscosity of a chemical product.

correlation function tails off with a sinusoidal decay, while the sample partial autocorrelation function cuts off after two lags. Thus, we would tentatively identify the underlying model of our series to be a stationary AR(2) model.

Occasionally in the identification phase it is useful to examine graphs of $|\hat{\rho}_k|$ and $|\hat{\phi}_{kk}|$, so that the effect of negative correlation will not confuse the analyst. Such graphs make the decay of the autocorrelation and/or partial autocorrelation function easier to see. For example, if we plot $|\hat{\rho}_k|$ for $k = 1, 2, \ldots, 36$, for our series we obtain the graph in Fig. 9-15. The sinusoidal decay of the autocorrelation function is now more apparent.

TABLE 9-2   Viscosity Data for Example 9-1 (100 Observations, Read Down from Left)

29.33	30.80	32.43	33.61	28.17
19.98	30.45	32.44	36.54	28.58
25.76	36.61	29.39	35.70	30.76
29.00	31.40	23.45	33.68	30.62
31.03	30.83	23.62	29.29	20.84
32.68	33.22	28.12	25.12	16.57
33.56	30.15	29.94	27.23	25.23
27.50	27.08	30.56	30.61	31.79
26.75	33.66	32.30	29.06	32.52
30.55	36.58	31.58	28.48	30.28
28.94	29.04	27.99	32.01	26.14
28.50	28.08	24.13	31.89	19.03
28.19	30.28	29.20	31.72	24.34
26.13	29.35	34.30	29.02	31.53
27.79	33.60	26.41	31.92	31.95
27.63	30.29	28.78	24.28	31.68
29.89	20.11	21.28	22.69	29.10
28.18	17.51	21.71	26.60	23.15
26.65	23.71	21.47	28.86	26.74
30.01	24.22	24.71	28.27	32.44

Sample autocorrelations:

Lags 1-12	0.51	−0.09	−0.33	−0.32	−0.07	0.26	0.25	0.04	−0.07	−0.13	−0.12	0.03
standard error	0.10	0.12	0.12	0.13	0.14	0.14	0.15	0.15	0.15	0.15	0.15	0.15
Lags 13-24	0.05	−0.08	−0.15	−0.12	−0.13	−0.03	0.16	0.22	0.06	−0.07	−0.18	−0.17
standard error	0.15	0.15	0.15	0.15	0.15	0.16	0.16	0.16	0.16	0.16	0.16	0.16
Lags 25-36	−0.01	0.08	0.01	0.03	0.02	−0.14	−0.16	0.00	0.05	0.06	0.02	−0.06
standard error	0.16	0.16	0.17	0.17	0.17	0.17	0.17	0.17	0.17	0.17	0.17	0.17

Sample partial autocorrelations (standard error ≈ 0.1):

Lags 1-12	0.51	−0.47	−0.03	−0.18	0.16	0.18	−0.17	0.05	0.06	−0.06	−0.01	0.04
Lags 12-24	−0.13	−0.08	−0.10	0.00	−0.18	0.06	0.13	0.10	−0.15	0.10	−0.09	0.02
Lags 25-36	−0.07	−0.12	−0.06	0.07	−0.06	−0.23	0.01	0.10	0.00	−0.05	−0.07	0.08

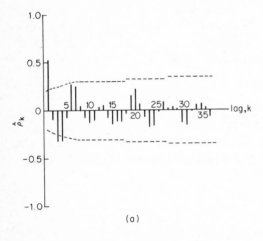

(a)

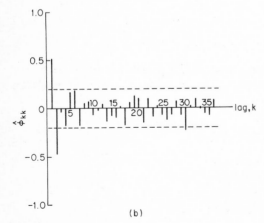

(b)

Fig. 9-14 Sample (a) autocorrelation and (b) partial autocorrelation functions for the time series in Example 9-1.

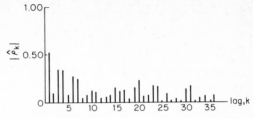

Fig. 9-15 Plot of $|\hat{\rho}_k|$ for the data in Example 9-1.

Having tentatively identified the model for this series as AR(2), we will now estimate the parameters ϕ_1, ϕ_2, and ξ. Parameter estimates may be easily obtained using a computer program prepared by the University of Wisconsin Computing Center [60]. This program is available commercially for a modest charge and is of considerable value to the analyst who wishes to use the Box-Jenkins approach to time series modeling.

Although linear least squares can be used to estimate the parameters of an AR(2) process, the University of Wisconsin program employs a nonlinear regression algorithm. We may find preliminary estimates of the model parameters of the AR(2) process from the *Yule-Walker* equations (9-23):

$$\rho_1 = \phi_1 + \phi_2\rho_1$$

$$\rho_2 = \phi_1\rho_1 + \phi_2$$

Using the estimates $\hat{\rho}_1 = 0.51$ and $\hat{\rho}_2 = 0.09$, we may solve the above equations to obtain $\hat{\phi}_1 = 0.751$ and $\hat{\phi}_2 = 0.473$. A preliminary estimate of ξ is obtained by solving (9-17) for ξ, which yields

$$\xi = E(x_t)(1 - \phi_1 - \phi_2)$$

Replacing $E(x_t)$ by $\bar{x}$ (the sample mean of the series) and ϕ_1 and ϕ_2 by $\hat{\phi}_1$ and $\hat{\phi}_2$, respectively, we obtain

$$\hat{\xi} = (28.68)(1 - 0.751 + 0.473) = 20.81$$

The actual least-squares estimates of the model parameters are obtained by using the preliminary parameter estimates as a starting point for the nonlinear regression algorithm. This results in

$$\hat{\phi}_1 = 0.777$$

$$\hat{\phi}_2 = 0.492$$

and

$$\hat{\xi} = 20.62$$

as the least-squares estimates. Note that the final estimates of the parameters

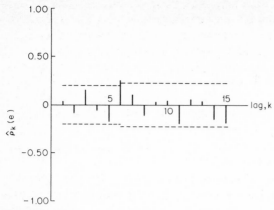

Fig. 9-16 Sample autocorrelation function of the residuals in Example 9-1.

are not far from the preliminary values. Thus, our tentative model is

$$x_t = 20.62 + 0.777x_{t-1} - 0.492x_{t-2} + \epsilon_t$$

The tentative model may be used to generate the fitted values of the time series and the residuals. For example, the first fitted value that can be computed is

$$\hat{x}_3 = 20.62 + 0.77x_2 - 0.492x_1$$

$$= 20.62 + 0.777(19.98) - 0.492(29.33)$$

$$= 21.72$$

and the corresponding residual is $x_3 - \hat{x}_3 = 25.76 - 21.72 = 4.04$.

The sample autocorrelation function of the residuals for this model is shown in Fig. 9-16. Of the 15 autocorrelations, only one at lag 6 is greater than its two-standard-error limit. We may consider simultaneously the effect of the first 15 autocorrelations by computing the approximate chi-square statistic

$$Q = (N - d) \sum_{k=1}^{K} \hat{\rho}_k^2(e)$$

$$= (100)\left[(0.03)^2 + (-0.09)^2 + \cdots + (-0.18)^2\right]$$

$$= 20.50$$

Comparing $Q = 20.50$ with a 5 percent value chi-square variable with 13 degrees of freedom, we find $\chi_{0.05,\,13}^2 = 22.36$, and so we would conclude that there is no strong evidence to reject the model.

EXAMPLE 9-2 The weekly demand for a small plastic container for the past 100 weeks is shown in Fig. 9-17. The container is manufactured by an injection molding process, and is widely used by several pharmaceutical houses as a package for a prescription drug. In examining Fig. 9-17, we note that the series tends to drift somewhat with no obvious mean. Thus, we suspect that the series is nonstationary.

From the listing of the time series in Table 9-4 we may calculate the sample autocorrelation function. This function is plotted in Fig. 9-18. We notice that the sample autocorrelation function dies down very slowly, which confirms our initial impression of nonstationarity.

The first difference of the plastic container demand data is listed in Table 9-5, and plotted in Fig. 9-19. Differencing seems to have been appropriate, as the

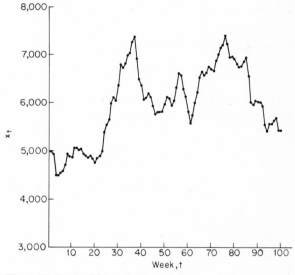

Fig. 9-17 Demand for a plastic container.

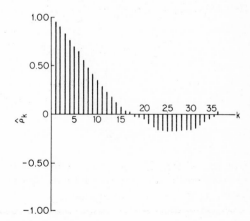

Fig. 9-18 Sample autocorrelation function of the time series in Fig. 9-17.

**TABLE 9-4 Weekly Demand for a Plastic
Container (100 Observations, Read Down
from Left)**

5,000	5,657	6,132	7,411
4,965	6,010	6,111	7,233
4,496	6,109	5,948	6,958
4,491	6,052	6,056	6,960
4,566	6,391	6,342	6,927
4,585	6,798	6,626	6,814
4,724	6,740	6,591	6,757
4,951	6,778	6,302	6,765
4,917	7,005	6,132	6,870
4,888	7,045	5,837	6,954
5,087	7,279	5,572	6,551
5,082	7,367	5,744	6,022
5,039	6,934	6,005	5,974
5,054	6,506	6,239	6,052
4,940	6,374	6,523	6,033
4,913	6,066	6,652	6,030
4,871	6,102	6,585	5,944
4,901	6,204	6,622	5,543
4,864	6,138	6,754	5,416
4,750	5,938	6,712	5,571
4,856	5,781	6,675	5,571
4,959	5,813	6,882	5,627
5,004	5,811	7,011	5,679
5,415	5,818	7,140	5,455
5,550	5,982	7,197	5,443

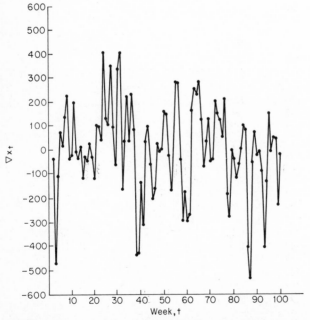

Fig. 9-19 First difference of weekly plastic container demand.

overall visual impression in Fig. 9-19 is that the series of first differences is stationary. This is confirmed by the sample autocorrelation and partial autocorrelation functions, which are shown in Fig. 9-20. We find that the sample autocorrelation function cuts off after lag one, while the sample partial autocorrelation function tails off. This is indicative of an MA(1) process. Furthermore, the sample mean of the series of first differences is 4.47, which is small relative to the observations, so that it is unlikely that a constant term is required in the model. Therefore, we would tentatively identify our time series as the ARIMA(0, 1, 1), or IMA(1, 1), process

$$\nabla x_t = (1 - B\theta)\epsilon_t$$

which we may write as

$$x_t = x_{t-1} + \epsilon_t - \theta\epsilon_{t-1}$$

The IMA(1, 1) process has only one parameter to estimate, θ. A preliminary estimate of this parameter can be found from the theoretical autocorrelation function of the MA(1) process, which is

$$\rho_1 = \frac{-\theta}{1 + \theta^2}$$

TABLE 9-5   The First Difference of Weekly Plastic Container Demand (99 Observations, Read Down from Left)

−35	353	−21	−178
−469	99	−163	−275
−5	−57	108	2
75	339	286	−33
19	407	284	−113
139	−58	−35	−54
227	38	−289	8
−34	227	−170	105
−29	40	−295	84
199	234	−265	−403
−5	88	172	−529
−43	−433	261	−48
15	−428	234	78
−114	−132	284	−19
−27	−308	129	−3
−42	36	−67	−86
30	102	37	−401
−37	−66	132	−127
−114	−200	−42	155
106	−157	−37	0
103	32	207	56
45	−2	157	52
411	7	129	−224
135	164	57	−12
107	150	214	

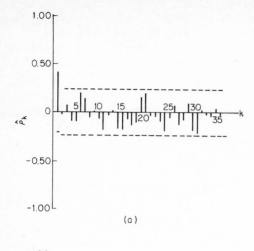

(a)

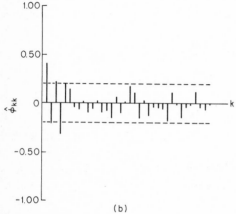

Fig. 9-20 Sample (a) autocorrelation and (b) partial autocorrelation functions for the first difference of weekly plastic container demand.

(b)

Substituting $\hat{\rho}_1 = 0.41$ we obtain a quadratic equation in θ whose roots are -1.9176 and -0.5215. Clearly only $\hat{\theta} = -0.5215$ satisfies the invertability condition $|\theta| < 1$ for an MA(1) process. Using the preliminary estimate of $\hat{\theta} = -0.5215$ and the University of Wisconsin program, we obtain the least-squares estimate of θ as $\hat{\theta} = -0.70$. Note that the preliminary estimate of θ differs considerably from the final least-squares estimate.

Our tentative model is

$$x_t = x_{t-1} + \epsilon_t + 0.70\epsilon_{t-1}$$

We next generate the residuals from this model and test the adequacy of the fit. No residual can be generated for $t = 1$; however, for $t = 2$ we find

$$\hat{x}_2 = x_1 + \epsilon_2 + 0.70\epsilon_1$$

and since our best estimate of both ϵ_2 and ϵ_1 is zero we find $\hat{x}_2 = x_1 = 5,000$. The actual observation in period 2 is $x_2 = 4,965$, so that the residual for period 2

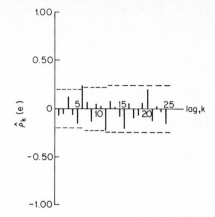

Fig. 9-21 Sample autocorrelation function of the residuals for Example 9-2.

is $e_2 = x_2 - \hat{x}_2 = 4{,}965 - 5{,}000 = -35$.   Similarly, for period 3 we find

$$\hat{x}_3 = x_2 + \epsilon_3 + 0.70\epsilon_2$$

$$= 4{,}965 + 0 + 0.70(-35)$$

$$= 4{,}940.5$$

and the residual $e_3 = x_3 - \hat{x}_3 = 4{,}496 - 4{,}941 = -445$.   The remaining residuals for periods $t = 4, 5, \ldots, 100$, may be generated similarly.

The sample autocorrelation function of the residuals is shown in Fig. 9-21. The overall impression is that the autocorrelations are those of a white noise process, although the autocorrelations at lags 6 and 11 are relatively large.   The chi-square statistic, applied to these auotcorrelations, is

$$Q = (n - d) \sum_{k=1}^{K} \hat{\rho}_k^2(e)$$

$$= (99)\Big[(-0.06)^2 + (-0.05)^2 + \cdots + (-0.15)^2\Big]$$

$$= 31.67$$

The 5 percent critical value of chi-square with 23 degrees of freedom is $\chi_{0.05,\,23}^2 = 35.172$, and so we have no evidence to reject the model.

9-3 FORECASTING

Once an appropriate model has been fit, it may be used to generate forecasts of future observations that are optimal in a minimum mean square error sense. Denote the current period by T, and suppose we wish to forecast the series in period $T + \tau$. Let $\hat{x}_{T+\tau}(T)$ represent the forecast for period $T + \tau$ made at origin T.

The forecast is generated by taking expectation at origin T of the model written at time $T + \tau$. Generally, the forecast for period $T + \tau$ must be built up successively from the forecasts for periods $T + 1, T + 2, \ldots, T + \tau - 1$. In this procedure, the x_{T+j} that have not occurred at time T are replaced by the forecasts $\hat{x}_{T+j}(T)$, the ϵ_{T+j} that have not occurred at time T are replaced by zero, and the ϵ_{T-j} that have occurred are replaced by the single-period forecast error $e_1(T - j) \equiv x_{T-j} - \hat{x}_{T-j}(T - j - 1)$. In starting the forecasting process, it will be necessary to assume that $\epsilon_{T-j} = 0$ for $T - j \leqslant 0$.

As an illustration, consider forecasting the ARIMA(1, 1, 1) process. At time $T + \tau$ the model is

$$(1 - \phi_1 B) \nabla x_{T+\tau} = (1 - \phi_1 B)\epsilon_{T+\tau}$$

or

$$x_{T+\tau} = (1 + \phi_1)x_{T+\tau-1} - \phi_1 x_{T+\tau-2} + \epsilon_{T+\tau} - \theta_1 \epsilon_{T+\tau-1}$$

Letting $\tau = 1$ and taking expectation at time T, we obtain

$$E[x_{T+1}] \equiv \hat{x}_{T+1}(T) = (1 + \phi_1)x_T - \phi_1 x_{T-1} - \theta_1 e_1(T)$$

since $E(\epsilon_{T+1}) = 0$, and at the end of time T, ϵ_T is estimated by $e_1(T) = x_T - \hat{x}_T(T - 1)$. For $\tau \geqslant 2$, we obtain by a similar procedure

$$E[x_{T+\tau}] \equiv \hat{x}_{T+\tau}(T) = (1 + \phi_1)\hat{x}_{T+\tau-1}(T)\phi_1\hat{x}_{T+\tau-2}(T) \qquad \tau \geqslant 2$$

since at origin T our best estimates of $x_{T+\tau-1}$ and $x_{T+\tau-2}$ are $\hat{x}_{T+\tau-1}(T)$ and $\hat{x}_{T+\tau-2}(T)$, respectively. This procedure is usually called forecasting with the difference-equation form of the model, because $\hat{x}_{T+\tau}(T)$ is simply a *difference equation* in the $\{x_t\}$ and $\{\epsilon_t\}$.

It is also possible to obtain forecasts using the model expressed in terms of the ψ weights. In general, at origin T, we may write

$$x_{T+\tau} = \psi_1 \epsilon_{T+\tau-1} + \psi_2 \epsilon_{T+\tau-2} + \cdots + \psi_{\tau-1}\epsilon_{T+1}$$

$$+ \psi_\tau \epsilon_T + \psi_{\tau+1}\epsilon_{T-1} + \cdots + \epsilon_{T+\tau} \qquad (9\text{-}48)$$

This is sometimes called the *random shock* form of the model. Now at times $t > T$ we may replace the corresponding ϵ_t by zero and at times $t \leqslant T$ we would replace ϵ_t by $e_1(t)$. Thus the forecasting function corresponding to (9-48) is

$$\hat{x}_{T+\tau}(T) = \psi_\tau e_1(T) + \psi_{\tau+1}e_1(T - 1) + \cdots \qquad (9\text{-}49)$$

The ψ weights in (9-49) can be found from the model parameters $\{\phi_i\}$ and/or $\{\theta_i\}$ very easily. Recall that the linear filter can be written as

$$x_t = \Psi(B)\epsilon_t$$

or

$$\epsilon_t = \frac{x_t}{\Psi(B)} \tag{9-50}$$

Substituting in (9-39), we obtain

$$\Phi_p(B)\nabla^d x_t = \Theta_q(B)\frac{x_t}{\Psi(B)}$$

or

$$\Psi(B)\Phi_p(B)(1-B)^d x_t = \Theta(B)x_t$$

Therefore, the ψ weights may be obtained by equating coefficients of like powers of B in the expansion

$$(\psi_0 + \psi_1 B + \cdots)(1 - \phi_1 B - \phi_2 B^2 - \cdots - \phi_p B^p)(1 - B)^d$$

$$= (1 - \theta_1 B - \theta_2 B^2 - \cdots - \theta_q B^q) \tag{9-51}$$

To illustrate the use of (9-51), consider the ARMA(1, 1) model

$$(1 - \phi_1 B)x_t = \xi + (1 - \theta_1 B)\epsilon_t$$

To calculate the ψ weights, we equate coefficients of like powers of B in

$$(\psi_0 + \psi_1 B + \cdots)(1 - \phi_1 B) = (1 - \theta_1 B)$$

For B^0, this yields $\psi_0 = 1$. For B^1, we obtain $\psi_1 = \phi_1 - \theta_1$. For B^2, we find

$$\psi_2 - \phi_1\psi_1 = 0$$

which yields $\psi_2 = \phi_1(\phi_1 - \theta_1)$. For this process, we may show in general that $\psi_j = \phi_1^{j-1}(\phi_1 - \theta_1)$.

There are two reasons why we are interested in the random shock form of the model. First, it admits a simple algorithm for updating the forecasts at the end of each time period. This procedure is described by Box and Jenkins ([6] pp. 132–135); see also Exercise 9-25. However, for simple forecasting problems, the difference-equation form of the model is most frequently used. Second, we may easily obtain probability limits on the τ-step-ahead forecast from the random shock form of the model. From (9-48) and (9-49), we find the τ-step-ahead forecast error as

$$e_\tau(T) = \epsilon_{T+\tau} + \psi_1\epsilon_{T+\tau-1} + \psi_2\epsilon_{T+\tau-2} + \cdots + \psi_{\tau-1}\epsilon_{T+1} \tag{9-52}$$

The variance of $e_\tau(T)$ is

$$V[e_\tau(T)] = \sigma_\epsilon^2\left(1 + \sum_{j=1}^{\tau-1}\psi_j^2\right)$$

Therefore, approximate $100(1 - \alpha)$ percent probability limits on the forecast for period $T + \tau$ would be computed from

$$\hat{x}_{T+\tau}(T) \pm u_{1-\alpha/2}\hat{\sigma}_{\epsilon}\left(1 + \sum_{j=1}^{\tau-1} \hat{\psi}_j^2\right)^{\frac{1}{2}} \tag{9-53}$$

where $u_{1-\alpha/2}$ is a $100(1 - \alpha/2)$ percentile of the standard normal distribution, $\{\hat{\psi}_j\}$ are the estimates of the $\{\psi_j\}$, and $\hat{\sigma}_{\epsilon}$ is an estimate of σ_{ϵ}. We usually estimate the variance of the white noise process by

$$\hat{\sigma}_{\epsilon}^2 = \frac{\mathrm{SS}(\hat{\phi}, \hat{\theta})}{r - m}$$

where $\mathrm{SS}(\hat{\phi}, \hat{\theta})$ = the value of the residual sum of squares function corresponding to the least-squares estimators of the model parameters
   r = the number of residuals
   m = the number of parameters in the model which have been estimated

---

EXAMPLE 9-3 We shall demonstrate forecasting with the Box-Jenkins models by forecasting the time series analyzed in Example 9-1. Recall that the model fit to the viscosity data in that example was the stationary AR(2) process

$$x_t = 20.62 + 0.777x_{t-1} - 0.492x_{t-2} + \epsilon_t$$

This is the difference-equation form of the model. To forecast for period $T + \tau$, we simply take expectation at origin T of

$$x_{T+\tau} = 20.62 + 0.777x_{T+\tau-1} - 0.492x_{T+\tau-2} + \epsilon_{T+\tau}$$

For $\tau = 1$ this yields

$$E[x_{T+1}] \equiv \hat{x}_{T+1}(T) = 20.62 + 0.777x_T - 0.492x_{T-1}$$

and for $\tau = 2$

$$E[x_{T+2}] \equiv \hat{x}_{T+2}(T) = 20.62 + 0.777\hat{x}_{T+1}(T) - 0.492x_T$$

Finally, for $\tau > 2$ we would obtain

$$E[x_{T+\tau}] \equiv \hat{x}_{T+\tau}(T) = 20.62 + 0.777\hat{x}_{T+\tau-1}(T) - 0.492\hat{x}_{T+\tau-2}(T) \qquad \tau > 2$$

The forecasts obtained from this model for $\tau = 1, 2, \ldots, 12$, using $t = 100$ as the time origin, are shown in Fig. 9-22. Notice that the curve projected by the forecast function $\hat{x}_{T+\tau}(T)$ depends upon the two previous realizations or their

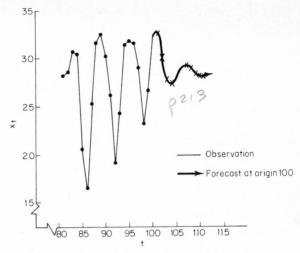

Fig. 9-22 Forecasts of viscosity data at origin $T = 100$, AR(2) model.

forecasts. Eventually, however, it will settle down to the estimate of the mean of the series, which is found from Eq. (9-17) as

$$\widehat{E(x_t)} = \frac{\hat{\xi}}{1 - \hat{\phi}_1 - \hat{\phi}_2}$$

$$= \frac{20.62}{1 - 0.777 - (-0.492)}$$

$$= 28.84$$

It is also possible to obtain probability limits on the forecasts at origin T from Eq. (9-53). The ψ weights for this model are found by equating like powers of B in the expansion

$$(\psi_0 + \psi_1 B^1 + \psi_2 B^2 + \cdots)(1 - \phi_1 B^1 - \phi_2 B^2) = 1$$

This yields

$$\psi_0 = 1 \qquad \psi_1 = \phi_1$$

$$\psi_2 = \phi_1 \psi_1 + \phi_2$$

and in general,

$$\psi_j = \phi_1 \psi_{j-1} + \phi_2 \psi_{j-2} \qquad j = 3, 4, \ldots$$

TABLE 9-6   Forecasts and 0.95 Probability Limits for the Viscosity Data at Origin $T = 100$

Lead time, τ	0.95 lower probability limit	Forecast, $\hat{x}_{100+\tau}(100)$	0.95 upper probability limit
1	26.64	32.66	38.69
2	22.40	30.03	37.66
3	20.22	27.87	35.53
4	19.63	27.50	35.36
5	20.21	28.26	36.31
6	20.98	29.04	37.11
7	21.20	29.27	37.35
8	20.97	29.07	37.17
9	20.69	28.80	36.90
10	20.58	28.68	36.79
11	20.63	28.73	36.84
12	20.72	28.84	36.93

Using $\hat{\phi}_1 = 0.777$ and $\hat{\phi}_2 = -0.492$ we obtain the following values of the weights:

$$\hat{\psi}_0 = 1$$

$$\hat{\psi}_1 = 0.777$$

$$\hat{\psi}_2 = 0.777(0.777) + (-0.492) = 0.111$$

and

$$\hat{\psi}_j = 0.777\hat{\psi}_{j-1} - 0.492\hat{\psi}_{j-2} \qquad \text{for } j = 3, 4, \ldots$$

An estimate of the variance of the white noise process is obtained by dividing the residual sum of squares (which for this series is 897.78) by the number of degrees of freedom (equal to the number of residuals minus the number of model parameters estimated from the data, or $98 - 3 = 95$). Thus $\hat{\sigma}_\epsilon^2 = 94.50$, and the 95 percent probability limits on the forecast can be directly computed from (9-53). These probability limits are shown in Table 9-6. Note that the limits increase in width as the forecast lead time τ increases.

Forecasts for each future observation may be easily revised as a new observation becomes available through the difference-equation form of the model. For example, if $x_{101} = 34.50$, then we may set the new origin of time equal to $T = 101$ and compute the new forecast for period 102 according to

$$\hat{x}_{102}(101) = 20.62 + 0.777x_{101} - 0.492x_{100}$$

$$= 20.62 + 0.777(34.50) - 0.492(32.44)$$

$$= 31.47$$

EXAMPLE 9-4 To demonstrate forecasting a nonstationary process, consider the IMA(1, 1) model

$$x_t = x_{t-1} + \epsilon_t + 0.70\epsilon_{t-1}$$

which we fit to the plastic container demand data in Example 9-2. If T is the time origin from which the forecast is to be made, then as usual we find the forecast $\hat{x}_{T+\tau}(T)$ by taking expectation of $x_{T+\tau}$. For example, if $\tau = 1$, then

$$\hat{x}_{T+1}(T) = x_T + 0.70e_1(T)$$

since $E(\epsilon_{T+1}) = 0$ and ϵ_T would be replaced by the one-step-ahead error for period T. For forecast lead times $\tau > 1$ we would obtain

$$\hat{x}_{T+\tau}(T) = E[x_{T+\tau-1} + \epsilon_{T+\tau} + 0.70\epsilon_{T+\tau-1}]$$

$$= \hat{x}_{T+\tau-1}(T)$$

since at origin T both $\epsilon_{T+\tau}$ and $\epsilon_{T+\tau-1}$ have zero expectation. Thus, for any lead time $\tau \geqslant 1$ the forecast function for an IMA(1, 1) process is the horizontal line $\hat{x}_{T+\tau}(T) = \hat{x}_{T+1}(T)$.

The forecasts at origin $T = 100$ for lead times $\tau = 1, 2, \ldots, 12$, are shown in Fig. 9-23. The 0.50 and 0.95 probability limits for the forecasts are also shown on the graph. Notice that the width of the probability limits increases as τ increases. Also, the 0.50 limits are considerably narrower than the 0.95 limits.

The forecasts shown in Fig. 9-23 may be easily computed using the difference-equation form of the model. At origin $T = 100$, we have

$$\hat{x}_{101}(100) = x_{100} + 0.70e_1(100)$$

The one-step-ahead forecast error at period 100 is not available, as no forecasts were made prior to $T = 100$, and so we approximate $e_1(100)$ by the residual for period 100, which is 137.8. Thus, since $x_{100} = 5,443$, we obtain

$$\hat{x}_{101}(100) = 5,443 + 0.70(137.8)$$

$$= 5,539.48$$

Since the eventual forecast function for IMA(1, 1) is the horizontal line $\hat{x}_{T+\tau}(T) = \hat{x}_{T+1}(T)$, we obtain

$$\hat{x}_{100+\tau}(100) = 5,539.48 \qquad \tau \geqslant 2$$

as the forecast for all future periods from origin 100.

Probability limits on the forecasts are computed from Eq. (9-53), where we have used $\hat{\sigma}_\epsilon^2 = 2.52$ as an estimate of the variance of the white noise process. This value is obtained by dividing the residual sum of squares from the fitted

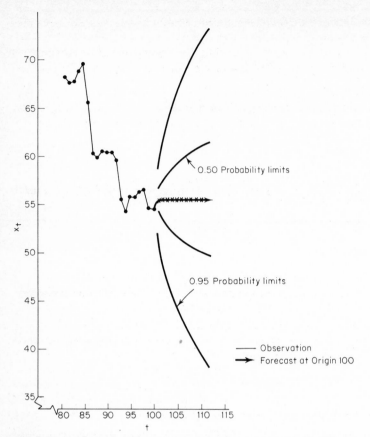

Fig. 9-23 Forecast of plastic container demand at origin 100, with 0.50 and 0.95 probability limits.

model (246.68) by the residual degrees of freedom (98). The ψ weights are obtained by equating like powers of B in the expansion

$$(\psi_0 + \psi_1 B + \psi_2 B^2 + \cdots)(1 - B) = (1 - \theta B)$$

which yields

$$\psi_0 = 1$$

$$\psi_1 = 1 - \theta$$

and

$$\psi_j = \psi_{j-1} \qquad j = 2, 3, \ldots$$

Substituting $\hat{\theta} = -0.70$, we find $\hat{\psi}_0 = 1$ and $\hat{\psi}_j = 1.70$ for $j = 1, 2, \ldots$. Substitution of $\hat{\psi}_j$ and $\hat{\sigma}_\epsilon^2$ into (9-53) will provide the probability limits shown in Fig. 9-23.

As new observations become available, the forecasts may be easily updated using the difference-equation form of the model.   For example, if the actual observation in period 101 is $x_{101} = 5,510$, then the one-step-ahead forecast error is $e_1(101) = 5,510 - 5,539.48 = -29.48$, and we would obtain a new forecast for period 102 as

$$\hat{x}_{102}(101) = x_{101} + 0.70e_1(101)$$

$$= 5,510 + 0.70(-29.48)$$

$$= 5,489.36$$

Therefore the forecast for all future periods at origin $T = 101$ is $\hat{x}_{101+\tau}(101)$ = 5,489.36.

9-4 SEASONAL PROCESSES

In previous sections we have discussed a class of time series models useful in representing stationary and nonstationary time series.   We shall now consider the extension of these ideas to seasonal time series.

Consider a *seasonal* autoregressive process with s observations per season, and let the only nonzero parameters be those with subscripts that are an integer multiple of s.   The process would be

$$x_t = \lambda_1 x_{t-s} + \lambda_2 x_{t-2s} + \cdots + \lambda_P x_{t-Ps} + \epsilon_t$$

This is a seasonal AR process of order P, and the $\{\lambda_i\}$ are the seasonal autoregressive parameters.   Similarly, a seasonal MA process of order Q could be written as

$$x_t = \epsilon_t - \gamma_1 \epsilon_{t-s} - \gamma_2 \epsilon_{t-2s} - \cdots - \gamma_Q \epsilon_{t-Qs} \qquad (9\text{-}54)$$

The autocorrelation function and partial autocorrelation functions for these seasonal models behave similarly to the nonseasonal case.   That is, the autocorrelation function of the seasonal AR process tails off, but the autocorrelations are nonzero only at lags that are integer multiples of s, while the autocorrelation function of the seasonal MA cuts off after lag Qs.

A logical extension of the seasonal AR and MA processes is a seasonal mixed model, say

$$x_t = \lambda_1 x_{t-s} + \lambda_2 x_{t-2s} + \cdots + \lambda_P x_{t-Ps} + \epsilon_t - \gamma_1 \epsilon_{t-s}$$

$$- \gamma_2 \epsilon_{t-2s} - \cdots - \gamma_{Qs} \epsilon_{t-Qs} \qquad (9\text{-}55)$$

In terms of the backshift operator, Eq. (9-55) can be written as

$$(1 - \lambda_1 B^s - \lambda_2 B^{2s} - \cdots - \lambda_P B^{Ps})x_t = (1 - \gamma_1 B^s - \gamma_2 B^{2s} - \cdots - \gamma_Q B^{Qs})\epsilon_t$$

or

$$\Lambda_P(B^s)x_t = \Gamma_Q(B^s)\epsilon_t \qquad (9\text{-}56)$$

where $\Lambda_P(B^s)$ and $\Gamma_Q(B^s)$ are polynomials in B^s of degree P and Q, respectively. This is a seasonal ARMA$(P, Q)_s$ model.

More generally, the series $\{x_t\}$ could be nonstationary. This can be treated by introducing an appropriate degree of *seasonal differencing*. Let $\nabla_s = (1 - B^s)$ be the seasonal difference operator. For example,

$$\nabla_s x_t = (1 - B^s)x_t = x_t - x_{t-s}$$

in the first seasonal difference. In general, D seasonal differences may be required to produce a stationary series. Then the seasonal difference operator of order D is $\nabla_s^D = (1 - B^s)^D$, and the general form of the seasonal autoregressive integrated moving average model of order P, D, Q, is

$$\Lambda_P(B^s)\nabla_s^D x_t = \Gamma_Q(B^s)\epsilon_t \qquad (9\text{-}57)$$

This is often called an ARIMA$(P, D, Q)_s$ model.

Unfortunately, observations in the model (9-57) are dependent only at multiples of seasonal lag. That is, observations *within* the season are independent. Box and Jenkins propose that this is unrealistic, and introduce a correlative structure between observations within a season by letting the noise input $\{\epsilon_t\}$ to (9-57) be represented by a second model

$$\Phi_p(B)\nabla^d \epsilon_t = \Theta_q(B)a_t \qquad (9\text{-}58)$$

where $\{a_t\}$ is a white noise process, and $\Phi_P(B)$ and $\Theta_q(B)$ are polynomials in B of order p and q, respectively. Substituting (9-58) into (9-57), we obtain

$$\Phi_q(B)\Lambda_P(B^s)\nabla^d\nabla_s^D x_t = \Theta_q(B)\Gamma_Q(B^s)a_t \qquad (9\text{-}59)$$

Equation (9-59) is called a *multiplicative* seasonal model of order $(p, d, q) \times (P, D, Q)_s$.

The approach to identification, estimation, diagnostic checking, and forecasting for multiplicative seasonal ARIMA models does not differ in principle from the corresponding procedures for nonseasonal series. However, the theory of multiplicative seasonal models is not well developed, and identifying an appropriate model by comparison of the sample autocorrelation and partial autocorrelation functions with theoretical patterns is frequently difficult. Box and Jenkins ([6], app. A9.1) present the autocovariances for several seasonal models. This is a useful aid in model identification.

The general approach to modeling a seasonal time series is to perform several iterations of the model-building process, and at each stage fit the most obvious characteristics of the series. Residual analysis should indicate any remaining structure at each interation, and a new model incorporating this structure can be obtained. Good examples of modeling seasonal time series are given in Box and Jenkins ([6], chap. 9) and Nelson ([45], chap. 7). It should be emphasized that, in general, simple models are often adequate to describe seasonal time series.

EXAMPLE 9-5 Figure 9-24 shown the monthly total airline miles flown in the United Kingdom for the seven years 1964–1970. Since airline travel is traditionally at its highest during the late summer months, a marked seasonal variation is observed in the series. The time series is also listed in Table 9-7. From examining Fig. 9-24, we note that the variability of the series increases as its general level increases throughout the period 1964–1970. This suggests that the logarithms of the mileage data should be analyzed, rather than the raw series. (As we noted in Sec. 9-1.5, the logarithms of data such as these are frequently simpler to analyze, because *percentage* fluctuation is relatively constant at different levels of the series.) The natural logarithms of the mileage

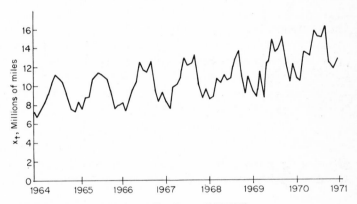

Fig. 9-24   United Kingdom miles flown, 1964–1970.

TABLE 9-7   United Kingdom Miles Flown, 1964–1970, in Millions of Miles

	1964	1965	1966	1967	1968	1969	1970
Jan.	7.269	8.350	8.186	8.334	8.639	9.491	10.840
Feb	6.775	7.829	7.444	7.899	8.772	8.919	10.436
Mar.	7.819	8.829	8.484	9.994	10.894	11.607	13.589
Apr.	8.371	9.948	9.864	10.078	10.455	8.852	13.402
May	9.069	10.638	10.252	10.801	11.179	12.537	13.103
June	10.248	11.253	12.282	12.953	10.588	14.759	14.933
July	11.030	11.424	11.637	12.222	10.794	13.667	14.147
Aug.	10.882	11.391	11.577	12.246	12.770	13.731	14.057
Sept.	10.333	10.665	12.417	13.281	13.812	15.110	16.234
Oct.	9.109	9.396	9.637	10.366	10.857	12.185	12.389
Nov.	7.685	7.775	8.094	8.730	9.290	10.645	11.594
Dec.	7.602	7.933	9.280	9.614	10.925	12.161	12.772

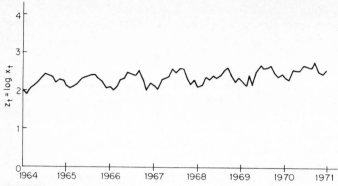

Fig. 9-25   Natural logarithms of United Kingdom miles flown.

TABLE 9-8   Natural Logs of United Kingdom Miles Flown, 1964–1970

	1964	1965	1966	1967	1968	1969	1970
Jan.	1.984	2.122	2.102	2.120	2.156	2.250	2.383
Feb.	1.913	2.058	2.007	2.067	2.172	2.188	2.345
Mar.	2.057	2.178	2.138	2.302	2.388	2.452	2.639
Apr.	2.125	2.297	2.289	2.310	2.347	2.181	2.595
May	2.205	2.364	2.328	2.380	2.414	2.529	2.573
June	2.327	2.421	2.508	2.561	2.360	2.692	2.704
July	2.401	2.436	2.454	2.503	2.379	2.615	2.650
Aug.	2.387	2.433	2.449	2.505	2.547	2.620	2.643
Sept.	2.335	2.367	2.519	2.586	2.626	2.715	2.787
Oct.	2.209	2.240	2.266	2.339	2.385	2.500	2.517
Nov.	2.039	2.051	2.091	2.167	2.229	2.365	2.451
Dec.	2.028	2.071	2.228	2.263	2.391	2.498	2.547

data are listed in Table 9-8 and shown in Fig. 9-25.   The log series $z_t = \log x_t$ does display less spatial variability than the raw series.

The strong increase in the level of the log series from 1964 to 1970 indicates that at least one difference will be required to achieve stationarity. This is borne out by the sample autocorrelation function of z_t and $(1 - B)z_t = \nabla z_t$ in Figs.

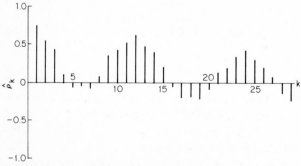

Fig. 9-26   Autocorrelation function for the log series.

Fig. 9-27 Autocorrelation function of the first difference of the log series $\nabla z_t = (1 - B)z_t$.

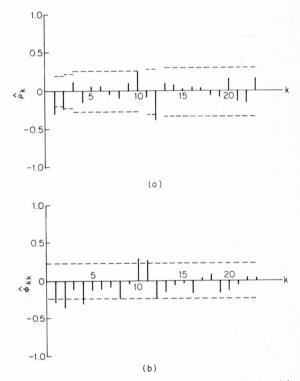

(a)

(b)

Fig. 9-28 Sample (a) autocorrelation and (b) partial autocorrelation functions for the series $(1 - B)(1 - B^{12})z_t$.

9-26 and 9-27, respectively. The sample autocorrelation function for the log series z_t decays slowly, due to nonstationarity, and displays large autocorrelations at seasonal lags. The sample autocorrelation function for the series of first differences $(1 - B)z_t$ still displays large autocorrelations, particularly at lags 12 and 24, indicating that seasonal differencing may be necessary.

The most pronounced seasonal effect is at lag 12. Thus, the seasonal difference $(1 - B^{12})$ seems appropriate. The sample autocorrelation and partial autocorrelation functions for the series $(1 - B)(1 - B^{12})z_t$ are shown in Fig. 9-28, along with the two standard error limits.

Since the autocorrelation function in Fig. 9-28a cuts off and the partial autocorrelation function decays more slowly, the model will be of moving average form. The only sample autocorrelations which exceed twice their standard errors are $\hat{\rho}_1$ and $\hat{\rho}_{12}$ (although $\hat{\rho}_2$ is almost equal to the two-standard-error limit), and thus a tentative model might be

$$(1 - B)(1 - B^{12})z_t = (1 - \theta_1 B)(1 - \gamma_{12} B^{12})\epsilon_t$$

Note that this is a multiplicative seasonal model of order $(0, 1, 1) \times (0, 1, 1)_{12}$. Using the data in Table 9-8, we may find the least-squares estimates of the model parameters as $\hat{\theta}_1 = 0.6966$ and $\hat{\gamma}_{12} = 0.5664$, and the residual mean square is 0.5852×10^{-2}. The autocorrelation function of the residuals for this model is plotted in Fig. 9-29. The largest autocorrelations are at lags 4 and 9, which suggest that perhaps the model may be improved by adding a seasonal moving average term at lag 4. Thus, the revised model is

$$(1 - B)(1 - B^{12})z_t = (1 - \theta_1 B)(1 - \gamma_4 B^4 - \gamma_{12} B^{12})\epsilon_t$$

The least-squares estimates of the parameters in this new model are $\hat{\theta}_1 = 0.6304$, $\hat{\gamma}_4 = 0.2503$, and $\hat{\gamma}_{12} = 0.5881$, and the residual mean square is 0.5615×10^{-2}.

The residual autocorrelations for this revised model are plotted in Fig. 9-30. None of these autocorrelations exceed twice their standard errors. Further-

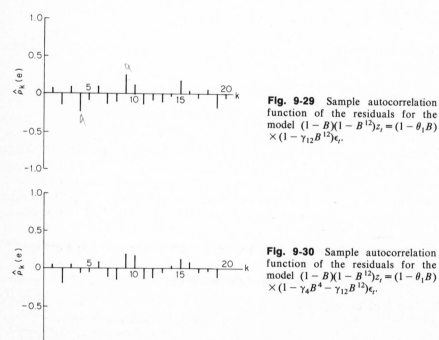

Fig. 9-29 Sample autocorrelation function of the residuals for the model $(1 - B)(1 - B^{12})z_t = (1 - \theta_1 B) \times (1 - \gamma_{12} B^{12})\epsilon_t$.

Fig. 9-30 Sample autocorrelation function of the residuals for the model $(1 - B)(1 - B^{12})z_t = (1 - \theta_1 B) \times (1 - \gamma_4 B^4 - \gamma_{12} B^{12})\epsilon_t$.

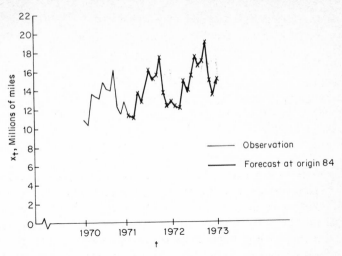

Fig. 9-31 Forecasts of United Kingdom miles flown at origin 84 (December 1970).

more, the chi-square statistic applied to the first 20 autocorrelations is $Q = 15.56$, with 17 degrees of freedom. Since the critical value of chi-square at 5 percent with 17 degrees of freedom is 27.59, we cannot reject the hypothesis that the residuals are a white noise series. Therefore, we conclude that the model

$$(1 - B)(1 - B^{12})z_t = (1 - 0.6304B)(1 - 0.2503B^4 - 0.5881B^{12})\epsilon_t$$

adequately describes the time series.

Forecasting with a seasonal model is conceptually the same as forecasting with any ARIMA(p, d, q) model. Forecasts are usually easier to compute using the model in difference equation form, or

$$z_t = z_{t-1} + z_{t-12} - z_{t-13} + \epsilon_t - 0.6304\epsilon_{t-1} - 0.2503\epsilon_{t-4} + 0.1578\epsilon_{t-5}$$

$$- 0.5881\epsilon_{t-12} + 0.3707\epsilon_{t-13}$$

The forecast for period $T + \tau$ made at origin T would be found by taking expectation at time T of this difference equation written at time $T + \tau$. The forecasts for periods 85, 86, ..., 108 at origin $T = 84$ are shown in Fig. 9-31. Recall that the difference equation produces forecasts of the natural logarithms of miles flown. Antilogs of $\hat{z}_{T+\tau}(T)$ must be taken to produce a forecast in units of miles flown.

9-5 A CRITIQUE OF THE BOX-JENKINS MODELS

The Box-Jenkins methodology is a powerful approach to the solution of many forecasting problems. It can provide extremely accurate forecasts of time series, and offers a formal, structured approach to model building and analysis.

However, the Box-Jenkins models are not without several important limitations.

In general, we require at least 50 and preferably 100 observations to develop an acceptable Box-Jenkins model. This is a moderately large amount of data, and there are many types of forecasting problems in which this much historical data would be unavailable. For example, in manufacturing seasonal style goods, the history of previous seasons is frequently of little value in forecasting the current season because of changes in styles, marketing strategies, etc. Even in forecasting demand for a fairly stable product on a monthly basis, we might not be able to accumulate 50 to 100 months of history that is completely reliable, as changes in the information processing system or the production control system may have modified the way data are collected or stored. For seasonal time series, the problem is even more complicated. So far as model identification and estimation are concerned, each complete season of history is much like a single observation. That is, in five years of monthly data, say, we have only five January observations, five February observations, etc. Thus many seasons of historical data may be required to build a suitable seasonal model. However, we should point out that in the absence of sufficient historical data, one can analyze the data available to obtain a preliminary model. This model can then be periodically revised as fresh data become available.

Another disadvantage of the Box-Jenkins models is that there is not, at present, a convenient way to modify or update the estimates of the model parameters as each new observation becomes available, such as there is in direct smoothing. One has to periodically completely refit the model. Perhaps even more serious is that we must assume that the future evolution of the time series will be identical to the past, that is, that the *form* of the model will not change over time. There are no systematic methods for monitoring the model performance or automatically adapting the parameter values to changes in the underlying process, such as those discussed for exponential smoothing in Chap. 8.

A final drawback of the Box-Jenkins models is the investment in time and other resources required to build a satisfactory model. This may not be important if only a few time series are under study. However, a typical forecasting application in the production-inventory systems environment might involve from a few hundred to several thousand different time series. It is doubtful that the improvements in forecast accuracy possible through the Box-Jenkins methodology could justify the cost of the model-building process in such a situation.

Despite these shortcomings, the Box-Jenkins models are probably the most accurate class of forecasting models available today. They are especially well suited for time series in which the sampling interval is very small, so that a relatively long history can be easily obtained. For this reason, they have been widely applied to series where hourly, daily, or weekly observations are of interest. For example, the time series of output characteristics of chemical processes, such as yield, purity, etc., are often of this general type. The Box-Jenkins models are also most profitably employed in situations where only a small number of time series are of interest, and management is willing to expend the resources necessary to achieve a high degree of forecast accuracy.

9-6 EXERCISES

9-1   Consider the AR(1) process

$$x_t = 20 + 0.6x_{t-1} + \epsilon_t, \qquad \sigma_\epsilon^2 = 4$$

a. Is this process stationary?
b. Estimate the moments μ, γ_0, γ_1, and γ_2. Graph the theoretical autocorrelation function.
c. If $x_{50} = 21$, would you expect x_{51} to be greater than or less than the mean?
d. Invert this process to moving average form. What are the values of the moving average parameters?

9-2   Consider the AR(2) process

$$x_t = 10 + 0.8x_{t-1} - 0.2x_{t-2} + \epsilon_t, \qquad \sigma_\epsilon^2 = 1$$

a. Is the process stationary?
b. Graph the theoretical autocorrelation function.
c. If $x_{45} = 12$, would you expect x_{46} to be greater than or less than the mean of the series?
d. Is the process invertible? If so, express the series in moving average form.

9-3   Consider the MA(1) process

$$x_t = 5 + \epsilon_t + 0.2\epsilon_{t-1}, \qquad \sigma_\epsilon^2 = 3$$

a. Is the process stationary?
b. Is the process invertible? If so, express the process in autoregressive form.
c. If x_{100} is greater than the mean of the process, would you expect x_{101} to be greater than the mean also? Explain your answer.

9-4   The linear filter model can be written in another form as a linear combination of the previous realizations $\{\tilde{x}_{t-j}\}$ and the current error ϵ_t, say

$$\tilde{x}_t = \sum_{j=1}^{\infty} \pi_j \tilde{x}_{t-j} + \epsilon_t$$

Find the general relationship between the ψ weights and the π weights.

9-5   Show that the AR(p) process can be inverted to an infinite-order moving average process. Are any conditions necessary on the parameters $\{\phi_j\}$ in the AR(p) process to ensure invertibility? Compare this with the invertibility conditions for a moving average process.

9-6   An important recurrence relation for the AR(p) process is the difference equation

$$\rho_k = \phi_1\rho_{k-1} + \phi_2\rho_{k-2} + \cdots + \phi_p\rho_{k-p} \qquad k \geqslant 1$$

Show that if we substitute $k = 1, 2, \ldots, p$, in this equation, we obtain a $p \times p$ set of simultaneous linear equations in $\{\rho_k\}$ and $\{\phi_j\}$. Given that the autocorrelations $\{\rho_k\}$ are replaced by their estimates, find a general solution for the estimates $\{\hat{\phi}_j\}$. Why are these estimates $\{\hat{\phi}_j\}$ sometimes called Yule-Walker estimates?

9-7   *Continuation of Exercise 9-6.* For the stationary AR(1) process, the difference equation in Exercise 9-6 becomes

$$\rho_k = \phi_1 \rho_{k-1} \quad k \geqslant 1$$

Show that the solution to this difference equation is

$$\rho_k = \phi_1^k \quad k \geqslant 0$$

Does this allow us to characterize the behavior of the theoretical autocorrelation of an AR(1) process?

9-8   *Continuation of Exercise 9-6.* Using the difference equation in Exercise 9-6, show that the Yule-Walker estimate of ϕ_1 in an AR(1) process is

$$\hat{\phi}_1 = \hat{\rho}_1$$

and the Yule-Walker estimates of ϕ_1 and ϕ_2 in an AR(2) process are

$$\hat{\phi}_1 = \frac{\hat{\rho}_1(1 - \hat{\rho}_1)}{1 - \hat{\rho}_1^2}$$

$$\hat{\phi}_2 = \frac{\hat{\rho}_2 - \hat{\rho}_1^2}{1 - \hat{\rho}_1^2}$$

Discuss the potential uses of these estimates.

9-9   Show that if an AR(2) process is stationary, then we must have

$$-1 < \rho_1 < +1$$

$$-1 < \rho_2 < +1$$

$$\rho_1^2 < \tfrac{1}{2}(\rho_2 + 1)$$

9-10   Use the theoretical autocorrelation function for the MA(1) process to find an estimator of θ_1 in terms of the sample autocorrelation coefficient $\hat{\rho}_1$. For an invertible process, find a range of feasible values for $\hat{\rho}_1$.

9-11   Write out the autocorrelation function for an MA(2) process. Show that for the process to be invertible, the feasible regions for the autocorrelations are bounded by segments of the curves

$$\rho_1 + \rho_2 = -0.5$$

$$\rho_2 - \rho_1 = -0.5$$

$$\rho_1^2 = 4\rho_2(1 - 2\rho_2)$$

9-12   Using the autocovariance function of an ARMA(1, 1) process, write out the theoretical autocorrelation function. Show that in order for the process to satisfy the stationarity and invertibility conditions, we must require

$$|\rho_1| > |\rho_2|$$

$$\rho_2 > \begin{cases} \rho_1(2\rho_1 + 1) & \text{for } \rho_1 < 0 \\ \rho_1(2\rho_1 - 1) & \text{for } \rho_1 > 0 \end{cases}$$

9-13 The data in Table B-1 in the Appendix represent the demand for a double-knit polyester fabric. Using the first 200 observations, tentatively identify an appropriate Box-Jenkins model. Estimate the parameters and perform diagnostic checks. Is the model adequate? Forecast the next 40 periods using a one-period lead time.

9-14 The weekly sales of a cutting tool are shown in Table B-2. Tentatively identify an appropriate model for this data. Estimate the parameters and perform diagnostic checks. Is the model adequate? Forecast the next 10 periods, using period 100 as the origin of time. Construct 50 percent probability for the forecasts.

9-15 The number of minutes of usage per day for a computer terminal are shown in Table B-3. Tentatively identify an appropriate model for this time series. Estimate the parameters and perform diagnostic checks. Forecast the next 10 periods, using day 100 as the origin of time. Construct 90 percent probability intervals for the forecasts.

9-16 The weekly demand for a particular type of crankshaft bearing is given in Table B-4. Tentatively identify an appropriate model for these data. Estimate the model parameters and perform diagnostic checking. Forecast the next 10 weeks of demand, using week 100 as the origin of time.

9-17 The temperature readings from a chemical process are taken every two minutes. A time series consisting of 100 successive observations is shown in Table B-6. Tentatively identify an appropriate model for this time series. Estimate the model parameters and perform diagnostic checking. Forecast the next 10 temperature readings, using period 90 as the origin of time, and compare the forecasts with the actual temperatures. Using period 100 as the origin of time, forecast the next 10 temperatures.

9-18 The monthly champagne sales of a French wine company for the last eight years are shown in Table B-9. Using the first seven years of data, fit an appropriate Box-Jenkins model to this process. Simulate a one-month lead time forecast for the last year of data.

9-19 Table B-10 contains the series of annual Wölfer sunspot numbers and measures the average number of sunspots on the sun during each year. Determine an appropriate Box-Jenkins model for this time series. (The Wölfer sunspot numbers have been the subject of considerable analysis; for example, see Yule [65], Moran [42], and Phadke and Wu [50].)

9-20 A time series model has been fit to historical data, yielding

$$x_t = 25 + 0.34x_{t-1} + \epsilon_t$$

Suppose that at time $t = 100$ the observation is $x_{100} = 28$.

a. Determine forecasts for periods 101, 102, 103, ..., from origin 100. What is the eventual shape of the forecast function from this origin?

b. Suppose $x_{101} = 32$. Revise your forecasts for periods 102, 103, ..., using period 101 as the new origin of time.

c. If $\hat{\sigma}_\epsilon^2 = 1.5$, find a 95 percent probability interval on the forecast for period 101 made at time 100.

9-21 The following time series model has been fit to historical data:

$$x_t = 15 + 0.86x_{t-1} - 0.32x_{t-2} + \epsilon_t$$

If $x_{50} = 32$ and $x_{51} = 30$, determine forecasts for periods 51, 52, ... What is the eventual forecast function for this model?

9-22 The following time series model has been fit to historical data:

$$x_t = 20 + \epsilon_t + 0.45\epsilon_{t-1} - 0.35\epsilon_{t-2}$$

If the first four observations are $x_1 = 17.50$, $x_2 = 21.36$, $x_3 = 18.24$, and $x_4 = 16.91$, compute forecasts for periods 5, 6, 7, ..., from origin 4. What is the eventual forecast function for this model?

9-23 A time series model has been fit to historical data, yielding

$$x_t = x_{t-1} + 0.83x_{t-1} - 0.24x_{t-2} + \epsilon_t$$

If $x_{100} = 620$ and $x_{99} = 624$, determine forecasts for periods 101, 102, ... What is the eventual forecast function for this model?

9-24 Give the forecasting equation for lead time $\tau = 1, 2, \ldots$, for the following models. In each case, discuss the eventual forecast function.

a. AR(1)
b. AR(2)
c. MA(1)
d. MA(2)
e. ARMA(1, 1)
f. IMA(1, 1)
g. ARIMA(1, 1, 0)

9-25 *Forecast updating.* Show that for any ARIMA model, the forecast for period $T + \tau + 1$ made at origin $T [\hat{x}_{T+\tau+1}(T)]$ and the forecast for period $T + \tau + 1$ made at origin $T + 1 [\hat{x}_{T+\tau+1}(T+1)]$ are related as follows:

$$\hat{x}_{T+\tau+1}(T+1) = \hat{x}_{T+\tau+1}(T) + \psi_\tau \epsilon_{T+1}$$

Discuss the practical use of this forecast updating result. Derive updating formulas for the AR(1) and MA(1) processes.

CHAPTER TEN

Bayesian Methods in Forecasting

In many forecasting problems, there is little or no useful historical information available at the time the initial forecast is required. Thus, the early forecasts must be based largely on subjective considerations. As time series information becomes available, we must modify our subjective estimates in light of the actual data. An example of this process is the forecasting of sales of seasonal products, which, because of style obsolescence, have a short life. A judgment forecast of total sales for a product during the season is made at the start of the season. As the season passes and actual orders are received, the original forecast should be modified in some manner.

Bayesian methods are often useful in statistical inference problems of this type. It is assumed that the original subjective forecast can be translated into a subjective estimate of the parameters of the forecasting model. The Bayesian procedures are then used to revise these parameter estimates when time series information is available. In this chapter, we give a general description of the Bayesian approach and demonstrate the methodology with several specific cases.

10-1 BAYESIAN ESTIMATION

The procedure for estimating parameters in the time series process makes use of Bayes' theorem. Let x be a random variable with probability density function f characterized by an unknown parameter θ. We shall write this density as $f(x \mid \theta)$ to indicate that the probability distribution depends upon the value of θ.

The parameter θ is assumed to be a random variable with probability density $h_0(\theta)$, which is called the *prior* density of θ. This probability distribution measures our subjective, or "degree-of-belief," information about θ. If we are relatively confident about the value of θ, we would choose a prior distribution with a small variance. If we are relatively uncertain about θ, we might choose a prior distribution with a larger variance.

In a forecasting situation, suppose the initial estimate of θ is given as a probability distribution $h_0(\theta)$, and that subsequently information about the time series process is obtained in the form of a statistic y whose probability distribution $f(y \mid \theta)$ depends upon θ. Typically y is a sample of observations, $x_1, x_2, \ldots, x_T$, from the time series, or some sufficient statistic computed from the sample. The new estimate of θ will be in the form of a revised distribution, $h_1(\theta \mid y)$, called the *posterior* distribution. Using Bayes' theorem, we have

$$h_1(\theta \mid y) = \frac{h_0(\theta)f(y \mid \theta)}{\int_\theta h_0(\theta)f(y \mid \theta) \, d\theta} = \frac{h_0(\theta)f(y \mid \theta)}{g(y)} \tag{10-1}$$

In the above,

$h_0(\theta) = $ *prior* distribution of θ (the marginal distribution of θ)

$f(y \mid \theta) = $ *likelihood* of y, given θ (the conditional distribution of y, given θ)

$g(y) = $ unconditional distribution of y, averaged over all θ (the marginal distribution of y)

$h_1(\theta \mid y) = $ *posterior* distribution of θ, given the information y (the conditional distribution of θ, given y)

Note that if θ is a discrete variable, the integral sign in Eq. (10-1) should be replaced by a summation sign.

Equation (10-1) provides a means for blending the observed data y with the prior information $h_0(\theta)$ to obtain a revised description of our uncertainty about θ. The *Bayes estimator* of θ, denoted θ^*, is defined as the expected value of the posterior density, or

$$\theta^* = \int_\theta \theta h_1(\theta \mid y) \, d\theta \tag{10-2}$$

Typically, we use θ^* as an estimate of θ in the forecasting model. For certain cases, it can be shown that θ^* is optimal in the sense of minimizing the variance of forecast error.

EXAMPLE 10-1 *Normal sampling process and normal prior.* Suppose y is normally distributed with mean θ and variance σ_y^2; that is,

$$f(y \mid \theta) = N(\theta, \sigma_y^2) \equiv (2\pi\sigma_y^2)^{-\frac{1}{2}} \exp\left[-\frac{1}{2}\left(\frac{y - \theta}{\sigma_y} \right)^2 \right] \tag{10-3}$$

where σ_y^2 is known. The prior distribution of θ is also normal with mean $\bar{\theta}'$ and variance v_θ'; that is,

$$h_0(\theta) = N(\bar{\theta}', v_\theta') = (2\pi v_\theta')^{-\frac{1}{2}} \exp\left[-\frac{(\theta - \bar{\theta}')^2}{2v_\theta'} \right] \tag{10-4}$$

The posterior distribution of θ, given y, is

$$h_1(\theta \mid y) = \frac{2\pi(v_\theta'\sigma_y^2)^{-\frac{1}{2}} \exp\left\{ -\frac{1}{2}\left[(\theta - \bar{\theta}')^2/v_\theta' + (y - \theta)^2/\sigma_y^2 \right] \right\}}{\int_{-\infty}^{\infty} 2\pi(v_\theta'\sigma_y^2)^{-\frac{1}{2}} \exp\left\{ -\frac{1}{2}\left[(\theta - \bar{\theta}')^2/v_\theta' + (y - \theta)^2/\sigma_y^2 \right] \right\} d\theta}$$

$$= \left(2\pi\, \frac{v_\theta'\sigma_y^2}{v_\theta' + \sigma_y^2} \right)^{-\frac{1}{2}} \exp\left\{ -\frac{1}{2}\, \frac{\left[\theta - (yv_\theta' + \bar{\theta}'\sigma_y^2)/(v_\theta' + \sigma_y^2) \right]^2}{v_\theta'\sigma_y^2/(v_\theta' + \sigma_y^2)} \right\}$$

which we recognize as a normal density with mean

$$\bar{\theta}'' \equiv E(\theta \mid y) = \frac{yv_\theta' + \bar{\theta}'\sigma_y^2}{v_\theta' + \sigma_y^2} \tag{10-5}$$

and variance

$$v_\theta'' \equiv V(\theta \mid y) = \frac{v_\theta'\sigma_y^2}{v_\theta' + \sigma_y^2} \tag{10-6}$$

We have found that the posterior distribution is normally distributed if the prior distribution is normal and the sampling process is normal with known variance.

Additional results for selected sampling processes and prior distributions are given in Exercises 10-1 to 10-4. More comprehensive coverage of Bayesian inference is given in Winkler [63], Raiffa and Schlaifer [53], and Pratt, Raiffa, and Schlaifer [51].

10-2 CONSTANT PROCESS

Suppose we believe the time series can be adequately described by the constant model

$$x_t = b + \epsilon_t \tag{10-7}$$

where b is the unknown mean and ϵ_t is the random component assumed to be normally distributed with mean 0 and known variance σ_ϵ^2. In simplified notation, we say that $\epsilon_t \sim N(0, \sigma_\epsilon^2)$. Thus, we are assuming that the demand in any period t has probability distribution

$$f(x_t \mid b) = N(b, \sigma_\epsilon^2) \tag{10-8}$$

Since the variance is assumed to be known, the problem is to estimate b.

10-2.1 Estimation

Assume that at the start of the forecasting process (time zero), we estimate the mean demand rate to be $\bar{b}'$. Assume that our uncertainty about this estimate is such that the true mean b is then assigned the following probability distribution:

$$h_0(b) = N\left(\bar{b}', v_b'\right) \tag{10-9}$$

where the variance v_b' is a measure of the uncertainty in the estimate.

After one period, the observation x_1 is known. The problem is to modify the estimate $\bar{b}'$ and the measure of uncertainty v_b' in light of this information. This can be done using the results of Example 10-1 to obtain the following:

$$h_1(\theta \mid x_1) = N\left[\bar{b}''(1), v_b''(1)\right]$$

where

$$\bar{b}''(1) \equiv E(b \mid x_1) = \frac{x_1 v_b' + \bar{b}' \sigma_\epsilon^2}{v_b' + \sigma_\epsilon^2}$$

$$v_b''(1) \equiv V(b \mid x_1) = \frac{v_b' \sigma_\epsilon^2}{v_b' + \sigma_\epsilon^2}$$

At the end of period 2, when x_2 is known, the Bayesian updating process transforms $h_1(b \mid x_1)$ into $h_2(b \mid x_1, x_2)$ in the following way:

$$h_2(b \mid x_1, x_2) = \frac{h_1(b \mid x_1) f(x_2 \mid b)}{\int_b h_1(b \mid x_1) f(x_2 \mid b)\, db}$$

Here h_1 is treated as a prior and, together with the likelihood of x_2, it is used to obtain the probability distribution of b at the end of period 2. Again using the results of Example 10-1, we find

$$h_2(b \mid x_1, x_2) = N\left[\bar{b}''(2), v_b''(2)\right]$$

$$\bar{b}''(2) \equiv E(b \mid x_1, x_2) = \frac{\bar{x} v_b' + \bar{b}'(\sigma_\epsilon^2/2)}{v_b' + (\sigma_\epsilon^2/2)}$$

$$v_b''(2) \equiv V(b \mid x_1, x_2) = \frac{v_b' \sigma_\epsilon^2}{2v_b' + \sigma_\epsilon^2}$$

where $\bar{x} = (x_1 + x_2)/2$. It is easily verified that $h_2(b \mid x_1, x_2) = h_2(b \mid \bar{x})$; that is, the same posterior is obtained using $\bar{x}$ as from using x_1 and x_2 sequentially (or jointly). This is because $\bar{x}$ is a sufficient statistic for estimating b.

To generalize, it may be shown that after observing x_T we calculate the posterior as

$$h_T(b \mid x_1, x_2, \ldots, x_T) = h_T(b \mid \bar{x}) = N\left[\bar{b}''(T), v_b''(T)\right] \tag{10-10}$$

where

$$\bar{b}''(T) = \frac{\bar{x}v_b' + \bar{b}'(\sigma_\epsilon^2/T)}{v_b' + (\sigma_\epsilon^2/T)} \tag{10-11}$$

$$v_b''(T) = \frac{v_b'\sigma_\epsilon^2}{Tv_b' + \sigma_\epsilon^2} \tag{10-12}$$

$$\bar{x} = \frac{\sum\limits_{t=1}^{T} x_t}{T}$$

The Bayes estimator of b after T periods is $b^*(T) = \bar{b}''(T)$.

By writing

$$b^*(T) = \frac{T}{n' + T}\bar{x} + \frac{n'}{n' + T}\bar{b}' \tag{10-13}$$

where $n' = \sigma_\epsilon^2/v_b'$, we see that the Bayes estimator of b is just a weighted average of the sample mean and the subjective initial estimate, $\bar{b}'$. Furthermore, $b^*(T)$ can also be expressed recursively as

$$b^*(T) = \alpha x_T + (1 - \alpha)b^*(T - 1) \tag{10-14}$$

where

$$\alpha = \alpha(T) = \frac{1}{n' + T} = \frac{v_b'}{Tv_b' + \sigma_\epsilon^2} \tag{10-15}$$

Equation (10-14) reveals that the estimate of the demand rate is updated each period by a form similar to exponential smoothing (see Sec. 3-1). However, we observe from Eq. (10-15) that α is a function of T, becoming smaller as T increases. Since $v_b''(T) = \alpha(T)\sigma_\epsilon^2$, the uncertainty in the estimate of b decreases to zero as T becomes infinitely large. Also the weight given to $\bar{b}'$, the initial estimate, decreases as T becomes large, and correspondingly more weight is given to the actual time series data. Eventually, at some point in time when enough data are available to reduce the posterior variance to the minimum level desired, a permanent forecasting procedure perhaps involving single exponential smoothing should be adopted. This can be accomplished by arbitrarily maintaining the variance $v_b''(T)$ at a given level, thereby keeping $\alpha(T)$ at a constant value.

Since the variance of the demand process, σ_ϵ^2, usually is not known, we must estimate it. If we are uncertain about its value, we could treat it as a random variable, just as we did b, and expand the unknown parameter set to $\theta = \{b, \sigma_\epsilon^2\}$. Then we would define a prior joint probability distribution on b and σ_ϵ^2. The updating process to calculate the posterior would utilize both the sample mean and the sample variance of the T observations. This is considerably more complex than in the known-variance case. Advice on the choice of a prior and details of computing the posterior are given by Raiffa and Schlaifer [53].

Cohen [17] shows that the estimator given in Eq. (10-13) is optimal in the sense that it minimizes the variance of forecast error even if the process is not normally distributed. In Exercise 10-9, the reader is asked to prove this.

10-2.2 Forecasting

Once the posterior distribution has been determined, it may be used as the basis for forecasting. For a constant process, the forecasting equation is

$$\hat{x}_{T+\tau}(T) = \hat{b}\,(T) \tag{10-16}$$

We use the Bayes estimator $b^*(T)$ as our estimator of b, so that our forecast for period $T + \tau$ is

$$\hat{x}_{T+\tau}(T) = b^*(T) \tag{10-17}$$

Our uncertainty in the estimate of b is measured by the posterior variance, $v_b''(T)$. Thus, from (10-17) we see that the forecast variance is $E[(b - b^*)^2]$, or

$$V[\hat{x}_{T+\tau}(T)] = v_b'' \tag{10-18}$$

The variance of the forecast error is

$$V[e_\tau(T + \tau)] = V[x_{T+\tau} - \hat{x}_{T+\tau}(T)] = \sigma_\epsilon^2 + v_b'' \tag{10-19}$$

Note that the forecast error variance is independent of the forecast lead time τ in the Bayesian case. Using (10-19) and assuming b and x are normally distributed, we can compute a $100(1 - \gamma)$ percent prediction interval for $x_{T+\tau}$ as

$$b^*(T) \pm u_{\gamma/2}\sqrt{\sigma_\epsilon^2 + v_b''} \tag{10-20}$$

where $u_{\gamma/2}$ is the $100(\gamma/2)$ percentile of the standard normal distribution.

EXAMPLE 10-2 We wish to forecast the demand for a new product. Time is measured in weeks. We believe that demand is normally distributed and that a constant model is appropriate, but no historical information is available. A reasonable prior density for b is thought to be $N(100, 25)$, and σ_ϵ^2 is estimated to be 150. The forecast for period 1 is

$$\hat{x}_1(0) = 100$$

The variance of forecast error is $150 + 25 = 175$, and so a 95% prediction interval for x_1 is

$$100 \pm (1.960)\sqrt{175} \qquad \text{or} \qquad [74.1, 125.9]$$

Suppose the actual demand in period 1 is 86. Then, using (10-14) with $n' = \sigma_\epsilon^2 / v_b' = 150/25 = 6$ and $\alpha(1) = 1/(6 + 1) = 0.143$, we have

$$b^*(1) = \bar{b}''(1) = \tfrac{1}{7}(86) + \tfrac{6}{7}(100) = 98.0$$

and

$$v_b''(1) = \tfrac{1}{7}(150) = 21.4$$

Therefore, the forecast for period 2 is

$$\hat{x}_2(1) = 98.0$$

and a 95% prediction interval for x_2 is

$$98.0 \pm (1.960)\sqrt{150 + 21.4} \qquad \text{or} \qquad [72.3, 123.7]$$

In period 2, the actual demand is 94. Then, $\alpha(2) = 1/(6 + 2) = 0.125$, and

$$b^*(2) = \tfrac{1}{8}(94) + \tfrac{7}{8}(98.0) = 97.5$$

$$v_b''(2) = \tfrac{1}{8}(150) = 18.8$$

The 95% prediction interval is

$$97.5 \pm 1.960\sqrt{150 + 18.8} \qquad \text{or} \qquad [72.0, 123.0]$$

This procedure would be continued until it was thought appropriate to switch to a more permanent forecasting system. For example, exponential smoothing with $\alpha = 0.1$ could be implemented when $\alpha(T)$ drops to that level.

10-3 GENERAL TIME SERIES MODELS*

We now give a Bayesian approach to parameter estimation and forecasting for time series models that are linear in the unknown parameters $b_1, b_2, \ldots, b_k$. The treatment of such models by classical regression methods was described in Sec. 4-1.

---

* Some of the material in this section is of a more advanced nature than the rest of the book. It may be omitted on first reading without loss of continuity.

10-3.1 Process Model

The time series model is

$$x_t = b_1 z_1(t) + b_2 z_2(t) + \cdots + b_k z_k(t) + \epsilon_t$$

$$= \sum_{i=1}^{k} b_i z_i(t) + \epsilon_t \tag{10-21}$$

where the $\{b_i\}$ are constants, the $\{z_i(t)\}$ are mathematical functions of t and are the independent variables in the model, and ϵ_t is $N(0, \sigma_\epsilon^2)$. We assume ϵ_t is independent of ϵ_{t+j}, for all j. Often $z_1(t) = 1$, so that b_1 is the constant term in the model.

It will be convenient to use matrix notation, and so we define

$$\mathbf{z}(t) = [z_1(t), z_2(t), \ldots, z_k(t)]^t$$

$$\mathbf{b} = [b_1, b_2, \ldots, b_k]^t$$

where the superscript t indicates "transpose" (all vectors are column vectors). Then (10-21) can be written as

$$x_t = \mathbf{b}'\mathbf{z}(t) + \epsilon_t \tag{10-22}$$

The probability distribution of x_t is

$$f(x_t \mid \mathbf{b}, \sigma_\epsilon^2) = N(\mathbf{b}'\mathbf{z}(t), \sigma_\epsilon^2) \tag{10-23}$$

In order to forecast this process, an estimate of $\mathbf{b}$ is required. We shall assume that σ_ϵ^2 is known. For the unknown-variance case, see Raiffa and Schlaifer ([53], chap. 13).

10-3.2 Prior Distribution

Prior to observing the time series, the $\{b_i\}$ are assumed to be jointly normally distributed with $E(b_i) = \bar{b}'_i$, $\text{Var}(b_i) = v'_{ii}$, and $\text{Cov}(b_i, b_j) = v'_{ij}$. That is, $\mathbf{b}'$ follows the multivariate normal distribution:

$$h_0(\mathbf{b}) = (2\pi)^{-\frac{1}{2}k} |\mathbf{V}'^{-1}|^{\frac{1}{2}} \exp\left\{ -\tfrac{1}{2} [\mathbf{b} - \bar{\mathbf{b}}']^t \mathbf{V}'^{-1} [\mathbf{b} - \bar{\mathbf{b}}'] \right\} \tag{10-24}$$

$$h_0(\mathbf{b}) = N(\bar{\mathbf{b}}', \mathbf{V}')$$

where $\bar{\mathbf{b}}' = E(\mathbf{b})$ and $\mathbf{V}'$ is the variance-covariance matrix of the prior distribution. The latter is a $k \times k$ symmetric matrix with elements v'_{ij}.

It will be convenient to define a matrix $\mathbf{G}'$ as follows:

$$\mathbf{G}' \equiv \sigma_\epsilon^2 \mathbf{V}'^{-1} \tag{10-25}$$

so that

$$G'^{-1} = \frac{V'}{\sigma_\epsilon^2} \tag{10-26}$$

We shall see that formulas for calculating the parameters of the posterior can be written in terms of G'.

10-3.3 Least-Squares Estimators

After T periods, we have observed $x_1, x_2, \ldots, x_T$, and wish to revise the prior distribution (10-24) in light of these actual data.   Define

$$\mathbf{x} = [x_1, x_2, \ldots, x_T]^t$$

and

$$Z = \begin{bmatrix} \mathbf{z}^t(1) \\ \mathbf{z}^t(2) \\ \vdots \\ \mathbf{z}^t(T) \end{bmatrix} = \begin{bmatrix} z_1(1) & z_2(1) & \cdots & z_k(1) \\ z_1(2) & z_2(2) & \cdots & z_k(2) \\ \cdots\cdots\cdots\cdots\cdots\cdots\cdots \\ z_1(T) & z_2(T) & \cdots & z_k(T) \end{bmatrix}$$

As shown in Sec. 4-1, we can estimate $\mathbf{b}$ from the actual time series data by solving the least-squares normal equations

$$Z^t Z \hat{\mathbf{b}} = Z^t \mathbf{x} \tag{10-27}$$

or, letting $\mathbf{G} = Z^t Z$ and $\mathbf{g} = Z^t \mathbf{x}$,

$$G\hat{\mathbf{b}} = \mathbf{g} \tag{10-28}$$

The least-squares estimators are

$$\hat{\mathbf{b}} = \mathbf{G}^{-1} \mathbf{g} \tag{10-29}$$

Since this computation is made at the end of period T, it is understood that $\hat{\mathbf{b}} = \hat{\mathbf{b}}(T)$.

The least-squares estimators are unbiased; that is,

$$E(\hat{\mathbf{b}} \mid \mathbf{b}) = \mathbf{b} \tag{10-30}$$

and have variance-covariance matrix

$$\text{Cov}(\hat{\mathbf{b}}) \equiv \mathbf{V} = \mathbf{G}^{-1}\sigma_\epsilon^2 \tag{10-31}$$

The elements of $\mathbf{V}$ are $v_{ij} \equiv \text{Cov}(\hat{b}_i, \hat{b}_j)$. $\mathbf{V}$ is symmetric.   It can be shown that

$\hat{\mathbf{b}}$ is sufficient for estimating $\mathbf{b}$ when σ_ϵ^2 is known and that it follows the multivariate normal distribution

$$f\left(\hat{\mathbf{b}} \mid \mathbf{b}; \mathbf{Z}, \sigma_\epsilon^2\right) = (2\pi)^{-\frac{1}{2}k}|\mathbf{V}^{-1}|\exp\left\{ \tfrac{1}{2}[\hat{\mathbf{b}} - \mathbf{b}]'\mathbf{V}^{-1}[\hat{\mathbf{b}} - \mathbf{b}]\right\} \quad (10\text{-}32)$$

$$f\left(\hat{\mathbf{b}} \mid \mathbf{b}; \mathbf{Z}, \sigma_\epsilon^2\right) = N(\mathbf{b}, \mathbf{V})$$

If we consider the prior distribution of $\mathbf{b}$, given by Eq. (10-24), the marginal distribution of $\hat{\mathbf{b}}$ can be computed, for fixed $\mathbf{Z}$ and σ_ϵ^2, by averaging over $\mathbf{b}$; that is,

$$g(\hat{\mathbf{b}}) = \int_{-\infty}^{\infty} f(\hat{\mathbf{b}} \mid \mathbf{b})h_0(\mathbf{b})\, d\mathbf{b}$$

$$= N(\bar{\mathbf{b}}', \mathbf{V}_m) \quad (10\text{-}33)$$

where

$$\mathbf{V}_m = \mathbf{V}' + \mathbf{V} = (\mathbf{G}'^{-1} + \mathbf{G}^{-1})\sigma_\epsilon^2 \quad (10\text{-}34)$$

10-3.4 Posterior Distribution

The posterior distribution of $\mathbf{b}$, given $\hat{\mathbf{b}}$, is computed at time T as

$$h_T(\mathbf{b} \mid \hat{\mathbf{b}}) = \frac{h_0(\mathbf{b})f(\hat{\mathbf{b}} \mid \mathbf{b})}{g(\hat{\mathbf{b}})} \quad (10\text{-}35)$$

It can be shown that

$$h_T(\mathbf{b} \mid \hat{\mathbf{b}}) = N(\bar{\mathbf{b}}'', \mathbf{V}'') \quad (10\text{-}36)$$

with mean $\bar{\mathbf{b}}''$ and variance-covariance matrix $\mathbf{V}''$ determined from

$$\mathbf{V}''^{-1} = \mathbf{V}'^{-1} + \mathbf{V}^{-1} \quad (10\text{-}37)$$

$$\bar{\mathbf{b}}'' = \mathbf{V}''(\mathbf{V}'^{-1}\bar{\mathbf{b}}' + \mathbf{V}^{-1}\hat{\mathbf{b}}) \quad (10\text{-}38)$$

Note that Eq. (10-37) can also be written as

$$\mathbf{G}'' = \mathbf{G}' + \mathbf{G} = \sigma_\epsilon^2\mathbf{V}'^{-1} + \mathbf{Z}'\mathbf{Z} \quad (10\text{-}39)$$

and Eq. (10-38) as

$$\bar{\mathbf{b}}'' = \mathbf{G}''^{-1}(\mathbf{G}'\bar{\mathbf{b}}' + \mathbf{G}\hat{\mathbf{b}}) = \mathbf{G}''^{-1}(\mathbf{G}'\bar{\mathbf{b}}' + \mathbf{g}) \quad (10\text{-}40)$$

The above results are derived in Raiffa and Schlaifer [53].

We have observed that when a normal prior distribution is selected, the posterior also will be normal and, more importantly, the parameters of the posterior can be determined from simple algebraic combinations of the prior parameters and the results of least-squares analysis of the time series data.

10-3.5 Forecasting

Equation (10-36) gives the posterior distribution of **b**, computed at time T. Our forecast for period $T + \tau$ is to be based on the posterior distribution of $x_{T+\tau}$, the demand in period $T + \tau$. Since

$$E(x_{T+\tau}) = \sum_{i=1}^{k} b_i z_i (T + \tau)$$

and the $\{b_i\}$ are jointly distributed according to (10-36), we (as Bayesians) consider $E(x_{T+\tau})$ to be a normally distributed random variable with mean

$$\sum_{i=1}^{k} \bar{b}_i'' z_i (T + \tau) = \mathbf{z}^t (T + \tau) \bar{\mathbf{b}}'' \tag{10-41}$$

and variance

$$\sum_{i=1}^{k} \sum_{j=1}^{k} z_i (T + \tau) z_j (T + \tau) v_{ij}'' = \mathbf{z}^t (T + \tau) \mathbf{V}'' \mathbf{z} (T + \tau) \tag{10-42}$$

Furthermore, since

$$x_{T+\tau} = E(x_{T+\tau}) + \epsilon_{T+\tau} \tag{10-43}$$

and $\epsilon_{T+\tau}$ is $N(0, \sigma_\epsilon^2)$ and assumed independent of **b**, we consider $x_{T+\tau}$ to be a normally distributed random variable having posterior mean given by (10-41) and variance

$$\mathbf{z}^t (T + \tau) \mathbf{V}'' \mathbf{z} (T + \tau) + \sigma_\epsilon^2 \tag{10-44}$$

Note that this statement about the distribution of $x_{T+\tau}$ is the same as the inference that the forecast error for period $T + \tau$,

$$e_\tau (T + \tau) = x_{T+\tau} - \hat{x}_{T+\tau} (T)$$

is normally distributed with mean 0 and variance given by (10-44), provided we use (10-41) as our forecast.

We may wish to make a probability statement about $x_{T+\tau}$, based on the posterior distribution at time T. To economize on notation, define $M(T + \tau)$ as the mean given by (10-41) and $S(T + \tau)$ as the square root of the variance given by (10-44). Then a $100(1 - \gamma)\%$ prediction interval for $x_{T+\tau}$ is

$$M(T + \tau) \pm u_{\gamma/2} S(T + \tau) \tag{10-45}$$

Cumulative forecast The cumulative demand in periods $T + 1$, $T + 2$, ..., $T + \tau$,

$$X_\tau(T) \equiv \sum_{j=1}^{\tau} x_{T+j} = \sum_{j=1}^{\tau} \mathbf{z}^t(T + j)\mathbf{b} \tag{10-46}$$

would be considered a random variable with mean

$$\sum_{j=1}^{\tau} \mathbf{z}^t(T + j)\bar{\mathbf{b}}'' \tag{10-47}$$

and variance

$$\left[\sum_{j=1}^{\tau} \mathbf{z}(T + j) \right]^t \mathbf{V}'' \left[\sum_{j=1}^{\tau} \mathbf{z}(T + j) \right] + \tau\sigma_\epsilon^2 \tag{10-48}$$

The cumulative demand is normally distributed; thus we can easily calculate a Bayesian prediction interval for $X_\tau(T)$ in a manner similar to (10-45) for the single-period demand.

To be more specific, we apply the preceding results to the analysis of a linear trend process in the following example.

EXAMPLE 10-3 A manufacturer of electrical appliances has introduced a new model ultrasonic oven. No similar item has been sold in the past, and so no historical data are available. The marketing manager wishes to forecast weekly sales of this item and requests assistance from a systems analyst. The manager tells the analyst that the initial sales rate will probably be between 200 and 300 units per week; but with the advertising program planned, the manager expects the sales rate to increase steadily and estimates the amount of increase from week to week at between 5 and 25 units.

The systems analyst interprets this information to mean that a linear trend model

$$x_t = b_1 + b_2 t + \epsilon_t$$

will be appropriate. In the notation of Eq. (10-21), $z_1(t) = 1$ and $z_2(t) = t$. Since the analyst thinks the assumption that ϵ_t is $N(0, \sigma_\epsilon^2)$ is reasonable, he/she uses a normal prior for $\mathbf{b} = [b_1, b_2]^t$. The prior means of b_1 and b_2 are taken as the midpoints of the ranges provided by the marketing manager. That is,

$$\bar{b}_1' = \frac{300 + 200}{2} = 250$$

$$\bar{b}_2' = \frac{5 + 25}{2} = 15$$

The prior standard deviations are assumed to be one-sixth of the ranges, since six standard deviations for all practical purposes constitute the spread of a normal distribution. The variances are then

$$\text{Var}(b_1) \equiv v'_{11} = \left(\frac{300 - 200}{6} \right)^2 = 277.78$$

$$\text{Var}(b_2) \equiv v'_{22} = \left(\frac{25 - 5}{6} \right)^2 = 11.11$$

The analyst has no rational basis for assigning a nonzero value to $\text{Cov}(b_1, b_2)$ $\equiv v_{12} = v_{21}$. Therefore, the prior variance-covariance matrix is

$$\mathbf{V}' = \begin{bmatrix} 277.28 & 0 \\ 0 & 11.11 \end{bmatrix}$$

To obtain a value for σ_ϵ^2, the analyst makes use of experience gained in forecasting other items of similar cost going to the same market and decides on $\sigma_\epsilon^2 = (50)^2 = 2,500$. Later, when actual sales results are available, the analyst may choose to revise this estimate.

Thus, at time 0, the demand in period τ, $x_{0+\tau}$, is estimated to be normally distributed with mean

$$M(0 + \tau) = \bar{b}'_1 + \bar{b}'_2 \tau = 250 + 15\tau$$

and variance given by (10-44), using $\mathbf{V}'$ instead of $\mathbf{V}''$:

$$S^2(0 + \tau) = \mathbf{z}'(0 + \tau)\mathbf{V}'\mathbf{z}(0 + \tau) + \sigma_\epsilon^2$$

$$= [1, \tau] \begin{bmatrix} 277.78 & 0 \\ 0 & 11.11 \end{bmatrix} \begin{bmatrix} 1 \\ \tau \end{bmatrix} + 2,500$$

$$= 277.78 + 11.11\tau^2 + 2,500$$

For example, the demand in the fourth period is assumed to be normal with mean and variance

$$M(0 + 4) = 250 + (15)(4) = 310$$

$$S^2(0 + 4) = 277.78 + (11.11)(4)^2 + 2,500 = 2,955.54$$

A 95% Bayesian prediction interval for x_4, made at a time 0, is given by

$$310 \pm 1.960\sqrt{2,955.54} \qquad \text{or} \qquad [203.44, 416.56]$$

Similarly, a 95% Bayesian prediction for x_{10}, made at time 0, is

$$400 \pm 1.960\sqrt{3{,}888.78} \quad \text{or} \quad [277.77, 522.23]$$

Now suppose that the actual demand for this product during the first 10 weeks is the following:

Week	Sales	Week	Sales
1	317	6	334
2	194	7	317
3	312	8	356
4	316	9	428
5	322	10	411

Using this information, the posterior distribution at $T = 10$ is computed in the following manner. First, the least-squares estimates are calculated from the data (see Sec. 2-1):

$$\mathbf{Z}' = \begin{bmatrix} 1 & 1 & 1 & \cdots & 1 \\ 1 & 2 & 3 & \cdots & 10 \end{bmatrix}$$

$$\mathbf{x}' = [317, 194, \ldots, 411]$$

$$\mathbf{G} = \mathbf{Z}'\mathbf{Z} = \begin{bmatrix} 10 & 55 \\ 55 & 385 \end{bmatrix}$$

$$\mathbf{g} = \mathbf{Z}'\mathbf{x} = \begin{bmatrix} 3{,}307 \\ 19{,}548 \end{bmatrix}$$

$$\mathbf{G}^{-1} = \begin{bmatrix} 0.46667 & -0.06667 \\ -0.06667 & 0.01212 \end{bmatrix}$$

$$\hat{\mathbf{b}} = \mathbf{G}^{-1}\mathbf{g} = \begin{bmatrix} 240.01 \\ 16.44 \end{bmatrix}$$

The sample variance-covariance matrix is

$$\mathbf{V} = \mathbf{G}^{-1}\sigma_\epsilon^2 = \begin{bmatrix} 1{,}166.68 & -166.68 \\ -166.68 & 30.30 \end{bmatrix}$$

Next, the parameters of the posterior distribution are computed using Eqs. (10-37) and (10-38):

$$\mathbf{V''}^{-1} = \mathbf{V'}^{-1} + \mathbf{V}^{-1}$$

$$= \begin{bmatrix} 0.00360 & 0 \\ 0 & 0.09001 \end{bmatrix} + \begin{bmatrix} 0.00400 & 0.02200 \\ 0.02200 & 0.15400 \end{bmatrix}$$

$$= \begin{bmatrix} 0.00760 & 0.02200 \\ 0.02200 & 0.24401 \end{bmatrix}$$

$$\mathbf{V''} = \begin{bmatrix} 178.05 & -16.05 \\ -16.05 & 5.55 \end{bmatrix}$$

$$\mathbf{\bar{b}''} = \mathbf{V''}(\mathbf{V'}^{-1}\mathbf{\bar{b}'} + \mathbf{V}^{-1}\mathbf{\hat{b}})$$

$$= \mathbf{V''}\left\{ \begin{bmatrix} 0.00360 & 0 \\ 0 & 0.09001 \end{bmatrix}\begin{bmatrix} 250 \\ 15 \end{bmatrix} + \begin{bmatrix} 0.00400 & 0.02200 \\ 0.02200 & 0.15400 \end{bmatrix}\begin{bmatrix} 240.01 \\ 16.44 \end{bmatrix} \right\}$$

$$= \begin{bmatrix} 178.05 & -16.05 \\ -16.05 & 5.55 \end{bmatrix}\begin{bmatrix} 0.90000 + 1.32172 \\ 1.35015 + 7.81198 \end{bmatrix}$$

$$= \begin{bmatrix} 248.53 \\ 15.19 \end{bmatrix}$$

The expected value of the posterior distribution of demand in period $10 + \tau$ is to be used as the point forecast for that period; that is,

$$\hat{x}_{10+\tau} = M(10 + \tau) = 248.53 + 15.19(10 + \tau)$$

$$= 400.43 + 15.19\tau$$

The posterior probability distribution of $x_{10+\tau}$ has variance given by (10-44):

$$S^2(10 + \tau) = [1, \ 10 + \tau]\begin{bmatrix} 178.05 & -16.05 \\ -16.05 & 5.55 \end{bmatrix}\begin{bmatrix} 1 \\ 10 + \tau \end{bmatrix} + 2{,}500$$

$$= 2{,}678.05 - 32.10(10 + \tau) + 5.55(10 + \tau)^2$$

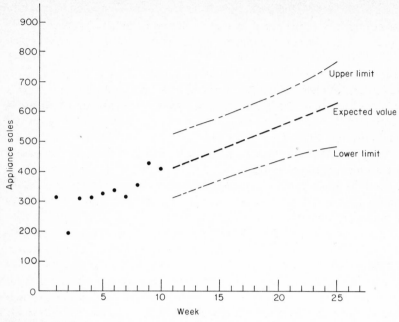

Fig. 10-1 Prediction made at the end of week 10 (Example 10-3).

TABLE 10-1   Predictions of Appliance Sales Made at the End of Week 10 (Example 10-3)

Week	Demand		95% prediction limits	
	Mean	Variance	Lower	Upper
11	415.62	2,996.50	308.33	522.91
12	430.81	3,092.05	321.82	539.80
13	446.00	3,198.70	335.15	556.85
14	461.19	3,316.45	348.32	574.06
15	476.38	3,445.30	361.33	591.43
20	552.33	4,256.05	424.46	680.20
25	628.28	5,344.30	484.99	771.57

Point forecasts and 95% prediction intervals for selected values of τ are given in Table 10-1 and illustrated in Fig. 10-1.

If, say at the end of the 20th week, the analyst again wanted to revise the probability distribution of **b**, he/she could either (1) use all 20 data points in the least-squares computation and revise the original prior, or (2) use only the data points for weeks 11 through 20 in the least-squares analysis and revise the probability distribution computed after the first 10 observations. Both approaches yield the same result.

10-4 EVALUATION OF BAYESIAN METHODS

The methods described in the previous section are applicable to process models that are linear in the $\{b_i\}$ and for which ϵ_t is normally distributed with known variance σ_ϵ^2. Nonlinear models are difficult to estimate by least-squares methods and, more importantly, the sampling distributions of estimators for parameters in such models generally do not have a normal distribution. This usually makes Bayesian methods impractical. Carter [12] attempted to use a Bayesian approach for forecasting the multiplicative seasonal model given by Eq. (5-1) and had only limited success.

The fact that the demand process was normally distributed led us to choose a multivariate normal distribution for **b**. This resulted in a normal posterior, with a relatively simple procedure for revising the parameters. Yet this procedure involved computation of least-squares estimators and additional matrix inversion to combine prior parameter values and sample results. So there is considerably more work required than in direct smoothing. However, if revisions are to be made infrequently, the Bayesian approach may be reasonable. Certainly it provides a rational way to blend prior information with newly observed data to make an inference about the probability distribution of demand in future periods. Some other common processes (besides the normal) and their associated prior distributions are described in Exercises 10-1 to 10-4.

Typically in Bayesian analysis, the variance of **b** becomes smaller as more data are obtained. This would be acceptable if the process model were correct and the parameters did not change over time. However, we cannot be sure that conditions will not change; hence, we really want the variance of **b**, which represents our uncertainty about the parameters, to remain at some nonzero level, or above. In fact, in times of considerable uncertainty, we may want the variance increased. A true Bayesian would then be willing to intervene and arbitrarily adjust the variance to the level he or she thinks appropriate.

10-5 EXERCISES

10-1 *Binomial sampling, beta prior.* Suppose that r is the number of favorable outcomes in n Bernoulli trials. Then r is a binomial variable having probability distribution

$$f(r \mid n, p) = \frac{n!}{r!(n-r)!} p^r (1-p)^{n-r} \qquad r = 0, 1, \ldots, p$$

where p is the probability of a favorable outcome on each trial. The prior distribution of p is assumed to be a beta distribution with parameters r' and n', written as follows:

$$h_0(p \mid r', n') = \frac{\Gamma(n')}{\Gamma(n')\Gamma(n'-r')} p^{r'-1}(1-p)^{n'-r'-1} \qquad \begin{array}{c} 0 \leqslant p \leqslant 1 \\ n' > r' > 0 \end{array}$$

Show that the posterior distribution of p after observing r successes in n trials is also beta with parameters $r'' = r' + r$ and $n'' = n' + n$.

10-2 *Pascal sampling, beta prior.* In Exercise 10-1, suppose the sampling process had been carried out until r successes were obtained. Then n is the random variable and it follows the Pascal distribution:

$$f(n \mid r, p) = \frac{(n-1)!}{(r-1)!(n-r)!} \, p^r (1-p)^{n-r} \qquad n = r, r+1, \ldots$$

Show that a beta prior for p results in a beta posterior with parameters $r'' = r' + r$ and $n'' = n' + n$. Note that this is the same as the result obtained in Exercise 10-1 assuming binomial sampling.

10-3 *Poisson sampling, gamma prior.* Suppose that r is the number of Poisson events observed in a time interval of fixed length T. Then r is a Poisson variable having probability distribution

$$f(r \mid \lambda T) = \frac{(\lambda T)^r e^{-\lambda T}}{r!} \qquad r = 0, 1, 2, \ldots$$

where λ is the "intensity" of the Poisson process, that is, the average number of events per unit time. Assume the prior distribution of λ is gamma with parameters r' and T'; that is,

$$h_0(\lambda \mid r', T') = \frac{(T')^{r'}}{(r'-1)!} \, \lambda^{r'-1} e^{-T'\lambda} \qquad \begin{array}{l} \lambda > 0 \\ r', T' > 0 \end{array}$$

Show that the posterior distribution of p after observing r events in n trials is also gamma with parameters $r'' = r' + r$ and $T'' = T' + T$.

10-4 *Gamma sampling, gamma prior.* In Exercise 10-3, suppose the process had been observed until the rth event occurred. The observation time T would then be a random variable having the gamma distribution (since the inter-event times are exponentially distributed):

$$f(T \mid r, \lambda) = \frac{\lambda^r}{(r-1)!} \, T^{r-1} e^{-\lambda T} \qquad T > 0$$

Show that a gamma prior for λ results in a gamma posterior with parameters $r'' = r' + r$ and $T'' = T' + T$. Note that this is the same as the result obtained in Exercise 10-3 assuming Poisson sampling.

10-5 Weekly demand for a spare part is assumed to have the following Poisson distribution:

$$f(x \mid \lambda) = \frac{e^{-\lambda} \lambda^x}{x!} \qquad x = 0, 1, 2, \ldots$$

The mean λ of the demand distribution is not known with certainty, but is assumed to have a gamma density

$$h(\lambda) = \frac{b^a}{(a-1)!} \, \lambda^{a-1} e^{-b\lambda} \qquad \lambda < 0$$

where a and b are parameters having subjectively established values. In the week following the establishment of this prior distribution, d parts were demanded. What is the revised (posterior) distribution of λ? What value would you use for the mean of the Poisson distribution in order to make probability statements about weekly usage? How would you operate this Bayesian procedure on a weekly basis?

10-6 Develop Eqs. (10-10) to (10-12) assuming that the only information available after T periods is the average demand $\bar{x}$, which is normally distributed with mean b and variance σ_ϵ^2 / T.

10-7 In Eq. (10-13), the quantity $n' = \sigma_\epsilon^2 / v_b'$ is defined. What happens to n' as v_b' increases? Could n' be interpreted as a measure of the relative value of prior information? Explain.

10-8 Derive the recursive relation given by Eq. (10-14) from Eq. (10-13).

10-9 *Blending prior information and observational data: the constant model.* Suppose that the demand for an item can be described by the constant model $x_t = b + \epsilon_t$, where $V(x_t) = \sigma_\epsilon^2$ is known and $E(x_t) = b$ is unknown. Management's subjective estimate of b is b' and their uncertainty is measured by $E[b - b')^2] = v'$. The analyst is a Bayesian, so that he or she assumes b to be a random variable with mean $\bar{b}' = b'$ and variance $v_b' = v'$. No assumption is made about the form of the prior distribution. After T periods, the average demand $\bar{x}$ is available. A reasonable approach to using both the prior estimate b' and the current observed average demand is to average them. That is, compute

$$b^* = (1 - \phi)\bar{x} + \phi b'$$

where $0 \leqslant \phi \leqslant 1$ is the weight attached to the prior estimate. One useful criterion for selecting ϕ is to minimize the variance of forecast error, that is, $V(x_t - b^*)$. Find an expression for the minimizing value of ϕ, assuming $\text{Cov}(\bar{x}, b') = 0$. Compare the solution with Eq. (6-13). $10-13 \ P245$

10-10 In the situation of Exercise 10-9, suppose the analyst had been of the classical school and definitely not a Bayesian. Then he or she would have interpreted management's estimate b' as the random variable, possibly assuming it to be unbiased so that $E(b') = b$ and $V(b') \equiv E[(b' - b)^2] = v'$. What would be the optimal weight ϕ? Compare this with the solution to Exercise 10-9.

10-11 A retailer has added a product to his/her line and wishes to forecast it weekly. He/she believes that the sales rate will remain constant over time. The retailer's initial feeling about the level of sales is that there is only a 0.10 probability that the average demand b will differ from 350 by more than 50 units. Sales are expected to be normally distributed about this average level with a standard deviation $\sigma_\epsilon = 50$.
  a. Choose a prior distribution for b.
  b. If sales in the first five weeks are 423, 403, 474, 451, and 465, what is the posterior distribution for b? Give a 95% prediction interval for x_6. Give a

95% prediction interval for the cumulative demand in periods 6 through 10.

c. If sales in the next five weeks (6 to 10) are 445, 459, 325, 331, and 350, what is the posterior distribution computed at $T = 10$?

10-12   In the situation described by Example 10-3, suppose that the actual sales in periods 11 to 20 were 494, 412, 460, 395, 392, 447, 452, 571, 517, and 397. Compute the posterior distribution at the end of week 20.

10-13   Use the table of random normal numbers (Appendix Table A-4) to generate observations for $t = 1, 2, \ldots, 10$, from the linear trend process

$$x_t = 400 + 20t + \epsilon_t$$

where ϵ_t is normally distributed with mean 0 and standard deviation $\sigma_\epsilon = 50$. Assume a normal prior with

$$\bar{b}' = \begin{bmatrix} 500 \\ 30 \end{bmatrix} \qquad V' = \begin{bmatrix} 900 & 0 \\ 0 & 40 \end{bmatrix}$$

Compute the posterior distribution at $T = 10$. Suppose the process changes so that subsequent to period 10 the mean is constant at 600, that is,

$$x_t = 600 + \epsilon_t \qquad t = 11, 12, \ldots$$

Generate five observations, $x_{11}, x_{12}, \ldots, x_{15}$, and compute the posterior at $T = 15$ (still assuming a linear trend model).

10-14   Assume a linear trend model for the spare part demand given in Table B-5 of the Appendix. The prior distribution is normal with

$$\bar{b}' = \begin{bmatrix} 250 \\ 0 \end{bmatrix} \qquad V' = \begin{bmatrix} 400 & 0 \\ 0 & 100 \end{bmatrix}$$

Using $\sigma_\epsilon = 30$, compute the posterior distribution at the end of 12 months. Give 90% prediction intervals for the demand in each of months 13 to 16, computed at $T = 12$. Give a 90% prediction interval for the cumulative demand in months 13 to 16, computed at the end of month 12.

10-15   The monthly sales for a soft drink are expected to be seasonal with a 12-month period and they are expected to be increasing with time because of population growth in the area. The following time series model seems appropriate for monthly sales in hundreds of cases:

$$x_t = b_1 + b_2 t + b_3 \sin \frac{2\pi}{12} + b_4 \cos \frac{2\pi}{12} + \epsilon_t$$

Suppose the prior distribution of model parameters is normal with

$$
\bar{b}' = \begin{bmatrix} 40 \\ 5 \\ 10 \\ -20 \end{bmatrix}
\qquad
V' = \begin{bmatrix} 25 & 0 & 0 & 0 \\ 0 & 4 & 0 & 0 \\ 0 & 0 & 100 & 0 \\ 0 & 0 & 0 & 100 \end{bmatrix}
$$

and assume $\sigma_\epsilon^2 = 40$. Use the data in Appendix Table B-7 to compute the posterior distribution at the end of 1973.

10-16 Discuss approaches for the rational selection of parameter values for the prior distribution described in Exercise 10-15.

10-17 Instead of using unweighted least squares to compute $\hat{b}$ from the data, suppose the discounted least-squares method is used, as in the direct smoothing models of Chap. 4. How would the Bayesian analysis proceed?

10-18 For a constant process, suppose the posterior distribution $h_T(b)$ has been computed. A single-value prediction of the demand in period $T + 1$ is desired. Two criteria for selecting this value are proposed: (1) Minimize the expected squared forecast error, $E[(x_{T+1} - \hat{x}_{T+1})^2]$; (2) minimize the expected absolute forecast error, $E[|x_{T+1} - \hat{x}_{T+1}|]$. Show that the former criterion leads to the forecast $\hat{x}_{T+1} = \bar{b}''$, the mean of the posterior, while the latter results in $x_{T+1} = \text{MED}(b)$. The mean and the median are the same value for normal posteriors, but not for nonsymmetrical distributions.

APPENDIX A

Statistical Tables

TABLE A-1 Distribution Function and Ordinates of the Standard Normal Density

$$\phi(z) = \frac{1}{\sqrt{2\pi}} \, e^{-(1/2)z^2}$$

$$\Phi(z) = \int_{-\infty}^{z} \phi(t) \, dt$$

z	$\Phi(z)$	$\phi(z)$	z	$\Phi(z)$	$\phi(z)$
0.00	0.500000	0.398942	0.15	0.559618	0.394479
0.01	0.503989	0.398922	0.16	0.563559	0.393869
0.02	0.507978	0.398863	0.17	0.567495	0.393219
0.03	0.511966	0.398763	0.18	0.571424	0.392532
0.04	0.515953	0.398623	0.19	0.575345	0.391806
0.05	0.519939	0.398444	0.20	0.579260	0.391043
0.06	0.523922	0.398225	0.21	0.583166	0.390242
0.07	0.527903	0.397966	0.22	0.587064	0.389404
0.08	0.531881	0.397668	0.23	0.590954	0.388529
0.09	0.535856	0.397330	0.24	0.594835	0.387617
0.10	0.539828	0.396953	0.25	0.598706	0.386668
0.11	0.543795	0.396536	0.26	0.602568	0.385684
0.12	0.547758	0.396080	0.27	0.606420	0.384663
0.13	0.551717	0.395586	0.28	0.610261	0.383606
0.14	0.555670	0.395052	0.29	0.614092	0.382515

TABLE A-1 (Continued)

z	$\Phi(z)$	$\phi(z)$	z	$\Phi(z)$	$\phi(z)$
0.30	0.617912	0.381388	0.79	0.785236	0.292004
0.31	0.621720	0.380227	0.80	0.788144	0.289692
0.32	0.625516	0.379031	0.81	0.791030	0.287369
0.33	0.629300	0.377801	0.82	0.793892	0.285037
0.34	0.633072	0.376537	0.83	0.796730	0.282695
0.35	0.636831	0.375241	0.84	0.799546	0.280344
0.36	0.640577	0.373911	0.85	0.802337	0.277985
0.37	0.644309	0.372548	0.86	0.805105	0.275618
0.38	0.648027	0.371154	0.87	0.807850	0.273245
0.39	0.651732	0.369728	0.88	0.810570	0.270864
0.40	0.655422	0.368270	0.89	0.813267	0.268478
0.41	0.659097	0.366782	0.90	0.815940	0.266085
0.42	0.662757	0.365263	0.91	0.818589	0.263688
0.43	0.666402	0.363714	0.92	0.821213	0.261286
0.44	0.670032	0.362135	0.93	0.823814	0.258881
0.45	0.673645	0.360527	0.94	0.826391	0.256471
0.46	0.677242	0.358890	0.95	0.828944	0.254059
0.47	0.680823	0.357225	0.96	0.831472	0.251644
0.48	0.684386	0.355533	0.97	0.833977	0.249228
0.49	0.687933	0.353813	0.98	0.836457	0.246810
0.50	0.691463	0.352065	0.99	0.838913	0.244390
0.51	0.694974	0.350292	1.00	0.841345	0.241971
0.52	0.698468	0.348493	1.01	0.843752	0.239551
0.53	0.701944	0.346668	1.02	0.846136	0.237132
0.54	0.705401	0.344818	1.03	0.848495	0.234714
0.55	0.708840	0.342944	1.04	0.850830	0.232297
0.56	0.712260	0.341046	1.05	0.853141	0.229882
0.57	0.715661	0.339124	1.06	0.855428	0.227470
0.58	0.719043	0.337180	1.07	0.857690	0.225060
0.59	0.722405	0.335213	1.08	0.859929	0.222654
0.60	0.725747	0.333225	1.09	0.862143	0.220251
0.61	0.729069	0.331215	1.10	0.864334	0.217852
0.62	0.732371	0.329184	1.11	0.866500	0.215458
0.63	0.735653	0.327133	1.12	0.868643	0.213069
0.64	0.738914	0.325062	1.13	0.870762	0.210686
0.65	0.742154	0.322973	1.14	0.872857	0.208308
0.66	0.745373	0.320864	1.15	0.874928	0.205936
0.67	0.748571	0.318737	1.16	0.876976	0.203572
0.68	0.751748	0.316593	1.17	0.879000	0.201214
0.69	0.754903	0.314432	1.18	0.881000	0.198863
0.70	0.758036	0.312254	1.19	0.882977	0.196521
0.71	0.761148	0.310060	1.20	0.884930	0.194186
0.72	0.764237	0.307851	1.21	0.886861	0.191860
0.73	0.767305	0.305628	1.22	0.888768	0.189543
0.74	0.770350	0.303389	1.23	0.890651	0.187236
0.75	0.773372	0.301138	1.24	0.892512	0.184937
0.76	0.776373	0.298873	1.25	0.894350	0.182649
0.77	0.779350	0.296595	1.26	0.896165	0.180371
0.78	0.782304	0.294305	1.27	0.897958	0.178104

TABLE A-1 Distribution Function and Ordinates of the Standard Normal Density (Continued)

z	$\Phi(z)$	$\phi(z)$	z	$\Phi(z)$	$\phi(z)$
1.28	0.899727	0.175848	1.76	0.960796	0.084777
1.29	0.901475	0.173602	1.77	0.961636	0.083293
1.30	0.903200	0.171369	1.78	0.962462	0.081828
1.31	0.904902	0.169147	1.79	0.963273	0.080380
1.32	0.906583	0.166937	1.80	0.964070	0.078950
1.33	0.908241	0.164740	1.81	0.964852	0.077538
1.34	0.909877	0.162555	1.82	0.965620	0.076143
1.35	0.911492	0.160384	1.83	0.966375	0.074766
1.36	0.913085	0.158225	1.84	0.967116	0.073407
1.37	0.914657	0.156080	1.85	0.967843	0.072065
1.38	0.916207	0.153948	1.86	0.968557	0.070741
1.39	0.917736	0.151831	1.87	0.969258	0.069433
1.40	0.919243	0.149728	1.88	0.969946	0.068144
1.41	0.920730	0.147639	1.89	0.970621	0.066871
1.42	0.922196	0.145564	1.90	0.971283	0.065616
1.43	0.923642	0.143505	1.91	0.971933	0.064378
1.44	0.925066	0.141460	1.92	0.972571	0.063157
1.45	0.926471	0.139431	1.93	0.973196	0.061953
1.46	0.927855	0.137417	1.94	0.973810	0.060765
1.47	0.929219	0.135418	1.95	0.974412	0.059595
1.48	0.930563	0.133435	1.96	0.975002	0.058441
1.49	0.931888	0.131469	1.97	0.975581	0.057304
1.50	0.933193	0.129518	1.98	0.976148	0.056183
1.51	0.934478	0.127583	1.99	0.976704	0.055079
1.52	0.935745	0.125665	2.00	0.977250	0.053991
1.53	0.936992	0.123763	2.01	0.977784	0.052919
1.54	0.938220	0.121878	2.02	0.978308	0.051864
1.55	0.939429	0.120009	2.03	0.978822	0.050824
1.56	0.940620	0.118157	2.04	0.979325	0.049800
1.57	0.941792	0.116323	2.05	0.979818	0.048792
1.58	0.942947	0.114505	2.06	0.980301	0.047800
1.59	0.944083	0.112704	2.07	0.980774	0.046823
1.60	0.945201	0.110921	2.08	0.981237	0.045861
1.61	0.946301	0.109155	2.09	0.981691	0.044915
1.62	0.947384	0.107406	2.10	0.982135	0.043984
1.63	0.948449	0.105675	2.11	0.982571	0.043068
1.64	0.949497	0.103961	2.12	0.982997	0.042166
1.65	0.950528	0.102265	2.13	0.983414	0.041280
1.66	0.951543	0.100587	2.14	0.983822	0.040408
1.67	0.952540	0.098926	2.15	0.984222	0.039550
1.68	0.953521	0.097282	2.16	0.984614	0.038707
1.69	0.954486	0.095657	2.17	0.984996	0.037878
1.70	0.955434	0.094049	2.18	0.985371	0.037063
1.71	0.956367	0.092459	2.19	0.985738	0.036262
1.72	0.957284	0.090887	2.20	0.986096	0.035475
1.73	0.958185	0.089333	2.21	0.986447	0.034701
1.74	0.959070	0.087796	2.22	0.986791	0.033941
1.75	0.959941	0.086277	2.23	0.987126	0.033194

z	$\Phi(z)$	$\phi(z)$	z	$\Phi(z)$	$\phi(z)$
2.24	0.987454	0.032460	2.68	0.996319	0.010997
2.25	0.987775	0.031740	2.69	0.996428	0.010706
2.26	0.988089	0.031032	2.70	0.996533	0.010421
2.27	0.988396	0.030337	2.71	0.996636	0.010143
2.28	0.988696	0.029655	2.72	0.996736	0.009871
2.29	0.988989	0.028985	2.73	0.996833	0.009606
2.30	0.989276	0.028327	2.74	0.996928	0.009347
2.31	0.989556	0.027682	2.75	0.997020	0.009094
2.32	0.989830	0.027048	2.76	0.997110	0.008847
2.33	0.990097	0.026427	2.77	0.997197	0.008605
2.34	0.990358	0.025817	2.78	0.997282	0.008370
2.35	0.990613	0.025218	2.79	0.997365	0.008140
2.36	0.990863	0.024631	2.80	0.997445	0.007915
2.37	0.991106	0.024056	2.81	0.997523	0.007697
2.38	0.991344	0.023491	2.82	0.997599	0.007483
2.39	0.991576	0.022937	2.83	0.997673	0.007274
2.40	0.991802	0.022395	2.84	0.997744	0.007071
2.41	0.992024	0.021862	2.85	0.997814	0.006873
2.42	0.992240	0.021341	2.86	0.997882	0.006679
2.43	0.992451	0.020830	2.87	0.997948	0.006491
2.44	0.992656	0.020328	2.88	0.998012	0.006307
2.45	0.992857	0.019837	2.89	0.998074	0.006127
2.46	0.993053	0.019356	2.90	0.998134	0.005953
2.47	0.993244	0.018885	2.91	0.998193	0.005782
2.48	0.993431	0.018423	2.92	0.998250	0.005616
2.49	0.993613	0.017971	2.93	0.998305	0.005454
2.50	0.993790	0.017528	2.94	0.998359	0.005296
2.51	0.993963	0.017095	2.95	0.998411	0.005143
2.52	0.994132	0.016670	2.96	0.998462	0.004993
2.53	0.994297	0.016255	2.97	0.998511	0.004847
2.54	0.994457	0.015848	2.98	0.998559	0.004705
2.55	0.994614	0.015449	2.99	0.998605	0.004567
2.56	0.994766	0.015060	3.00	0.998650	0.004432
2.57	0.994915	0.014678	3.10	0.999032	0.003267
2.58	0.995060	0.014305	3.20	0.999313	0.002384
2.59	0.995201	0.013940	3.30	0.999517	0.001723
2.60	0.995339	0.013583	3.40	0.999663	0.001232
2.61	0.995473	0.013234	3.50	0.999767	0.000873
2.62	0.995604	0.012892	3.60	0.999841	0.000612
2.63	0.995731	0.012558	3.70	0.999892	0.000425
2.64	0.995855	0.012232	3.80	0.999928	0.000292
2.65	0.995976	0.011912	3.90	0.999952	0.000199
2.66	0.996093	0.011600	4.00	0.999968	0.000134
2.67	0.996208	0.011295			

TABLE A-2 Percentage Points of the χ^2 Distribution*

ν \ α	0.995	0.990	0.975	0.950	0.500	0.050	0.025	0.010	0.005
1	0.00+	0.00+	0.00+	0.00+	0.45	3.84	5.02	6.63	7.88
2	0.01	0.02	0.05	0.10	1.39	5.99	7.38	9.21	10.60
3	0.07	0.11	0.22	0.35	2.37	7.81	9.35	11.34	12.84
4	0.21	0.30	0.48	0.71	3.36	9.49	11.14	13.28	14.86
5	0.41	0.55	0.83	1.15	4.35	11.07	12.83	15.09	16.75
6	0.68	0.87	1.24	1.64	5.35	12.59	14.45	16.81	18.55
7	0.99	1.24	1.69	2.17	6.35	14.07	16.01	18.48	20.28
8	1.34	1.65	2.18	2.73	7.34	15.51	17.53	20.09	21.96
9	1.73	2.09	2.70	3.33	8.34	16.92	19.02	21.67	23.59
10	2.16	2.56	3.25	3.94	9.34	18.31	20.48	23.21	25.19
11	2.60	3.05	3.82	4.57	10.34	19.68	21.92	24.72	26.76
12	3.07	3.57	4.40	5.23	11.34	21.03	23.34	26.22	28.30
13	3.57	4.11	5.01	5.89	12.34	22.36	24.74	27.69	29.82
14	4.07	4.66	5.63	6.57	13.34	23.68	26.12	29.14	31.32
15	4.60	5.23	6.27	7.26	14.34	25.00	27.49	30.58	32.80
16	5.14	5.81	6.91	7.96	15.34	26.30	28.85	32.00	34.27
17	5.70	6.41	7.56	8.67	16.34	27.59	30.19	33.41	35.72
18	6.26	7.01	8.23	9.39	17.34	28.87	31.53	34.81	37.16
19	6.84	7.63	8.91	10.12	18.34	30.14	32.85	36.19	38.58
20	7.43	8.26	9.59	10.85	19.34	31.41	34.17	37.57	40.00
25	10.52	11.52	13.12	14.61	24.34	37.65	40.65	44.31	46.93
30	13.79	14.95	16.79	18.49	29.34	43.77	46.98	50.89	53.67
40	20.71	22.16	24.43	26.51	39.34	55.76	59.34	63.69	66.77
50	27.99	29.71	32.36	34.76	49.33	67.50	71.42	76.15	79.49
60	35.53	37.48	40.48	43.19	59.33	79.08	83.30	88.38	91.95
70	43.28	45.44	48.76	51.74	69.33	90.53	95.02	100.42	104.22
80	51.17	53.54	57.15	60.39	79.33	101.88	106.63	112.33	116.32
90	59.20	61.75	65.65	69.13	89.33	113.14	118.14	124.12	128.30
100	67.33	70.06	74.22	77.93	99.33	124.34	129.56	135.81	140.17

ν = degrees of freedom.

* Adapted from E. S. Pearson and H. O. Hartley, *Biometrika Tables for Statisticians*, vol. 1, Cambridge University Press, London, 1958, with permission of the publisher.

TABLE A-3 Percentage Points of the t Distribution*

	α										
ν	0.45	0.40	0.35	0.30	0.25	0.125	0.05	0.025	0.0125	0.005	0.0025
1	0.158	0.325	0.510	0.727	1.000	2.414	6.314	12.71	25.45	63.66	127.3
2	0.142	0.289	0.445	0.617	0.817	1.604	2.920	4.303	6.205	9.925	14.09
3	0.137	0.277	0.424	0.584	0.765	1.423	2.353	3.183	4.177	5.841	7.453
4	0.134	0.271	0.414	0.569	0.741	1.344	2.132	2.776	3.495	4.604	5.598
5	0.132	0.267	0.408	0.559	0.727	1.301	2.015	2.571	3.163	4.032	4.773
6	0.131	0.265	0.404	0.553	0.718	1.273	1.943	2.447	2.969	3.707	4.317
7	0.130	0.263	0.402	0.549	0.711	1.254	1.895	2.365	2.841	3.500	4.029
8	0.130	0.262	0.399	0.546	0.706	1.240	1.860	2.306	2.752	3.355	3.833
9	0.129	0.261	0.398	0.543	0.703	1.230	1.833	2.262	2.685	3.250	3.690
10	0.129	0.260	0.397	0.542	0.700	1.221	1.813	2.228	2.634	3.169	3.581
11	0.129	0.260	0.396	0.540	0.697	1.215	1.796	2.201	2.593	3.106	3.500
12	0.128	0.259	0.395	0.539	0.695	1.209	1.782	2.179	2.560	3.055	3.428
13	0.128	0.259	0.394	0.538	0.694	1.204	1.771	2.160	2.533	3.012	3.373
14	0.128	0.258	0.393	0.537	0.692	1.200	1.761	2.145	2.510	2.977	3.326
15	0.128	0.258	0.393	0.536	0.691	1.197	1.753	2.132	2.490	2.947	3.286
20	0.127	0.257	0.391	0.533	0.687	1.185	1.725	2.086	2.423	2.845	3.153
25	0.127	0.256	0.390	0.531	0.684	1.178	1.708	2.060	2.385	2.787	3.078
30	0.127	0.256	0.389	0.530	0.683	1.173	1.697	2.042	2.360	2.750	3.030
40	0.126	0.255	0.388	0.529	0.681	1.167	1.684	2.021	2.329	2.705	2.971
60	0.126	0.254	0.387	0.527	0.679	1.162	1.671	2.000	2.299	2.660	2.915
120	0.126	0.254	0.386	0.526	0.677	1.156	1.658	1.980	2.270	2.617	2.860
∞	0.126	0.253	0.385	0.524	0.674	1.150	1.645	1.960	2.241	2.576	2.807

ν = degrees of freedom.

* Reproduced from William W. Hines and Douglas C. Montgomery, *Probability and Statistics in Engineering and Management Science*, The Ronald Press Company, New York, 1972, with permission of the publisher.

TABLE A-4 Random Normal Numbers

2.616	−.118	−.553	−.008	.492	−1.279	.503	.583	−.342
.220	−.064	−2.074	−.794	−.413	.281	1.873	−.508	.719
1.954	1.022	−.710	1.758	−.380	−.304	−.673	.073	−.603
−.773	−.558	1.661	1.389	−.133	.511	.252	.010	−.258
.815	.351	2.163	−.234	.728	.252	−1.738	−.656	.093
−.545	.086	.175	.298	−.260	−.138	−.466	.834	.390
−.771	−.432	−1.967	−.431	.504	.956	−.190	2.382	1.121
.081	.416	−.039	−.805	−.778	.526	−.470	−.702	1.241
1.114	−.865	−.801	.509	2.448	−.239	1.969	−.279	.362
.362	.882	−.661	.152	−2.205	−.503	1.454	−.381	−.854
−1.212	−1.759	−.974	.445	.154	.195	−.111	1.215	−.083
2.439	1.017	−1.532	.874	.919	.018	.483	2.391	−.257
2.131	−.172	−.553	1.664	−.017	−1.374	−.746	−.1740	−.227
.455	1.015	−.226	−.412	.262	−.589	−.801	−.088	.060
.221	−.952	−.865	1.878	.919	−.877	−.535	−1.512	−.908
.163	−.534	.136	−.276	−1.599	−.102	−.512	−1.584	1.466
−.364	.604	−.872	.127	−.320	−1.673	−.839	.042	.144
−.716	1.537	−.226	.838	−.993	1.285	.138	.636	.452
1.542	.544	−1.700	.717	.680	.504	.502	1.312	1.135
.925	1.080	.260	.547	−.392	−.606	−.347	−.638	−1.967
−.848	.863	−.276	−.075	.812	.084	−1.790	−.311	−.176
.652	−.179	−.194	.654	.587	−.628	−1.090	−1.070	.349
1.500	−1.390	1.171	1.013	1.033	.620	−.784	−.280	−1.755
−1.165	−.563	.554	1.355	−1.151	.312	.513	.280	−2.212
1.437	1.436	−3.334	.307	−1.299	−1.487	.833	−.021	−.951
.879	1.153	−.572	−.622	1.214	.837	−1.002	.246	−.486
−.607	.504	−.082	.059	−.015	.001	−.445	−.136	.730
−.251	−.801	−1.610	1.207	−.193	1.029	−1.811	2.270	−.343
−1.504	−.585	−1.211	1.347	−.493	1.333	−.982	−.862	−1.003
−.652	−.409	1.210	.482	1.117	.303	−1.360	1.001	−.236
−.649	−1.315	1.406	1.013	−.189	.913	.382	−.264	−.663
.628	1.419	−.233	−.666	.371	−1.105	1.304	−.263	.071
−.615	.550	−.115	.861	.666	.069	1.193	.116	−.519
.049	2.063	.649	.165	−1.550	.859	.722	.129	.427
.538	−.162	.884	1.246	.193	.479	−.069	−.657	.556
−1.514	−.423	−.202	−.420	.192	−2.496	1.495	−1.912	1.017
.318	−.314	.748	3.515	.303	.371	1.531	−.513	.471
−.776	1.730	.457	−.071	−.378	−.054	.816	.531	−1.081
1.527	2.022	−.657	−.932	.071	−.096	−.700	−.322	−.322
−1.264	−.053	1.141	−1.281	.328	.641	.082	.208	−1.228
.045	−2.465	−1.440	−1.492	−.783	.883	.987	1.870	−1.230
−1.638	−1.153	.518	−1.321	1.588	−.224	−1.888	−.368	.605
.517	−.182	.692	−.711	.377	1.025	−1.463	−.810	1.125
−.244	−.215	.490	.754	−1.467	−1.194	−.524	.066	−.565
−.044	−1.069	−.424	−.408	.327	−1.075	1.714	−2.023	.045
−.138	.865	−2.034	.073	.381	.960	1.300	−.098	1.062
.010	.987	−2.424	1.439	1.038	1.460	.064	1.044	−.017
−.081	.283	1.219	.070	−1.491	−1.781	−.253	1.069	1.773
.698	−.547	1.300	.105	−.867	.783	.058	−.887	−1.003
−.536	−1.536	.809	1.635	1.806	1.121	−.121	−.188	.379
−.599	−.106	−1.552	−1.271	−1.797	−.213	1.011	.900	.807

APPENDIX B

Collection of Time Series for Exercises

TABLE B-1 Demand for a Double-Knit Polyester Fabric (240 Observations, Read Down from Left)

656	561	588	513	577	627	585	640	620	590
659	556	609	584	552	597	598	616	645	600
601	505	632	537	593	564	613	563	628	644
624	704	550	656	628	604	687	608	637	640
545	641	505	478	594	552	689	561	592	506
502	632	625	629	540	560	600	624	641	577
565	644	549	592	526	593	604	583	633	606
577	677	600	601	576	576	481	560	615	621
549	574	549	582	555	609	513	632	577	614
624	624	684	514	651	624	635	640	632	581
521	529	613	569	504	579	622	698	583	614
520	512	648	612	609	507	576	592	637	627
594	576	652	545	612	543	539	603	570	640
620	547	669	608	625	564	620	481	505	602
537	561	588	581	517	552	613	492	632	597
640	592	624	700	556	645	648	629	648	636
513	481	513	625	577	600	520	585	697	572
639	574	536	636	600	569	561	575	604	625
600	490	585	632	577	630	606	531	624	556
617	614	552	657	616	625	609	640	467	488
636	529	597	546	609	563	619	641	622	642
603	624	612	597	684	568	625	636	613	668
497	506	569	497	634	577	614	535	528	677
600	617	496	544	628	624	614	565	568	637

TABLE B-2 Weekly Sales of a Cutting Tool (100 Observations, Read Down from Left)

100	101	115	125	137
94	100	122	126	138
90	102	118	129	140
96	110	120	132	139
91	104	116	131	131
94	110	118	130	129
95	113	119	133	134
99	112	118	134	133
95	113	120	133	133
98	120	123	135	134
100	121	124	138	132
97	118	123	137	126
99	123	121	140	130
98	124	126	138	131
96	123	128	144	130
98	129	124	135	133
96	125	122	138	132
99	119	123	137	129
97	118	119	136	135
98	120	120	136	136

TABLE B-3 Minutes of Usage Per Day for a Computer Terminal (100 Observations, Read Down from Left)

160	184	187	212
158	186	185	211
150	187	188	210
151	195	192	208
150	202	198	205
151	203	197	202
153	205	193	201
157	208	190	203
156	209	183	205
158	214	178	197
162	215	180	188
161	209	183	186
162	203	187	185
163	199	193	184
161	192	196	183
160	193	197	187
158	190	198	173
159	189	201	171
157	185	200	173
159	182	201	172
160	181	204	174
162	180	206	175
170	181	210	171
172	184	211	172
177	186	216	175

TABLE B-4 Weekly Demand for Crankshaft Bearings (100 Observations, Read Down from Left)

599	1,052	902	480
840	780	922	1,231
1,482	1,018	1,293	1,060
742	1,372	995	922
1,140	876	1,058	968
1,026	703	697	1,059
1,098	1,293	951	1,010
716	991	1,095	1,091
1,197	865	774	936
1,084	1,296	1,130	574
778	694	1,293	1,090
1,116	710	918	1,312
968	1,121	1,083	900
897	1,125	1,038	990
1,136	710	875	1,019
884	1,486	918	903
1,145	733	1,148	735
830	1,039	998	1,380
1,029	826	853	981
1,177	1,124	1,100	882
895	1,070	1,176	1,138
1,036	923	876	911
1,350	1,063	1,090	796
561	1,114	891	1,310
1,307	939	1,244	1,020

TABLE B-5 Monthly Demand for a Spare Part (60 Observations, Read Down from Left)

260	285	399
251	265	361
235	251	380
234	278	394
287	347	368
314	339	359
304	312	374
310	274	418
272	285	429
330	318	448
315	326	420
330	331	442
327	335	457
320	310	477
282	325	443
250	355	410
285	391	399
335	412	424
330	349	468
290	365	480

TABLE B-6   Chemical Process Temperature Readings, Every Two Minutes, °F (100 Observations, Read Down from Left)

153	150	137	144	159	148	156	128
145	148	146	145	156	137	158	138
142	157	152	150	159	155	155	157
145	140	135	143	139	137	147	170
175	133	141	156	148	140	141	133
170	165	137	159	158	162	138	135
159	178	151	169	168	163	145	170
173	149	182	174	173	147	162	160
140	141	148	141	149	150	167	120
136	166	129	133	142	138	149	134
185	166	138	160	165	158	143	128
173	134	149	168	167	153	152	138
155		161		162		133	

TABLE B-7   Monthly Sales of a 32-oz Soft Drink in Hundreds of Cases (48 Observations, Read Down)

	1972	1973	1974	1975
Jan.	28	35	45	52
Feb.	31	40	49	60
Mar.	36	46	57	66
Apr.	43	55	68	80
May	46	60	78	85
June	52	68	80	95
July	55	72	88	100
Aug.	59	75	90	104
Sept.	58	70	84	101
Oct.	55	66	80	94
Nov.	47	58	57	81
Dec.	40	50	60	70

TABLE B-8   Monthly Demand for Carpet (48 Observations, Read Down)

	1970	1971	1972	1973
Jan.	31	43	55	66
Feb.	30	42	54	67
Mar.	35	47	60	71
Apr.	42	54	70	78
May	45	57	69	81
June	52	64	76	88
July	58	70	81	93
Aug.	60	71	84	96
Sept.	57	69	80	93
Oct.	51	65	76	87
Nov.	52	60	75	88
Dec.	47	61	71	83

TABLE B-9   Monthly Champagne Sales (in 1000's of Bottles)*

Year	Month	Sales	Year	Month	Sales	Year	Month	Sales
1962	Jan.	2.851	1963	Jan.	2.541	1964	Jan.	3.113
	Feb.	2.672		Feb.	2.475		Feb.	3.006
	Mar.	2.755		Mar.	3.031		Mar.	4.047
	Apr.	2.721		Apr.	3.266		Apr.	3.523
	May	2.946		May	3.776		May	3.937
	June	3.036		June	3.230		June	3.986
	July	2.282		July	3.028		July	3.260
	Aug.	2.212		Aug.	1.759		Aug.	1.573
	Sept.	2.922		Sept.	3.595		Sept.	3.528
	Oct.	4.301		Oct.	4.474		Oct.	5.211
	Nov.	5.764		Nov.	6.838		Nov.	7.614
	Dec.	7.132		Dec.	8.357		Dec.	9.254
1965	Jan.	5.375	1966	Jan.	3.633	1967	Jan.	4.016
	Feb.	3.088		Feb.	4.292		Feb.	3.957
	Mar.	3.718		Mar.	4.154		Mar.	4.510
	Apr.	4.514		Apr.	4.121		Apr.	4.276
	May	4.520		May	4.647		May	4.968
	June	4.539		June	4.753		June	4.677
	July	3.663		July	3.965		July	3.523
	Aug.	1.643		Aug.	1.723		Aug.	1.821
	Sept.	4.739		Sept.	5.048		Sept.	5.222
	Oct.	5.428		Oct.	6.922		Oct.	6.873
	Nov.	8.314		Nov.	9.858		Nov.	10.803
	Dec.	10.651		Dec.	11.331		Dec.	13.916
1968	Jan.	2.639	1969	Jan.	3.934			
	Feb.	2.899		Feb.	3.162			
	Mar.	3.370		Mar.	4.286			
	Apr.	3.740		Apr.	4.676			
	May	2.927		May	5.010			
	June	3.986		June	4.874			
	July	4.217		July	4.633			
	Aug.	1.738		Aug.	1.659			
	Sept.	5.221		Sept.	5.951			
	Oct.	6.424		Oct.	6.981			
	Nov.	9.842		Nov.	9.851			
	Dec.	13.076		Dec.	12.670			

* Adapted from Wheelwright and Makridakis [62].

TABLE B-10 Yearly Wölfer Sunspot Numbers (Average Number of Sunspots/Year)

Year	No.	Year	No.	Year	No.	Year	No.
1770	101	1795	21	1820	16	1845	40
1771	82	1796	16	1821	7	1846	62
1772	66	1797	6	1822	4	1847	98
1773	35	1798	4	1823	2	1848	124
1774	31	1799	7	1824	8	1849	96
1775	7	1800	14	1825	17	1850	66
1776	20	1801	34	1826	36	1851	64
1777	92	1802	45	1827	50	1852	54
1778	154	1803	43	1828	62	1853	39
1779	125	1804	48	1829	67	1854	21
1780	85	1805	42	1830	71	1855	7
1781	68	1806	28	1831	48	1856	4
1782	38	1807	10	1832	28	1857	23
1783	23	1808	8	1833	8	1858	55
1784	10	1809	2	1834	13	1859	94
1785	24	1810	0	1835	57	1860	96
1786	83	1811	1	1836	122	1861	77
1787	132	1812	5	1837	138	1862	59
1788	131	1813	12	1838	103	1863	44
1789	118	1814	14	1839	86	1864	47
1790	90	1815	35	1840	63	1865	30
1791	67	1816	46	1841	37	1866	16
1792	60	1817	41	1842	24	1867	7
1793	47	1818	30	1843	11	1868	37
1794	41	1819	24	1844	15	1869	74

TABLE B-11 Reported Cases of Rubella by Two-Week Periods, East North-Central United States (Ohio, Indiana, Illinois, Michigan, Wisconsin)*

Period	1966	1967	1968
1	420	180	125
2	550	195	210
3	610	300	300
4	910	445	505
5	1,115	440	500
6	1,210	435	1,500
7	1,190	520	980
8	1,080	775	1,000
9	1,175	640	900
10	1,195	775	1,075
11	1,280	650	990
12	1,200	760	520
13	395	390	395
14	360	200	190
15	220	130	140
16	230	100	150
17	150	90	140
18	165	20	155
19	150	50	194
20	160	90	154
21	110	130	162
22	110	80	164
23	140	160	160
24	150	120	180
25	190	202	185
26	195	200	181

* Center for Disease Control, Atlanta, Georgia

TABLE B-12 Monthly Demand for a Plastic Container (48 Observations, Read Down)

	1971	1972	1973	1974
Jan.	337	480	545	645
Feb.	185	420	581	700
Mar.	315	382	615	690
Apr.	325	487	583	675
May	340	584	580	625
June	350	542	614	729
July	320	585	547	785
Aug.	380	405	610	771
Sept.	448	420	612	745
Oct.	420	588	780	795
Nov.	505	584	724	799
Dec.	415	565	685	784

APPENDIX C

Computer Programs

C-1 MULTIPLE EXPONENTIAL SMOOTHING

Description

This program performs either single, double, or triple exponential smoothing for a time series consisting of n observations. It is also capable of optimizing the smoothing constant over a specified range and estimating the starting values of the smoothed statistics from the input data.

If smoothing constant optimization is desired, then the user must identify the portion of the time series to be analyzed in the optimization scheme. This segment is the first $n_1 (< n)$ observations. The optimum smoothing constant is selected as the value which results in a minimum forecast error sum of squares for the first n_1 observations.

If the starting values of the smoothed statistics are to be estimated from the data, the first six observations are used and least-squares estimates of the parameters of the postulated time series model are obtained. We have arbitrarily selected the number of observations used in this phase. The user may easily change the number of observations employed in the parameter estimation process. However, the value chosen seems to work reasonably well in practice. The least-squares estimates are used to obtain the starting values of the smoothed statistics. If this option is not selected, the user must provide starting values of the smoothed statistics.

The last $n - n_1$ observations are used in a forecast simulation. The forecast lead time must be specified by the user. Output of this phase includes forecast errors and both smoothed error and cumulative error tracking signals.

Input Data Preparation

Card 1

Column 1	Degree of smoothing (1, 2, or 3).
Columns 2–5	Number of observations in the time series (integer, right justified).
Columns 6–9	Number of observations to be used in smoothing constant optimization and/or estimating starting values of the smoothed statistics (integer, right justified).
Columns 10–13	Forecast lead time (integer, right justified).
Column 14	0 if the starting values of the smoothed statistics are specified by the user, or 1 if the starting values of the smoothed statistics are estimated from the data.
Column 15	0 if smoothing constant optimization is desired, or 1 if a specified smoothing constant is to be used.

Card 2

Columns 1–4	If the smoothing constant is specified, enter the desired value (F4.0 Format). If smoothing constant optimization is desired, enter the lower limit for the smoothing constant.
Columns 5–8	Amount by which the smoothing constant is to be incremented in each iteration of the optimization routine (F4.0 Format).
Columns 9–12	Upper limit for the smoothing constant (F4.0 Format).

If a value is specified for the smoothing constant, columns 5–12 are left blank.

Card 3 Data Cards

Enter the data, 10 observations per card in F8.0 Format, beginning with the first observation and proceeding to the end of the time series. Use as many cards as necessary.

Card 4

If starting values of the smoothed statistics are to be estimated from the data, this card is deleted. If starting values are specified, they are entered on this card as follows:

Columns 1–4	Starting value of the first-order exponentially smoothed statistic (F4.0 Format).
Columns 5–8	Starting value of the double exponentially smoothed statistic (F4.0 Format). Entered only if double or triple smoothing is desired.
Columns 9–12	Starting value of the triple exponentially smoothed statistic (F4.0 Format). Enter only if triple smoothing is desired.

Program Listing

```
       IMPLICIT INTEGER (E-D)
       DIMENSION X(500),S(500),S2(500),S3(500),R(500),F(500),FFP(500)
C
C
C                        MULTIPLE SMOOTHING PROGRAM
C
C      WILL PERFORM CONSTANT, LINEAR, OR QUADRATIC SMOOTHING, DEPENDING
C         ON THE VALUE OF K
C
C      F(I) IS THE FORECAST MADE AT PERIOD I FOR PERIOD I+L
C      R(I) IS THE ERROR DERIVED AT PERIOD I CALCULATED BY
C      SUBTRACTING THE ESTIMATED VALUE ( MADE L PERIODS BEFORE)
C      FFP(I) IS THE FORECAST FOR PERIOD I  ( MADE L PERIODS AGO )
C      X(I) IS THE ACTUAL DATA FOR PERIOD I
C
C
       READ(5,1) K,N,N1,L,KN,KS
       XL=L
       XLSQ=XL*XL
       N1ML=N1-L
1      FORMAT(I1,3I4,2I1)
C
C      N IS THE NUMBER OF DATA ENTRIES TO BE PROCESSED
C      N1 IS THE NUMBER OF DATA ENTRIES TO BE USED IN THE PARAMETER
C         ESTIMATION PHASE
C      L IS THE LEAD TIME USED FOR FORECASTING
C      EST IS THE NUMBER OF POINTS IN THE ESTIMATION PHASE
C         TO BE USED IN PERIOD '0' ESTIMATION.
C      THE REMAINDER OF THE N1-EST POINTS ARE USED IN THE
C      ALPHA OPTIMIZATION SECTION
C
       IF(N1.LT.L)N1=L
       EST=6
       ESTP1=EST+1
       ESTP2=EST+2
       ESTPL=EST+L
       WRITE(6,111)
111    FORMAT(1H1,50X,'MULTIPLE SMOOTHING PROGRAM')
C
C      IF KS = 0 READ IN AU,D,AL  ..  ELSE READ IN SELECTED ALPHA
       IF(KS.EQ.0) GO TO 3
       READ(5,2)A
2      FORMAT(3F4.0)
       GO TO 4
3      READ(5,2) AL,D,AU
C      AL IS THE LOWER BOUND FOR THE ALPHA SEARCH
C      D IS THE DELTA CHANGE BETWEEN ALPHA SIMULATIONS
C      AU IS THE UPPER BOUND ON POSSIBLE ALPHA'S
C
C      INPUT THE DATA VALUES FOR DEMAND
4      READ(5,6)(X(J),J=1,N)
6      FORMAT(10F8.0)
       WRITE(6,112)K
112    FORMAT(1H0,10X,'DEGREE OF SMOOTHING SELECTED=',I2/)
       IF(KN.EQ.1) GO TO 10
C
C      READ IN THE REQUIRED PARAMETERS (KN = 1)
C
       IF(K-2)7,8,9
7      READ(5,2)S0
       WRITE(6,113)S0
113    FORMAT(1H0,10X,'STARTING VALUE OF THE SMOOTHED STATISTIC SPECIFIED
      * AS S1=',F10.4)
       GO TO 11
8      READ(5,2)S0,S20
       WRITE(6,114) S0,S20
114    FORMAT(1H0,10X,'STARTING VALUES OF THE SMOOTHED STATISTIC SPECIFI
      *ED AS S1=',F10.4,5X,'S2=',F10.4)
       GO TO 11
```

```
562    FFP(I+L)=F(I)
C
C      BEGIN FORECAST SIMULATION
C
       J=N1+1
       DO 60 I=J,N
       S(I)=A*X(I)+AA*S(I-1)
       IF(K-2)57,58,59
57     FFP(I)=S(I-L)
       GO TO 60
58     S2(I)=A*S(I)+AA*S2(I-1)
       FFP(I)=(2.0+XL*A/AA)*S(I-L)-(1.0+XL*A/AA)*S2(I-L)
       GO TO 60
59     S2(I)=A*S(I)+AA*S2(I-1)
       S3(I)=A*S2(I)+AA*S3(I-1)
       AHAT=3.0*S(I-L)-3.0*S2(I-L)+S3(I-L)
       BHT=A/(2.0*AA**2)*((6.0-5.0*A)*S(I-L)-2.0*(5.0-4.0*A)*S2(I-L)
      **+(4.0-3.0*A)*S3(I-L))
       CHAT=(A/AA)**2*(S(I-L)-2.0*S2(I-L)+S3(I-L))
       FFP(I)=AHAT+XL*BHT+0.5*XL**2*CHAT
60     CONTINUE
C
C      LOGIC TO PRINT OUT PAGE 2
70     T=0.0
       T2=0.0
       TA=0.0
       WRITE(6,121)
121    FORMAT(1H1,10X,'OUTPUT OF MODEL INITIALIZATION PHASE')
       WRITE(6,122)K,A
122    FORMAT(1H0,'DEGREE OF SMOOTHING=',I2,5X,'SMOOTHING CONSTANT=',F10.
      *2//)
       WRITE(6,143) EST
143    FORMAT(I8,' SAMPLES WERE USED IN ESTIMATION OF INITIAL CONSTANTS')
       WRITE(6,123)
123    FORMAT(1H0,'PERIOD',5X,'DATA',10X,'SMOOTHED STATISTICS',13X,'FITTE
      *D MODEL',5X,'RESIDUAL')
       IF(K.EQ.1)WRITE(6,124)
124    FORMAT(24X,'FIRST'/)
       IF(K.EQ.2)WRITE(6,125)
125    FORMAT(24X,'FIRST',5X,'SECOND'/)
       IF(K.EQ.3)WRITE(6,126)
126    FORMAT(24X,'FIRST',5X,'SECOND',5X,'THIRD'/)
       DO 75 I=1,EST
75     WRITE(6,1299)I,X(I)
       DO 71 I=ESTP1,N1
       T=T+R(I)
       T2=T2+R(I)**2
       TA=TA+ABS(R(I))
       IF(K.EQ.1)WRITE(6,127)I,X(I),S(I),FFP(I),R(I)
       IF(K.EQ.2)WRITE(6,128)I,X(I),S(I),S2(I),FFP(I),R(I)
       IF(K.EQ.3)WRITE(6,129)I,X(I),S(I),S2(I),S3(I),FFP(I),R(I)
127    FORMAT(1X,I4,2X,F10.2,2X,F10.2,28X,F10.2,5X,F10.2)
128    FORMAT(1X,I4,2X,F10.2,2X,F10.2,2X,F10.2,16X,F10.2,5X,F10.2)
129    FORMAT(1X,I4,2X,F10.2,2X,F10.2,2X,F10.2,2X,F10.2,2X,F10.2,5X,F10.2
      *)
1299   FORMAT(1X,I4,F12.2)
71     CONTINUE
       V=N1-EST
       TA=TA/V
       TH=T/V
       VAR=(T2-V*TB**2)/(V-1.0)
       STD=SQRT(VAR)
       WRITE(6,130)T,T3
130    FORMAT(1H0,'SUM OF RESIDUALS=',F10.2,
      *5X,'AVERAGE OF RESIDUALS=',F10.5)
       WRITE(6,131)T2,VAR,STD,TA
131    FORMAT(1X,'RESIDUAL SUM OF SQUARES=',E14.7,3X,'VARIANCE=',F13.2,
      *3X,'STANDARD DEVIATION=',F10.2,3X,'MEAN ABS. DEV.=',
      *F10.2)
```

279

```
C
C         LOGIC TO PRINT OUT PAGE 3
          KNTR=0
          V=2.0*STD
          W=-V
          DO 72 I=ESTP1,N1
          IF(R(I).GT.V.OR.R(I).LT.W)KNTR=KNTR+1
72        CONTINUE
          WRITE(6,132)KNTR
132       FORMAT(1X,'NUMBER OF RESIDUALS EXCEEDING TWO STANDARD DEVIATIONS='
         *,I4)
          WRITE(6,133)
133       FORMAT(1H1,10X,'OUTPUT OF FORECASTING PHASE'/)
          WRITE(6,134)K,A,L
134       FORMAT(10X,'DEGREE OF SMOOTHING=',I2,5X,'SMOOTHING CONSTANT=',F10.
         *2,10X,'FORECAST LEAD TIME=',I2,1X,'PERIODS')
          WRITE(6,135)
135       FORMAT(1H0,'PERIOD',5X,'DATA',13X,'SMOOTHED STATISTICS',12X,'FOREC
         *AST',6X,'ERROR',12X,'TRACKING SIGNALS')
          IF(K.EQ.1)WRITE(6,136)
          IF(K.EQ.2)WRITE(6,137)
          IF(K.EQ.3)WRITE(6,138)
136       FORMAT(24X,'FIRST',55X,'CUMULATIVE ERROR',2X,'SMOOTHED ERROR'/)
137       FORMAT(24X,'FIRST',6X,'SECOND',44X,'CUMULATIVE ERROR',2X,'SMOOTHE
         *D ERROR')
138       FORMAT(24X,'FIRST',6X,'SECOND',6X,'THIRD',35X,'CUMULATIVE ERROR'-
         *2X,'SMOOTHED ERROR'/)
          J=N1+1
          Z=0.0
          T=0.0
          T2=0.0
          DO 73 I=J,N
          Q=X(I)-FFP(I)
          T=T+Q
          T2=T2+Q**2
          TA=A*ABS(Q)+AA*TA
          Z=A*Q+AA*Z
          TSC=T/TA
          TSS=Z/TA
          IF(K.EQ.1)WRITE(6,139)I,X(I),S(I),FFP(I),Q,TSC,TSS
          IF(K.EQ.2)WRITE(6,140)I,X(I),S(I),S2(I),FFP(I),Q,TSC,TSS
          IF(K.EQ.3)WRITE(6,141)I,X(I),S(I),S2(I),S3(I),FFP(I),Q,TSC,TSS
139       FORMAT(1X,I4,2X,F10.2,2X,F10.2,28X,F10.2,2X,F10.2,5X,F10.2,5X,F10.
         *2)
140       FORMAT(1X,I4,2X,F10.2,2X,F10.2,2X,F10.2,16X,F10.2,2X,F10.2,5X,F10.
         *2,5X,F10.2)
141       FORMAT(1X,I4,2X,F10.2,2X,F10.2,2X,F10.2,2X,F10.2,4X,F10.2,2X,F10.2
         *,5X,F10.2,5X,F10.2)
73        CONTINUE
          V=N-N1
          TB=T/V
          VAR=(T2-V*TB**2)/(V-1.0)
          STD=SQRT(VAR)
          WRITE(6,142)T,TB,VAR,STD
142       FORMAT(1H0,'SUM OF FORECAST ERRORS=',F10.4,5X,
         *'AVERAGE FORECAST ERROR=',F10.4,5X,'VARIANCE=',F10.4,5X,
         *'STANDARD DEVIATION=',F10.4)
          STOP
          END
```

```
          WRITE(6,117)B,T
117       FORMAT(12X,F10.4,10X,E16.7)
          IF(T.GE.TBEST)GO TO 14
          TBEST=T
          ABEST=B
14        IF(ABS(B-AU).LE.0.0001 .OR. B.GT.AU) GO TO 15
          B=B+D
          GO TO 12
C
C         BEST SMOOTHING CONSTANT HAS BEEN FOUND AND STORED IN A
C         ESTIMATION USING THE OPTIMUM ALPHA
C
15        A=ABEST
16        WRITE(6,118)A
118       FORMAT(1H0,10X,'SMOOTHING CONSTANT=',F10.4)
          AA=1.0-A
          IF(KN.EQ.0)GO TO 50
          IF(K-2)50,25,400
25        S0=B0-AA/A*B1
          S20=B0-2.*AA/A*B1
          WRITE(6,119)S0,S20
119       FORMAT(1H0,'STARTING VALUES OF THE SMOOTHED STATISTICS ESTIMATED F
         *ROM THE DATA AS S1=',F10.4,5X,'S2=',F10.4)
          GO TO 50
400        S0=B0-AA/A*B1+AA*(2.0-A)/(2.0*A**2)*B2
          S20=B0-2.*AA/A*B1+2.0*AA*(3.0-2.0*A)/(2.0*A**2)*B2
          S30=B0-3.*AA/A*B1+3.0*AA*(4.0-3.0*A)/(2.0*A**2)*B2
          WRITE(6,152)S0,S20,S30
152       FORMAT(1H0,'STARTING VALUES OF THE SMOOTHED STATISTICS ESTIMATED F
         *ROM THE DATA AS S1=',F10.4,5X,'S2=',F10.4,5X,'S3=',F10.4)
50        S(ESTP1)=A*X(ESTP1)+AA*S0
          IF(K.GT.1)GO TO 51
          F(ESTP1)=S(ESTP1)
          GO TO 53
51        S2(ESTP1)=A*S(ESTP1)+AA*S20
          IF(K.EQ.3) GO TO 52
          F(ESTP1)=(2.+XL*A/AA)*S(ESTP1)-(1.+XL*A/AA)*S2(ESTP1)
          GO TO 53
52        S3(ESTP1)=A*S2(ESTP1)+AA*S30
          AHAT=3.*S(ESTP1)-3.*S2(ESTP1)+S3(ESTP1)
          BHT=A/AA/AA/2.*((6.-5.*A)*S(ESTP1)-2.*(5.-4.*A)*S2(ESTP1)+
         *(4.-3.*A)*S3(ESTP1))
          CHAT=A*A/AA/AA*(S(ESTP1)-2.*S2(ESTP1)+S3(ESTP1))
          F(ESTP1)=AHAT+BHT*XL+.5*CHAT*XL*XL
53        R(ESTP1+L)=X(ESTP1+L)-F(ESTP1)
          DO 56 J=ESTP2,N1
          JL=J+L
          S(J)=A*X(J)+AA*S(J-1)
          IF(K.GT.1)GO TO 54
          F(J)=S(J)
          GO TO 56
54        S2(J)=A*S(J)+AA*S2(J-1)
          IF(K.EQ.3)GO TO 55
          F(J)=(2.+A*XL/AA)*S(J)-(1.+XL*A/AA)*S2(J)
          GO TO 56
55        S3(J)=A*S2(J)+AA*S3(J-1)
          AHAT=3.*S(J)-3.*S2(J)+S3(J)
          BHT=A/AA/AA/2.*((6.-5.*A)*S(J)-2.*(5.-4.*A)*S2(J)+(4.-3.*A)*S3(J))
          CHAT=A*A/AA/AA*(S(J)-2.*S2(J)+S3(J))
          F(J)=AHAT+BHT*XL+.5*XL*XL*CHAT
56        R(JL)=X(JL)-F(J)
          DO 561 I=1,ESTPL
          FFP(I)=0.
561       R(I)=0.
          DO 563 I=1,EST
          S(I)=0.
          S2(I)=0.
563       S3(I)=0.
          DO 562 I=1,N1ML
```

Example

We shall illustrate the data card layout for using the multiple smoothing program for double smoothing. The time series has 48 observations, the forecast lead time is one period, and the smoothing constant is specified as 0.08. We wish to use the first 24 periods' data to initialize the model, and simulate forecasting for the last 24 periods. Notice that only the first 6 periods' data will be used to estimate the model parameters and the starting values of the smoothed statistics. These starting values will be successively smoothed through the end of period 24, when a forecast simulation will begin. The required data cards are given below:

```
2  48  24  111
0.08
555.   570.   549.   574.   558.   580.   587.   603.   583.   628.
597.   568.   598.   628.   577.   604.   513.   620.   627.   625.
667.   693.   633.   652.   637.   598.   601.   647.   665.   648.
665.   651.   655.   642.   669.   680.   701.   720.   676.   646.
692.   736.   713.   724.   705.   708.   757.   734.
↑
```
Card Column 1

The output for the multiple smoothing program is shown on pages 285–286. Notice that in the model initialization phase, no forecasts are provided for periods one through six. The first forecast is for period $7 + \tau$, where τ is the specified lead time. We see that only one residual (or forecast error) exceeds two standard deviations of the forecast error. The results of the forecast simulation are summarized on the last page of output. The forecasts produced by this model seem reasonably good, although in periods 32 through 36 several large values of the cumulative error tracking signal are generated.

MULTIPLE SMOOTHING PROGRAM

DEGREE OF SMOOTHING SELECTED= 2

STARTING VALUES OF THE SMOOTHED STATISTICS TO BE ESTIMATED FROM   6 DATA POINTS

ESTIMATES OF PARAMETERS IN LINEAR MODEL-INTERCEPT= 572.4762   SLOPE=   3.2571

   SMOOTHING CONSTANT=   .0800

STARTING VALUES OF THE SMOOTHED STATISTICS ESTIMATED FROM THE DATA AS S1= 535.0190   S2= 497.5619

   OUTPUT OF MODEL INITIALIZATION PHASE

DEGREE OF SMOOTHING= 2   SMOOTHING CONSTANT=   .08

   6 SAMPLES WERE USED IN ESTIMATION OF INITIAL CONSTANTS

PERIOD	DATA	SMOOTHED STATISTICS FIRST	SECOND	FITTED MODEL	RESIDUAL
1	555.00				
2	570.00				
3	549.00				
4	574.00				
5	558.00				
6	580.00				
7	587.00	539.18	500.89	.00	.00
8	603.00	544.28	504.36	580.79	22.21
9	583.00	547.38	507.80	587.68	-4.68
10	628.00	553.83	511.49	590.40	37.60
11	597.00	557.28	515.15	599.86	-2.86
12	568.00	558.14	518.59	603.08	-35.08
13	598.00	561.33	522.01	601.13	-3.13
14	626.00	566.66	525.58	604.07	23.93
15	577.00	567.49	528.93	611.32	-34.32
16	604.00	570.41	532.25	609.40	-5.40
17	513.00	565.82	534.94	611.89	-98.89
18	620.00	570.15	537.75	599.38	20.62
19	627.00	574.70	540.71	605.37	21.63
20	625.00	578.72	543.75	611.65	13.35
21	667.00	585.79	547.11	616.74	50.26
22	693.00	594.36	550.89	627.82	65.18
23	633.00	597.45	554.62	641.61	-8.61
24	652.00	601.82	558.39	644.01	7.99

SUM OF RESIDUALS=   69.80   AVERAGE OF RESIDUALS=   3.87763
RESIDUAL SUM OF SQUARES=   .271958+05   VARIANCE=   1320.53   STANDARD DEVIATION=   36.34   MEAN ABS. DEV.=   25.32
NUMBER OF RESIDUALS EXCEEDING TWO STANDARD DEVIATIONS=   1

OUTPUT OF FORECASTING PHASE

DEGREE OF SMOOTHING= 2   SMOOTHING CONSTANT= .08   FORECAST LEAD TIME= 1 PERIODS

PERIOD	DATA	SMOOTHED STATISTICS		FORECAST	ERROR	TRACKING SIGNALS	
		FIRST	SECOND			CUMULATIVE ERROR	SMOOTHED ERROR
25	637.00	604.63	562.09	649.02	-12.02	-.50	-.04
26	596.00	604.10	565.45	650.87	-52.87	-2.44	-.19
27	601.00	603.65	568.53	646.11	-45.11	-3.92	-.30
28	647.00	607.31	571.63	642.25	4.75	-4.02	-.28
29	665.00	611.92	574.85	646.08	18.92	-3.37	-.20
30	646.00	614.81	578.05	652.21	-4.21	-3.79	-.21
31	616.00	616.82	581.31	654.76	10.24	-3.52	-.17
32	651.00	621.40	584.52	659.60	-8.60	-4.11	-.20
33	655.00	624.09	587.68	661.48	-6.48	-4.67	-.22
34	642.00	625.52	590.71	663.65	-21.65	-5.70	-.28
35	669.00	629.06	593.77	663.35	5.65	-5.76	-.25
36	680.00	633.08	596.92	667.28	12.72	-5.25	-.19
37	701.00	638.51	600.24	672.38	28.62	-3.58	-.05
38	720.00	645.03	603.83	680.10	39.90	-1.42	.11
39	670.00	647.51	607.32	689.82	-13.82	-2.13	.05
40	646.00	647.34	610.53	691.19	-45.19	-3.95	-.12
41	592.00	656.96	613.76	687.45	4.55	-4.00	-.10
42	736.00	657.76	617.28	691.39	44.61	-1.74	.07
43	712.00	662.18	620.87	701.76	11.24	-1.30	.11
44	724.00	667.12	624.57	707.08	16.92	-.55	.17
45	705.00	670.15	628.22	713.38	-8.38	-.98	.13
46	708.00	673.18	631.82	715.74	-7.74	-1.43	.09
47	757.00	679.89	635.66	718.14	38.86	.52	.23
48	734.00	684.22	639.55	727.96	6.04	.85	.24

SUM OF FORECAST ERRORS=   16.9376   AVERAGE FORECAST ERROR=   .7057   VARIANCE=   651.6340   STANDARD DEVIATION=   25.5271

NORMAL EXIT. EXECUTION TIME: 391 MI.SEC.
FIN

C-2 WINTERS' METHOD

Description

This computer program uses Winters' method for forecasting a time series of length n consisting of a permanent component, an additive trend component, and a multiplicative seasonal component. The length of the season must be specified by the user. The program is capable of optimizing the smoothing constants over specified ranges and estimating the starting values of the model parameters from the input data.

If smoothing constant optimization is desired, then the user must identify the portion of the time series to be analyzed in the optimization scheme. This segment is the first $n_1(<n)$ observations. The optimum combination of smoothing constants are those values which result in a minimum forecast error sum of squares for the first n_1 periods. The initial model parameters are estimated from the first n_1 observations, if this option is utilized. If initial model parameters are to be estimated, then n_1 must be a multiple of the length of the season.

The last $n - n_1$ observations are used in a forecast simulation. The forecast lead time must be specified by the user. Output of this phase includes the forecast errors and both smoothed error and cumulative error tracking signals. The smoothing constant used in tracking signal computations is arbitrarily set at 0.10.

Input Data Preparation

Card 1

Columns 1–3   Length of time series (integer, right justified).

Columns 4–6   Length of time series to be used in model initialization and smoothing constant calculations (integer, right justified).

Column 7   0 if the smoothing constants are specified by the user, or 1 if smoothing constant optimization is desired.

Column 8   0 if the initial values of the model parameters are specified by the user, or 1 if the initial values of the model parameters are estimated from the data.

Columns 9–11   Length of the season (integer, right justified).

Columns 12–14   Forecast lead time (integer, right justified).

Card 2

If smoothing constants are specified by the user:

Columns 1–4   Smoothing constant for permanent component (Alpha), F4.0 Format.

Columns 5–8   Smoothing constant for trend component (Beta), F4.0 Format.

Columns 9–12   Smoothing constant for seasonal component (Gamma), F4.0 Format.

If smoothing constant optimization is desired (all F4.0 Format):

Columns 1–4   Lower limit for Alpha.

Columns 5–8   Step size for Alpha.

Columns 9–12   Upper limit for Alpha.

Columns 13–16   Lower limit for Beta.
Columns 17–20   Step size for Beta.
Columns 21–24   Upper limit for Beta.
Columns 25–28   Lower limit for Gamma.
Columns 29–32   Step size for Gamma.
Columns 33–36   Upper limit for Gamma.

Caution: The program tries all possible combinations of smoothing constants, and unless the ranges and step sizes are carefully chosen a large number of relatively uninformative calculations will be made. For example, if you specify the range of each smoothing constant as 0.00 to 0.99 in steps of 0.01, then $(100)^3$ or 1,000,000 trials will be made. It is better to use a coarse grid at first, and make a second run (if necessary) with a fine grid restricted to a narrow interval.

Card 3 Data Cards

Enter the data, 10 observations per card in F8.0 Format, beginning with the first observation. Use as many cards as necessary.

If initial values of the model parameters (permanent component, trend, and L seasonal factors) are specified by the user, the following additional cards are required:

Card 4

Columns 1–4   Initial value of the permanent value, F4.0 Format.

Card 5

Columns 1–4   Initial value of the trend component, F4.0 Format.

Card 6

Columns 1–4   Initial seasonal factor, 1st period, F4.0 Format.

Card 7

Columns 1–4   Initial seasonal factor, 2nd period, F4.0 Format.
$\vdots$

Card $L + 5$

Columns 1–4   Initial seasonal factor, Lth period, F4.0 Format.

Program Listing

```
      DIMENSION X(500),A(500),B(500),S(24),V(10),FF(10,24),R(500),F(500)
      DIMENSION FFP(500),SAVE(24),SS(500)
      REAL ONEMAA,ONEMBB,ONEMGG
C
C
C     WINTERS' METHOD- ADDITIVE TREND AND MULTIPLICATIVE SEASONALS
C
C     F(I) IS THE FORECAST MADE IN PERIOD I
C     FFP(I) IS THE FORECAST MADE FOR PERIOD I
C     X(I) IS THE DATA WHICH IS RECIEVED IN PERIOD I
C     R(I) IS X(I)-FFP(I)
C
      READ(5,1)N,N1,KS,KN,L,LT
1     FORMAT(2I3,2I1,2I3)
      XLT=LT
      IF(KS.EQ.0)READ(5,2)ALPHA,BETA,GAMMA
2     FORMAT(9F4.0)
      IF(KS.EQ.1)READ(5,2)AL,AD,AU,BL,BD,BU,GL,GD,GU
      READ(5,4)(X(I),I=1,N)
4     FORMAT(10F8.0)
      WRITE(6,5)
5     FORMAT(1H1,25X,'WINTERS'' METHOD FOR FORECASTING A SEASONAL TIME S
     *ERIES'/)
      IF(KN.EQ.1)GO TO 12
      WRITE(6,6)
6     FORMAT(1H0,10X,'INITIAL VALUES OF THE PERMANENT, TREND AND SEASONA
     *L COMPONENTS SPECIFIED')
      READ(5,2)A0
      READ(5,2)B0
      DO 7 I=1,L
      READ(5,2)S(I)
7     SAVE(I)=S(I)
      WRITE(6,8)A0
8     FORMAT(1H0,20X,'INITIAL PERMANENT COMPONENT=',F10.4)
      WRITE(6,9)B0
9     FORMAT(1H0,20X,'INITIAL TREND COMPONENT=',F10.4)
      DO 10 I=1,L
10    WRITE(6,11)I,S(I)
11    FORMAT(1H0,20X,'INITIAL SEASONAL FACTOR FOR PERIOD',I3,1X,'=',
     *F10.4)
      GO TO 22
12    WRITE(6,13)
13    FORMAT(1H0,10X,'INITIAL VALUES OF THE PERMANENT, TREND AND SEASONA
     *L COMPONENTS TO BE ESTIMATED FROM THE DATA.')
      KK=N1/L
      WRITE(6,14)N1,KK
14    FORMAT(1H0,10X,'THE FIRST',I3,1X,'PERIODS OF DATA WHICH CORRESPOND
     * TO,'I3,1X,'SEASONS WILL BE USED')
      RL=L
      J1=1
      J2=L
      DO 16 I=1,KK
      V(I)=0.0
      DO 15 J=J1,J2
15    V(I)=V(I)+X(J)
      V(I)=V(I)/RL
      J1=J2+1
      J2=J1+L-1
16    CONTINUE
      RR=N1-L
      B0=(V(KK)-V(1))/RR
      A0=V(1)-RL/2.*B0
      J1=0
      DO 18 I=1,KK
      DO 17 J=1,L
      JT=J+J1*L
      RJ=J
17    FF(I,J)=X(JT)/(V(I)-(((RL+1.0)/2.0)-RJ)*B0)
      J1=J1+1
```

289

```
18      CONTINUE
        SUMS=0.0
        RKK=KK
        DO 20 J=1,L
        SUM=0.0
        DO 19 I=1,KK
19      SUM=SUM+FF(I,J)
        S(J)=SUM/RKK
20      SUMS=SUMS+S(J)
        WRITE(6,8)A0
        WRITE(6,9)B0
        DO 21 J=1,L
        S(J)=S(J)*(RL/SUMS)
        SAVE(J)=S(J)
21      WRITE(6,11)J,S(J)
22      IF(KS.EQ.0) GO TO 32
        WRITE(6,23)
23      FORMAT(1H1,10X,'SMOOTHING CONSTANT OPTIMIZATION ROUTINE')
        WRITE(6,24)
24      FORMAT(1H0,10X,'ALPHA',10X,'BETA',10X,'GAMMA',10X,
       *'RESIDUAL SUM OF SQUARES'/)
C
C       SEARCH FOR OPTIMUM VALUES
C
        KA=(AU-AL)/AD+1.0
        KB=(BU-BL)/BD+1.0
        KG=(GU-GL)/GD+1.0
        AA=AL
        AREST=0.0
        BREST=0.0
        GREST=0.0
        EREST=1.0E+38
        DO 30 II=1,KA
        ONEMAA=1.0-AA
        BB=BL
        DO 29 IJ=1,KB
        ONEMBB=1.0-BB
        GG=GL
        DO 28 IK=1,KG
        DO 205 IL=1,L
205     S(IL)=SAVE(IL)
        ONEMGG=1.0-GG
        A(1)=AA*(X(1)/S(1))+ONEMAA*(A0+B0)
        B(1)=BB*(A(1)-A0)+ONEMBB*B0
        S(1)=GG*(X(1)/A(1))+ONEMGG*S(1)
        XHAT=(A(1)+XLT*B(1))*S(1+LT)
        E=(X(1+LT)-XHAT)**2
        DO 26 I=2,N1
        IL=MOD(I,L)
        IF(IL.EQ.0) IL=L
25      A(I)=AA*(X(I)/S(IL))+ONEMAA*(A(I-1)+B(I-1))
        B(I)=BB*(A(I)-A(I-1))+ONEMBB*B(I-1)
        S(IL)=GG*(X(I)/A(I))+ONEMGG*S(IL)
        ILLT=IL+LT
        IF(ILLT.GT.L) ILLT=ILLT-L
        XHAT=(A(I)+XLT*B(I))*S(ILLT)
26      E=E+(X(I+LT)-XHAT)**2
        WRITE(6,27)AA,BB,GG,E
27      FORMAT(8X,F10.4,5X,F10.4,5X,F10.4,15X,E15.7)
        IF(E.GE.EREST)GO TO 28
        ALPHA=AA
        BETA=BB
        GAMMA=GG
        EREST=E
28      GG=GG+GD
29      BB=BB+BD
30      AA=AA+AD
        WRITE(6,31)
31      FORMAT(1H0,10X,'THE OPTIMUM SMOOTHING CONSTANTS ARE')
```

290

```
32      IF(KS.EQ.0)WRITE(6,33)
33      FORMAT(1H0,10X,'THE SMOOTHING CONSTANTS ARE SPECIFIED AS')
        WRITE(6,34)ALPHA,BETA,GAMMA
34      FORMAT(1H0,10X,'ALPHA=',F10.4,5X,'BETA=',F10.4,5X,'GAMMA=',
       *F10.4)
        IF(N1.EQ.0)N1=L
C
C       FORECAST WITH OPTIMUM SMOOTHING CONSTANTS
C
        DO 305 IL=1,L
305     S(IL)=SAVE(IL)
        ONEMAA=1.0-ALPHA
        ONEMBB=1.0-BETA
        ONEMGG=1.0-GAMMA
        A(1)=ALPHA*(X(1)/S(1))+ONEMAA*(A0+B0)
        B(1)=BETA*(A(1)-A0)+ONEMBB*B0
        S(1)=GAMMA*(X(1)/A(1))+ONEMGG*S(1)
        F(1)=(A(1)+XLT*B(1))*S(LT+1)
        SS(1)=S(1)
        FFP(1+LT)=F(1)
        R(1+LT)=X(1+LT)-F(1)
        SUM=R(1)
        SUMSQ=R(1)**2
        XMAD=ABS(R(1))
        DO 36 I=2,N1
        IL=MOD(I,L)
        IF(IL.EQ.0) IL=L
35      A(I)=ALPHA*(X(I)/S(IL))+ONEMAA*(A(I-1)+B(I-1))
        B(I)=BETA*(A(I)-A(I-1))+ONEMBB*B(I-1)
        S(IL)=GAMMA*(X(I)/A(I))+ONEMGG*S(IL)
        SS(I)=S(IL)
        ILLT=IL+LT
        IF(ILLT.GT.L) ILLT=ILLT-L
        F(I)=(A(I)+XLT*B(I))*S(ILLT)
        FFP(I+LT)=F(I)
        R(I+LT)=X(I+LT)-F(I)
        SUM=SUM+R(I)
        XMAD=XMAD+ABS(R(I))
36      SUMSQ=SUMSQ+R(I)**2
        DO 306 I=1,LT
        R(I)=0.
306     FFP(I)=0.
        J=N1+1
        SUME=0.0
        SUME2=0.0
C
C       START THE FORECASTING PHASE
C
        DO 38 I=J,N
        IL=MOD(I,L)
        IF(IL.EQ.0)IL=L
37      FFP(I)=(A(I-LT)+XLT*B(I-LT))*S(IL)
        A(I)=ALPHA*(X(I)/S(IL))+ONEMAA*(A(I-1)+B(I-1))
        B(I)=BETA*(A(I)-A(I-1))+ONEMBB*B(I-1)
        S(IL)=GAMMA*(X(I)/A(I))+ONEMGG*S(IL)
        SS(I)=S(IL)
        R(I)=X(I)-FFP(I)
        SUME=SUME+R(I)
38      SUME2=SUME2+R(I)**2
        WRITE(6,39)
39      FORMAT(1H1,50X,'OUTPUT OF THE INITIALIZATION PHASE'//)
        WRITE(6,40)
40      FORMAT(1H0,10X,'PERIOD',5X,'OBSERVATION',5X,'PERMANENT COMPONENT',
       *2X,'TREND',7X,'SEASONAL FACTOR',5X,'FITTED MODEL',4X,
       *'RESIDUAL'/)
        DO 41 I=1,N1
41      WRITE(6,42) I,X(I),A(I),B(I),SS(I),FFP(I),R(I)
42      FORMAT(12X,I3,6X,F10.4,11X,F10.4,4X,F10.4,7X,F10.4,7X,F10.4,
       *5X,F10.4)
```

```
        T=N1
        AVE=SUM/T
        VAR=(SUMSQ-T*AVE**2)/(T-1.0)
        STD=SQRT(VAR)
        XMAD=XMAD/T
        WRITE(6,43)SUM,AVE,VAR,STD
43      FORMAT(1H0,5X,'SUM OF RESIDUALS=',F10.4,5X,'AVERAGE RESIDUAL='
       *,F10.4,5X,'VARIANCE=',F10.4,5X,'STANDARD DEVIATION=',F10.4)
        WRITE(6,3)XMAD
3       FORMAT(1H0,5X,'MEAN ABSOLUTE DEVIATION=',F10.4)
        KTR=0
        STDM=STD*(-2.0)
        STD=2.0*STD
        DO 44 I=1,N1
        IF(R(I).GT.STD.OR.R(I).LT.STDM)KTR=KTR+1
44      CONTINUE
        WRITE(6,45)KTR
45      FORMAT(1H0,5X,'NUMBER OF RESIDUALS EXCEEDING TWO STANDARD DEVIATIO
       *NS=',I3)
        WRITE(6,46)
46      FORMAT(1H1,50X,'OUTPUT OF FORECASTING PHASE'//)
        WRITE(6,47)L,LT
47      FORMAT(1H0,40X,'LENGTH OF THE SEASON IS',I3,1X,'PERIODS',5X,
       *'FORECAST LEAD TIME IS',I3,1X,'PERIODS')
        WRITE(6,48)
48      FORMAT(1H0,'PERIOD',5X,'OBSERVATION',5X,'PERMANENT COMPONENT',
       *5X,'TREND',5X,'SEASONAL FACTOR',5X,'FORECAST',5X,'ERROR',
       *10X,'TRACKING SIGNALS')
        WRITE(6,49)
49      FORMAT(104X,'CUM. ERROR',2X,'SMOOTHED ERROR')
        Y=0.0
        Z=0.0
        DO 51 I=J,N
50      Y=Y+R(I)
        Z=0.1*R(I)+0.9*Z
        XMAD=0.1*ABS(R(I))+0.9*XMAD
        TC=Y/XMAD
        TS=Z/XMAD
51      WRITE(6,52)I,X(I),A(I),B(I),SS(I),FFP(I),R(I),TC,TS
52      FORMAT(3X,I3,6X,F10.4,11X,F10.4,5X,F10.4,7X,F10.4,5X,F10.4,2X,
       *F10.4,1X,F10.4,2X,F10.4)
        XN=N-N1
        AVG=SUME/XN
        VAR=(SUME2-XN*AVG**2)/(XN-1.0)
        STD=SQRT(VAR)
        WRITE(6,53)SUME,AVG,VAR,STD
53      FORMAT(1H0,'SUM OF FORECAST ERRORS=',F10.4,5X,'AVERAGE FORECAST ER
       *ROR=',F10.4,5X,'VARIANCE=',F10.4,5X,'STANDARD DEVIATION=',
       *F10.4)
        STOP
        END
```

Example

We shall illustrate the data card layout for using the Winters' method program. The time series has 48 observations, the length of the season is 12 periods, and the forecast lead time is one period. The smoothing constants are specified as $\alpha = 0.15$, $\beta = 0.10$, and $\gamma = 0.15$. We wish to estimate the model parameters from the first 24 observations, and simulate forecasting for the last 24 periods. The required data cards are given below:

```
48  2401  12  1
0.150.100.15
290.  246.  290.  186.  225.  200.  189.  210.  200.  255.
225.  300.  285.  270.  264.  235.  201.  164.  225.  214.
240.  297.  275.  292.  300.  250.  280.  245.  250.  202.
220.  225.  250.  287.  285.  312.  315.  271.  300.  241.
244.  206.  218.  252.  265.  301.  296.  304.
↑
```
Card Column 1

  The output for Winters' method is shown on pages 294–296. The first page of output summarizes the parameter estimation process. Results of the model initialization phase are shown on the second page of output. Notice that no residuals exceed two standard deviations of forecast error. In general, there are no forecasts produced for the first τ periods, where τ is the forecast lead time. The forecast simulation is summarized on the third page. The cumulative error tracking signal is rather large in periods 39 through 44. This is due to several successive negative errors preceding period 39, and very small forecast errors in periods 40 through 42, which reduce the mean absolute deviation. Notice that the smoothed error tracking signal reacts correctly during these periods. See Sec. 7-3 for further discussion of this point.

WINTERS' METHOD FOR FORECASTING A SEASONAL TIME SERIES

INITIAL VALUES OF THE PERMANENT, TREND AND SEASONAL COMPONENTS TO BE ESTIMATED FROM THE DATA.
THE FIRST 24 PERIODS OF DATA WHICH CORRESPOND TO, 2 SEASONS WILL BE USED

        INITIAL PERMANENT COMPONENT= 228.5833

        INITIAL TREND COMPONENT=   1.0139

        INITIAL SEASONAL FACTOR FOR PERIOD 1 =   1.2234

        INITIAL SEASONAL FACTOR FOR PERIOD 2 =   1.0916

        INITIAL SEASONAL FACTOR FOR PERIOD 3 =   1.1697

        INITIAL SEASONAL FACTOR FOR PERIOD 4 =   .8814

        INITIAL SEASONAL FACTOR FOR PERIOD 5 =   .8920

        INITIAL SEASONAL FACTOR FOR PERIOD 6 =   .7598

        INITIAL SEASONAL FACTOR FOR PERIOD 7 =   .8565

        INITIAL SEASONAL FACTOR FOR PERIOD 8 =   .8752

        INITIAL SEASONAL FACTOR FOR PERIOD 9 =   .9026

        INITIAL SEASONAL FACTOR FOR PERIOD 10 =   1.1281

        INITIAL SEASONAL FACTOR FOR PERIOD 11 =   1.0170

        INITIAL SEASONAL FACTOR FOR PERIOD 12 =   1.2026

THE SMOOTHING CONSTANTS ARE SPECIFIED AS

ALPHA=   .1500   BETA=   .1000   GAMMA=   .1500

OUTPUT OF THE INITIALIZATION PHASE

PERIOD	OBSERVATION	PERMANENT COMPONENT	TREND	SEASONAL FACTOR	FITTED MODEL	RESIDUAL
1	290.0000	230.7154	1.1257	1.2284	.0000	.0000
2	246.0000	230.8697	1.0286	1.0877	253.0687	-7.0687
3	290.0000	234.3014	1.2689	1.1799	271.2600	18.7400
4	186.0000	231.8876	.9006	.8695	207.6400	-21.6400
5	225.0000	235.7045	1.1922	.9014	207.6571	17.3429
6	200.0000	240.8460	1.5872	.7704	179.9957	20.0043
7	189.0000	239.1677	1.2606	.8466	207.6457	-18.6457
8	210.0000	240.3545	1.2532	.8750	210.4306	-.4306
9	200.0000	238.6029	.9528	.8930	218.0819	-18.0819
10	255.0000	237.5286	.7500	1.1199	270.2451	-15.2451
11	225.0000	235.7222	.4944	1.0076	242.3326	-17.3326
12	300.0000	236.2042	.6932	1.2111	284.0656	15.9344
13	285.0000	237.8641	.5898	1.2239	293.4620	-8.4620
14	270.0000	239.9218	.7366	1.0933	259.3561	10.6439
15	264.0000	238.1208	.4829	1.1692	283.9613	-19.9613
16	235.0000	243.3519	.9577	.8840	207.4748	27.5252
17	201.0000	241.1103	.6378	.8913	220.2266	-19.2266
18	164.0000	237.4174	.2047	.7585	186.2418	-22.2418
19	225.0000	241.8457	.6271	.8591	201.1631	23.8369
20	214.0000	242.7874	.6585	.8760	212.1646	1.8354
21	240.0000	247.2441	1.0383	.9046	217.3888	22.6112
22	297.0000	250.8195	1.2920	1.1296	278.0581	18.9419
23	275.0000	255.2321	1.6041	1.0181	254.0373	20.9627
24	292.0000	254.4764	1.3681	1.2015	311.0525	-19.0525

SUM OF RESIDUALS= 10.9901   AVERAGE RESIDUAL= .4579   VARIANCE= 325.0569   STANDARD DEVIATION= 18.0293

MEAN ABSOLUTE DEVIATION= 16.0737

NUMBER OF RESIDUALS EXCEEDING TWO STANDARD DEVIATIONS= 0

OUTPUT OF FORECASTING PHASE

LENGTH OF THE SEASON IS 12 PERIODS   FORECAST LEAD TIME IS 1 PERIODS

PERIOD	OBSERVATION	PERMANENT COMPONENT	TREND	SEASONAL FACTOR	FORECAST	ERROR	CUM. ERROR	TRACKING SIGNALS SMOOTHED ERROR
25	300.0000	254.2366	1.2073	1.2173	313.1195	-13.1195	-.8315	-.0631
26	250.0000	251.4267	.8056	1.0785	279.2803	-29.2803	-2.4754	-.2399
27	280.0000	250.3180	.6142	1.1616	294.9218	-14.9218	-3.3903	-.3070
28	245.0000	254.8667	1.0076	.8956	221.8137	23.1863	-1.9466	-.1342
29	250.0000	259.5686	1.3771	.9020	228.0498	21.9502	-.6778	.0043
30	202.0000	261.7536	1.4578	.7604	197.9147	4.0853	-.4883	.0288
31	229.0000	262.1405	1.3508	.8562	230.1339	-6.1339	-.9158	-.0118
32	225.0000	262.4964	1.2513	.8731	230.8098	-5.8098	-1.3758	-.0512
33	250.0000	265.6391	1.4404	.9101	238.5929	11.4071	-.6059	-.0330
34	287.0000	265.1299	1.2455	1.1225	301.6811	-14.6811	-1.6311	-.0731
35	285.0000	268.4086	1.4488	1.0247	271.1995	13.8005	-.6681	.0308
36	312.0000	268.3286	1.2959	1.1957	324.2464	-12.2464	-1.5494	-.0590
37	315.0000	267.9966	1.1331	1.2110	328.2103	-13.2103	-2.5048	-.1481
38	271.0000	266.4527	.8654	1.0693	290.2471	-19.2471	-3.7417	-.2612
39	300.0000	265.9585	.7294	1.1566	310.5291	-10.5291	-4.5939	-.3164
40	241.0000	267.0507	.7657	.8966	238.8345	2.1655	-4.8508	-.2943
41	244.0000	268.2187	.8059	.9032	241.5808	2.4192	-5.0757	-.2679
42	206.0000	269.3052	.8340	.7611	204.5776	1.4224	-5.4338	-.2512
43	218.0000	267.8126	.6013	.8498	231.2798	-13.2798	-6.5135	-.3411
44	252.0000	271.4435	.9043	.8814	234.3644	17.6356	-4.6424	-.1393
45	265.0000	275.1721	1.1867	.9180	247.8640	17.1360	-3.0391	-.0200
46	301.0000	275.1279	1.0636	1.1182	310.2116	-9.2116	-3.8872	-.0586
47	296.0000	278.0940	1.2539	1.0306	283.0041	12.9959	-2.7757	.0555
48	304.0000	275.5815	.8772	1.1818	334.0241	-30.0241	-4.5829	-.1732

SUM OF FORECAST ERRORS= -63.4911   AVERAGE FORECAST ERROR= -2.6455   VARIANCE= 238.3617   STANDARD DEVIATION= 15.4390

NORMAL EXIT. EXECUTION TIME: 482 MSEC.
@FIN

RUNID: ILDCM   ACCT: 011A0936   PROJECT: MONTGOMERY

TIME: TOTAL: 00:00:36.939

        CPU: 00:00:05.237   I/O: 00:00:12.314

        CC/ER: 00:00:19.387   WAIT: 00:00:00.107

IMAGES READ: 277   PAGES: 9

START: 10:19:53 DEC 13,1974   FIN: 10:20:38 DEC 13,1974

References

1. Bamber, D. J., "A Versatile Family of Forecasting Systems," *Operational Research Quarterly*, vol. 20, pp. 111–121, April, 1969.
2. Bartlett, M. S., "On the Theoretical Specification of Sampling Properties of Autocorrelated Time Series," *Journal of the Royal Statistical Society*, ser. B, vol. 8, 1946.
3. Bossons, J., "The Effects of Parameter Misspecification and Non-stationarity on the Applicability of Adaptive Forecasts," *Management Science*, vol. 12, no. 9, pp. 659–669, 1966.
4. Bowker, A. H., and G. J. Lieberman, *Engineering Statistics*, 2d ed., Prentice-Hall, Inc., Englewood Cliffs, N.J., 1972.
5. Box, G. E. P., and N. R. Draper, *Evolutionary Operation: A Method for Increasing Industrial Productivity*, John Wiley & Sons, Inc., New York, 1969.
6. Box, G. E. P., and G. M. Jenkins, *Time Series Analysis, Forecasting, and Control*, Holden-Day, Inc., San Francisco, 1970.
7. Box, G. E. P., and D. A. Pierce, "Distribution of Residual Autocorrelations in Autoregressive-Integrated Moving Average Time Series Models," *Journal of the American Statistical Association*, vol. 64, 1970.
8. Brown, R. G., *Statistical Forecasting for Inventory Control*, McGraw-Hill Book Company, New York, 1959.
9. Brown, R. G., *Smoothing, Forecasting and Prediction of Discrete Time Series*, Prentice-Hall, Inc., Englewood Cliffs, N.J., 1962.
10. Brown, R. G., *Decision Rules for Inventory Management*, Holt, Rinehart and Winston, Inc., New York, 1967.
11. Brown, R. G., and R. F. Meyer, "The Fundamental Theorem of Exponential Smoothing," *Operations Research*, vol. 9, no. 6, pp. 673–685, 1960.
12. Carter, R. F., "A Bayesian Approach to Seasonal Style Goods Forecasting," unpublished M.S. thesis, Georgia Institute of Technology, Atlanta, 1971.
13. Chambers, J. C., S. K. Mullick, and D. D. Smith, "How to Choose the Right Forecasting Technique," *Harvard Business Review*, vol. 65, no. 4, pp. 45–74, 1971.
14. Chen, G. K. C., and P. R. Winters, "Forecasting Peak Demand for an Electric Utility with a Hybrid Exponential Model," *Management Science*, vol. 12, no. 12, pp. 531–537, 1966.
15. Chow, W. M., "Adaptive Control of the Exponential Smoothing Constant," *Journal of Industrial Engineering*, vol. 16, no. 5, pp. 314–317, 1965.
16. Cogger, K. O., "The Optimality of General-Order Exponential Smoothing," *Operations Research*, vol. 22, no. 4, pp. 858–867, 1974.
17. Cohen, G. D., "Bayesian Adjustment of Sales Forecasts in Multi-item Inventory Control Systems," *Journal of Industrial Engineering*, vol. 17, no. 9, pp. 474–479, 1966.
18. Cox, D. R., "Prediction by Exponentially Weighted Moving Averages and Related Methods," *Journal of the Royal Statistical Society*, ser. B, vol. 23, no. 2, pp. 414–422, 1961.
19. Crane, D. B., and J. R. Crotty, "A Two-Stage Forecasting Model: Exponential Smoothing and Multiple Regression," *Management Science*, vol. 13, no. 8, pp. 501–507, 1967.
20. Davenport, W. B., and W. L. Root, *An Introduction to the Theory of Random Signals and Noise*, McGraw-Hill Book Company, New York, 1958.
21. D'Esopo, D. A., "A Note on Forecasting by the Exponential Smoothing Operator," *Operations Research*, vol. 9, no. 5, pp. 686–687, 1961.
22. Dobbie, J. M., "Forecasting Periodic Trends by Exponential Smoothing," *Operations Research*, vol. 11, no. 6, pp. 908–918, 1963.
23. Draper, N. R., and H. Smith, *Applied Regression Analysis*, John Wiley & Sons, Inc., New York, 1968.

24. Dubin, J., "The Fitting of Time Series Models," *Revue of the International Institute of Statistics*, vol. 28, 1960.

25. Goodman, M. L., "A New Look at Higher-Order Exponential Smoothing for Forecasting," *Operations Research*, vol. 22, no. 4, pp. 880–888, 1974.

26. Grenander, V., and M. Rosenblatt, *Statistical Analysis of Stationary Time Series*, John Wiley & Sons, Inc., New York, 1957.

27. Gross, D., and J. L. Ray, "A General Purpose Forecast Simulator," *Management Science*, vol. 11, no. 6, pp. 119–135, 1965.

28. Guttman, I., S. S. Wilks, and J. S. Hunter, *Introductory Engineering Statistics*, 2d ed., John Wiley & Sons, Inc., 1971.

29. Harris, L., "A Decision-Theoretic Approach on Deciding When a Sophisticated Forecasting Technique Is Needed," *Management Science*, vol. 13, no. 2, pp. 66–69, 1966.

30. Harrison, P. J., "Exponential Smoothing and Short-Term Sales Forecasting," *Management Science*, vol. 13, no. 11, pp. 821–842, 1967.

31. Harrison, P. J., and O. L. Davies, "The Use of Cumulative Sum (CUSUM) Techniques for the Control of Routine Forecasts of Product Demand," *Operations Research*, vol. 12, no. 2, pp. 325–333, 1964.

32. Hertz, D. B., and K. H. Schaffir, "A Forecasting Method for Management of Seasonal Style Goods Inventories," *Operations Research*, vol. 8, no. 1, pp. 45–52, 1960.

33. Hicks, C. R., *Fundamental Concepts in the Design of Experiments*, 2d ed., Holt, Rinehart and Winston, Inc., New York, 1973.

34. Hines, W. W., and D. C. Montgomery, *Probability and Statistics in Engineering and Management Science*, The Ronald Press Company, New York, 1972.

35. Jenkins, G. M., and D. G. Watts, *Spectral Analysis and Its Applications*, Holden-Day, Inc., San Francisco, 1968.

36. Johnson, L. A., and D. C. Montgomery, *Operations Research in Production Planning, Scheduling, and Inventory Control*, John Wiley & Sons, Inc., New York, 1974.

37. Kalman, R. E., "A New Approach to Linear Filtering and Prediction Problems," *Journal of Basic Engineering*, ser. D, vol. 82, 1960.

38. Kirby, R. M., "A Comparison of Short and Medium Range Statistical Forecasting Methods," *Management Science*, vol. 13, no. 2, pp. B202–B210, 1966.

39. Milne, W. E., *Numerical Calculus*, Princeton University Press, Princeton, N.J., 1949.

40. Montgomery, D. C., "An Introduction to Short-Term Forecasting," *Journal of Industrial Engineering*, vol. 19, no. 10, pp. 500–503, 1968.

41. Montgomery, D. C., "Adaptive Control of Exponential Smoothing Parameters by Evolutionary Operation," *AIIE Transactions*, vol. 2, no. 3, pp. 268–269, 1970.

42. Moran, P. A. P., "Some Experiments in the Prediction of Sunspot Numbers," *Journal of the Royal Statistical Society*, ser. B, vol. 16, 1954.

43. Morrison, N., *Introduction to Sequential Smoothing and Prediction*, McGraw-Hill Book Company, New York, 1969.

44. Muth, J. F., "Optimal Properties of Exponentially Weighted Forecasts of Time Series with Permanent and Transitory Components," *Journal of the American Statistical Association*, vol. 55, no. 290, pp. 299–306, 1960.

45. Nelson, C. R., *Applied Time Series Analysis for Managerial Forecasting*, Holden-Day, Inc., San Francisco, 1973.

46. Nerlove, M., and S. Wage, "On the Optimality of Adaptive Forecasting," *Management Science*, vol. 10, no. 2, pp. 207–224, 1964.

47. Pandit, S. M., and S. M. Wu, "Exponential Smoothing as a Special Case of a Linear Stochastic System," *Operations Research*, vol. 22, no. 4, pp. 868–879, 1974.

48. Pegels, C. C., "A Note on Exponential Forecasting," *Management Science*, vol. 15, no. 5, pp. 311–315, 1969.

49. Peterson, R., "A Note on the Determination of Optimal Forecasting Strategy," *Management Science*, vol. 16, no. 4, pp. B165–B169, 1969.

50. Phadke, M. S., and S. M. Wu, "Modeling of Continuous Stochastic Processes from Discrete Observations with Applications to Sunspot Data," *Journal of the American Statistical Association*, vol. 69, no. 346, pp. 325–329, 1974.

51. Pratt, J. W., H. Raiffa, and R. Schlaifer, *Introduction to Statistical Decision Theory*, McGraw-Hill Book Company, 1965.

52. Quenouille, M. H., "Approximate Tests of Correlation in Time Series," *Journal of the Royal Statistical Society*, ser. B, vol. 11, 1949.

53. Raiffa, H., and R. Schlaifer, *Applied Statistical Decision Theory*, Harvard University Press, Cambridge, Mass., 1961.

54. Roberts, S. D., and R. Reed, "The Development of a Self-Adaptive Forecasting Technique," *AIIE Transactions*, vol. 1, no. 4, pp. 314–322, 1969.

55. Schussel, G., "Sales Forecasting with the Aid of a Human Behavior Simulator," *Management Science*, vol. 13, no. 10, pp. B593–B611, 1967.

56. Theil, H., and S. Wage, "Some Observations on Adaptive Forecasting," *Management Science*, vol. 10, no. 2, pp. 198–206, 1964.

57. Thompson, H. E., and W. Beranek, "The Efficient Use of an Imperfect Forecast," *Management Science*, vol. 13, no. 3, pp. 233–243, 1966.

58. Trigg, D. W., "Monitoring a Forecasting System," *Operational Research Quarterly*, vol. 15, no. 3, pp. 271–274, 1964.

59. Trigg, D. W., and A. G. Leach, "Exponential Smoothing with an Adaptive Response Rate," *Operational Research Quarterly*, vol. 18, no. 1, pp. 53–59, 1967.

60. University of Wisconsin Computing Center, *Computer Programs for the Analysis of Univariate Time Series Using the Methods of Box and Jenkins*, Supplementary Program Series No. 517, 1970.

61. Wheelwright, S. C., and S. Makridakis, *Forecasting Methods for Management*, John Wiley & Sons, Inc., New York, 1973.

62. Wheelwright, S. C., and S. Makridakis, "Forecasting with Adaptive Filtering," *Revue Française d'Automatique, d'Informatique et de Recherche Operationelle*, Winter, 1973.

63. Winkler, R. L., *Introduction to Bayesian Inference and Decision*, Holt, Rinehart and Winston, Inc., New York, 1972.

64. Winters, P. R., "Forecasting Sales by Exponentially Weighted Moving Averages," *Management Science*, vol. 6, no. 3, pp. 324–342, 1960.

65. Yule, G. U., "On a Method of Investigating Periodicities in Disturbed Series, with Special Reference to Wölfer's Sunspot Numbers," *Philosophical Transactions of the Royal Society (London)*, ser. A, vol. 226, 1927.

Index